T0283294

Joel, Obadiah, and Micah

FACING THE STORM

MAGGID

Yaakov Beasley

JOEL, OBADIAH, AND MICAH

FACING THE STORM

Maggid Books

Joel, Obadiah, and Micah
Facing the Storm

First Edition, 2024

Maggid Books
An imprint of Koren Publishers Jerusalem Ltd.

POB 8531, New Milford, CT 06776–8531, USA
& POB 4044, Jerusalem 9104001, Israel
www.korenpub.com

The publication of this book was made possible
through the generous support of *The Jewish Book Trust*.

ISBN 978-1-59264-597-8, *hardcover*

Printed and bound in the United States

Lovingly dedicated in memory of

Chaim Yaakov Weisz ז"ל

*who had a deep love of Torah learning,
Yiddishkeit, and Israel.*

*By his daughter and son-in-law
Vivian & Lewis Dubrofsky
and their children
Yehuda, Akiva,
and Hadassa & Miles Peller*

Contents

OBADIAH

MICAH

Preface

"Those who don't study history are doomed to repeat it."[1]

And the few that do study it are depressed as they watch others make the same mistakes over and over.

"We need our prophets back!" It was two weeks after the holiday of Purim, 2020. The holiday itself was a joyous affair – raucous and boisterous dancing in the streets combined with family get-togethers and festive meals. Then, suddenly, Israel shut down. COVID-19 hit the country with a vengeance, as it did worldwide. Schools were shuttered, businesses closed. My overseas students had less than a week to evacuate the country, and my wife's place of employment suddenly fired more than half of its staff, including her. Faces disappeared, covered instead by paper masks; papers told of ever-rising numbers of sick and dying. No one knew what was happening, or why. My wife Devorah and I were walking (within 100 meters radius from our house, as far as we were permitted go). Trying to make sense of the upheaval, Devorah suggested the obvious: "We need our prophets back!"

---

1. Generally attributed to philosopher George Santayana, as paraphrased by Winston Churchill in an address to the House of Commons in 1948. Mark Twain's variant reads "History doesn't repeat itself, but it does rhyme" (https://bigthink.com/ culture-religion/those-who-do-not-learn-history-doomed-to-repeat-it-really/).

I immediately understood her sentiments. After all, we were always taught that the prophets were nothing less than conduits of the divine word, making order of chaos and providing answers to life's mysteries. Obviously, their guidance championed the path of morality and righteousness. Yet, a question remained: "Why didn't the Jewish people ever listen to them?" To this, I know of several partial answers: The powers that be did not wish to lose their authority/wealth. False prophets misled the populace. The people were too attached to idol worship/immorality/generic sin to consider change willingly.

All these answers are accurate. Yet, I always felt that another missing factor contributed to the difficulties the biblical prophets faced, and why their books are often overlooked even today. The more I studied, an insight began to crystalize in my mind. My teachers had always emphasized the timelessness of the prophets' eternal message. However, I was never taught how their message was timely to their listeners as well. Prophets spoke to real people, struggling with the vicissitudes and challenges of daily living.[2] Emphasis on the prophets' literary skills without context is a study of their poetry, not their passion. More importantly, understanding their history helps make the prophets' message relevant to our own. Which alliances should Israel pursue? How should we react to the growing inequality in income distribution in Western society? What exemplifies the truly religious personality that we should aspire to? The prophets addressed these issues in their time, yet the same challenges and issues reappear again and again. Hopefully, through properly studying the prophets and internalizing their message, we will find the relevant answers and begin to break the cycle.

This volume is my second study on the Twelve Minor Prophets (Trei Asar). My first book investigated the messages of Nahum, Habakkuk, and Zephaniah. In addition to the literary and moral messages they contained, the work emphasized the history of their time, focusing on how their surroundings inspired and formed their messages. These

---

2. Therefore, we begin with a fictional narrative illustrating the thoughts of the average citizen during the period described.

three prophets lived during the seventh century BCE, facing challenges unimaginable to the modern-day listener. In their time, the average Judean would have likely spent his entire life under Assyrian rule (ruthlessly administered by Judah's idolatrous puppet king, Manasseh), with no hope or expectation of a change for the better. Prophets who dared speak about upcoming upheavals and revolutions were not only foolhardy but suicidal.[3] Additionally, after the Assyrian destruction of the Northern Kingdom of Israel in 721 BCE and the near obliteration of the Kingdom of Judah in 701 BCE, the average citizen would have likely doubted that God still cared for His people. Indeed, they probably believed that God had been defeated by Ashur, the Assyrian god, decades before. These three prophets had to use God's words to rebuild a people, physically and spiritually. Many readers responded that this was the most meaningful section of the book, opening their eyes to a time that they had not known existed.

The three prophets in this volume – Joel, Obadiah, and Micah – faced different challenges. However, they all had one thing in common. All three prophesied not after a calamity struck but right before or during a potential crisis. Facing potential catastrophe, the Jewish people

---

3. And yet, they persevered – compelled by their message. As Maimonides writes in his *Guide for the Perplexed* (2:37):

> It is further the nature of this element in man that he who possesses an additional degree of that influence is compelled to address his fellowmen, under all circumstances, whether he is listened to or not, even if he injures himself thereby. Thus we find prophets that did not leave off speaking to the people until they were slain; it is this divine influence that moves them, that does not allow them to rest in any way, though they might bring upon themselves great evils by their action. E.g., when Jeremiah was despised, like other teachers and scholars of his age, he could not, though he desired it, withhold his prophecy, or cease from reminding the people of the truths which they rejected. "For whenever I speak prophecy, I shout; I call out, Injustice! Violence! The Lord's word has brought upon me derision and scorn all day long. I said to myself: I will not make mention of it. I will no longer speak in His name. But it resides within me like a flaming fire, locked into my bones. I wearied of holding it back. I could not" (Jer. 20:8–9). This is also the meaning of the words of another prophet (Amos 3:8), "A lion roars; who would not fear? The Lord God speaks; who would not prophesy?" (Friedländer tr. [1904], at https://www.sacred-texts.com/jud/gfp/gfp124.htm)

had to decide where their loyalties lay and had to demonstrate that they understood their moral and ethical responsibilities. To be successful, our prophets had to persuade the people to abandon decades of habitual behavior and indifferent attitudes towards God and towards each other. At least two, Joel and Micah, successfully effected change among their listeners, and this work will investigate how this was achieved.

It is impossible to state with certainty that Joel, Obadiah, and Micah were contemporaries. Micah's years are the easiest to determine; he lived during the second half of the eighth century BCE (approx. 750–700 BCE). Though most scholars place Obadiah in the time of the First Temple's destruction in 586 BCE, we argue that Obadiah was contemporary with Micah. Joel represents the greatest enigma regarding the years in which he prophesied. Scholars have offered dates ranging from before Saul in the eleventh century BCE to after the rebuilding of the Second Temple almost seven centuries later. One rabbinic tradition dates Joel to the second half of the eighth century BCE as well (we recognize that this is only speculation and is not relevant to his message). During this period, the two kingdoms of Israel and Judah underwent irreversible transformations. In 750 BCE, they were prosperous, powerful, and at peace. Half a century and three devastating wars later, the Northern Kingdom had been erased from history, crushed by the ruthless Assyrian military machine. In Judah, only Jerusalem remained – Sennacherib's armies had razed the rest of the country.

The prophets, however, are not passive onlookers, content to chronicle the people's tribulations and sufferings. To the contrary, they confidently outline the people's moral failings and faults that allowed this catastrophe to happen. Joel attempts to shake a lethargic people out of its slumber while facing an existential threat; Obadiah describes the immoral behavior of Israel's neighbors during the crisis that led to their downfall; Micah protests the social inequities and corruption that plagued Judah. A hardened reader may mock the prophets' obsession with improving the behavior of the Jewish people: Could two minuscule nations have stood a chance against the Assyrian behemoth that enveloped the ancient world? Yet, at its core, Joel, Obadiah, and Micah's message empowers. Small acts of kindness and simple acts of justice can withstand the force of the mightiest empires. Sincere prayer can avert catastrophe. Though we live in a world where chaos runs amok and might makes right, the Jewish people can still guide humanity to a world in which morality reigns supreme. This volume contains their message. And yes – we need our prophets back today, and their message is as relevant as ever.

ACKNOWLEDGMENTS

טוב להודות לה׳ ולזמר לשמך עליון ולהגיד בבוקר חסדך ואמונתך בלילות.

It is an honor to begin the acknowledgments by recognizing the person to whose memory the book is dedicated, Mr. Chaim Yaakov Weisz. I was privileged to meet Mr. Weisz when I was in high school along with his daughter Vivian, and the hospitality Mr. and Mrs. Weisz showed to a young small-town boy remains fondly remembered. To this day, Devorah and I are privileged to still count Vivian and her husband Lewis Dubrofsky, as valued friends, and thank them for their generous sponsorship of this volume. Mr. Weisz was a hardworking, honest Jew, who, along with Mrs. Weisz, raised an exceptional family in Toronto after emigrating from Romania via Israel. I remember his good humor, how he always greeted everyone with a warm smile and a twinkle in his eye. His loss saddened all who knew him, and I hope that having this commentary serve as a merit for his memory brings comfort to all his family.

Many people have taken the time to contact me after the publication of the first volume, *Nahum, Habakkuk, and Zephaniah* (Maggid, 2020), with comments, thoughts, questions (and more than a few criticisms). I thank each one of you and welcome all continued communication to discuss ideas found in this work.

In the previous volume, I noted that the book you hold in your hands is not my work alone. While I bear sole responsibility for the material presented within, this book would not have come to fruition without the support and encouragement of many people along the way. First and foremost, I thank Matthew Miller, publisher, and Rabbi Reuven Ziegler and his wonderful and professional team at Maggid Books, including Caryn Meltz, Ita Olesker, Rachelle Emanuel, and Ruth Pepperman. Thanks to their continuous publication of intelligent and thought-provoking Torah literature, the English-speaking Torah world is enriched beyond measure. Personally, Rabbi Ziegler has not only pushed me forward professionally at many key junctures but has also been a dear friend and colleague.

I was privileged to mention the vast array of teachers and friends who have taught and supported me throughout the years in the first volume, and now wish to note that the feelings of appreciation and gratitude have only grown. You accompanied and guided me from a small town in Canada to Alon Shevut, Israel, with many fun and fascinating stations along the way. Specifically, I wish to mention my parents and grandparents whose patience for me I still marvel at. You provided me with unconditional love, a thirst for knowledge, and a healthy dose of curiosity. You managed to weather my terrible twos (which apparently lasted over a decade, if the rumors are true).

I am fortunate to have had the opportunity to teach in amazing institutions both here in Israel and abroad; Toronto, New Jersey, Minnesota, to name a few. Many of the ideas in this book have been battle-tested in the classroom over time by excellent students whose insights and questions have often forced me to sharpen and revise my thoughts. I am grateful to Yeshivat AMIT Nachshon under Rabbis Noam Krigman and Yaakov Grunsfeld, where in addition to my regular teaching responsibilities I am responsible for guiding the participants in the Yom HaAtzma'ut national Bible quiz. My greatest appreciation is to Yeshivat Hesder Lev HaTorah, where for the past decade I have been given the tremendous responsibility and opportunity to introduce the students to the beauty and the depths of serious and meaningful Tanakh study, while basking in the warmth and friendship of the amazing staff. I wish to express my admiration for my incredible students, specifically those brave souls willing to enroll in the Power Tanakh class. To Rabbis Mori, Cytrin, and Kwalwasser – thank you for making this possible.

Several talented scholars generously donated of their time to read, edit, and critique this manuscript. As a result of the efforts and insights of Rabbanit Mali Brofsky and Rabbi Moshe Debow, this book is a much-improved product. Thank you.

Most importantly, I wish to extend my most sincere thanks to all my family members, whose unstinting support provided me with the strength to persevere and complete this work. Recently, we lost two valued family members. Two years ago, my mother-in-law Matilde Nowosiolski passed away, and her absence and caring is still felt by everyone who knew and loved her. To my father-in-law Alberto Nowosiolski: I wish you many years of enjoyment from all your grandchildren and great-grandchildren. Recently, my mother Adela Zur lost her husband Zwi Zur, a Holocaust survivor whose pure appreciation for living brought cheer to everyone. Ima, I wish you many more years of health and happiness. To my amazing and generous siblings, Dr. Kenneth and Laura Beasley, Steven and Natalie Beasley, Sara Beasley, and Scott and Leah Leckie – many years more of happiness, health, and shared *semaḥot*. To my incredible children, Mordechai, Shabtai, Michaya, Yair, and Yoshiyahu, and my amazing daughters-in-law, Noa, Sara Leeba, and Tamar – may God fulfill all the requests of your hearts – so ask for the sky! To our newest members, little Ari Oz and Uriel Natan – welcome to the family. Discussions around the Shabbat table inevitably revolve around the Tanakh, and you'll get used to the noise quickly! I look forward to learning with you as soon as you are ready!

Finally, to my wife, Devorah: Without your love and faith, this book would never have come into being. I only hope that I continue to be worthy of being together with you and deserving of your love for many decades to come.

Yaakov Beasley
Alon Shevut
25 Elul, 5783

Methodology[1]

"They [the prophets] have a queer way of talking, like people who,
instead of proceeding in an orderly manner, ramble off from one thing
to the next so that you cannot make heads or tails of them or see
what they are getting at."[2]

For most modern readers, the prophetic books are among the difficult works to approach. They are rarely taught as whole entities in most schools; at best, for regular synagogue attendees, they hear several verses as part of the *haftara* reading after the recital of the weekly Torah portion. We can point to three intimidating obstacles that stand between today's readers and the prophets: (1) a faulty understanding of the purpose of the prophets and their works, (2) the historical distance between their time and ours, and (3) a lack of knowledge

---

1. In *Nahum, Habakkuk, and Zephaniah: Lights in the Valley* (Jerusalem: Maggid Books, 2020), pp. xiii–xviii, we have already discussed the general approach by which we study prophetic literature, emphasizing knowledge of the historical background, literary, and rhetorical techniques, as well as clarifying the prophet's moral and religious message. However, we wish to emphasize certain issues that reappear in this volume, with emphasis on the challenges faced by the reader as well as the literary issues that will arise.
2. Gerhard von Rad quoting Martin Luther, in *Old Testament Theology*, vol. 2, trans. D. M. G. Stalker (New York: Harper & Row, 1965), 2:33n1.

of the literary devices and spoken techniques the prophets used to convince their listeners.

First, many people approach prophetic books with an inaccurate understanding of the words "prophet" and "prophecy," and thereby don't understand the nature of the texts they are reading. In English, the word prophet connotes one who foretells the future, and the dominant image is one of a seer immersed in predicting acts and events in the far distance. However, while the prophets did indeed announce the future, they generally described the immediate future of Israel, Judah, and the surrounding nations. As noted above, their message was both timeless and timely. More importantly, seeing the prophets as primarily predictors of future events misses their primary function, which was, in fact, to speak for God to their contemporaries. This function is clear from Rashi's understanding of the Hebrew word for prophet (*navi*, נביא):

> "[And Aaron] will be your spokesman (*nevi'ekha*)": [We should understand this word] like the Targum: your interpreter. Every appearance of *nevua* (prophecy) [in the Tanakh] denotes a man who publicly announces to the people words of reproof. It is derived from the root of "I form the speech (*niv*) of the lips" (Is. 57:19); "speaks (*yanuv*) wisdom" (Prov. 10:31); "and he [Samuel] finished prophesying (*mehitnavut*)" (I Sam. 10:13). (Rashi on Ex. 7:1)

The Ibn Ezra advances a different understanding of the word *navi*. Unlike Rashi, whose understanding of *navi* deriving from the word for speech (Heb., *niv*) ignores the letter *alef*, Ibn Ezra prefers inferring the meaning of the word from its context in Amos 3:7, which states that God does not act with revealing "his secret to His servants, the *nevi'im*." Ibn Ezra deduces that a *navi* is someone who is the recipient of God's secrets.

Modern interpretations connect the word *navi* to similar words in Akkadian (and other Semitic languages e.g., the Akkadian *nabu* [to call, announce, proclaim], Arabic *naba'a* [he uttered with a low voice, announced], *nab'ah* [a low sound]). There the root word connotes "to call" – so a *navi* is someone who is either called (appointed) or calls to the people.[3]

What connects all these interpretations is that they avoid connotations of predicting the future and focus the meaning of being called or appointed to deliver God's message to his people. Reading prophetic texts as primarily prognosticators of future events misses their primary function, that of delivering God's message to their listeners. Many of their grim predictions are meant to serve to warn the people of the consequences of continuing in the wrong direction, not as guarantees of a dire future. Similarly, many of the positive promises given to Israel were meant to inspire; but if the people of the prophet's time failed to seize the opportunity presented to them, the visions of redemption and hope would not come to pass, to be delayed until a later generation would aspire to live according to the moral and ethical standards God demanded of them.[4]

---

3. Summarized from Mitchell First's article "What Is the Meaning of the Word Navi?" available online at https://jewishlink.news/features/26051-what-is-the-meaning-of-the-word-navi.
4. This principle explains many of the difficult passages in the prophets that describe glorious periods of peace and prosperity that did not materialize in the time of their listeners, whether Isaiah's vision of the messianic era where "the wolf will lie down beside the lamb, the leopard will lie beside the young goat.... There will be no wrong or violence on all My holy mountain, for knowledge of the Lord will fill the earth" (Is. 11:6–9), or Haggai's promise to the original settlers during the period of the return to Judah regarding the Second Temple that "the glory of this latter House will be greater than the glory of the first, says the Lord of Hosts, and I will bestow peace upon this place" (Hag. 2:9). While earlier commentators debate whether the prophets directed these prophecies to their contemporaries or towards future generations, the Malbim in both places notes the prophecies were given conditionally, dependent on the people's behavior:

    With the proper outlook, we find in these matters a powerful principle, that from the moment of the first exile in Sennacherib's time, began the time of redemption...from that time, prophets began to prophesy that there would come a redeemer who would gather these exiles from the four corners of the earth. The potential for redemption based on good deeds and repentance already began in Hezekiah's time. This is what [the Sages] said...that "the Holy One, blessed be He, wished to appoint Hezekiah as the Messiah, and Sennacherib as Gog and Magog, except that a sin interfered" (Sanhedrin 94a). They intended to teach that *had they merited, Hezekiah himself would have been that redeemer,*

The second issue that complicates comprehending the prophetic books is the problem of historical distance. At first glance, our world is too far removed from the religious, historical, and cultural life of ancient Israel. We lack the context of the prophet's world, and therefore, their words lack relevance for ours (at first glance). Therefore, this volume contains a brief introduction to the history of Israel and Judah in the eighth century, focusing on the political, social, and religious challenges facing the Jewish people at that time. These years were years of unprecedented upheaval, as long-standing political boundaries, economic standards, and religious behaviors would change irrevocably within the space of a few decades. The prophet's words provided an anchor to a people adrift in these stormy seas. Therefore, with continued study and reflection, the parallels and relevance of our prophets to our time will grow clearer and clearer.

The final difficulty faced by the reader is a lack of knowledge of the literary devices and spoken techniques used. This difficulty is compounded by the fact that though the prophecies are before us in written form, most of them were first delivered orally as speeches. As such, they differ from the stories of the prophets that appear in the narrative histories of the Tanakh (i.e., Elijah and Elisha in the book of Kings), where what they did becomes much more significant than what they said. In contrast, the prophetic books contain prophecies, but generally do not discuss the prophets who uttered them. Joel, Obadiah, Nahum,

---

and all these futuristic prophecies would have been fulfilled in his day. Since they did not merit [that redemption] the prophecy remains suspended and in its potential state until its proper time. (Malbim's commentary on Isaiah 11:1)

[Haggai calls this building, the Second Temple,] "the last house," for it destined not to be destroyed and there would be peace, [should there not be] baseless hatred [among Jews towards each other] which was the cause of its destruction – *for the entire prophecy was conditional... [however] once the condition was not fulfilled, for they did not honor the covenant and did not behave peacefully toward each other, resulting in the proliferation of sects and baseless hatred, this destiny disappeared until a later generation would fulfill the conditions necessary to rebuild it.* (Malbim's commentary on Haggai 2:8)

For further discussion and sources regarding this issue, see Hayyim Angel, "Prophecy as Potential: The Consolations of Isaiah 1–12 in Context," first appearing in *Jewish Bible Quarterly* 37:1 (2009): 3–10.

Habakkuk, and Malachi are only names in a book. This results in the difficulty of locating the prophecies within their historical context, with few exceptions. (Isaiah contains several prophecies that stem from specific situations faced by kings Ahaz and Hezekiah. Similarly, Jeremiah and Ezekiel date several of their prophecies, as do Haggai and Zechariah in the first half of his book.) Additionally, as the prophetic books are collections of spoken oracles, they generally do not appear in the original chronological sequence by when they were first proclaimed, as other factors may have played a role in their compilation into book form.[5] Therefore, the first step is identifying the individual speeches within the overall structure, and when possible, locating the individual speeches in their historical context.

Locating the individual units within the prophetic work is a difficult task, as many sections do not contain clear markers that delineate where one oracle ends, and another begins. In the introduction to each prophet's book, we attempt to identify the various discourses and speeches as originally uttered by the prophets. To do so, we have noted both literary markers (the call to "Hear" in Micah 1:2, 3:1, 6:1), changes in speaker (the shift in Joel 2:18 and 2:19 when God addresses the people), and thematic shifts (the shift in Obadiah 1:9 and 1:10 from Edom's pride to its betrayal of brotherly bonds); as well as the appearance of several literary forms that can signify the beginning of a new discourse: formulaic phrases ("so says the Lord"), commands to the audience, imperatives, changes in time, etc. Additionally, dividing the text into its original speeches requires noting shifts or discontinuities with respect to form (e.g., a shift to direct speech), content (e.g., a new topic), function (e.g., an example given to illustrate a prior exposition), and genre (the shift

---

5. For example, in the book of Micah, several scholars suggest an overall literary structure of three alternating sections of prophecies of doom and judgment with prophecies of redemption and hope – 1:1–2:13, 3:1–5:15, and 6:1–7:20, which they argue is an editorial decision made in the text's compilation despite the individual units emanating from different time periods (J. T. Willis, quoted by Bruce Waltke, *A Commentary of Micah* [Grand Rapids, MI: Eerdmans, 2007], 13–15). Closer investigation of the sections, however, reveals that the artificial attempt to create larger thematic units fails to account for the changes in topic, audience, and style of the individual speeches, as will be demonstrated.

from the "lawsuit oracle" form in Micah 6 to the individual laments and tribulations of the abandoned prophet in Micah 7).

Among the rhetorical devices the prophet uses to convey his message are specific discourse genres that their audiences would readily recognize. Several of the most common forms in prophetic literature include announcements of judgment and/or salvation, the messenger speech, the lawsuit oracle, vision reports, symbolic acts, and woe oracles. The most common, announcements of judgment and salvation, almost always include the reason for the judgment to come, and then an announcement of judgment. As noted above, these proclamations were rarely irrevocable; the people's repentance (or backsliding) could overturn the divine decree. For example, Amos declares:

> [You] who lie on beds of ivory, lounge upon your couches, feasting on the choicest of sheep and calves taken from their feeding stalls, who play the harp – with instruments they think themselves like David – who guzzle wine from bowls, anoint yourselves with the finest of oils, but are not heartsick over Joseph's ruin – therefore, you will now be the first of exiles, a coterie of loungers removed, the Lord God swears by Himself; the Lord, God of Hosts, has spoken. (Amos 6:4–7)

The prophetic messenger speech is possibly modelled after diplomatic messages sent from one king or prince to another, and it serves to add authority to the prophet, who does not act on his own accord, but solely as God's dispassionate messenger. Obadiah begins as follows: "So says the Lord God to Edom – we have heard tidings from the Lord: and an envoy has been sent among the nations, 'Come, let us rise up in battle against her.'"

In the lawsuit oracle, the prophet portrays God and the people as antagonists in a courtroom. Rhetorically, this allows the prophet to provide a third person portrayal of the Divine decision making, beginning with the outlining of the charges against the people, a listing of the charges and evidence for and against, concluding with a Divine verdict. In many of the texts, the Hebrew word for lawsuit, *riv*

(Heb., רִיב) appears (e.g., Is. 3, Jer. 2, Hos. 4, 12, and Mic. 6). The commentary to Micah 6 provides a full explanation of the lawsuit oracle. To appreciate its effectiveness, Isaiah's attack on Judah's corrupt leadership and their wives provides an excellent example:

> The Lord is ready for His case (רִיב) to be heard: He stands up now to judge nations. The Lord is coming to trial with His people's elders, its princes: "It is you who ravaged the vineyard; the plunder of the poor is in your homes. By what right do you crush My people, grinding the faces of the poor?" So speaks the Lord God of Hosts.... Because the daughters of Zion are proud, walking with their heads poised, casting their eyes around them, walking their dainty walk, their feet ringing with anklets – the Lord will scab over the skulls of the daughters of Zion; the Lord will lay their heads bare. (Is. 3:13–17)

Two final factors complicate the reader's task – the abundance of poetic techniques and devices within the prophecies, and a lack of familiarity with the earlier biblical texts that the prophets allude to in order to strengthen their message. All prophetic books contain a substantial amount of poetry; several are exclusively poetic. Several scholars estimate that poetry comprises almost one-third of the Tanakh text.[6] As expected, the prophet chooses poetic imagery in order to stir his listeners' emotions. We will investigate the many devices used by the prophet to engage his audience's imagination, including similes, metaphor, personification, alliteration and assonance, symbolism, and wordplay. These devices serve to make the prophet's message easier to remember. Underlying of almost all prophetic poetry lies parallelism[7] – where two or more successive lines strengthen, reinforce, and develop each other. The prophets employ several forms of parallelism: synonymous

---

6. J. B. Gabel and C. B. Wheeler, *The Bible as Literature*, 2nd ed. (New York: Oxford University Press, 1990), 37 and 293.

7. James Kugel, *The Idea of Biblical Poetry: Parallelism and Its History* (New Haven: Yale University Press, 1981); Leland Ryken, *How to Read the Bible as Literature* (Grand Rapids, MI: Zondervan Academic Books, 1984), 103.

parallelism, antithetical (contrasting) parallelism, and synthetic parallelism, and we shall endeavor to identify them in the text.[8]

Finally, we shall attempt to locate the textual parallels, echoes, and allusions to previous sources found within our books. As master rhetoricians, our prophets clearly drew upon previous texts and traditions to formulate their message. In doing so, they are able to evoke the ideas and emotions that their listeners would associate with these recognizable passages; on occasion, the prophet makes subtle changes in the earlier text to create a sense of dissonance in his listeners. Joel's constant references to the Exodus from Egypt clearly intends to create hope in his listeners that a redemption of historical dimensions will surely come; his declaration that a time is coming when people would "Beat [their] plowshares into swords and [their] pruning hooks into spears" would clearly shock them. At the conclusion of his book, Micah's call for God's mercy cleverly intertwines allusions from both the familiar and expected Thirteen Attributes of Mercy with an unexpected source, the triumphant Song of the Sea which the Jewish people sang at the Red Sea. Throughout the work, we shall identify the biblical antecedents for the prophets' words.

---

8. In synonymous parallelism, the second or subsequent line repeats or reinforces the sense of the first line:

> Hear the Lord's word, you rulers of Sodom!
> Listen to the law of our God, you people of Gomorrah! (Is. 1:10)
> I have swept your offenses like a cloud,
> your sins like the morning mist. (Is. 44:22)
> Then I shall turn your festivals into mourning
> And all your songs into lamentation. (Amos 8:10).

In contrast, antithetical parallelism occurs when where the second or subsequent line contrasts or negates the previous idea:

> They do not cry out to me from their hearts,
> but wail upon their beds. (Hos. 7:14)
> A wise man's mind is to his right,
> as the mind of a fool is to his left. (Eccl. 10:2)

Finally, in synthetic parallelism, related thoughts are brought together to emphasize similarities, contrasts, or correlations of degree:

> Acquiring wisdom is much better than refined gold;
> acquiring understanding is superior to silver. (Prov. 16:16)
> It is better to heed the rebuke of the wise
> than to hear the song of fools. (Eccl. 7:5)

Prologue

"Coming, coming…" As heavy rain pounded the roof, Yeter stumbled over the sparse wooden furniture in his stone hut and opened the door. Three dark silhouettes, two large and one small, stood on the threshold. "What do you want?"

"Please," two voices begged. "We need a place for the night. Can you help?"

"Come in," responded Yeter instinctively, standing aside to allow the three to pass. They entered his hut quickly, and Yeter shut the door to the howling winds and raging storm outside. "What are you doing outside in the rain? No one wanders around these hills at nighttime, especially in this weather." He turned around to greet his guests and gasped. "But you're…you're…."

"Yes. We are from Manasseh," answered the tallest figure, an elderly gentleman carrying a bent walking staff. The colors on the guests' garments were faded, torn, and covered with mud, but still noticeably not a southern weave. "I am Yishi, this is my daughter Shua, and the boy is Asrael." He looked up and noticed that Yeter had turned his eyes away. "Thank you for letting us in. I know this cannot be easy for you. We have been walking for days, maybe weeks. Most people that we met turn us away."

"Nonsense," interrupted She'erah, Yeter's wife, emerging from the corner where a pot hung over a small fire. "In the rain and the wind at night, with no place for shelter. Would leaving you outside be appropriate for the children of Abraham and Sarah?"

"Children of Abraham and Sarah? Was it appropriate for children of Abraham and Sarah to invade our lands, burn our cities, and take our people captive?" blurted out Yeter. "Their twisted worship of our God, golden calves and clay figures, and doing who knows what. If it weren't for the weather, you'd be out in the mud already!" He turned away, and an uncomfortable pause filled the air. Suddenly, the room became much smaller. Only She'erah remained unperturbed, and she began to ladle stew into small bowls.

"You will have to forgive my husband, Yeter. When your King Pekah invaded, two of his brothers were killed, and the Edomites took several of my cousins captive." She instinctively spat on the grounds when she uttered the king's name. "Only last year," she continued, all the while efficiently bringing dry garments to the bewildered guests, "Philistine raiding parties came within two hilltops of our village, Mareisha. Our two children have had to leave because we can barely get by. Hezekiah drafted one, and he is now in Lakhish. The other works as a laborer digging wells near Jerusalem. But don't worry," she smiled, "we have enough for tonight, thank God. And with God's help, we will have for tomorrow as well. Come and sit. We have enough."

The two families sat together quietly for several minutes, awkwardly picking at the simple meal she placed in front of them. The boy Asrael barely raised his eyes – but it was clear that he had seen horrors beyond his years. Finally, Shua spoke. "I'm sorry for your loss. Many of us in Samaria did not want Pekah to attack. We were once one family. But Pekah told us that it was necessary – if Judah didn't join us to fight Assyria, both Israel and Judah would die. He promised that people in Judah would stand up against your young king, Ahaz, and that replacing him would be a mere formality. You know, when Pekah took Judeans captive, our prophets stood up against him. No one expected Ahaz to surrender to Assyria instead. When we heard that he had placed an altar to Ashur in the Temple courtyard, we realized that in the end Pekah was right about one thing: Without Judah's help, we would fall to the

Assyrians. And we did. My husband died last year while defending our
capital, Samaria, waiting for the Egyptians to come. Fortunately for him,
he died in battle. The survivors suffered much worse. The Assyrians took
most of my family northwards; I don't know to where. We only found
out later. We lived in the hills some distance away – the Assyrians did
not bother coming after us after they torched the city. I guess they don't
consider us farmers important enough to take."

"If you're a farming family, you won't get much justice in Judah
either," Yeter mumbled bitterly, his voice echoing off the mud walls. "For
years, Jerusalem's rich have been slowly driving up the price of grain.
When family farmers like us need to buy goods, they advance us money
in exchange for the next year's crops – and many have had to mortgage
family lands to do so. Whether the harvest is good or bad, they always
get paid first. If you don't pay, the judges are no use. Who wants to listen
to a poor country worker, standing covered in dirt and sweat and rags,
when his silk-clad noble buddy stands opposite him?"

"The same thing happened to us!" Yishi exclaimed. "Samaria's palaces were a sight to behold. The pride of Israel, we called them. I could
never look at those atrocities, though, built on the blood and sweat of
honest workers like ourselves."

"And now rumors have it that Hezekiah is planning to shake the
Assyrian lion's tail. We hear that he is seeing Babylonian envoys for that
purpose!" Yeter was warming up – no matter who his audience was, he
always enjoyed being allowed to rail against life's injustices. "It was nice
to eat a proper Pesah offering again, and he did good by removing that
despicable altar from the Temple once and for all. Now Jerusalem is
overrun by northerners. If war with Assyria is coming, Hezekiah will
build new walls, store rations, buy arms. And when the rich plan war,
the poor pay the price. First, they raise taxes, and then they draft an
army. Of course, it's our boys who serve on the front line, not the rich
kids. That means fewer people working the field, less harvest brought
in, and again, it's the rich that profit in the end." Yeter paused, and for a
minute, the table was still.

"You know," Yishi continued quietly, "you Judeans did try to warn
us. That shepherd from Tekoa … What was his name? Amos. My father
told me how he came into the city center and threatened us that God

would destroy Samaria if we didn't change. But everyone only laughed. We accused him of being a rabble-rouser, a populist, a southern collaborator." Yishi shook his head. "We should have listened when we had the chance."

"Our neighbor does the same thing!" exclaimed She'erah. "Micah. He has been traveling around the cities in Judah, speaking to anyone, anywhere. Sometimes they laugh, one or two listen – but most times, people turn away. I asked his wife Ahlai how he continues, day after day. Wouldn't he do better at home, bringing in a crop or working a craft? She just smiled and said that Micah told her that his strength was not his own. It was a gift from God. Yeter doesn't believe in that," she added, glancing at her husband. "He says, 'Just be a good person, just, kind, and humble – that's all you need.' Not to worry about God – leave that to the priests."

"God hasn't been too interested in us these days," Yeter growled. "Besides, I don't trust voices when I can't see the speaker."

"I do!" piped up Asrael. Everyone turned to look at the gaunt young boy, whose face had lit up for the first time since entering the house. "When Moses went up to Mount Sinai to receive the commandments, no one saw God then – yet we heard him. Micah always says that God will remember us and that some of us will always survive. And when God wants, we will be saved – you wait and see."

Silence fell over the table. Suddenly, Yeter began to chuckle, and Yishi quickly joined in. "Look at us, a couple of wise old men, yet it is the young one who speaks clearly. Maybe there is hope for us after all."

Introduction

A Brief History of Israel and Judah

Because the prophets' messages are timeless, they have fascinated and inspired humanity for almost three thousand years. Challenges of social justice and religious integrity, of maintaining optimism in the darkest times, of ethics and morality – all these speak as powerfully to us as they did to struggling farmers eking out a living in the Judean mountains during the eighth century BCE. Yet, as timeless as the prophets' words are, they were always timely as well. We argued in the preface that to fully appreciate a prophet, we must understand his *Sitz im Leben*. This includes the setting when he spoke, the various forces at play during his career, including political maneuvering (internal and external), the competing religious trends and beliefs, and the socio-economic condition of the nation. These factors constitute the unwritten background for the prophet's words.

We must remember that no matter how powerful or persuasive his message, a prophet could only do so much. The prophets were not the leaders, making the decisions that affected the kingdom. That role was the province of the kings. Like monarchs everywhere, the kings of Israel and Judah faced tremendous challenges. They had to meet the needs and desires of the populace, maintain good relations with neighboring countries, prepare for future threats, select between different policies and potential alliances – all the while attempting to ensure that their behavior was acceptable to God. Unlike other ancient empires, where the religious establishment was subservient to the ruling polity and existed to strengthen the existing institutions, the Jewish king was subservient to God; and true prophets of God were not obedient lackeys. No foreign prophet in ancient times could have rebuked his sovereign so fearlessly and harshly as Nathan spoke to David after the Bathsheba affair. Therefore, despite their lack of political power, the prophets played a crucial role in guiding the nation. Sometimes they were court insiders, sometimes charismatic outsiders, and sometimes a lonely voice in the desert.[1] Whatever role they played, it was their voice that provided the spiritual direction and guidance for the king and the people, according to the needs of their times. We begin our study by summarizing the turbulent history of the kingdoms of Israel and Judah, and how the almost fifty years from 745 BCE to 701 BCE led to calamities and upheavals from which the Jewish people never recovered.

In 750 BCE, the Jewish people found themselves paradoxically in both their strongest yet weakest state ever.[2] Having enjoyed over a half-century of peace and prosperity, they were fractured and fragmented

---

1. For scholarly discussion and different understandings of the prophets' roles, see Abraham Joshua Heschel, *The Prophets* (New York: Harper & Row, 1962); Norman Podhoretz, *The Prophets: Who They Were, What They Are* (New York: Simon & Schuster, 2002); Brad E. Kelle, "Ancient Israelite Prophets and Greek Political Orators: Analogies for the Prophets and Their Implications for Historical Reconstruction," in *Israel's Prophets and Israel's Past: Essays on the Relationship of Prophetic Texts and Israelite History*, ed. Brad E. Kelle and Megan Moore (New York: T&T Clark International, 2006), 57–82; J. Blenkinsopp, *A History of Prophecy in Israel* (Louisville, KY: Westminster John Knox, 1996), 40–64; J. H. Hayes, "Prophecy and Prophets, Hebrew Bible," in D. L. Petersen, *The Prophetic Literature: An Introduction* (Louisville, KY: Westminster John Knox, 2002), 215–38.

2. Here is historian John Bright's concise evaluation: "The eighth century in Israel reached its mid-point on a note of hideous dissonance. The state of Israel, externally strong, prosperous, and confident of the future, was inwardly rotten and sick past curing.... It was thanks primarily to the prophets that, as the northern state went to her grave ... Israel's faith received a new access of life" (*A History of Israel* [Louisville, KY: Westminster John Knox, 2000], 266).

instead of unified. They were divided geographically and politically into two small kingdoms. They were divided religiously between Judah's pure worship of God and the northern tribes' syncretic approach, which combined worship of God with the local deities. They were divided politically between differing factions bickering over how to deal with a new threat – the steady encroachment of Assyria, whose borders were becoming ever closer. Most crucially, to the prophets, the people were divided socially, as the traditional gap between urban and rural dwellers grew into an economic chasm. How did this situation develop? We begin with the formation of the twin kingdoms of Israel and Judah. We continue through alternating periods of war and peace, poverty and prosperity, until we arrive at the end of the eighth century BCE, a period of destruction and tragedy unparalleled until then in Tanakh. When the dust settled in the year 700 BCE, the former mighty Kingdom of Israel was no longer, her inhabitants exiled forever. Judah barely fared better, having been reduced to Jerusalem and its immediate surroundings. As Isaiah plaintively describes, "Your land is laid waste, your towns burned up in fire; your own land – before your eyes strangers consume it – laid waste: a vision of strangers' overturning. Only daughter Zion stands like the watchman's shack in a vineyard, like the hut in a cucumber field – a town besieged" (Is. 1:7–8).

FROM TRIBES TO KINGDOMS

Kingship first appeared in Israel in the tenth century BCE, when the people demanded a king from Samuel. The nation was weary of the instability that characterized the tumultuous rule of the judges during the previous centuries. They needed protection, so Samuel appointed Saul of Benjamin to lead them. However, only under his successor David of Judah did the new kingdom grow in power and prestige. David's son Solomon would enjoy a lengthy period of peace and prosperity, which allowed him to complete the First Temple's building and develop Jerusalem into a cosmopolitan, international city. However, at the beginning of the reign of his son Rehoboam in 931 BCE, ancient fissures between the tribes split the kingdom apart into two separate entities. Ten northern tribes united and formed the Kingdom of Israel under Jeroboam son of Nebat, with only the tribe of Judah remaining loyal to David's grandchild Rehoboam.

THE EARLY DIVIDED KINGDOM:
REHOBOAM UNTIL JEHU

The Kingdom of Israel struggled to find its footing during the first century after the schism, despite being the stronger and more prosperous of the two nations. The primary reason was its inability to maintain political stability. While Asa (912–871 BCE) reigned over Judah in the south, seven kings sat on Israel's throne.[3] Coups were frequent; so much so, that the name of one would-be northern conspirator, Zimri, became a synonym for assassin (II Kings 9:27). Both kingdoms, however, remained vulnerable to attack and extortion by external enemies – from the Egyptian empire in the south to Aram (modern-day Syria) and Assyria in the northeast. The constant worries of invasion and instability were probable factors in Omri's eventual decision to ally himself with the Phoenicians and marry his son Ahab to the Sidonian princess Jezebel. The alliance brought Israel temporary stability, but at the expense of religious fidelity to God. During Ahab's reign (874–853), Israel became a regional superpower. At the same time, marriage between the children of Ahab and King Jehoshaphat of Judah temporarily allied the two kingdoms and led to a period of relative quiet for the two countries.

The Tanakh remembers Ahab's reign for his never-ending clashes with the prophet Elijah. At stake was nothing less than the allegiance of the people. Were they loyal to God, or would they serve Ahab and Jezebel's new gods? Due to Ahab's religious infidelity and social abuses, God decreed that his reign would end. Nevertheless, Ahab repented and humbled himself after Elijah confronted him in the vineyard of Naboth, and God chose to suspend His sentence of destruction. Once Ahab's children returned to idol worship, Elijah's disciple Elisha inspired Jehu to seize power in a bloody coup, wiping out all of Ahab's descendants. Ahab's daughter Athaliah attempted to seize the throne in Judah, slaughtering all her grandchildren. A quick-thinking girl spirited one baby away, and the people would rebel against Athaliah and restore the Davidic dynasty.

---

3. Jeroboam I, Nadab, Baasha, Elah, Zimri, Omri, and Ahab (as listed in I Kings 13–16).

List of Kings from the Mid-Eighth Century[4]

Year	King of Israel	King of Judah	Prophet	King of Assyria Who Threatens Israel or Judah
840	Jehu	[Athaliah]	Elisha	
835	843–814	Joash		
830		836–797		
825				
820				
815				
810	Jehoahaz			
805	814–798			
800		Amaziah		
795	Jehoash	797–768		
790	798–782			
785		Azariah		
780	Jeroboam II	(Uzziah)[5]	Jonah	
775	793–753	793–742		

4. Questions abound regarding the exact years when the kings reigned, both from textual inconsistencies in the book of Kings and attempts to synchronize these dates with the available outside evidence. The appendix to this book is dedicated to outlining the various issues and suggesting solutions. In the main body of this work we maintain the accepted historical chronology.
5. As we shall explain in the appendix, most of Uzziah's reign overlaps with either his father's or his children's. Regarding the two names for Uzziah (Azariah in Kings, Uzziah in Chronicles), one popular explanation is that the book of Chronicles consistently uses "Uzziah" to distinguish the king Azariah from the high priest Azariah (II Chr. 26:17, 20). A scholarly discussion of the differing names Azariah and Uzziah, which regards one as a birth name and the other as a throne name taken at the time of his accession, can be found in A. Honeyman, "The Evidence for Regnal Names among the Hebrews," *Journal of Biblical Literature* 67 (1948): 13–25. Other possible examples of dual names in the Tanakh include the cases of Shallum-Jehoahaz (Jer. 22:11), Eliakim-Jehoiakim (II Kings 23:34), and Mattaniah-Zedekiah (II Kings 24:17).

Year	King of Israel	King of Judah	Prophet	King of Assyria Who Threatens Israel or Judah
770				
765			Amos	
760				
755			Isaiah	
750	Final years of strife and instability – six kings reign		Hosea	
745		Jotham 752–736	Micah	Tiglath-Pileser III
740		Ahaz 742–727		
735				
730				
725		Hezekiah 727–698		Salmanazar V
720	Downfall and exile			Sargon II
715				
710				
705				Sennacherib
700				

THE LATER DIVIDED KINGDOM: STABILITY AND STRENGTH

Starting with the mid-ninth century BCE, however, both Israel and Judah enjoyed a period of relative tranquility. This "silver age" lasted almost a century, from 843 BCE until 745 BCE. Two new kings appeared. In Judah, Jehoash concentrated on the rebuilding of the Temple. Jehu and his descendants would rule for almost a century in the north, becoming Israel's longest unchallenged dynasty. However, recovery from the upheavals extracted a high cost. Jehu's killing of Jezebel meant that Israel renounced its alliance with the Phoenicians and forced Jehu to conclude an alliance with Assyria, just as Assyrian power waned.[6] Israel would suffer

---

6. As recorded on the Black Obelisk of Salmanazar III, on display in the British museum today. It bears the inscription concerning "the tribute of Jehu, son of Omri: I received

many defeats at the hand of Aram during the following years,[7] while Judah suffered losses to Edom and the Philistines in the south. Under Elisha's patient guidance, however, Israel managed to regain its former prosperity while the boy king, Jehoash, slowly rebuilt Judah. External threats from neighboring countries began to dwindle. Egypt to the south was no longer a danger. Both the Philistine coastal cities and the desert kingdoms of Ammon, Moab, and Edom to the east slowly diminished in strength. The leaders rebuilt the tattered relationships with the Phoenicians, and they became valued trading partners, bringing new riches into the cities.

Most importantly, Aram in the north turned its attentions elsewhere, facing the growing threat of the Assyrian Empire to the east. The

---

from him silver, gold, a golden bowl, a golden vase with pointed bottom, golden tumblers, golden buckets, tin, a staff for a king [and] spears." In addition, one panel, the Jehu Relief panel, contains the earliest surviving representation of a biblical character, with "a bearded Semite in royal attire bowing with his face to the ground before King Salmanazar III, with Hebrew servants standing behind him bearing gifts." For further information, see http://www.bible-history.com/black-obelisk/what-is-the-black-obelisk.html.

Black Obelisk relief showing a prostrate King Jehu offering tribute to Assyria

7. Archaeological evidence of which was discovered in 1993 with the discovery in Tel Dan of a stele belonging to Hazael, king of Aram. In its text, he boasts of having killed two kings, the rulers of Israel and of Judah. Since he had apparently defeated Jehu, conquering territory in the process, he appropriated for himself Jehu's accomplishments!

one blemish in this period was a foolhardy attempt by Amaziah son of Jehoash of Judah to invade Israel (II Kings 14). Some suggest that this was an attempt to remove Judah's status as the lesser kingdom; however, it nearly led to the Southern Kingdom's collapse. Amaziah was deposed, and both countries enjoyed an extended period of tranquility and prosperity under the lengthy reigns of Azariah (Uzziah) in the south (fifty-two years) and Jeroboam II in the north (forty-one years). With a favorable international political situation, the disappearance of external threats and conflicts, Israel and Judah enjoyed a mini golden age, unseen since the days of David and Solomon. Both kings expanded their borders considerably (II Kings 14; II Chr. 26) and established political hegemony in the region. With control of the major trade routes spanning the Transjordan and northern Arabia, the coastal plains, and the Phoenician ports, both countries could generate considerable wealth and tremendous economic prosperity.[8] Amos describes Samaria's fortified cities, vacation homes, luxury homes, vast vineyards, and elaborately catered feasts.[9] Isaiah similarly

MeLeCH ISRaEL
King of Israel

BeIT DaViD
House of David

Line 6: *of my kings. And I killed two [power]ful kin[gs], who harnessed two thou[sand cha-]*
Line 7: *riots and two thousand horsemen. [I killed Jo]ram son of [Ahab]*
Line 8: *king of Israel, and I killed [Achaz]yahu son of [Joram kin]g*
Line 9: of the House of David

8. John Bright, *A History of Israel*, 3rd ed. (Philadelphia: Westminster Press, 1981), 258.
9. Amos 3:11, 15; 5:11; 6:4–7.

mocks the opulence of Judah's upper class. However, these new riches created a sharp social divide between the city-dwelling urban elite and the rural residents of the countryside. With the quickly growing gap between the economic elite and the farming poor, the Jewish people faced an existential peril, not from external enemies but from inside their own borders.

SOCIAL DIVIDE

In the eyes of the eighth-century prophets, the growing chasm between Israel and Judah's rich and poor represented a vital threat that would lead the kingdoms to ruin.[10] Amos, Hosea, Isaiah, and Micah critiqued not the riches but the covetousness and selfishness of the beneficiaries of the economic upheaval. Prosperity and affluence do not automatically lead to economic injustice unless the newfound gains occur through the exploitation of others. Recent scholarship suggests that in addition to the ever-present factors of human avarice and greed, the prophets were railing against larger economic structural forces that inevitably led to economic inequality. For example, Marvin Chaney argues that the very institution of the monarchy with its accompanying centralized government set in motion forces that led to the schism between the urban elite and the rural peasants.[11] Other social scientists who study the modern effects of urbanization on highly rural, agrarian communities argue, with

---

10. Summarized nicely by Samuel Yeivin in "The Divided Kingdom: Rehoboam-Ahaz/ Jeroboam-Pekah," in *The World History of the Jewish People*, vol. 4:1: *The Age of Monarchies: Political History*, ed. A. Malamat and I. Ephcal (Jerusalem: Masada Press, 1979), 126–78:

    > Prosperity brought in its wake a much more acute differentiation between the agricultural population, which became more and more landless, and the nouveaux-riche absentee landlords, living in cities as large dealers and high-grade bureaucrats exploiting their privileged economic position to the detriment of the population as a whole.

11. Marvin Chaney writes:

    > The full-blown monarchy from the Solomonic reign down to the ninth and eighth century put severe pressure on peasants when a subsistence economy [transformed] into a market economy to serve the lifestyle of the local elite and export to other neighboring countries as well. Peasants were forced into debt slavery when natural disaster like famine and drought struck them. The unfortunate situation was followed by the process of foreclosure and land acquisition, which was accelerated by a corrupted court system, and ultimately led to the process of latifundialisation. ("Systemic Study of the Israelite Monarchy," *Semeia* 37 [1986]: 72)

some possible merit, that the same economic forces of wealth concentration were at play during this period in eighth-century Israel and Judah.
Oswald Lorezt suggests that "rent-capitalism," where moneylenders
ultimately reduced the helpless peasants into bonded laborers, was the
primary factor behind the increasing gulf between the upper and lower
classes.[12] Similarly, D. N. Premnath suggests that a process of latifun-
dialisation occurred (defined as the accumulation of land in the hands
of a wealthy minority elite). Based on the insights derived from social
anthropology, Bernhard Lang compares ancient Israel to modern "peasant
societies." These societies consist of two different social classes: peasants
who maintain themselves on a subsistence economy and a propertied,
merchant elite who live in cities and control public affairs. Occasional
periods of poor climate and resulting crop failures often compel peasants to borrow from urban lenders, causing farmers to gradually fall into
debt.[13] Forced to sell off their ancestral holdings to cover their debts, the
farmers became bonded laborers to absentee urban landowners, tilling
land they once owned. Other forces accelerated the impoverishment of
the rural farmers: the growth of urban centers, taxation, luxurious life-
styles, and the elite's control over both trade and commerce and courts.[14]

In chapters 7 and 8 of *Peasants, Prophets, & Political Economy* (Eugene, OR: Cascade
Books, 2017), Chaney argues that the intensification of agriculture that occurred during the reigns of Jeroboam II and Uzziah, increasing their participation in international
trade, was the main factor behind the social crisis encountered by the prophets.

12. O. Lorezt, "Die prophetische Kritik des Rentenkapitalismus," *Ugarit-Forschungen* 7
(1975): 271–78.

13. B. Lang, "The Social Organization of Peasant Poverty in Biblical Israel," in *Anthro-
pological Approaches to the Old Testament* (Philadelphia: Fortress Press, 1985), 83ff.

14. D. N. Premnath, *Eighth Century Prophets: A Social Analysis* (St. Louis, MO: Chalice
Press, 2003). Recent archaeological discoveries generally affirm these descriptions of
the social situation in eighth-century BCE Judah and Israel. Excavations at Samaria
reveal that houses of the tenth century were of uniform size throughout the city. By
the mid-eighth century, the size of the residences varied widely, and larger houses
became a distinctive feature of Israelite lifestyle (see D. N. Freedman, ed., *The Anchor
Bible Dictionary* [New York: Doubleday, 1992], s.v. "Amos, Book of"). Additionally,
archaeologists have noticed changes in the sizes of storage pots and jars dated to the
eighth century. Storage containers from earlier periods would vary greatly in size
and shape. When the agricultural economies of Israel and Judah only functioned at
subsistence level, and foodstuffs were stored and consumed close to where they were

As noted above, the prophets do not attack wealth per se, but rather the self-indulgence of the affluent and their expressed indifference towards the plight of the nation's poor. In doing so, they ignored traditional Jewish values of community and interdependence and a fundamental sense of compassion for others. Whether the underlying corruption stems from human nature or economic structures, it is clear from a quick overview of the prophets' critiques, as seen in the table below, that systematic corruption and social injustice prevailed in Israel and Judah at this time.

Verse	Phenomenon Described by the Prophet
"Woe to those who add house to house, join field to field until no space is left; you are settled there alone on the face of the land." Isaiah 5:8	Isaiah is referring to the large-scale accumulation of lands in the hands of a limited group of people that deprived the common populace, or the formation of large, cultivated estates by absorbing neighboring property, or the intentional buying up of fields, thereby crowding out smaller farmers.
"The princes of Judah have become like those who move back the boundary stones; upon them I will pour out My wrath like water." Hosea 5:10	The Torah forbids removing the landmarks that delineated the boundaries between people (Deut. 19:14) and curses them in Deut. 27:17. Proverbs also warns, "Do not remove an ancient boundary that your forefathers set." Hosea emphasizes how the powerful were able to enlarge their properties at the expense of others.

---

grown, there was no need for storage jars to be identical in volume. However, finds dated to the eighth century show a standardization of sizes and shapes, reflecting the demands of interregional trade and economic efficiency. However, see recent critiques by Philippe Guillaume in *Land, Credit and Crisis: Agrarian Finance in the Hebrew Bible* (Sheffield: Equinox, 2012); Walter J. Houston, "Was There a Social Crisis in the Eighth Century?" *In Search of Pre-Exilic Israel: Journal for the Study of the Old Testament*, Supplement Series 406 (2004), 130–49; Houston, "Exit the Oppressed Peasant? Rethinking the Background of Social Criticism in the Prophets," in John Day, ed., *Prophecy and the Prophets in Ancient Israel* (London: T&T Clark, 2010), 101–16.

Verse	Phenomenon Described by the Prophet
"Hear this, O cows of the Bashan who are on Mount Shomron, who oppress the poor, who break the poverty stricken, who say to their masters, 'Bring wine and let us drink.'" Amos 4:1	Amos berates the wives of the elites for their materialistic lifestyle, which led them to pressure their husbands to make even more massive profits to satisfy them without being concerned about the effects of their demands on the oppressed poor whose labor they exploited.
"Woe to those who plot wicked deeds, who plan evildoing from their beds; come morning light they carry it out merely because they have the power. They lust for others' fields and seize them, eye others' homes and assume them as theirs; they exploit men and their households, both man and his estate." Micah 2:1–2	Like Isaiah above, Micah decries the behavior of the rich who plotted and planned on how they could expand their estates by depriving the legitimate owners of their ancestral homes and fields. That they acted at dawn, in the morning, is significant because it was at this time that the courts traditionally met to decide legal disputes. The control the wealthy exercised over the judicial system ensured that their greedy schemes would receive stamps of approval from the legal establishment.
"Your ministers are wayward, friends to thieves, loving corruption, all of them, chasing bribes. They do not judge an orphan's case; a widow's claim does not even come before them." Isaiah 1:23	Corruption was endemic, permeating all layers of society. Both the government (the princes) and the judicial system functioned only with bribes and kickbacks, and no one represented the interests or protects society's weaker elements.
"Who lie on beds of ivory, lounge upon your couches, feasting on the choicest of sheep and calves taken from their feeding stalls, who play the harp – with instruments they think themselves like David – who guzzle wine from bowls, anoint yourselves with the finest of oils, but are not heartsick over Yosef's ruin." Amos 6:4–6	The saying "eat, drink, and be merry" summarizes Amos's description of Samaria's elite citizens, who enjoyed a luxurious and opulent lifestyle while the poor suffered.

The relative calm enjoyed by Israel and Judah would end in 745 BCE when Tiglath-Pileser III (called Pul in II Kings 15:19) took the Assyrian throne. Capable and ruthless, he turned Assyria into the most powerful empire the Middle East had ever known, and for the first time, Israel and Judah were facing an existential threat.

The two kingdoms at the height of their dominion

THE ASSYRIANS – THE WORLD SUDDENLY CHANGES

Though Assyria existed as an independent (and often powerful entity) since the third millennium BCE, the rise to power of King Adad Nirari II (912–891 BCE) signifies the beginning of the neo-Assyrian Empire. Under Adad Nirari II and his successors, Assyria managed to expand its borders, from Babylon in the east to modern-day Turkey in the west. A century later, Shalmaneser III would expand the empire even further, eventually reaching the Mediterranean and receiving tribute from the wealthy Phoenician cities of Tyre and Sidon. Simultaneously, the Assyrians built numerous highways across the Middle East, equipping them with supply centers and granaries. These technological advancements enabled their armies to travel long distances without needing to replenish their supplies. More importantly, they were able to engage in their favorite military tactic – siege warfare.[15] Once successful in conquering a city, the victorious Assyrians would establish shrines to Ashur in the vanquished temples. Thus, many of the conquered peoples slowly assimilated into the worship of Ashur, which created a common religious framework for the empire. However, the Assyrian westward expansion halted abruptly during the mid-ninth century, as civil wars and disputes over succession crippled the empire. Assyria's misfortunes were good fortune for Israel and Judah, providing them with a lengthy period of relative quiet and prosperity during the first half of the eighth century BCE described above.

"Sennacherib Came and Mixed Up the Nations of the World" (Mishna Yadayim 4:4)[16]

It is impossible to overstate the extent that Tiglath-Pileser III's rise to the Assyrian throne in 745 BCE overthrew the established world order. Within half a century, the entire ancient Near East fell under the yoke of the neo-Assyrian Empire. While kingdoms had extended their reach before, for the first time an empire arose that not only conquered most of the region but aggressively engaged in forced exile and resettlement of all its conquered peoples. For centuries, a people's sense of identity

---

15. Discussing ancient military tactics and the development of siege warfare, Simon Anglim writes:

> More than anything else, the Assyrian army excelled at siege warfare, and was probably the first force to carry a separate corps of engineers…. Assault was their principal tactic against the heavily fortified cities of the Near East. They developed a great variety of methods for breaching enemy walls: sappers were employed to undermine walls or to light fires underneath wooden gates, and ramps were thrown up to allow men to go over the ramparts or to attempt a breach on the upper section of wall where it was the least thick. Mobile ladders allowed attackers to cross moats and quickly assault any point in defenses. These operations were covered by masses of archers, who were the core of the infantry. But the pride of the Assyrian siege train were their engines. These were multistoried wooden towers with four wheels and a turret on top and one, or at times two, battering rams at the base. (World History Encyclopedia, s.v. "Assyrian Warfare," https://www.worldhistory.org/Assyrian_Warfare/)

16. In rabbinic thought, the name Sennacherib became synonymous with all the Assyrian kings (see Numbers Rabba 23; Sanhedrin 94a). As such, the quotation from the mishna can be understood to mean that it was the Assyrian empire that mixed up (lit., confused) the nations of the world.

(language, culture) and religious beliefs (each city-state had a local deity that resided within its borders and protected its inhabitants) had developed naturally from their place of residence. Now, the Assyrians scattered them throughout their empire. Only the Akkadian language of their conqueror, and the worship of Ashur, the head of the Assyrian pantheon, united them.[17] This upheaval began with the decision of Tiglath-Pileser III (745–727 BCE) to restructure Assyria's vast military so that within decades the Assyrian army became the most effective military force ever known. Quickly and efficiently, he subjugated Babylon, southern Turkey, and Aram (Syria). Ultimately, the Assyrian armies reached Israel's borders in the north and exiled the tribes that dwelled in the Transjordan region (Reuben, Gad, and Manasseh).

Shalmaneser V (727–722 BCE) followed, punishing Israel's desperate and foolhardy attempt to rebel by laying siege to the capital city of Samaria. During the siege, he was abruptly succeeded by his brother Sargon II (722–705 BCE), possibly in a violent coup. Sargon's descendants ruled the Assyrian Empire until its fall at the end of the seventh century. In 722 BCE, Sargon defeated the last remnants of the Northern Kingdom, sending its inhabitants into exile (II Kings 17–18).

Sargon II was succeeded by his son Sennacherib (705–681 BCE), who continued to campaign extensively and ruthlessly, conquering the Philistine cities, sections of Judah, and Anatolia between 714–712 BCE. He also moved the capital to Nineveh, which remained Assyria's political capital until its fall in 612 BCE. The Taylor Prism, a cuneiform describing Sennacherib's military exploits, details his siege of Jerusalem in 701 BCE. Discovered in 1830 CE by Britain's Colonel Robert Taylor, the prism records Sennacherib's claims that he captured 46 cities and trapped the people of Jerusalem inside the city "like a bird in a cage." The Tanakh also describes this pivotal campaign in II Kings 18–19, II Chronicles 32, and Isaiah 37. Ultimately, Sennacherib's older children assassinated him in 681 BCE (II Kings 19:37). They rationalized it as an act to appease the wrath of the Babylonian gods after Sennacherib sacked

---

17. It is possible that it was this development that caused the prophets of Israel at this time (i.e., Amos and Isaiah) to begin to articulate the universal characteristics of God, which wasn't needed previously.

Babylon. Most likely, though, their motive was revenge, as Sennacherib chose his youngest son, Esarhaddon, to succeed him.

The Taylor Prism, recording the first eight campaigns of King Sennacherib

ISRAEL SELF-DESTRUCTS

Just as the Assyrian lion began to raise its head, the Northern Kingdom began a slow collapse into anarchy. After Jeroboam II's relatively stable and prosperous reign, an earthquake devastated parts of the country's infrastructure in 760 BCE. At the same time, assassinations, internal turmoil, and power struggles left Israel politically unprepared to cope with the growing Assyrian menace. Meanwhile, as Amos and Hosea emphasize, social injustice and Baal worship were rampant, weakening Israel's national identity and resolve, ultimately sealing its downfall.

Zechariah (746–745) and Shallum (745)

In the thirty-eighth year of Azaryahu, king of Judah, Zechariahu son of Yorovam became king over Israel in Shomron for six months. He did what was evil in the eyes of the Lord, as his ancestors did; he did not turn away from the sins of Yorovam son of Nevat, who led Israel to sin. Then Shalum son of Yavesh formed a conspiracy against him; he struck him down before the people and assassinated him and reigned in his place. As for the rest of Zechariah's history – it is recorded in the Book of the History of the Kings of Israel. This was the word of the Lord as promised to Jehu: "Four generations of your line will sit on the throne of Israel," and it had come to pass. Shalum son of Yavesh became king in the thirty-ninth year of Uzziah, king of Judah, and for one month, he reigned in Shomron. (II Kings 15:8–13)

Israel's disintegration began with the ascension of Zechariah, the son of Jeroboam II and the fourth king in the Jehu dynasty, who ascended the throne after his father's forty-year reign. However, after only half a year, he was assassinated by Shallum son of Jabesh. In turn, Shallum was murdered after only a month by Menahem son of Gadi.

Menahem (745–737) and Pekahiah (737–736)

Then Menahem son of Gadi marched up from Tirtza and entered Shomron. He struck down Shalum son of Yavesh in Shomron and assassinated him, and he reigned in his place.... It was then that Menahem attacked Tifsah and everything in it and its territories from Tirtza; they would not yield, so he attacked – he even slashed open its pregnant women. In the thirty-ninth year of Azarya, king of Judah, Menahem son of Gadi became king over Israel, for ten years in Shomron. He did what was evil in the eyes of the Lord; all his days, he did not turn away from the sins of Yorovam son of Nevat. When Pul, king of Assyria, invaded the land, Menahem gave Pul one thousand talents of silver to gain his support in maintaining control of the kingdom. Menahem exacted the silver from Israel; every able man had to pay fifty shekel of silver to the king of Assyria. Then the king of Assyria withdrew and did not remain there in the land. (II Kings 15:14–20)

Having assassinated his predecessor, Menahem began his reign by cruelly subjugating those who opposed him. Though he ruled for almost a decade, he was weak, bribing the Assyrians to maintain power. Menahem taxed the wealthy to pay tribute to Tiglath-Pileser, thus avoiding a direct invasion. He functionally made Israel a vassal state of the Assyrian Empire and sowed opposition to his rule. We can only speculate about Israel's national mood, but unfolding events suggest strong resentment against subjugation to Assyria.

Pekah (736–732) and the Syro-Ephraimite War

And Menahem slept with his ancestors, and his son Pekahiah reigned in his place.... Then Pekah son of Remaliah, his adjutant, formed a conspiracy against him; he struck him down in the citadel of the royal palace in Shomron. With him were Argov and Aryeh and fifty men of the Gileadites; they assassinated him, and he reigned in his place.

In the fifty-second year of Azarya, king of Judah, Pekah son of Remaliah became king over Israel in Shomron for twenty years. He did what was evil in the eyes of the Lord; he did not turn away from the sins of Yorovam son of Nevat, who led Israel to sin. In the days of Pekah, king of Israel, Tiglath-Pileser, king of Assyria, came and seized Iyon, Avel Beit Maakha, Yanoaḥ, Kedesh,

Hazor, the Gilad, the Galil, and all the region of Naftali, and had them exiled to Assyria. (II Kings 15:22–29)

Assassination not only signifies an abrupt transfer of power but also entails a dramatic reversal of policy. In this instance, Pekah's assassination of Menahem's son, Pekahiah, set the nation on a dangerous course. Pekahiah maintained the peace by appeasing the Assyrians. Pekah chose to engage them directly. Scholars suggest that Pekah was already ruling over the tribes on the eastern side of the Jordan when he assassinated Pekahiah (hence the twenty-year reign attributed to him).[18] Now, having assumed complete control over Israel's foreign policy, Pekah began an aggressive anti-Assyrian program that would ultimately prove fatal. Though Israel was in no condition to embark on this course, Pekah formed an anti-Assyrian alliance with Rezin of Damascus and tried to recruit others into open warfare against the empire. He appealed to Judah, now ruled by Uzziah's son Jotham, but Jotham refused. As a result, the two monarchs decided to remove Jotham by force, probably hoping to replace him with someone more sympathetic to their plans (Is. 7:6). Meanwhile, other nations such as Edom and the Philistines took the opportunity to also wage war against Judah to strengthen their borders (II Kings 16:6; II Chr. 28:17–18). Jotham died suddenly, replaced by Ahaz.

During the invasion, Pekah managed to lay siege to Jerusalem. While II Kings says that Pekah could not defeat Ahaz (16:5), Chronicles describes a great slaughter of civilians and the looting of Jerusalem as punishment for Ahaz's idolatry (II Chr. 28:1–15). Under pressure, Ahaz appealed to Assyria for assistance in repelling the invading coalition armies. Accordingly, Tiglath-Pileser's troops destroyed the Philistine city-states along the coast in 734, cut off any potential Egyptian aid, and then turned back north to deal with Pekah. By 733, the Assyrians had taken most of Israel's territories. Only the Samarian hill country remained. Just as the Assyrians were poised to capture Samaria (II Kings 15:29), Pekah was assassinated by Hoshea. Upon

---

18. A full discussion of the issues involved in establishing a set chronology can be found in the appendix.

taking control, Hoshea changed policy toward Assyria and saved the nation temporarily.[19]

Hoshea (731–722) and the End

> Then Hoshea son of Ela formed a conspiracy against Pekah son of Remaliah; they struck him down and assassinated him, and he reigned in his place in the twentieth year of Jotham son of Uzziah.... In the twelfth year of Ahaz, king of Judah, Hoshea son of Ela became king over Israel in Shomron for nine years. He did what was evil in the eyes of the Lord, though not to the extent of the kings of Israel who preceded him. Shalmaneser, king of Assyria, marched up against him, and Hoshea became his vassal and paid him tribute. But when the king of Assyria discovered that Hoshea had betrayed him by sending envoys to So, king of Egypt, and by failing to pay his annual tribute to the king of Assyria, he had him seized and thrown into prison. Then the king of Assyria marched against the whole land and marched up to Shomron and besieged it for three years. In the ninth year of Hoshea, the king of Assyria captured Shomron. He exiled Israel to Assyria and settled them in Ḥalaḥ, the Ḥavor, the Gozan River, and the cities of Media. This came to pass because the Israelites had sinned against the Lord their God – who had brought them out from the land of Egypt and the oppression of Pharaoh, king of Egypt – by revering other gods. (II Kings 15:30; 17:1–8)

---

19. According to Assyrian records, Tiglath-Pileser receives the credit for the murder of Pekah and his replacement by Hoshea instead:

> The land Bit-Humri [or Beit-Omri – the name of the Kingdom of Israel], all of whose cities I had utterly devastated in my former campaigns, whose [people] and livestock I had carried off and whose (capital) city Samaria alone had been spared: (now) they overthrew Pekah, their king. (*Tiglath-Pileser III 44*, 171–78)

> The land Bit-Humri (= Israel): I brought to Assyria [...], its auxiliary army, [...] and an assembly of its people. [They (or: I) killed] their king Pekah and I placed Hoshea [as king] over them. (*Tiglath-Pileser III 42*, 15'b–17'a)

Available online at http://www.ucl.ac.uk/sargon/essentials/countries/israel/.

Hoshea's immediate surrender and payment of tribute (II Kings 17:1-3) probably saved Samaria from destruction, at least for a while. However, some in Israel still wanted complete independence. Hoshea eventually chose to take advantage of a brief period of Assyrian distraction, the transfer of leadership after Tiglath-Pileser's death, in what Hoshea assumed was an opportunity to regain freedom. He allied with Egypt, depended on them for military assistance, and withheld tribute from Assyria (II Kings 17:4). However, Egypt was unreliable. Salmanazar's army attacked the reduced territory in 724, captured most of the land, and took Hoshea prisoner. Only the capital Samaria remained. It was besieged for three years, finally falling in 722-721 BCE (II Kings 17:5-6). With the city destroyed and many of its inhabitants taken as prisoners to Assyria, the Northern Kingdom ceased to exist. However, remnants of the population remained in the area (II Chr. 30), joined by other peoples transferred into the area by successive Assyrian monarchs (II Kings 17:24; Ezra 4).

JUDAH UNDER SIEGE – FATEFUL DECISIONS

Like Israel after Jeroboam's reign, Judah after Uzziah's illness felt that it could not ignore the increasing turmoil in the north, despite being geographically isolated.[20] With the Assyrian threat looming over them, Judah's kings faced crucial decisions in which direction to lead their country – to join an anti-Assyrian alliance with their neighbors, to surrender and pledge loyalty to Assyria, or to stay neutral, hoping to wait out the storm. Isaiah championed a third approach – have patience and trust in God. Both were in short supply.

---

20. My teacher, Rabbi Yaakov Medan, speculates that the reason that Uzziah entered the Temple against protocol and dictate, resulting in Uzziah contracting leprosy, was to entreat the Lord for protection against the rumblings in the east as the Assyrians began to turn their attention to the region. He similarly suggests that Hezekiah did the same in order to pray for deliverance from Sannecherib's armies six decades later. If so, then the first warning signs of impending trouble would have occurred in the year of Jotham's ascension to the throne in 758-57 BCE as a caretaker for his father (heard orally).

In the days of Ahaz son of Jotham son of Uzziah, king of Judah, Retzin, king of Aram, and Pekah son of Remaliah, king of Israel, launched an attack on Jerusalem, but they could not conquer it. The House of David was told, "Aram is allied with Ephraim." And his heart swayed, and the hearts of his people, as trees of the forest will sway with the wind.

And the Lord said to Isaiah: Go out now to meet Ahaz, you and She'ar Yashuv your son, to the end of the Upper Pool's conduit, by the road to the Fuller's Field. And say to him: Be guarded, stay still, do not fear, and let your heart not soften before these smoking tails of firebrands, before the rage of Retzin and Aram and the son of Remaliah. For Aram has conspired to harm you, along with Ephraim and Remaliah's son: "We shall go up to Jerusalem, bring about her end; we shall break her walls open for ourselves and set a new king over her: the son of Taval."

Thus says the Lord God: It will not come to pass; it will not be. For the head of Aram is Damascus, and the head of Damascus, Retzin, and in another five and sixty years Ephraim will be shattered as a nation. The head of Ephraim is Shomron, the head of Shomron is Remaliah's son – and if you have no faith, you have no future. (Is. 7:1–9)

Jotham (757–742)

In the second year of Pekah son of Remaliah, king of Israel, Jotham son of Uzziah, king of Judah, became king. He was twenty-five years old when he became king, and for sixteen years he reigned in Jerusalem. His mother's name was Yerusha daughter of Tzadok. He did what was right in the eyes of the Lord, just as his father Uzziah had done. Yet the high shrines were not removed; the people still offered sacrifices and incense at the high shrines. He built the upper gate of the House of the Lord. As for the rest of Jotham's history and all his deeds – they are recorded in the Book of the History of the Kings of Judah. (II Kings 15:32–36)

Judah's "silver age" ended with Azariah/Uzziah's downfall.[21] During the latter part of his reign, King Uzziah contracted leprosy, which placed his son Jotham as co-regent for Uzziah's last years. Given the monumental shifts in the balance of power and upheavals that rocked the region, it is surprising that the Tanakh does not invest much energy in describing Jotham's reign. The book of Kings assigns Jotham mixed reviews – giving credit for following Uzziah's religious practices, but not dealing with the issue of the private altars (*bamot*) that decentralized worship of God away from Jerusalem.[22] Both Kings and Chronicles describe impressive building projects under Jotham (II Chr. 27:1–5; II Kings 32–35), with Chronicles adding a victory over the Ammonites that resulted in three years of tribute. While we date Jotham's reign earlier, others date it ending in 732, having Jotham die just as Pekah's armies reached Jerusalem, leaving his son Ahaz alone to deal with the threat. With either approach, Jotham becomes the transitional figure between Uzziah's period of glory and the tribulations that awaited Judah afterward, as the Tanakh states:

> At that time the Lord began to rouse Retzin, king of Aram, and Pekah son of Remaliah against Judah. And Jotham slept with

---

21. David Ben-Gurion saw Uzziah as the model for Israel's leadership, noting his proficiency in both strengthening Judah militarily and developing the country economically. See his address "The Significance of the Negev," in Yoel Bin-Nun and Binyamin Lau, *Isaiah: Prophet of Righteousness and Justice* (Jerusalem: Maggid Books, 2020), 1.
22. The Talmud describes Jotham as one of the three greatest righteous people to ever walk the planet, and Rashi on II Chronicles 27:2 writes that Jotham is the only king of Judah to never sin: "[Jotham did] as all that his father Uzziah did." Rashi: [Only] the good deeds that his father had done.

> That is what R. Simeon ben Yohai said: I can absolve the entire world from judgment for sins committed from the day I was created until now. The merit that he accrued through his righteousness and the suffering that he endured atone for the sins of the entire world. And were the merit accrued by Eliezer, my son, calculated along with my own, we would absolve the world from judgment for sins committed from the day that the world was created until now. And were the merit accrued by the righteous king, Jotham ben Uzziah, calculated with our own, we would absolve the world from judgment for sins committed from the day that the world was created until its end. (Sukka 45b)

his ancestors and was buried with his ancestors in the City of David, his ancestor. And his son Ahaz reigned in his place. (II Kings 15:36–37)

Ahaz (742–726)

In the seventeenth year of Pekah son of Remaliah, Ahaz son of Jotham, king of Judah, became king. Ahaz was twenty years old when he became king, and for sixteen years he reigned in Jerusalem. But he did not do what was right in the eyes of the Lord his God, like his ancestor David; he followed in the ways of the kings of Israel and even passed his son through the fire, imitating the horrors of the nations whom the Lord had dispossessed before the Israelites. He offered sacrifices and incense at the high shrines and on hilltops and under every shady tree. It was then that Retzin, king of Aram, and Pekah son of Remaliah, king of Israel, launched an attack on Jerusalem. They besieged Ahaz, but they could not conquer him. (II Kings 16:1–6)

Tanakh remembers Ahaz as one of Judah's worst kings. Not only did Ahaz surrender his country to Assyria, but he was the first of Judah's kings to wholeheartedly align himself both politically and religiously with Assyria, shattering the religious covenant between God and his people. Ahaz came to the throne at a young age and immediately faced the challenge of either resisting the overtures from the Israel-Syrian coalition or joining it. As mentioned above, Isaiah desperately pleaded with Ahaz to remain neutral and trust in God's protection. However, the king hesitated, and the resulting invasion (known historically as the Syro-Ephraimite war) was devastating for tiny Judah. Not only did the invaders reach the gates of Jerusalem, but they killed the king's son Maaseyahu along with much of Judah's leadership (II Chr. 28:7). Additionally, since Judah's army had to move to its northern border due to the invasion, the southwest and southeast were left unprotected, vulnerable to raids from Judah's historical enemies, Edom and Philistia. They exploited Judah's temporary weakness to plunder the land and its people.

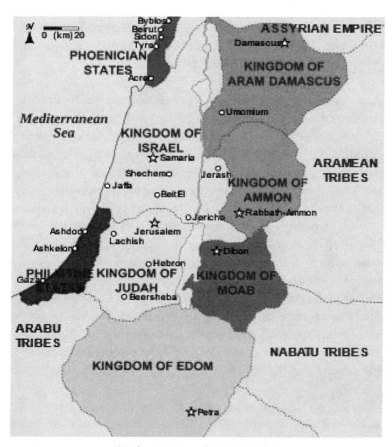

Map of countries surrounding Israel and Judah

Then Ahaz sent messengers to Tiglath-Pileser, king of Assyria, saying, "I am your servant and your son; come up and rescue me from the hand of the king of Aram and the hand of the king of Israel, who threaten me." And Ahaz took the silver and gold that was in the House of the Lord and the royal treasuries of the palace, and he sent them to the king of Assyria as a bribe. The king of Assyria acceded to him; the king of Assyria launched an attack on Damascus, captured it, and exiled its people to Kir. As for Retzin – he put him to death. King Ahaz went to meet Tiglath-Pileser, king of Assyria, in Damascus. When he saw the altar in Damascus, King Ahaz sent an image of the altar to Uriya

> the priest with its design, down to every last detail of its construc-
> tion. The priest Uriya then built the altar exactly as King Ahaz
> had instructed from Damascus... (II Kings 16:7–11)

Facing unprecedented pressure, Ahaz chose to ignore Isaiah's advice to stay neutral and appealed to Tiglath-Pileser III of Assyria for assistance. To demonstrate his loyalty, Ahaz traveled to Damascus and acknowl-edged the Assyrian gods as his own. There, Ahaz saw an altar to Ashur, Assyria's patron deity. He sent plans of this altar to Jerusalem, instructing that a copy be built and placed in the Temple for his use, converting it into a shrine to Ashur. Thus, he willingly surrendered Judah to Assyrian control, becoming a vassal to the superpower. In doing so, the young king saved his throne, but at the cost of Judah's political and religious independence. Following the king's example, Baal worship and other foreign religious practices flourished (Ahaz even offered one of his sons as a sacrifice [II Kings 16:3]). Rabbi Binyamin Lau speculates that Ahaz's efforts to thwart the Assyrian invasion boosted his popularity among the populace.[23] However, the Tanakh remembers Ahaz's reign as one of apostasy from God, rivaled only by the reign of Manasseh a half-century later.[24]

---

23. Bin-Nun and Lau, *Isaiah: Prophet of Righteousness*, 85.
24. According to rabbinic thought, Ahaz closed the doors of the study halls. One midrash portrays Ahaz as the tutor of a king's son who planned to kill the son. Realizing that if he himself did the deed he would be executed, the tutor instead separated the son from his wet-nurse in order to let him die by malnutrition. Similarly, Ahaz reasoned that without children studying Torah, there would be no disciples capable of becoming sages; if there were no sages, there would be no prophets; if there were no prophets, the Holy One, blessed be He, would have no one upon whom to cause His Divine Presence to dwell (Genesis Rabba 42:3; Jerusalem Talmud 51a; see also Josephus, *Antiquities of the Jews* XI, 12:3). However, most views in the Talmud do not believe that Ahaz lost his share in the World to Come, either because he behaved with humility and shame in front of Isaiah, or that the loss of his son served as an atonement (Sanhedrin 104a). (A minority opinion in Leviticus Rabba 36:3 disagrees.)
   Ahaz first appeared in archaeological records in 1873, when a clay tablet was dis-covered in the ancient Assyrian palace at Nimrud. On it, Tiglath-Pileser III boasts of the tribute paid to him by Ahaz (mentioned in II Kings 16:8). In part, the inscrip-tion reads: "From these I received tribute... Jehoahaz [Ahaz] of Judah... including gold, silver, iron, fine cloth and many garments made from wool that was dyed in

Hezekiah (725–697)

> In the third year of Hosea son of Ela, king of Israel, Hezekiah son of Ahaz, king of Judah, became king. He was twenty-five years old when he became king, and for twenty-nine years he reigned in Jerusalem. His mother's name was Avi daughter of Zecharia. He did what was right in the eyes of the Lord just as his ancestor David did. He removed the high shrines and tore down the worship pillars and cut down the sacred tree. And he crushed the bronze serpent that Moshe had made.... In the Lord, God of Israel, he placed his trust; there were none like him among all the kings of Judah who succeeded him or those who came before him. He clung to the Lord and never turned away from him and kept the commandments that the Lord had commanded Moshe. And the Lord was with him; wherever he turned, he was successful. He rebelled against the king of Assyria and did not serve him. (II Kings 18:1–7)

As bad as Ahaz's reign was, his son Hezekiah is remembered as one of Judah's greatest kings. Judah was anxious to be free after over a decade of Assyrian rule. A new Assyrian king, Sargon II, came to power about the time Samaria fell. He quickly became embroiled in Assyria's other provinces, quelling revolts and consolidating his reign. Taking advantage of the opportunity, Hezekiah began to engage in massive religious reform. He removed the altar to the Assyrian gods that Ahaz had set up. In addition, Hezekiah decided to try to do what no king of Judah had dared to do before him – remove the *bamot* that dotted the countryside while renewing the covenant at the massive Passover celebration in Jerusalem. Wisely, Hezekiah remained neutral when Egypt encouraged the region's nations to rebel (presumably to establish a buffer zone between

---

purple...." In the mid-1990s a very important bulla (a hardened clay seal used to seal papyrus documents before being tied up) was discovered. A mere centimeter in diameter, it still had the imprint of the papyrus it once sealed, and an inscription that read, "Belonging to Ahaz [son of] Yehotam, King of Judah." Recently, in 2015, another such bulla was discovered, with the inscription "Belonging to Hezekiah [son of] Ahaz king of Judah." Given the process used to create and preserve bullae, they are virtually impossible to forge, and most scholars believe these bullae to be authentic.

Egypt and Assyria), and the Philistine city-states revolted. However, Sargon ruthlessly vanquished them in 612 BCE, when promised Egyptian assistance never arrived to assist them. However, Hezekiah's nationalist fervor awoke with dangerous consequences.[25]

By 704 BCE, an opportunity to rid Judah of the Assyrian rule arrived. Sargon II died in battle, and his son Sennacherib found that the Assyrian armies were spread too sparsely across the empire. Sensing the time was right, Hezekiah withheld tribute, signaling rebellion. Despite Isaiah's strenuous objections, Hezekiah joined Egypt (Is. 30–31) and became the revolt's leader. Only in 701 did Sennacherib turn his attention to Judah, but the results of Hezekiah's defiance would devastate Judah for generations. The Assyrian army marched from the north into Israel, intent on ravaging the rebellious cities and states. Sennacherib quickly defeated the Phoenician seaport Tyre, causing Moab, Ammon, and others to reassert their allegiance to Assyria. However, the Philistine cities, along with Judah, stood defiant. Sennacherib continued moving southward, quickly securing all the Philistine territory along the coast, finally turning inland to deal with Hezekiah and Judah. The Assyrians destroyed most of Judah's cities, left the countryside devastated, and laid siege to Jerusalem. Only God's miraculous intervention saved the city (II Kings 19:35–37), just as Isaiah had promised Hezekiah (Is. 37:33–35). In Chronicles, the message is that God spared the city because of Hezekiah's faithfulness and his religious reforms (II Chr. 31:20–21). However, Hezekiah would die soon afterwards, leaving the young child Manasseh alone to rebuild the devastated country of Judah under the Assyrian yoke.

---

25. According to Rabbi Yoel Bin-Nun, this change in policy from religious reforms to militant nationalism was rebuked by Isaiah, causing a split between prophet and king. See Bin-Nun and Lau, *Isaiah*, 133–45.

Joel

Introduction

Perhaps no prophet encapsulates Tanakh's prophetic message better than the second of the Twelve Minor Prophets,[1] Joel. We know little

---

1. In the Septuagint sequence, Joel occupies the fourth position in the Twelve Minor Prophets, immediately following Micah and preceding Obadiah. The reason for the variation in order is not fully understood, and appears to be the result of the overall theological conception that informs each respective version. See M. A. Sweeney, *The Twelve Prophets*, vol. 1 (Hosea, Joel, Amos, Obadiah, and Jonah), Berit Olam: Studies in Hebrew Narrative and Poetry, ed. David W. Cotter (Collegeville, MN: The Liturgical Press, 2000), 147. Several scholars explain Joel's early placement in the Twelve Minor Prophets to literary links between the book of Joel with its predecessor Hosea and the book of Amos which follows it. For example, Amos Hakham notes several literary parallels between Joel 4:16–18 and Amos 1:2, 9:13, and how the blessing described at the end of Joel is similar to Hosea 14:8 (*Daat Mikra: Trei Asar* I [Jerusalem: Mossad Harav Kook, 1973], introduction to Joel, 3). James Nogalski notes the thematic links: "Hosea ends with an extended call to repentance, while Joel begins with the same genre. Joel ends with an extended pronouncement of eschatological judgment against the nations, while Amos begins with an extended group of oracles against the nations" ("Joel as 'Literary Anchor' for the book of the Twelve," in Nogalski and Sweeney, *Reading and Hearing the Book of the Twelve* [Atlanta: Society of Biblical Literature, 2000], 92).

Recent scholarship has approached the Twelve Minor Prophets as a unified whole, and explains the early placement by showing how Joel's message presents

about Joel or when he lived, yet we can quickly close our eyes and envision dark clouds of locusts slowly approaching on the horizon, quietly blotting out the sun. Listen carefully, and we hear the sound of the distant echo of what sounds like approaching hooves and chariots, a dull, deep rhythmic sound that slowly gets louder, though our eyes cannot yet identify the threat. Is that the sound of a horde of locusts, or the noise of Sennacherib's chariots and legions? Joel contains chilling portrayals of destruction and devastation, but he also manages to reinforce our belief in God's mercy, using some of the most magnificent expressions of comfort found in the prophetic works.[2] The language is poetic and inspiring, though we sense that we have encountered it before.[3] Both philosophical and practical, Joel dares to ask perhaps the most critical

---

the major themes for later books to develop and expand (including themes such as "the day of the Lord," repentance, the nature of God, and the eschatology of Israel and the nations). A leading proponent of this approach, James Nogalski, writes that the book of Joel serves as the "interpretive key for unifying major literary threads in the Twelve ... [and is] the writing through which all major themes of the Twelve must travel." See Nogalski, "Joel as 'Literary Anchor,'" in *Reading and Hearing*, 92, 105.

2. The following midrash (*Sifrei Devarim* 342) reflects this tension between the two messages, finding the echoes of Joel's message in Moses's valedictory address:
   "This is the blessing with which Moshe, man of God, blessed the Israelites before he died" (Deut. 33:1): Because Moses spoke harsh things to Israel first ... he then went back and told them consoling things ... and from him all of the prophets learned to first address the Jews with harsh words and then to return with consoling words. No prophet spoke harsher words than Hosea, who began with, "Give them, O Lord – what can I ask you to give them? Give them a grieving womb and shriveled breasts gone dry..." (Hos. 9:14). And so Joel said to them, "Listen, O elders; take heed, all those who live on the land. Has there been anything like this in your lifetimes or in the lifetimes of your parents? You will tell your children of this, and your children will tell their children of this, and their children will tell a different generation of this: 'What remains after the chewer-locusts will be eaten by the locusts; what remains after the locusts will be eaten by the springing-locusts; what remains after the springing-locusts will be eaten by the finisher-locusts'" (Joel 1:2–4). But he then spoke consoling words to them: "I will repay you for all the seasons consumed by the locusts, the springing-locusts, the finisher-locusts, and the chewer-locusts" (2:25).

3. More than a third of Joel's seventy-three verses appear in various forms elsewhere in the Tanakh. Most famous of these is the reversal of Isaiah and Micah's famous prophecy in Joel 4:10: "Beat your plowshares into swords and your pruning hooks into spears."

question facing humanity in times of crisis: When catastrophe strikes, how do we react? Do we give in to despair in times of trouble, or do we find new reservoirs of faith and persevere forward and grow? His 73 verses contain 43 separate commands to his listeners: weep, awake, lament, assemble, repent, sound an alarm, fast, return, and ultimately rejoice.[4] We traditionally read Joel in synagogues on the Shabbat after Rosh HaShana, *Shabbat Shuva* – the Sabbath of Repentance. The first section of the haftara for *Shabbat Shuva*, Hosea 14, assures us that repentance is possible, but it is Joel who challenges us to seize that opportunity.

The book of Joel itself, despite its short length of only four chapters, has often proved problematic to interpret. Who was Joel? When did he live? He spoke of the Temple – but was it is the First or Second that he saw? What was the threat that he faced that led him to warn the people to pray – a locust invasion or an army invasion, or both? Did the people sin, and is Joel calling them to repentance – or are they simply called to pray? The book clearly has two halves, but where – at 2:17 or 2:27? And despite all these questions, Joel is that rarity in Tanakh – a successful prophet. How he accomplished this, and why this is relevant for us, is the subject of our study.

WHO WAS JOEL? WHEN DID HE LIVE?

Joel ranks among the hardest prophets to identify; his book references no specific historical event or figure. Fortunately, this lack does not hamper us from appreciating Joel's message. The name Joel means the

---

Some scholars suggest that Joel is less a prophet than an interpreter of prophecy. For example, Leslie Allen writes that this is part of Joel's role: "It is essential to Joel's purpose that he should not be original. His deliberate aim is to make a deep impression by using stereotyped, well-known language to show that *in the present situation venerated prophecies were on the verge of fulfillment. His newness lies in the application of the old words*" (*The Books of Joel, Obadiah, Jonah and Micah*, NICOT (Grand Rapids, MI: Eerdmans, 1976), 68.

4. When Stephen Langton divided the Bible into chapters in the thirteenth century, he followed the Vulgate's division of Joel into three chapters, appending chapter 3 to the second chapter. However, in the Bomberg edition of the Hebrew Bible published in 1526, Jacob ben Hayyim divided Joel into four chapters, a practice followed by all later Hebrew publishers (J. L. Crenshaw, *Joel: A New Translation with Introduction and Commentary* [Yale University Press, 1995], 11).

Lord is God, combining a shortened form of the divine name (*yo*) and the word (*el*) for "God" (his father's name, Pethuel, means "persuaded of God").[5] Almost a dozen individuals in Tanakh bear the name Joel.[6] As Joel makes many references to Judah and Jerusalem,[7] he was in all likelihood a resident of Judah. Because of his focus on Temple rituals, some scholars suggest that he was either a Levite or a priest. While this is speculation, it is important to note that Joel contains none of the criticisms of the sacrificial service and rituals common in other prophets. Instead, he calls upon the community to gather at the Temple to pray and beseech God for His mercy.

When did Joel live? Answers range from before the establishment of the kingdom to well into the Second Temple period. In the absence of explicit textual evidence, we will have to examine the circumstantial evidence from within the text. The evidence includes (a) the early placement of Joel within the book of the Twelve Prophets, (b) the depiction of a functioning Temple, (c) the fact that there is no mention of a king, (d) the absence of traditional sins like idolatry or social injustice, (e) the mention of the Greeks, (f) the absence of the Northern Kingdom, (g) the list of foreign nations mentioned, (h) the absence of Assyria or Babylonia, and (i) the numerous literary parallels between Joel and other texts, which would imply a later date for Joel.[8] Different interpreters understand the evidence in a variety of ways resulting in different conclusions, which we shall list below.

Seder Olam, the traditional midrashic work of chronology, based on the failure to mention a king, locates Joel in the reign of Manasseh in the seventh century BCE.[9] This view has its difficulties – Joel

---

5. *The Anchor Bible Dictionary*, s.v. "Joel, Book of."
6. Cf. I Sam. 8:2; Ezra 10:43; Neh. 11:9; I Chr. 4:35, 5:4, 7:3, 11:38, 15:7, 26:22, 27:20; II Chr. 29:12.
7. See 1:9, 13–14, 16; 2:1, 9, 14–15, 17, 23; 3:5, 4:1–8, 12, 14, 17–21.
8. For example, Joel Barker argues that Joel's "numerous allusions to other prophetic literature, including Isaiah, Ezekiel, Amos, Micah, and Obadiah" point toward an early postexilic date of composition (*Joel: A Discourse Analysis of the Hebrew Bible* [Grand Rapids, MI: Zondervan, 2020], 31).
9. *Seder Olam* 20: "Joel, Nahum, and Habakkuk prophesied during the days of Manasseh, but they did not identify him because he was a wicked king [and therefore not worthy of having his name mentioned in the prophetic books]."

continuously pleads with the people to gather at the Temple. During Manasseh's reign, the Temple was a center of idolatry and foreign worship, making this request near impossible.

In his introduction to Joel, Rashi quotes a midrash that equates our prophet with the prophet Samuel's son, who lived near the beginning of the millennium (approx. 1000 BCE):

> "When Samuel grew old, he appointed his sons to be Israel's judges. The name of his elder son was Joel, and the name of his second was Aviah" (I Sam. 8:1–2). The Sages said: Just as the eldest son was a wicked person, so the second was also wicked. R. Yudin said, in the name of R. Simon: They repented in the end, which is why he was called *sheni* (the second – see I Chr. 6:13), for his deeds changed [*nishtanu*]. [Due to their repentance] they merited receiving divine inspiration, as it is written, "This is the word of the Lord that came to Joel the son of Pethuel" (Joel 1:1). [Who was Pethuel?] This was Samuel. Why was he called Pethuel? Because he seduced [Heb., *pitah*] God with his prayer. (Numbers Rabba 10:5)

However, though the midrash declares that Samuel's sons repented, this is not mentioned in the text, nor is Samuel ever identified by Pethuel. For these reasons, Ibn Ezra explicitly rejects this identification.

Another rabbinic attempt equates the locust plague that Joel so vividly describes with the famine depicted in II Kings 6:24–8:1, sometime between 850–800 BCE (Taanit 5a).[10] Both Rashi and Radak present this approach:

---

10. The actual period in which the plague (and these chapters in Kings, which belong to what is known as the Elisha cycle of stories) occurred is under dispute. Most of the commentators assume that the king in Israel at the time was Jehoram, the second son of Ahab, who ruled after his father. This assumption, however, as my teacher Rabbi Yoel Bin-Nun has pointed out, has two major difficulties. First, the name of the king in these chapters is not explicitly mentioned; second, many of the events (namely, the repeated Aramean invasions and political dominion as described in chapters 5–7) would likely not have occurred during the prosperity and security that occurred under the rule of the Omri dynasty, but under the following dynasty

[He] prophesied first about the locusts which God would bring to Israel for their sins. Then he prophesied about the future, the days of Messiah. Some say he presented this prophecy in the days of Jehoram son of Ahab, when there was a famine in the land, as it is written: "for the Lord has decreed a seven-year famine on the land" (II Kings 8:1). Four years were the four types of locusts, and three years were of drought. (Introduction to Radak's commentary to Joel)

Abrabanel understands that the sequence of the prophets in the Twelve Minor Prophets reflects a chronological basis. Therefore, as the books of Hosea and Amos flank Joel at the beginning of the Twelve Minor Prophets, he would place Joel in the middle of the eighth century BCE. However, attempting to maintain the *Seder Olam* chronology as well, Abrabanel suggests that Joel enjoyed tremendous longevity, prophesying for almost a century until Manasseh's reign.[11]

Some modern scholars also place Joel in pre-exilic times, advocating dates during King Jehoshaphat's reign (872–848 BCE, concurrent with Jehoram of Israel above) or his grandson's, King Joash (835–796 BCE).[12] Arguments in favor of this period include the early

---

with Jehu and his descendants, when the Northern Kingdom was temporarily but significantly weakened, and regularly suffered from invasions from their northern neighbor. (For a full discussion of these issues, see Rabbi Alex Israel's study, available online at https://etzion.org.il/en/tanakh/neviim/sefer-melakhim-bet/melakhim-b-2-8-chronology-structure-and-two-judean-kings.)

11. In our work, we have cautiously adopted Abrabanel's approach. Obviously this is not a purely chronological order, as Jonah is the earliest of the prophets listed (see II Kings 14:23–28). However, four out of the first six books (excepting the undated Joel and Obadiah) definitely occur during the eighth century BCE, at a time when the Assyrian empire was the major threat; the next three books all occur during the seventh century BCE, when the Babylonians were ascendant; and the final three works occur during the period of the return to Zion, in the second half of the sixth century BCE. With this as a guideline, we see no reason to postdate Obadiah and Joel outside the Assyrian period. We bring additional proofs in the commentary.

12. The earliest commentator to suggest this was brought by Ibn Ezra in his commentary almost a millennium ago:

Rabbi Yeshuah said: This prophecy was entirely for the future. Rabbi Moshe HaKohen said: If so, why did it say "After this" (Joel 3:1) instead of "And it will

position of Joel in the listing of the prophets in Trei Asar, the mention of Jehoshaphat in chapter 4, the enemies that Joel names: Tyre, Sidon, Philistia (cf. II Chr. 21:16–17), Egypt (cf. I Kings 14:25–26), and Edom (cf. II Kings 8:20–22), all of whom were enemies of Israel during this time. Finally, Joel gives Judah's priests and elders a prominent role, but not to her king (Joash was a boy king, allowing the elderly high priest Jehoiada to run the country).

However, most modern commentators and scholars place Joel much later, generally after the completion of the building of the Second Temple in 516 BCE. The word Judah repeatedly appears with the connotation of "all of the land." The preponderance of verses from other prophets (over a third of the verses in Joel appear elsewhere in various forms) implies that Joel summarizes the teachings of all those who preceded him. Finally, Joel does not mention kingship.[13] In his commentary in *Daat Mikra*, Amos Hakham observes:

> Some say that Joel prophesied soon after the construction of the Second Temple. There is evidence for this view: Joel used the name of Judah even when referring to Israel's entire promised land (4:20).
>
> Also, in his appeal to the people to repent, he does not enumerate specific sins nor does he mention idolatry (which the prophets rebuked [the people] at length during the time of the First Temple, but) which was uprooted from Israel in the Second Temple. Joel does not mention the king when he speaks about the nation gathering to pray in the House of God. [However], these proofs are not decisive.
>
> [Similarly], the mention of the Greeks (4:6) is not proof to date [Joel] later [until the Greek invasion of Judah], but rather

---

be at the end of days?" Perhaps this prophet lived in the days of Jehoshaphat, which is why he mentioned the Valley of Jehoshaphat (4:2). There were many prophets and student prophets in those days, for many went to speak with Elisha, and Obadiah alone hid them. (Ibn Ezra on 3:1)

13. Scholars note that the *terminus ante quem* (latest possible date) of Joel has to be the mid-fourth century BCE, as Tyre and Sidon fell in 343 and 332 BCE respectively (H. W. Wolff, *Joel and Amos* [Philadelphia: Fortress Press, 1977], 4).

to date him earlier, because Greece is described as a distant land, such that one who was exiled there could not return to his land easily. Additionally, the Greeks are not present in the land [in Joel's prophecy], but are the buyers of the Jewish slaves from the Phoenicians.[14]

Placing Joel in the period of the Second Temple is the favored approach among most scholars. Professor Elie Assis argues for a novel approach: Joel prophesied during the inter-exilic period between the First Temple's destruction in 586 BCE and the return to Zion almost half a century later. He interprets Joel as tailoring his message for the small remnant of Jews who remained behind in Judah after the destruction and exile.[15] He posits that the remaining Jews were able to maintain offering sacrifices and libations on the spot of the Temple's altar, even without the Temple building. Joel emphasizes not sin, but the restoration of the relationship between the Jewish people and God. Additionally, Joel shares metaphors with books from that period, Ezekiel and Lamentations, increasing the likelihood that they were contemporaries. Assis argues that this serves a rhetorical purpose: "Joel sought to establish a line of continuity between him and the earlier prophets in response to the feeling of rupture with the past that gripped the people."[16]

However, many of the verses imply that the Temple was fully functional in Joel's time. For example, several of the opening verses describe how the famine's severity caused the halt of the sacrifices customarily offered on the Temple:

> Don sackcloth – mourn, O priests. Wail, attendants of the altar. Come sleep in sackcloth, attendants of my God, for grain offerings and libations have been cut off from the House of your God. (1:13; see also 1:9, 16; 2:14)

---

14. *Daat Mikra*, Joel 5.
15. Elie Assis, *The Book of Joel: A Prophet Between Calamity and Hope,* The Library of Hebrew Bible/Old Testament Studies (New York: Bloomsbury, 2013), adapted into Hebrew: *Yoel: Bein Mashber LeTikva* (Jerusalem: Maggid, 2015).
16. Assis, *Book of Joel*, 23.

Based on this, in his commentary on 1:1 and 3:1, the medieval commentator Ibn Caspi observes that these verses indicate that a Temple was standing when Joel spoke (whether it was the first or second is immaterial), which would negate the approach suggested by Professor Assis above. However, Assis valiantly argues that even "after the destruction of the Temple, the people [did not cease] ... calling the Temple area 'the House of the Lord.' The habit of calling a place by a certain name is not easily changed, even when there are substantial changes in the character of the place.... [I]n order to strengthen the people's feeling that the Lord still dwells in Jerusalem despite the exile, the prophets might well continue to call the place 'the House of the Lord.' Indeed, in Ezra, the Temple precinct was called the House of God before the Temple was built on it (3:8; 5:8) and also in Haggai (2:3)."[17]

In summary, we've seen a range of almost eight hundred years (!) in the attempts to date when Joel spoke. Later, we will express a tentative preference for dating Joel to the Assyrian invasion of Judah in 701 BCE. Fortunately, unlike other prophets, establishing Joel's time period is not relevant for its universal message. We argue that the difficulty in determining Joel's date is not an interpretive liability; instead, the ambiguity is intentional, establishing a universal typology of God's rule and how to react in a crisis.[18]

JOEL'S MESSAGE

At first glance, the message of Joel appears clear: There is a locust plague approaching, and the people should repent if they wish to be spared. Today, we cannot fully appreciate the import of Joel's dire message, as modern technology has managed to control, if not eliminate, the devastating effect of a locust swarm. Their appearance on an ancient

---

17. Elie Assis, "The Date and Meaning of the Book of Joel," *Vetus Testamentum* 61 (2011): 169.
18. Nogalski, "Joel as 'Literary Anchor,'" in *Reading and Hearing*, 107. Similarly, Colin Toffelmire suggests that the effect of removing almost all concrete evidence for dating the book gives the book "rhetorical flexibility" so that it is "continually re-applicable, because of its de-historicized nature" (Colin M. Toffelmire, "A Discourse and Register Analysis of the Prophetic Book of Joel," *Studia Semitica Neerlandica*, vol. 66 (Leiden: Brill, 2016), 7.

horizon was a calamity. Swarms can contain over a billion members, leaving mass destruction and starvation in their wake.[19] Ancient monarchs used locust imagery to threaten those who would violate a signed treaty.[20] To Joel's audience, the appearance of locusts (like

---

19. Describing locust plagues, Raymond Dillard writes:

> In our generation areas having the potential for a locust outbreak are monitored by international agencies using satellite reconnaissance and other technology; incipient swarms are met by aircraft and trucks carrying powerful pesticides. However, if the locusts are not destroyed or contained shortly after they hatch, once the swarm has formed, control efforts are minimally effective even today. For example, in 1988 the civil war in Chad prevented international cooperation in attacking the hatch, and a destructive swarm spread throughout North Africa devastating some of the poorest nations and threatening Europe as well. It is difficult for modern Western people to appreciate the dire threat represented by a locust plague in earlier periods. Such outbreaks had serious consequences for the health and mortality of an affected population and for a region's economy. Scarcity of food resulting from the swarm's attack would bring the population to subsistence intake or less, would make the spread of disease among a weakened populace easier, would eliminate any trade from surplus food products, and would stimulate high inflation in the costs of food products. Disease outbreaks are further aggravated when swarms die; the putrefaction of the millions of locust bodies breeds typhus and other diseases that spread to humans and animals.... It was only in 1921 that the mystery of the locust was solved. Prior to this date researchers wondered what became of the locust during the years in which there were no outbreaks. In 1921 B. P. Uvarov demonstrated that the swarming locust was none other than an ordinary species of grasshopper. However, when moisture and temperature conditions favored a large hatch, the crowding, unceasing contact, and jostling of the nymphs begin to stimulate changes in coloration, physiology, metabolism, and behavior, so that the grasshopper nymphs make the transition from solitary behavior to the swarming gregarious and migratory phases of the dreaded plague. Plagues continue as long as climatic conditions favor the large hatches. Once entering their gregarious phase, swarms of locusts can migrate great distances and have even been observed twelve hundred miles at sea. The swarms can reach great sizes: a swarm across the Red Sea in 1889 was estimated to cover two thousand square miles. A swarm is estimated to contain up to 120 million insects per mile.

(*The Minor Prophets*, "Joel," 255–56, online at https://bible.org/seriespage/joel)

20. For example, the Sefire Treaty (dated from the mid-eighth century BCE), between the king of Arpad named Mati'ilu with the Mesopotamian ruler Bir-Ga'yah, threatened the following affliction on those who would not comply with the treaty's terms: "*For seven years may the locust devour,* and for seven years may the worm eat, and for seven years may [*tevi* – meaning unknown] come upon the face of the land" (Moshe

any natural disaster) would signify divine judgment being meted out against them. However, Joel continues, moving from describing the locust swarm in chapter 1 to describing a significant military invasion, with an additional call for repentance, hoping that God will respond to the people's cries.

The tone of the second half of the book shifts dramatically from mourning to hope. Joel describes not only God's forgiveness of the people, but continues with a dramatic vision of the end of days. How Joel links these disparate ideas represents the core of his message. Even in the book's first chapter, we sense that something larger is at work than a simple locust plague. Joel begins by emphasizing the unique nature of this natural phenomenon. And within chapter 1's descriptions of the effects of the approaching locust storm, we find scattered verses alluding to something even more foreboding: "For a nation has risen up against My land – innumerable, mighty, with lion's teeth" (1:6).

This verse describes the locusts as an invading nation, emphasizing their lion-like ability to wreak havoc and destruction. Combined with Joel's second chapter describing an army of raiders that will plunder the land, Joel clearly states that something more ominous is occurring. Joel himself declares: "O, for the day, *the day of the Lord is nigh*; like havoc from Shaddai it will come" (1:15).

Mentioning the upcoming "day of the Lord" suggests that the impact of the impending tragedy will contain ramifications beyond the natural disaster. In prophetic literature, "the day of the Lord" encompasses many ideas, including devastating military conquest and supernatural calamity. It is characterized by the pouring of divine wrath on God's enemies, whether Jewish or Gentile (Amos 5:18–20; Zech. 1:14–15), and the pouring out of blessings on those faithful to God.[21] It is not a one-time event; the prophets use the term "day of the Lord" to describe anytime God intervenes to save or judge.[22]

Weinfeld, *Deuteronomy and the Deuteronomic School* [Winona Lake, IN: Eisenbrauns, 1992], 124).

21. See Is. 4:2–6, 30:26; Hos. 2:18–23; Amos 9:11–15; Mic. 4:6–8; Zeph. 2:7; Zech. 14:6–9.
22. Leland Ryken, James C. Wilhoit, and Tremper Longman, eds., *Dictionary of Biblical Imagery* (Downers Grove, IL: InterVarsity, 1998), s.v. "Day of the Lord."

Based on this structure, many assert that the "day of the Lord" is Joel's primary message.[23] In the Tanakh, the phrase "day of the Lord" appears fifteen times; thirteen in the Twelve Minor Prophets, five of these in Joel.[24] Additionally, Joel contains six other allusions to days with divine intervention: the day (1:15), a day of darkness and gloom (2:2), a day of clouds and thick darkness (2:2), in those days (3:2, 4:1), and on that day (4:18). Thus, Joel's "day of the Lord" is both imminent, as well as indicative of a great day at the end of days. Read in this manner, chapter four functions as a climax to all of Joel's prophecy, telescoping from the immediate (and escalating) events of chapters one and two to the distant future of chapters three and four.

However, Joel is doing more than simply describing the terror of the upcoming "day of the Lord." Significantly, he does not expect his listeners to passively wait for the calamity to occur. Instead, he challenges them to respond. Noticeably, only in Joel does the entire Jewish people survive the "day of the Lord." The reason may be another anomaly in the prophet's message. Rabbi Hayyim Angel credits his teacher, Rabbi Shalom Carmy, with observing that "the book of Joel is unique in prophetic literature in not identifying any sin as the cause for a specific disaster nor as impetus for repentance."[25] We will examine some theological

---

23. Jeremias for example, notes, "The one and only subject of the book of Joel is the 'Day of the Lord'" (J. Jeremias, "The Function of the Book of Joel for Reading the Twelve," in R. Albertz, J. D. Nogalski, and J. Wöhrle, eds., *Perspectives on the Formation of the Book of the Twelve – Methodological Foundations – Redactional Processes – Historical Insights* [Berlin: De Gruyter], 77). Douglas Stuart in turn, explains, "This concept is so prominent in Joel that it may be likened to an engine driving the prophecy" (*Word Biblical Commentary* 31: *Hosea – Jonah* [Nashville: Thomas Nelson, 1987], 230).
24. Joel 1:15; 2:1, 11; 3:4; 4:14.
25. Hayyim Angel, *The Book of Joel: Anticipating a Post-Prophetic Age*, available online at https://library.yctorah.org/files/2016/09/The-Book-of-Joel-Anticipating-a-Post-Prophetic-Age.pdf. It can be argued that other prophets also do not mention sin (e.g., Nahum does not accuse the Jewish people directly of any wrongdoing but is simply heralding the eventual destruction of Assyria). However, Rabbi Carmy's fundamental point remains valid. See also R. A. Simkins, "'Return to [the Lord]': Honor and Shame in Joel," *Semeia* 68 (1996): 42–43:

> Evidently, it was sufficient for Joel's purpose merely to call the people to return to [the Lord], and consequently, to offer the hope that the terrible catastrophe – the day of [the Lord] – would be averted. Perhaps this was sufficient for the

ramifications of this idea in our conclusion. Based on the book's structure, we suggest that Joel downplays neither the severity of the destruction nor the need to pray. Instead, he invites his audience to reframe how they see their sufferings. Their troubles are not retribution for personal failings. Rather, Joel challenges his listeners to broaden their perspective and place them within a grander scheme of things still to come.

Finally, Joel creatively embellishes his central theme, "the Day of the Lord," with numerous allusions to major biblical motifs – including creation, the exodus, the covenant, and redemption. Before the coming "Day of the Lord," Joel describes a locust plague, an invasion, and the exiling of captives – integral components of the covenantal curses. (Cf. Deut. 28:38, 41, 47–9 – "You will carry much seed into the field but gather little, because locusts will eat it. … You will bear sons and daughters, but they will not remain yours, for they will be taken into captivity. … Because you did not serve the Lord your God with joy… the Lord will bring against you a nation from afar.") The locusts play a dual role, combining the covenant curses with the plagues of Egypt. However, when the people genuinely repent, the wrath of "the Day of the Lord" will be averted – instead, God will restore the people (2:18), bestow the covenantal blessing on the land (2:21), and increase the knowledge of the Lord (2:27). The restoration will be accompanied by signs, fire, and a pillar of smoke (3:3), which like the locusts allude to the exodus from Egypt, and present to the people the possibility of a second exodus. Through his portrayal of "the Day of the Lord," Joel reveals his vision – from their present state of crisis and calamity, there will be a new exodus, a new covenant, and ultimately a new creation.

---

people, Joel's original audience, as well. After all, in the midst of suffering the struggle for deliverance often overrides any need for justification.

Some scholars attempt to argue that the sin in Joel exists, but is assumed, given prior knowledge of the covenantal agreements as outlined in Leviticus 26 and Deuteronomy 28, both of which mention locusts as a punishment. Hays explains that the reason Joel does not explicitly mention the covenant is that he assumes his audience is well aware that they have been disobedient, therefore "Joel skips over listing many covenant violations and simply focuses on the resultant curse" (J. D. Hays, *The Message of the Prophets: A Survey of the Prophetic and Apocalyptic Books of the Old Testament* [Grand Rapids: Zondervan, 2010], 276–77).

LOCUSTS OR ASSYRIANS?

> What remains after the chewer-locusts will be eaten by the
> locusts; what remains after the locusts will be eaten by the
> springing-locusts; what remains after the springing-locusts will
> be eaten by the finisher-locusts. (1:4)

> For a nation has risen up against My land – innumerable, mighty,
> with lion's teeth – its fangs the fangs of a lioness. (1:6)

One of the fundamental questions facing every reader of Joel is the nature
of Judah's enemy. Chapter 1 introduces the enemy as four types of locusts.
Yet immediately, they are described as a mighty nation. However, the
explicit description of the damage caused by these locusts suggests that
the plain reading of the text is the advent of a locust plague. The situation is more complex in chapter 2. There, with meticulous detail as to
the military nature of its advance, Joel describes an enemy approaching
Jerusalem. The enemy resembles "horses – like war-horses, so they run.
Theirs is the pounding of chariots dancing over the mountain peaks…
theirs is the shout of a vast nation ready for battle. Nations tremble before
them; they are all ashen faced. They race like warriors; like soldiers they
ascend the wall: Every soldier moving forward in position, not one
strays from the route. They advance untouching, every warrior moving
forward…. They rush into the city, race over the wall, ascend into the
houses like thieves through the windows" (2:4–9). But is Joel describing an army – either a historical foe of the Jewish people (Assyrian or
Babylonian) or a future unidentified apocalyptic enemy? Or is Joel cleverly comparing the locust swarm to an enemy invasion?[26]

---

26. Elie Assis, for example, notes the constant repetition of the comparative word "like"
(Hebrew – כ) in the description above: "Their appearance is *like* the appearance
of horses; and *like* horsemen…. *Like* the rumbling of chariots…they leap, *like* the
crackling of a flame of fire devouring the stubble, *like* a powerful army drawn up
for battle. They run *like* mighty men, they climb the wall *like* men of war" (2:4–9;
translation is Assis's); he argues that this proves that the army is only a metaphor for
the locusts. Elie Assis, "The Structure and Meaning of the Locust Plague Oracles in
Joel 1, 2–2, 17," *ZAW* 122 (2010): 401.

Locusts previously appeared in several significant historical places. When Moses warns the Jewish people of the consequences of abandoning the covenant, he lists locusts as an instrument that God will use to discipline them: "You will carry much seed into the field but gather little, because locusts will eat it" (Deut. 28:38). However, the book of Judges compares the invading Midian armies to locusts as well:

> Whenever Israel would sow, Midyan, Amalek, and the peoples of the East would come up and raid them. They attacked them and destroyed the land's produce all the way to Aza; they left no sustenance in Israel.... For they would ascend with their cattle and tents *like a swarm of locusts*; they and their camels were innumerable.... Israel was reduced to destitution by Midyan, and the Israelites cried out to the Lord. (Judges 6:3–6)

In the first description of the redemption, Joel appears to imply that a literal swarm of locusts was the meaning all along: "I will repay you for all the seasons consumed by the locusts, the springing-locusts, the finisher-locusts, and the chewer-locusts – My great army, which I sent among you" (2:25).

According to this approach, the only enemy was the locusts. Any previous references to a human army were metaphors. This is the Talmud's approach, adopted by most medieval commentators (including Rashi and Radak)[27] and most modern commentators.[28] However, some commentators (including R. Eliezer of Beaugency and Abrabanel) argue the opposite approach that the references to locusts in the

---

27. Explaining the appearance of the word "nation" in chapter 1 to describe the locusts, Radak writes, "All gatherings of living creatures are called *goy*, therefore Joel said *goy* regarding the locusts. And so too regarding ants, it says in Proverbs 30:25, "Ants are not a strong species (lit., A nation that is not mighty)."

28. Additionally, Assis argues that the descriptions of effects of the locust invasion are too realistic to be understood metaphorically. For sources on both sides of the issue in scholarship, see Assis, "The Structure and Meaning of the Locust Plague Oracles," 401–2, notes 1–3.

first two chapters are a metaphor describing an enemy invasion.[29] Abrabanel interprets the four distinct types of locusts listed in chapter 1 as the four kingdoms that traditional scholarship states would dominate Israel – Babylonia, Persia, Greece, and Rome. A midrash is even more specific in identifying the locusts as the invading army of the Assyrians that invaded Judah in 701 BCE:

> R. Abba bar Kahana cited R. Shmuel bar Naḥman: Three decrees were sealed on that day. The decree that the ten tribes would fall to Sennacherib was sealed, the decree that Sennacherib would fall to Hezekiah was sealed, and the decree that Uzziah [Shebna] would be struck with leprosy was sealed. It is written, "And on nation [goy] and man together" (Job 34:29). *Goy* refers to Sennacherib [and his forces], regarding whom it is written (Joel 1:6), "For a *goy* has risen against My land." (Leviticus Rabba 5:3)

An additional proof for understanding the locust invasion as a metaphor for human armies is found in Joel's reference to the invader as emanating from the north: "I will drive the *northerners* away from you" (2:20). In the Bible, north traditionally refers to Assyria or Babylonia and their military invasions. Locusts, however, traditionally come from the south, not the north.[30]

---

29. Among modern scholars, Stuart argues that the description of the devastation caused by the locusts in 1:7 ("He has laid my vine waste, and my fig tree into a disappointment; he has peeled it and cast it off; its branches have become white") is incongruent with the observed behavior of locusts (D. Stuart, *Word Biblical Commentary* 31: *Hosea – Jonah*, 243). Additionally, both ancient Egyptian and Assyrian records describe marauding armies as locusts. (The Egyptian records use the locust metaphor to describe a large army of relatively weak soldiers, while the Assyrian records use the metaphor to emphasize the devastation left behind when a large army marches across a land.) For further discussion, see John A. Thompson, "Joel's Locusts in the Light of Near Eastern Parallels," *Journal of Near Eastern Studies* 14 (1955): 55; Victor Avigdor Hurowitz, "Joel's Locust Plague in Light of Sargon II's Hymn to Nanaya," *Journal of Biblical Literature* 112:4 (Winter, 1993): 597–603; R. A. Simkins, "God, History, and the Natural World in the Book of Joel," *The Catholic Bible Quarterly* 55 (1993): 437, note 9.
30. The Tanakh employs the idea of the north or the northerner to refer to Israel's great historical enemies Assyria and Babylonia, whose invasions typically came from

Finally, other commentators and scholars prefer an exegetical middle ground: chapter 1 describing an upcoming locust plague and chapter 2 switching to an enemy invasion. In this approach, Joel's announcement of the locust outbreak was only a harbinger of an impending even greater catastrophe. The announcement leads to the people's repentance and the restoration of the land from both of these catastrophes at the end of chapter 2.

Returning to the midrash above, we find the understanding that Joel prophesied during the reign of Hezekiah appealing. The Assyrian invasion of 701 BCE devastated the Judean countryside, and the few starving survivors huddled in Jerusalem, waiting for the inevitable approach of the enemy chariots. Under siege, the people waited nervously for the breaching of the walls described in chapter 2 and the resulting slaughter of the remaining population. Joel mentions no sin – indeed, Hezekiah was widely considered a righteous king who had purged Assyrian influences and idolatries from the Temple[31] – yet the nation was on the verge of extinction. Assyria destroyed the Northern Kingdom; only Judah and Jerusalem remained (hence, Joel makes no mention of Israel). Only a few years earlier, the nations mentioned by Joel in chapter 4 betrayed Judah, taking advantage

---

the north due to the implausibility of attack across the eastern desert (Is. 41:25; Jer. 1:13–15, 4:6, 6:22, 10:22; Ezek. 26:10, 38:6, 15; Zech. 2:10). According to Jamieson-Fausset-Brown Bible Commentary:

> The Hebrew expresses that the north in relation to Palestine is not merely the quarter whence the invader comes, but is his native land, "the Northlander"; namely, the Assyrian or Babylonian (compare Jer. 1:14, 15; Zeph. 2:13). The locust's native country is not the north, but the south, the deserts of Arabia, Egypt, and Libya. Assyria and Babylon are the type and forerunner of all Israel's foes. (http://biblehub.com/commentaries/jfb/joel/2.htm)

31. Not only the Tanakh is effusive in its praise of Hezekiah: "He did what was right in the eyes of the Lord just as his ancestor David did. He removed the high shrines and tore down the worship pillars.... In the Lord, God of Israel, he placed his trust; *there were none like him* among all the kings of Judah who succeeded him or those who came before him. He clung to the Lord and never turned away from him and kept the commandments that the Lord had commanded Moses" (II Kings 18:3–6). The Talmud credits Hezekiah with creating a universal school system that achieved educational heights unreached since in Jewish history: "From the territory of Dan in the north to Beersheba in the south...there was not a child who did not know the most complex laws of purity and impurity" (Sanhedrin 94b).

of its weakened state to plunder the land and its inhabitants (these nations would have been relevant during the eighth-century, and not at a later date). Overnight, however, God heard the nation's prayers and decimated the Assyrian camp (II Kings 19). This sudden turnaround in their fortune is reflected in the sudden switch between the two halves of Joel's prophesy. The first half is all destruction; the second half describes an immediate salvation, with the potential for even greater redemption on the horizon.[32]

In the commentary, we will treat each chapter without its metaphorical overtones, explaining chapter 1 as referring to a locust invasion and chapter 2 to the invasion of a human army.

STYLE AND STRUCTURE

Establishing the structure of the book of Joel based on subject matter should be a relatively easy task. The first two chapters contain two portrayals of a devastating locust plague on the land of Judah, interspersed with Joel's appeals to the people as to what their response should be, and concluding with God's response – the restoration of the country. The final two chapters shift to a description of Joel's vision of the end of days. He foresees widespread prophecy resting on the people, a major battle between the nations, and concludes triumphantly with peace and prosperity for those loyal to God. With two completely different subjects matters, some early secular scholars posited that the book is a composite of two separate works; however, later scholarship recognizes the book's fundamental unity.[33]

However, we shall divide the book differently, based not on the subject matter (locusts vs. Messianic redemption) but rather on the

---

32. Indeed, rabbinic thought views Hezekiah as a "potential" Messiah, and suggests that had he praised God properly for the miracle that occurred, a total redemption (as described in Joel 4) could have occurred (Sanhedrin 94b).

33. For an excellent summary of the history of secular scholarship regarding the book's composition, see Joel Barker's chapter "The Unity of Joel," in *Joel: A Discourse Analysis of the Hebrew Bible* (Grand Rapids, MI: Zondervan, 2020), 6–122, in which he concludes "the weight of the argument regarding Joel's composition seems to fall on the side of the scholars who consider it a unified work"; see also Assis, "The Structure and Meaning of the Locust Plague Oracles," 39–42.

content of Joel's message.[34] We place God's response in chapter 2 as the hinge around which the book revolves. In the first half of the book (1:1–2:17), God is absent. The verses describe how Joel urges the people to do everything in their power to petition God to relent as the invading locusts/armies approach. As a result, the people mourn, cry, lament, and repent, uncertain whether God would heed their prayers "Who knows? Maybe He will reconsider and relent" (2:14). Suddenly, "Then the Lord will be fiercely zealous toward His land, and He will have mercy upon His nation" (2:18). For the first time, the Lord becomes the active party. Throughout Joel's second half, God moves to respond to their cries and prayers – from restoring the grains and harvests destroyed by the invaders to bestowing His spirit upon the people, and ultimately defeating their enemies so that the Jewish people can finally live in peace. As such, we divide the book in the following manner:

A. The Jewish people turn to God in times of catastrophe
    i.   Urge to lament (1:2–14)
    ii. Outline of the lamentation (1:15–20)
    iii. Invasion of Judah by a foreign nation (2:1–11)
    iv. Joel leads the people's repentance (2:12–17)
B. God responds to the Jewish people's cries
    i.   God restores the harvests destroyed by the locusts (2:18–27)
    ii. God promises to pour out His spirit on the people (ch. 3)
    iii. God judges the nations (4:1–17)
    iv. God provides peace and prosperity to Judah (4:18–21)

In the commentary, we shall outline the many parallels and links between the sections, how each section builds upon the previous ones, and the literary and textual criteria and markers that support this delineation.

---

34. We have adopted Nogalski's approach (with a change in nomenclature), as he writes that separating chapters 1–2 from chapters 3–4 is to divide it by content (locust invasion vs. future eschatology), while separating 1–2:17 from 2:18–4:21 is to divide it by form (emphasis on the people's actions vs. emphasis on God's actions). See Nogalski, *Redactional Processes in the Book of the Twelve* (Berlin: De Gruyter, 1993), 2.

Joel's poetic style is clear, vivid, and moving. Half-prose, half-poetry, but all passion – his account of the effects of the locust swarm is heartrending; his description of the invasion is terrifying. His words capably arouse the required emotions in his listeners – first fear for the future, and then, in the darkest moment – hope that all is not lost – if only they choose to act. His descriptions of redemption inspire and uplift. A master wordsmith, he was creative in his phrasing – one verse alone, 1:17, contains three hapax legomena (words that do not appear elsewhere in Tanakh). As noted previously, his book contains many verbal and literal parallels and allusions to other biblical texts (often the Garden of Eden and the Exodus narrative) – yet it is his creativity with them that allows him to formulate his own unique vision, just as a painter mixes colors on the canvas to create an original composition. We will note the various poetic devices that he uses throughout the text.

Joel's Call to Prayer

LOCUSTS ARE COMING! (JOEL 1:1–14)

"This is the word of the Lord that came to Joel son of Pethuel." (1:1)[1]

Joel's superscription is simple, devoid of any identifying details. Unlike other prophetic books, it tells us nothing of who Joel was or where and when he lived.[2] The only information given is that his message comes from God.

The first chapter is divided into two clear parts: In verses 2–14, Joel calls the people to prayer; in verses 15–20, he leads them in a collective lament. In the first part's first section (vv. 2–4), Joel outlines the reason for his call. Then, in the following section (vv. 5–14), Joel

---

1. Interestingly, the Septuagint identifies the name of Joel's father as Bethuel, the name of Rebecca's father (see Gen. 22:22–23; 24:15, 24, 47, 50). Possibly, the Septuagint copyist chose to transform an unknown name into a name that had previously occurred in the Bible.
2. Six prophets in the Twelve Minor Prophets – Joel, Obadiah, Jonah, Nahum, Habakkuk, and Malachi – do not provide a regnal formula that would assist in identifying the king under whom they prophesied. Three other prophets – Hosea, Micah, and Zephaniah – have the phrase "The word of the Lord, which came to…." For a full listing of the variations between the prophetic superscriptions, see Beasley, *Nahum, Habakkuk, and Zephaniah*, 40–41.

cleverly alternates between different groups in society, encouraging them to react (mourn, wail, be ashamed, lament) while continually adding horrific descriptions of the devastation to justify his call to action. The emphasis on action creates an optimistic undertone for his message – act now when something can be done! – while the constant addition of terrifying imagery and descriptions, piled one upon another, creates a sense of urgency. The first section culminates in verse 14 when Joel calls for a communal assembly to engage in prayer and lamentation.

Two textual markers indicate that verse 14 concludes the first part.[3] First, there is an *inclusio*[4] that surrounds verses 2–14. Verse 2 calls to the "elders" and the "inhabitants of the land" to establish the veracity of Joel's message; verse 14 calls upon the "elders" and the "inhabitants of the land" to assemble with Joel to pray to God to lament the impending devastation (and by implication, be saved). Second, the two parts have two different subjects. Verses 2–14 are Joel's call to communal lamentation, while verses 15–20 are the actual lamentation. Thus, the first part is divided as follows:

> **ACTION**: "Listen, O elders; take heed, all those who live on the land. Has there been anything like this in your lifetimes or in the lifetimes of your parents? You will tell your children of this, and your children will tell their children of this, and their children will tell a different generation of this." (vv. 2–3)
>
> **DESCRIPTION**: "What remains after the chewer-locusts will be eaten by the locusts; what remains after the locusts will be

---

3. Many scholars argue that the first section ends with verse 12, and that the call for the priests to lead the people in prayer begins the second section. Assis, for example, argues that the first verses (3–12) are a description of the tragedy, followed by a call to prayer (Assis, "The Structure and Meaning of the Locust Plague Oracles," 403). As we demonstrate, the first verses contain more than a simple description, alternating between descriptions of the tragedy and calls for the people to react.

4. Wendland defines an *inclusio* as when "[A ... A'] – [identical] elements demarcate the beginning and ending of the same discourse unit." Ernst Wendland, *Translating the literature of Scripture* (Dallas: SIL International), 123–37.

eaten by the springing-locusts; what remains after the springing-locusts will be eaten by the finisher-locusts." (v. 4)

ACTION: "Wake, drunkards, and weep; wail, drinkers of wine, over the sweet wine you are denied drinking." (v. 5)

DESCRIPTION: "For a nation has risen up against My land – innumerable, mighty, with lion's teeth – its fangs the fangs of a lioness. It has laid My vines to waste and splintered My fig trees. It has stripped them bare and cast them down, their cuttings bleached." (vv. 6–7)

ACTION: "Wail like a young woman donning sackcloth for her husband in her youth." (v. 8)

DESCRIPTION: "Grain offerings and libations have been cut off from the House of the Lord. The priests, attendants of the Lord, are in mourning. The field has been devastated; the earth is in mourning. The grain is devastated, the young wine has dried up, and the oil languishes." (vv. 9–10)

ACTION: "Farmers, be ashamed; vintners, bewail the wheat, the barley, the harvest of the field – destroyed." (v. 11)

DESCRIPTION: "The vine has withered, and the fig tree languishes; the pomegranate; also the date. The apple and all the orchard trees wither. Truly man is parched of joy." (v. 12)

ACTION: "Don sackcloth – mourn, O priests. Wail, attendants of the altar. Come sleep in sackcloth, attendants of my God, for grain offerings and libations have been cut off from the House of your God. Sanctify a fast day, convene an assembly, gather the elders and all those who live on the land to the House of the Lord, your God, and cry out to the Lord." (vv. 13–14)

Joel directs his first words at both "the elders" and all the inhabitants of the land. There is a clear chiastic temporal framework in this opening unit. Joel begins with a call to the past [A – elders], then to the present [B – the present inhabitants of the land], and continues with an appeal to the present [B' – your days], and concludes with a return to past events [A' – your parents' days]. The dual command formula appears throughout the Bible, including diplomatic discourse (II Kings 18:28–29), wisdom instruction (Prov 4:1; 7:24), as well as prophetic oracles,[5] and serves to emphasize the importance of the message to be delivered. Joel demands that his audience listen and pay attention, asking rhetorical questions about the impending calamity to shock them into action. He must convey to them a sense of urgency; what awaits them is unparalleled. Should the people doubt his words, they can turn to the elders for verification.[6] In the Tanakh, elders are more than old people with long memories. Elders serve as counselors (Judges 9:2; I Kings 12:6), participate in electing kings (I Sam. 8:4; I Kings 12:1–15), and occasionally represent the people in the Temple service (Lev. 9:1–2; I Kings 8:3). Here, Joel relies on their implied authority to verify his words. It is so shocking, so gigantic, that people will tell of it to the generations that follow, moving from the past/present to the future. Yet Joel hasn't yet revealed the true nature of the crisis – the repetition being "a rhetorical strategy of delay to heighten the tension."[7]

In verse 3, Joel continues to delay divulging the nature of the incomparable event at which he hinted in the previous verse. Instead, he commands his listeners to communicate this message to their children. Their children should retell it to the next generation and it should be retold again to a fourth generation. Verse 2 ended with the previous generations never having seen anything like the event – verse 3 fixes the event's uniqueness in history by referring to future generations. The motif of instructing the children and retelling God's greatness and actions draws a link to the Exodus.[8] The purpose of this allusion is not simply to emphasize the event's importance. Rather, Joel means to create a dramatic shock, an intellectual earthquake among his listeners.

5. Cf. Is. 1:1; Ezek. 6:3; Hos. 4:1; Amos 3:1; Mic. 6:1.
6. Alsheikh presents a different understanding as to why Joel singles out the elders for consideration. He argues that unlike younger listeners, who had never seen destruction and devastation on a large scale before, the elders had a tendency to dismiss any bad tidings that they heard ("You think *that* plague was bad? When I was a young boy in the year 913 BCE, there were so many locusts that…")
7. J. Barker, *Joel*, 53.
8. See Ex. 12:26–27; 13:8, 14; Deut. 6:2–3.

In verse 4, Joel reveals what the incomparable event is: An invasion of locusts is about to hit Israel. To Joel's listeners, the very idea that locusts would attack the Jewish people would be nothing less than a dramatic inversion and repudiation of the Exodus.[9] Once, God sent locusts to strike the Egyptians; now Judah and Jerusalem face a locust plague sent by God. Joel uses four separate terms to describe the locusts. Some commentators suggest that Joel refers to four subspecies of locusts or four stages of the locusts' maturity.[10] However, Joel is more likely to be describing the locust invasion as coming in four waves upon the helpless populace: gnawing, swarming, creeping, and stripping, devouring every leaf and kernel along the way. Other prophets, too, use the imagery of four waves of invasion to present a picture of complete devastation (Jer. 15:3; Ezek. 14:21).

Once the elders have verified Joel's words about the uniqueness of the impending calamity that they face, Joel addresses four groups of people in turn: drunkards (vv. 5–7), the people of Jerusalem (vv. 8–10), farmers (vv. 11–12), and priests (v. 13). Each address contains three elements: a call to lament, a description of who is to lament, and an explanation that details the reason for each group to lament. All these groups have intimate ties to the land, whether as a source of sustenance or as

---

9. Commentators wrestle with reconciling Joel's claim that this locust plague was the worst ever (Joel 2:2) with Exodus 10:14, which states that "The locusts ascended over the entire land of Egypt…before them, there was never such a locust [plague], and after it, there will never be one like it." A brief summary of their responses appears here:

   Rashi, Radak: The plague in Joel's time consisted of many species together, but in Egypt only one species of locust was involved.

   Ramban: Locust swarms will occur, but at random, and never at God's command, like in Egypt.

   Rabbeinu Hananel, Abrabanel: Exodus is referring specifically to a locust plague in Egypt, not the rest of the world (he argues that the uniqueness is in the way the winds blow). It should be noted that Abrabanel avoids the issue of a global sense, as he understands the locusts as a metaphor for an invading army, with each type of locust representing a different world power that invaded Israel (the shearing locust – Babylonia; the increasing locust – Persia; the nibbling locust – Greece; and the finishing locust – Rome).

10. J. Barker quotes Sellers, "Stages of Locust," *The American Journal of Semitic Languages and Literatures* 52:2 (1936): 81–85.

their occupation. We suggest that this order reflects the ascending order in severity and importance in which the locust plague affects the people.

Joel curiously begins the second section by singling out Judah's drunkards and wine drinkers. He exhorts them to "wake, weep and wail!"[11] As extensive drinkers, they will be the first to feel the effect of the plague. Typically, drunkards have no concern for the general wellbeing of society around them. Indeed, Joel uses a particular verb in addressing them – *hakitzu!* "Wake up!"[12] However, they will not be immune from the effects of the invasion, as the first item to disappear will be the luxury product, the grapes. First, regular freshly produced wine will disappear, and then the strong wine in storage will also vanish from the shelves as the effects of the locusts begin to be felt.[13] Thus, Joel's goading of the drunkards serves a dual purpose. They are the first to notice the loss of wine; however, since wine played an important role in traditional celebrations, every one of Joel's listeners would commiserate with their plight.

In verses 6–7, Joel enumerates the reasons why the drunkards should mourn. The locusts are an invading army, "innumerable and mighty," equated with the ferocity of wild lions, destroying everything in their path. Barker writes that "these two images [a vast army and ravenous lions] poetically describe the two most distinctive features of locust infestations: vast numbers and voracious appetite." The locusts' teeth are compared to lions' teeth in how they destroy their prey, stripping the vines and fig trees so thoroughly bare that their branches were barkless, left gleaming white. Cleverly, Joel also shows how he personally relates to the suffering of the people – he describes the Land of Israel, helpless under the onslaught of the locusts, as "my land," "my vine," and "my fig

---

11. Malbim suggests that Joel is addressing two groups of individuals – both the habitual drunkards and the moderate drinkers.
12. The word *hakitzu* carries several connotations. In many places it refers to awaking from sleep (I Sam. 26:12; Is. 29:8; Ps. 3:6; 7:20). However, in Proverbs it specifically denotes awakening from a drunken stupor (Prov. 23:25).
13. There are several interpretations regarding the two types of wine Joel mentions – *yayin* and *assis*. Rashi understands *assis* as being a superior wine. Modern commentators understand it as being either a stronger wine or a sweeter beverage produced from younger grapes (though still intoxicating). See Isaiah 49:26.

tree."[14] In doing so, he makes the people more receptive to his message and more likely to heed his plea to join him in prayer.

Joel's agricultural references, specifically the combination of "vine and fig tree," draw upon common biblical metaphors for peace and prosperity – the wish of the people that everyone should dwell in peace "each man under his vine and his fig tree" (I Kings 5:5; Mic. 4:4). However, the usage of these fruits to convey the scope of the destruction cleverly reverses the imagery from peace and prosperity to destruction, devastation, and desolation.[15] Continuing his approach that the first chapter is a metaphor for the invasion of an enemy army, Abrabanel suggests that the fig trees and vines symbolize the Jewish people (described by the prophets as God's vineyard; see Is. 5), who the invader will completely raze. Dillard poetically develops this approach: "God had planted a garden in Eden, and he had also planted his vine in the Land of Israel.... The locust plague represents the undoing of the paradisiacal abundance of God's garden."[16]

After the drunkards, Joel turns to his second audience, an unnamed feminine entity he tells to mourn like a young maiden who discovers that her fiancé has died. One can imagine her tragedy. She has planned for her wedding, prepared her trousseau, anticipating a life of

---

14. Some commentators suggest that God is the subject of "My land," "My vine," and "My fig tree," demonstrating the fusion of the prophet and the divine message giver. Barker notes that this fusion is built into the "nature of prophetic authority and the necessity for close identification with a deity"; see Thomas Overholt, *Channels of Prophecy: The Social Dynamics of Prophetic Activity* (Minneapolis, MN: Augsburg Fortress, 1989), 69–70. Concerning the juxtaposition of human words and the divine word in prophetic proclamation, see the discussion of Jeremiah's commissioning in R. W. L. Moberly, *Prophecy and Discernment*, CSCD 14 (Cambridge: Cambridge University Press, 2006), 43–47, and J. Barker, *Joel*, 144.

15. Malbim in his commentary goes even further, suggesting that the speaker of the calls to lament were in fact the land's fruits:

    [Joel] offered a parable, speaking as if the grape and the fig were wailing these words! The grape of the vine was telling the drunkards to weep, for a nation had ascended upon the land...destroying its grapes. These words are spoken by the grape and fig which are being destroyed.... This is an incredible parable.

16. Raymond Dillard, *The Minor Prophets*, "Joel," 258. We will see Joel use additional Garden of Eden imagery in the following chapters, specifically referring to Eden in 2:3.

happiness and intimacy with her husband. Suddenly, right before her wedding, he dies.[17] Having never enjoyed her beloved's company, she must nonetheless mourn, replacing her lace wedding gown with sackcloth. One of the traditional roles of a woman in ancient society was bearing and raising children for the family unit.[18] Left without children, the young woman now faces a future of poverty, reliant on others for her sustenance. Similarly, the people have toiled the land, anticipating a bountiful harvest that will sustain them through the long winter. Now, they face a bleak future without food stored away.

To whom is Joel speaking? One possibility is that he is speaking to his human audience. Ibn Ezra suggests that Joel is now speaking directly to the land. Another intriguing possibility is that Joel is addressing the city of Jerusalem (and its inhabitants). The comparison of Jerusalem to a virgin daughter appears in several places in the Bible (e.g., II Kings 19:21, Lam. 1:15). If so, the potential allusion to Jerusalem in verse 8 foreshadows the mourning in the Temple in the following verse. Though they did not work the land themselves, Jerusalem's inhabitants began to sense the lack of grain, wine, and oil. These three food groups represent Israel's three major forms of vegetation in Israel: grasses, shrubs, and trees. While it does not say that Jerusalem's inhabitants are yet directly suffering, they begin to sense the magnitude of the impending catastrophe both in their marketplaces and in the decline in the number of the offerings brought in the Temple (if not their total disappearance). Joel mentions two offerings, grain offerings and wine libations, that require flour and oil (Num. 28:5) and wine (Ex. 29:40; Num. 28:7), respectively, as part of the daily offerings.

The locust plague's adverse effect on the daily service in the Temple leads Joel to mention another group of mourners – the priests. Radak notes that the priests were reliant on the daily offerings for their sustenance. Additionally, the cessation of the daily offerings suggests that the Temple service, the way the people communicate with God,

---

17. R. Eliezer of Beaugency suggests that based on this metaphor, we can identify when the locusts arrived – right before the holiday of Sukkot, when all the wheat is in the field waiting to be harvested, only to be devoured in an instant.
18. Gen. 30:1; I Sam. 2:5; Ps. 127:3–5, 128:3–4.

has come to a halt. It was restoring this channel and reconnecting the people with God that would become Joel's primary mission. Based on a homiletic in the commentary of Rabbi Moshe Alsheikh, we suggest that Joel was advancing another rhetorical goal. Joel uses similar language in his address to the drunkards and his description of the halt of the Temple service. Verse 6 states, "over the sweet wine you are denied (*niKHRaT*) drinking"; regarding the Temple service, verse 9 states, "Grain offerings and libations have been cut off (*hoKHRatT*) from the House of the Lord." Alsheikh suggests that Joel wishes to compare and contrast the two situations. The Alsheikh homiletically indicates that the young widow could have chosen to mourn the loss of her soon-to-be husband and the personal pleasure that she was to enjoy with him (like the drunkards and their wine). Yet, she chooses to focus on the loss of her partner instead. Similarly, Joel suggests that what should motivate the people's repentance are not their personal losses but rather the calamity of the cessation of offerings in the Temple.

Joel's description of the expanded devastation of the land in verse 10 is one of the most poetic verses in prophetic literature. He uses five agricultural images, each containing only two words, to emphasize the scope of the devastation the locusts left behind. Each begins with a verb that either describes destruction or lamentation, followed by the verb's subject. The rhythm of these brief phrases reads like a steady, staccato drumbeat that emphasizes the thorough nature of the desolation. The first two images – "the earth has been devastated; the land is mourning" – *shudad sadeh, avla adama* – start with the passive description [has been plundered], and then with the land actively responding by mourning.[19] By describing the earth as engaging in mourning, Joel suggests that the behavior that he is asking the people to employ is a natural reaction, innate in the natural order.

Similarly, the earth mourns just like the priests in the previous verse. All society has been leveled; nothing (mineral, plant, animal, or human) has escaped destruction. The final three images list which crops

---

19. We have translated the Hebrew word *avla* as "mourning," following Ibn Ezra, for the reason outlined above. Radak and the Targum, however, translate the Hebrew word *avla* as "destroyed."

the earth mourns; again, like humanity, it mourns the loss of grains, wine, and oil.

In the third section, Joel switches his attention from the city-dwellers to the farmers. The people most directly affected by the locust invasion are to despair; the fruits of their labors have perished. Verse 11 describes how the locusts have decimated the wheat and barley. Verse 12 expands the extent of the devastation to all the fruits: grapes, figs, pomegranates, dates, and apples. The first verse describes the staples on which human survival depends (Genesis 42 tells about the famine Jacob's family faced in Canaan due to the lack of grains, even though Jacob and his family had dried fruits and nuts available).[20] Malbim notes that Joel lists all produce – first, the seven species for which Israel is praised (Deut. 8:8): wheat, barley, grapes, figs, pomegranates, and dates (with olives included in the word "vineyards"). Second, the phrase "the harvest of the field" includes all vegetables, and the apple represents all fruit, as the most important of the tree species. The verses are tied together nicely by a clever wordplay: Verse 11 begins with the imperative *hoViSH*, be ashamed, from the root B-SH-SH; verse 12 concludes with the word *hoViSHu*, the fruit has dried, from the root Y-B-SH.

In verses 13 and 14, Joel turns his attention again to the priests. Contrasted with his opening call to the drunkards (vv. 5–7), Joel has moved from the most ungodly citizens to the godliest (ideally), effectively including all of Judah's citizens in his call. Referring to "my God" and "your God" in the same verse, Joel demonstrates that his concerns and the people's concerns are the same. Another reminder of the lack of produce dramatically outlines the crisis facing the people. They need to call out to God for help, yet without any offerings to bring, the people cannot approach the Lord as required. Joel focuses on the priests again, but the religious leaders are to set an example for the rest of the nation. Joel has achieved his goal at this point – he has convinced the people to pray to the Lord.

---

20. Heard orally from Professor Yonatan Grossman.

THE DAY OF THE LORD (JOEL 1:15–20)

> O, for the day, the day of the Lord is nigh; like havoc from Shaddai
> it will come. Is not food cut off in front of our very eyes; happi-
> ness and joy from the House of our God? The seeds have shriv-
> eled under the clods. The storehouses are desolate. The granaries
> have been destroyed; the grain has dried up. O, the animals, how
> they moan. Herds of cattle are in confusion, for they are without
> pasturage; even the flocks of sheep suffer.
>
> To You, my Lord, I cry out. Fire has consumed the desert
> pasture, and flame has been ignited in all the orchard trees. Even
> the animals of the fields long for You – for the riverbeds are dry,
> and fire has consumed the desert pasture. (1:15–20)

Having gathered the people, Joel now leads them in prayer, describing
the devastating effects of the locust plague before turning directly to
God in the last two verses. No longer does Joel divide the people into
its subgroups; more importantly, he does not divide himself from them.
Instead, he now identifies himself with his audience (e.g., v. 16, "*our* eyes,"
"from the house of *our* God"). No longer does Joel command the people
to mourn; instead, he provides the prayer they are to recite together.

The prayer starts with the cry "Alas!" – a common word that signifies the beginning of a new section and indicates lament or mourning.[21]
Joel describes the day of the devastation of the land as being nothing less
than the harbinger of an imminent "day of the Lord,"[22] a theme he will
return to in chapter 2 (vv. 1, 11). The locusts are not the pinnacle of the
people's troubles, but a mere prelude to something even worse. As discussed in the introduction, the phrase "the day of the Lord" becomes the
theme around which Joel builds his message. In the Tanakh, it generally
refers to any period in which God delivers judgment on the people. In
Joel, the phrase "the day of the Lord" appears five times (1:15; 2:1, 11; 3:4;
4:14). It first appears here in verse 15, which has an almost exact parallel

---

21. See Josh. 7:7; II Kings 3:10; 6:5; Jer. 4:10; 14:13; Ezek. 9:8; 11:13.
22. Abrabanel interprets the double usage of the word "day" in verse 15 as referring to
 the destruction of the two Temples, both of which, according to tradition, were
 destroyed on the ninth of Av (Tisha B'Av).

in Isaiah: "Wail, for the day of the Lord is nigh; like assault from Shaddai it strikes" (Is. 13:6). Though directed at different nations, both Joel and Isaiah stress the day's inevitable nature as one of divinely inspired destruction. However, Isaiah describes the judgment and destruction that approaches Babylon as inevitable. Joel uses his pronouncement to inspire the people to pray, repent, and avoid judgment. Both verses contain the wordplay of "raid" (SHoD) and "Almighty" (SHaDai), emphasizing that the plague is from God, not simply occurring due to natural causes.

Verse 16 contains two rhetorical questions: "Is not food cut off in front of our very eyes?" and "[has not] happiness and joy from the House of our God [been cut off]?" Joel once again affirms that the service in the Temple is unable to function – but as opposed to describing the lack of offerings, Joel focuses on the lack of "joy and happiness," feelings that the service should engender (Deut. 12:5–7) among the people. Radak interprets this verse as alluding to the festival of Sukkot – the festival of the harvest and the only holiday where the commandment to rejoice is doubled (Deut. 15). The following two verses continue to describe the effects of the locusts, as silos lie empty of grain and empty casks begin to gather mold.[23] Joel expands the realms affected by the locusts to the animal and natural realm. With vivid imagery, he describes the barren countryside: fields are aflame, beasts die of thirst. Malbim interprets this verse as Joel questioning God – "If the people deserve to be punished, why are the animals made to suffer so?"

Finally, the prayer concludes with a first-person appeal from the prophet to God. This shift in voice highlights the belief that only God can provide relief for the people's suffering, and allows Joel to model for the Jewish people their response to the calamity – a heartfelt prayer to God. In his prayer, he adds to the description of the destruction: fires

---

23. True to form, Abrabanel describes the granaries and silos as sitting empty not due to the locusts, but rather due to the people being too terrified to harvest their grain as the enemy advances. The fires ablaze in all directions are the armies themselves; the other animals fleeing in panic symbolize the other nations of the world, attempting to flee as Babylonia lays waste their countries in turn.

rage out of control, burning pastures and trees.[24] The conflagration has spread from the farmyards with the domesticated animals to the wilderness and all the beasts that live there. Finally, his imagery of the animals panting for water (*ta'ARoG elekha*) reinforces the message that Joel has been trying to convey to the people – call to God! His words allude to Psalms 42, the only other occurrence of the root (A-R-G) in the Tanakh. Psalms 42:2 has David declare, "As a deer pines (*ta'ARoG*) for flowing streams, my soul pines (*ya'ARoG*) for You, God; my soul thirsts for God, the living God – oh, when will I come and appear before God?" Both Joel and Psalms describe the presence (or absence) of God as "streams of water" (*afikei mayim*). Joel reuses this metaphor at his book's end: "On that day, the mountains will drip with sweet wine, the hills will flow with milk, and all of Judah's rivers will flow, full of water. A spring will surge forth from the House of the Lord and irrigate the Valley of Acacias" (4:18). In chapter 2, we will see if the prayer offered was successful.

ARMIES APPROACH (JOEL 2:1–11)

Blow a ram's horn in Zion; sound a horn on My holy mountain. Let all those who live on the land tremble, for the day of the Lord is coming; it is nigh. It is a day of darkness and blinding black, a day of clouds and mist like dawn spread over the mountains. There will be a great and mighty nation, the likes of which has never been before nor will ever be again until the end of time. Before it, the consuming fire; after it, a burning flame. The land, like Eden, before it; after it, a barren desert. It leaves not one survivor. Its resemblance is to horses – like war-horses, so they run. Theirs is the pounding of chariots dancing over the mountain peaks; theirs is the crackle of a flame as it consumes straw; theirs is the shout of a vast nation ready for battle.

Nations tremble before them; they are all ashen faced. They race like warriors; like soldiers they ascend the wall: Every soldier moving forward in position, not one strays from the route. They advance untouching, every warrior moving forward

---

24. Cf. "The Lord God showed me this: He was calling to fight with fire. It consumed the mighty deep; it consumed the allotted land" (Amos 7:4).

in position along the track. They fall on the sword but are not wounded. They rush into the city, race over the wall, ascend into the houses like thieves through the windows. The earth trembles before Him, the skies thunder, the sun and the moon go dark, and the stars draw in their light. Then the Lord raises His voice before His troops – for His camp is vast, and mighty are the ones who carry out His words. For great and terrifying is the day of the Lord – who could withstand it? (2:1–11)

At the end of chapter 1, the people prayed to God, hoping to avoid the impending calamity. Chapter 2 provides a startling response to their prayer. An invading army approaches, the alarm is to be sounded. The initial appeals to cry out to God, including Joel's lament, have not been successful; in fact, the opposite has occurred, and the situation has considerably deteriorated. The first section of this chapter is demarcated, in its first and last verses, with the dramatic phrase that these crises are again nothing less than the "day of the Lord." In verse 2 Joel describes the devastating darkness that this day brings. The following several verses describe the invading army, with verse 6 shifting perspective briefly to the inhabitants' reaction. Verses 7–9 describe the enemy's assault on Zion, focusing on the invader's ability to overcome any defenses. The section's last two verses return to the "day of the Lord" theme; it is as if the entire cosmos has joined the battle against the Jewish people, culminating with the dramatic revelation in verse 11 that God is the one who leads all the host against Zion.

There are several differences between Joel's descriptions in this chapter and the previous one. First, the enemy is no longer a horde of locusts, but an efficient and terrifying human army. Second, the target is no longer the countryside, but Jerusalem. Most significantly, God leads the enemy's assault. Finally, unlike in chapter 1, Joel does not intersperse descriptions of the calamity with calls for prayer. The implicit message is that Joel's audience is no longer capable of preventing their eventual demise.

This section begins with three commands: Blow the shofar (the ram's horn), blow the horn, and tremble. Joel has effectively become the city's watchman,[25] and God himself shouts out the warning ("My holiness"). In Tanakh, the command to blow the shofar can signify an alarm, a call to war, and also a call to bring the people to religious observance.[26] Traditional commentators, including Rashi, view the blowing of the shofar as a call to repentance. Malbim argues that Joel's double command, "Blow the shofar! Sound the trumpet!" represents two steps that the people must take to avoid the calamity – first assembling in the Temple, and then prayer and repentance. However, this verse contains several literary parallels with two other verses. Zephaniah 1:14–16 also includes the immediacy of an upcoming "day of the Lord," with imagery of blackness and darkness, and an assault against fortified cities, including Jerusalem. Jeremiah 4:5 describes a city under siege and the command to blow the shofar. Therefore, it is likely that the order here to sound the shofar denotes a call to alarm.

Joel then emphasizes that the "day of the Lord" is near. Unlike chapter 1, which did not elaborate on the nature of this day, Joel begins to describe what will happen when the "day of the Lord" comes. Amos describes the "day of the Lord" as one of darkness and not light (Amos 5:18–20; cf. Zeph 1:15–16). Joel provides four different synonyms for the word "darkness" and then details what will occur when this day dawns. Radak suggests that this verse can be understood symbolically, with light equivalent to happiness and darkness equivalent to suffering, and literally, with the darkness occurring when the horde of locusts block out the sunlight. Joel asks rhetorically whether such an event had happened before, just as he did at the beginning of chapter 1. He then commands the audience to tell of this event to succeeding generations.

The following verses continue to describe the approaching horde and the havoc they wreak on the land. Verse 3 employs a "before and after" strategy to describe the progression across the landscape. Continuing this strategy, Joel compares the land to the Garden of Eden and then to a desolate wasteland. Joel then switches to describe the invaders as

---

25. See Is. 21:11–12; Jer. 6:17; Ezek. 3:17.
26. For the shofar as an alarm, see Jer. 4:5; 6:1; Hos. 8:1; as a call to war, Judges 3:27; 6:34; 7:8; Jer. 51:27; and as a call for religious observance, Lev. 25:9; Ps. 47:6; 81:4; II Chr. 15:14.

an approaching cavalry, both in appearance and speed. Slowly, the dark cloud on the distance can now be heard – the noisy clamor of hooves and wheels, conveying the sense of impending dread felt by the city's inhabitants. Suddenly, they appear in their full glory – a division of chariots arrayed on the mountaintops. In Tanakh, chariots represent the most potent military instrument available (Ex. 14:6–7; Judges 4:3, 5:28; I Sam. 13:5), and they also describe the heavenly host (II Kings. 2:11–12, 6:17; Ezek. 1). The location of these chariots on the mountaintops is shocking; they are generally used for battles in the plains and are not mobile in mountainous terrain (Judges 1:19, 4:3; see Ibn Ezra, Radak here). If the enemy can bring chariots to Jerusalem, skipping over the hilltops along the way, then stopping the invader would seem impossible. Joel then compares the noise to that of a raging fire that scorches the ground, recalling not only verse 3 above, but Joel's descriptions of rampaging fires in chapter 1. This first subsection concludes with Joel labeling the invader "like a vast nation," again drawing upon militaristic overtones (Num. 20:20, 21:33; Judges 5:13; II Kings 18:26).

Verse 6 temporarily delays the assault, focusing instead on the terrified reactions of the helpless citizens. The following verses explain why these reactions are fitting. The invading army is now prepared to overwhelm the city's defenses. The attackers are relentless, fighting with unparalleled discipline. The army breaches the outer walls. Once having penetrated through all the futile fortifications erected by the inhabitants, they systematically traverse unimpeded throughout the city streets and upon the city walls. With no resistance, they raid and pillage every building and dwelling place. Joel uses short and staccato phrases to describe this invasion, imitating the relentless and disciplined trek of an army marching through the cobble-stoned streets. The description of their entry through the windows recalls Jeremiah 9:20, "For death has climbed into our windows, arrived in our palaces, to cut down babes from the outdoors and youth from the town squares." Verse 10 describes how even the heavenly host – the sun, moon, and stars – quake in fear before the invaders. The implication is that there is nothing in nature that can halt the enemy's advance.

Verse 10 begins with the word "before him/it [Him?]." This ambiguous pronominal suffix in the word *lefanav*, could refer to the invading army or foreshadow God's explicit appearance in the next verse. The trembling of the heavenly bodies often precedes God's appearance (cf. Ps 77:16; Is. 13:10, 13; Mic. 1:4). All this leads to the climactic reveal of this section – God is leading the invading army Himself! Given that the target is Zion, God's own holy mountain (as Joel stated in verse 1), the portrayal of God authorizing the assault on Jerusalem is stunning. The effect of this revelation on Joel's listeners must have been disheartening. Together with the prophet, they prayed to God in chapter 1 to stave off the calamity.[27] Now, they discover that God is leading the enemy force against them! Against this force, there is no escape. To whom can the Jewish people now turn for assistance?[28] The section ends with Joel's poignant rhetorical question, "Who could withstand it?"

REPENT WHILE YOU CAN (JOEL 2:12–17)

Even now, so says the Lord, return to Me wholeheartedly, with fasting, weeping, and grief. Rend your hearts, not your clothing, and come back to the Lord your God. For He is gracious and compassionate, slow to anger and abounding in kindness; He may well relent and forswear the evil. Who knows? Maybe He will reconsider and relent, and leave behind blessings; offer grain offerings and libations to the Lord, your God.

Blow a ram's horn in Zion, sanctify a fast day, convene an assembly, gather the people, sanctify the masses, convene the old, and gather the children and infants. Let the groom come from his room and the bride from her wedding chamber. Let the priests, attendants of the Lord, weep between the hallway and the altar. Let them say: "Have compassion, O Lord, upon Your people, and do not allow Your possession to become a reproach – ruled

---

27. Ernst Wendland succinctly describes Joel 2:11 as the "emotive psychological nadir of the entire prophecy" (*Prophetic Rhetoric: Case Studies in Text Analysis and Translation* [Maitland, FL: Xulon Press, 2009], 25).

28. However, Malbim here suggests that the appointment of God as the army's supreme Commander contains a hint of potential consolation. If the army/locust horde were unstoppable, then hope would indeed be lost. Once God is placed in charge, then the possibility that God will be open to repentance remains.

by nations." Why should it be said among the peoples, "Where is their God?" (2:12–17)

The previous section left the Jewish people facing annihilation, and with Joel's revelation that God was leading the armies against them, feeling a sense of hopelessness and despair. Now, this final section of the first half of the book of Joel provides one last surprise, and its message is the heart of this book. Despite everything, even when it appears that God Himself stands against a person, there is still hope. All a person has to do is pray. In this section, Joel intertwines the human and divine perspectives. He begs the people to return sincerely to God, even providing the words of the prayer that they should offer. He indicates that this is God's real desire and suggests that should the people return to God, God would respond reciprocally. Why is Joel so assured? Joel reveals the source of his confidence – the nature of God's character.

This section has two distinct subunits. The first three verses are a general call for repentance and prayer, guided by two commands using the word "return" (SH-U-V). The speaker of these verses shifts from first-person divine address ("return to Me," v. 12) to Joel's exhorting the people ("come back to the Lord your God," v. 13).[29] The second section, verses 15–17, expands upon Joel's initial call to return by providing a specific procedure on how people should respond and what they should say.[30]

The section begins with the phrasal hapax legomenon (*vegam ata* – "even now"), as well as a change in speaker, marked by "the word of the Lord." That God assumes the role of the speaker is necessary once Joel declared that God is leading the invading army. The previous

---

29. Malbim notes a subtle distinction between the "returns" of verses 12 and 13. In verse 12, the Hebrew reads *shuvu adai*, which Malbim interprets as a general change of direction – return **toward** Me. In verse 13, the Hebrew reads "*shuvu el Hashem*," return **to** God – in full and complete repentance (see similar change of wording between Deut. 30:2, "and you will return toward [ad] the Lord, your God," and Deut. 30:10, "when you return to [el] the Lord, your God").
30. Abrabanel suggests that the verses until verse 14 discuss the destruction of the First Temple by Babylonia, and from verse 15 onwards the prophet discusses the destruction of the Second Temple by Rome centuries later. We mention this view in passing, but prefer to read the text as one continuous unit.

section lacked any imperatives. As far as Joel was concerned, there was nothing left for the people to do. However, God Himself injects – even now, there is still hope! With God's approval, Joel can resume his role in instructing the people in their repentance and prayer.

God's instruction in verse 12 is for the Jewish people to "return to Me wholeheartedly."[31] Generally, this common prophetic word ("return") implies repentance from sins[32] and the reestablishment of the reciprocal relationship between God and the Jewish people.[33] The book of Joel, however, lacks any specific mention of sin. This lacuna suggests a broader understanding of his call to return. Unlike chapter 1, Joel's emphasis here is not on the external performance of the traditional triad of actions that generally accompanies repentance (fasting, weeping, and mourning). These actions certainly appear in the Tanakh: David fasted for the child conceived as a result of his adultery with Bath-Sheba (II Sam. 12:16), and the prophets often called upon the people to weep (Is. 22:12; Jer. 31:9) and mourn (Jer. 6:26; Amos 5:16, 17; Mic. 1:8). Notably, the only other occurrence of these three terms together in Tanakh is in the book of Esther 4:3, where the exiled Jewish community engages in these activities in the wake of learning about Haman's plot. Similarly, the Jewish people undertake these actions facing mortal peril, yet the book of Esther does not identify what specific sin they committed to warrant Haman's decree.

As noted, Joel focuses not only on external actions but also on the people's internal motivations. Verse 12 urges them to return to God

---

31. The centrality of these verses in rabbinic conceptions of repentance is underlined by the fact that the Midrash identifies these verses with the holidays that center around repentance:

"And the Lord gave forth His voice" (v. 11): this is Rosh HaShana, when the shofar sounds; "the great Day of the Lord" (v. 11): this is Yom Kippur, when the final judgment is pronounced and sealed; "even now return to me with all your hearts" (v. 12): even after Yom Kippur, as long as you repent and return with all your heart. (*Pesikta DeRav Kahana* 157b)

32. See Is. 1:27, 6:10, 9:12, 10:21, 19:22, 31:6; Jer. 3:1, 7, 10, 12, 14, 22; 24:7; Hos. 3:5, 5:4, 6:1; Amos 4:6, 8–11; Zech. 1:3; Mal. 3:7; II Chr. 30:6.

33. The reciprocal nature of this relationship is evident here, as God also becomes the subject of the word "return" (*yaSHUV*); see also Zech. 1:3; Mal. 3:7; II Chr. 30:6 (J. Barker, *Joel*, 212).

"wholeheartedly," and the beginning of verse 13 begs them to "rend" their hearts and not simply their clothes.[34] This demand is a consistent theme in the Tanakh. Repentance must be genuine and not merely the correct external performance of rituals and rote.[35] However, it should be noted that the place for this repentance to occur is in the Temple. Joel is not engaging in "anticultic" prophecy; indeed, he laments the Temple's inability to function. Instead, the call here is for sincerity and genuineness, not solely external gestures.

Verse 13 restates the command to return to God – this time in Joel's voice. Joel now provides a reason for this second call for return – the very nature of God Himself, as described in Ex. 34:6–7 where, in the aftermath of the sin of the Golden Calf, Moses receives the second copy of the tablets. Despite Israel's sin, God remains "the Lord," compassionate and gracious, slow to anger, abounding in lovingkindness, and one who both forgives iniquity and punishes the unrepentant. This summary of God's character is known as the *yud gimel middot haraḥamim*, the thirteen attributes of mercy. Variations of this list appear throughout the Tanakh, and it is central to understanding God's character.[36]

Joel, however, makes two significant changes to the listing of God's attributes of mercy. First, he omits the declaration that God will visit punishment on the generations following those who disobey – likely a result of his desire to encourage his listeners that they can still avoid penalty should they return properly. The second significant change is Joel's addition of the phrase that God "relents from evil," not found in Ex. 34:6–7. The verbal root for relent (N-Ḥ-M) occurs several times in the Tanakh with God as its subject, generally implying that God either changes his mind or relents concerning punishment that he was going to

---

34. Most commentators, including Rashi, understand Joel as exhorting the people to be sincere in their repentance, or thorough to the depths of their souls. Rashi brings another interpretation: If you repent now sincerely, you won't have to rend your garments in mourning [for your children, who will die of hunger] (Rashi quoting *Pesikta DeRav Kahana* 161b).

35. Amos 4:4–5 and 5:21–23 exemplify the tradition of castigating the community for performance of ritual without the proper accompanying spirit (cf. Is. 58:1–12; Jer. 7:1–8; Hos. 6:6; Mic 6:1–8). See J. Barker, *Joel*, 214.

36. Cf. Num. 14:18; Jonah 4:2; Nahum 1:3; Ps. 86:15, 103:8, 145:8 and Neh. 9:17, 31.

visit upon either his people or foreign nations.[37] It also appears in Jonah, where the disgruntled prophet uses it as an accusation against God for showing mercy to Nineveh, much to Jonah's chagrin and disappointment. Thus, while Joel illustrates God's compassionate nature towards His covenant people, Jonah demonstrates the universal extent of God's mercy (even including enemies of the Jewish people).

The word relent (N-Ḥ-M) also occurs in the episode of the sin of the Golden Calf, before God reveals to Moses his thirteen attributes of mercy, when Moses pleads for the Jewish people's survival. In Ex. 32:12, Moses uses the imperative form, asking God to relent of the planned evil towards His people, and the success of Moses's plea appears in v. 14, where it states that "Then the Lord relented from the evil He had spoken of doing to His people." It should be noted that while this managed to delay the punishment, only the thorough cleansing of the people in Ex. 32:19–29 allowed the regiving of the tablets and the renewal of the covenant. Similarly, the strategic placement of the keyword "relent" here allows Joel to outline a complete and detailed program of what the people must perform before God can choose to restore the relationship and save them from their tribulations.

Alluding and evoking the episode of the Golden Calf to his listeners, Joel reminds them that the Jewish people faced the threat of complete annihilation before – however, due to Moses's intercession, the danger was averted. The situation is dire, but destruction is not inevitable. Moses prayed, and the punishment was waived. Perhaps, Joel hints to his listeners, God will do the same, and the covenant will be preserved.[38]

In Joel's rewording of the attributes of mercy, he puts forth a question that emphasizes the complete inscrutability of God's character – *mi yodea* – "Who knows?" Perhaps God may change his mind, but perhaps not.[39] This emphasis on the total freedom of God's choices

---

37. See Jer. 4:28; 15:6, 20: 16; Amos 7:3, 6; Zech. 8:14.
38. Assis, *The Book of Joel*, 140–41.
39. Angel points out that the subject of the phrase "Who knows" is ambiguous. It can be read regarding God, and is therefore understood as a question – "Perhaps God will relent, perhaps not." This is the reading adopted by Ibn Ezra and *Daat Mikra*, and it's the one we have adopted in our commentary. However, Rashi, Rabbi Yosef Kara, Rabbi Eliezer of Beaugency, and Malbim read it as an imperative directed at

appears throughout the Tanakh.[40] Significantly, Joel's plea to the people to "return" (*shuvu*) in verse 13 is a wordplay where the return of the community through fasting, weeping, and mourning allows for verse 14, God's return (*yashuv*) in response.

Verse 14 concludes with the mention of a blessing, defined as a grain offering and a drink offering, recalling Joel's earlier laments in 1:9 and 1:13 that the locust infestation has destroyed so much that the priests cannot offer these gifts in the Temple. It is also a challenge to God – for the Jewish people to properly appease Him, God must first replace and restore the destroyed harvest. As such, blessings for the people and offerings to God are two sides of the same coin, indicating the renewed and reciprocal relationship between God and the Jewish people.[41]

The following three verses detail the specifics of the actions that Joel wants the people to perform while alluding to exactly how God will respond positively to their overtures. While at first glance, these verses appear to repeat the previous three verses, with the communal assembly and the summons to prayer, their focus is different. Verses 12–14 discuss God's compassionate nature and conclude with a plea for repentance – since God is merciful, He will accept your atonement. Verses 15–17 repeat the calls for communal prayer, but this time, the focus of the prayer is to request pity and express the hope that if God does not act to save them for His people's sake, at least He may consider doing so to prevent the desecration of His holy name.

The first command Joel issues is to "Blow a ram's horn in Zion" but instead of warning of an invasion, he calls the people to gather at the Temple. Joel then repeats his commands from 1:14, summoning the community to fast and assemble. In the next verse he expands further, detailing who is

---

the people: "He [who] knows [what his sin is] must repent, and He [God] will have mercy." Both Radak and Abrabanel present both options without stating their preference. Based on the literary parallel with Jonah 3:9, and the unannounced switch in the verses' subject the second reading requires, we adopt the first understanding in the commentary. For further development of this discussion, see Hayyim Angel, "The Uncertainty Principle in Repentance," in *Revealed Texts, Hidden Meanings: Finding the Religious Significance in Tanakh* (Jersey City, NJ: Ktav Publishing House, 2009), 15–34.

40. Cf. II Sam. 12:22; Jonah 3:9; Ps. 90:11; Eccl. 2:19, 3:21, 6:2, 8:1; Est. 4:4.

41. J. Barker, *Joel*, 219.

supposed to gather. Everyone is to attend, from elders to children and nursing infants. Even those about to be married are to pause their preparations and join the rest of the community. However, unlike the mourning bride of 1:8, here the bride and groom have not lost their partners. Even though newly married couples generally received an exemption from communal activities (Deut. 20:7; 24:5), at this moment, all individual considerations are banished for the needs of the general community.[42]

Verse 17 outlines the assembly's performance with tremendous detail. He states the exact location where the petitions are to be uttered – between the Temple hall and the altar.[43] He appoints the priests responsible for leading the community, recalling the similar command in 1:13 for the priests to don sackcloth and cry out to God. Then Joel provides the precise words that the priests are to pronounce. Two short petitions ask God to show mercy, and he concludes with a variation of the classic rhetorical question, "What will the nations say?" Completely omitted are the people's fasting and repentance. The only issue before God is His honor. The pronominal suffix of *amekha*, "*Your* people," alludes to God's relationship and ownership of the Jewish people.[44] The term "Your inheritance" can refer to either to the Jewish people or the Land of Israel, reflecting the interconnected relationship between God, His people, and His land.

Joel concludes his plea to spare the people with a negated imperative – "[at least,] do not give the Jewish people over into disgrace." Should Judah become a public spectacle among the foreign nations, their humiliation reflects on God as well – for He permitted the Jewish people to sink to this pathetic state. Again, as in verse 14, Joel ends with a rhetorical question, this time directed at God. Why would he allow the nations of the world to wonder, "Where is their God?" His conclusion

---

42. Rabbinic thought understands this verse metaphorically. The Mishna (Taanit 2:1) describes how the Holy Ark containing the Torah is taken out of the synagogue and placed in the center of the town square to inspire the community to repent (with the Ark compared to a bridegroom and the Torah being the bride).

43. Radak suggests that this central location was meant to remind the people of how they used to properly offer sacrifices before their supplies ran out. Ibn Ezra suggests that this location is chosen because it is forbidden to be sad in the Temple building.

44. Cf. I Sam. 10:1; I Kings 8:53; II Kings 21:14; Is. 19:25; Mic. 7:18; Ps. 33:12, 68:10, 106:5.

alludes to Moses's plea to God to preserve the Jewish people after the sin of the Golden Calf (Ex. 32:12 – "Why, O Lord, unleash Your anger against Your people … *Why should the Egyptians be able to say that You brought them out with evil intent,* to kill them in the mountains and purge them from the face of the earth?"; and to Moses retelling of the his prayer to God after the people's failures in the desert [Deut. 9:26–28] – "when the Lord had said He would destroy you, I prayed to the Lord – 'Lord God,' I said, 'do not destroy the people, Your heritage,' … *otherwise the nation from which You brought us will say, "It was because the Lord was unable to bring them into the land that He promised them, and because He hated them, that He took them out to kill them in the wilderness"*). In both cases, Moses equates the possibility of the destruction of the Jewish people with the impression of God's apparent powerlessness.[45]

In this section, Joel has successfully gathered the people to prayer and repentance, persuading them that despite the bleakness and hopelessness of their situation, if they repent and return correctly, they can be saved. Now, the onus is on God to "return" to the Jewish people in response.

---

45. See also Ezekiel 36, where the prophet explicitly equates the state of exile with a desecration of God's name ("There, in whichever nations they came to, they desecrated My holy name because it was said of them: These are the Lord's people, and they have left His land," Ezek. 36:20), and plays a pivotal role in the Ramban's commentary to Deut. 32:26:

> The expression that "I will cause their memory to cease from among humanity" refers to our current state of exile. We, the remnants of the tribes of Binyamin and Yehuda, have no renown among the peoples, and are not considered to be a people or a nation at all. The verses here declare that according to the strict attribute of justice, we ought to remain in exile forever, were it not for the "anger" of the enemy. This indicates that in our present exile, the merit of our ancestors has been exhausted. Our only hope of preservation and salvation from the hands of the nations is for God to act on behalf of His great Name. So too says the Prophet Yechezkel, when God proclaims that "I will gather you from the lands into which you have been scattered, and I will be sanctified through you in the eyes of the nations … and you shall know that I am God when I act with you for the sake of My name, and not in accordance with your evil ways and corrupt deeds, O House of Israel!" (translation by Rabbi Michael Hattin, available online at https://etzion.org.il/en/tanakh/torah/sefer-devarim/parashat-haazinu/haazinu-eternity-jewish-people)

Response and Redemption

RESTORATION OF THE LAND (JOEL 2:18–27)

Then the Lord will be fiercely zealous toward His land, and He will have mercy upon His nation.

He will reply and say to His nation: Behold – I will send to you grain, and sweet wine, and young oil. You will be sated with it. I will no longer allow you to become a reproach among the nations. I will drive the northerner away from you – I will banish them to a dry and desolate land; their vanguard to the east sea, their rearguard to the west sea. Their foul smell will ascend, their stench will rise, for they have done terrible things.

Fear not, earth. Rejoice! Be glad! For the Lord has done great things. Fear not, animals of My fields, for the desert pasture is green with grass; the tree has borne fruit: the fig and vine have blossomed. Rejoice and be glad in the Lord, your God, children of Zion. For He has given you the first rain out of generosity. He will rain down for you the first and last rain as it was in the beginning. The granaries will fill with grain, and the press will overflow with sweet wine and young oil.

I will repay you for all the seasons consumed by the locusts, the springing-locusts, the finisher-locusts, and the chewer-locusts – My great army, which I sent among you. You will eat, eat and be sated, and you will praise the name of the Lord, your God, who

> has done wonders for you, for My nation will never be ashamed.
> You will know that I am among Israel, and I am the Lord, your
> God; there is no other. (2:18–27)

Verse 18 introduces the book's second half. No longer is Joel begging, prompting, guiding the people to act. From here until the end of the book, Joel declares God's positive responses regarding both the immediate invasion and the ultimate redemption in the future. No more threats await the Jewish people, just promises of peace and prosperity. This section deals specifically with the restoration of the land and its produce after the locusts. However, its real purpose is to convince the people that just as God intends to act on their behalf now, they should trust as well in the final redemption, which Joel will detail in chapters 3 and 4.

As noted above, Joel presented the people with two prayer options. First, he summoned them together to repent their sins and rely on God's merciful nature (2:12–14). Second, he also gathered them to pray, the second time asking God to save them and thereby prevent the desecration of His holy name. What causes God to respond positively to their plea, and which plea does He react to? According to Rashi, Yosef Kara, and Radak, the two prayers are functionally one, and without the people's act of repentance, God would not redeem them. According to Abrabanel and Malbim, God chose to act to prevent the desecration of His name. This is not to suggest that these commentators felt that repentance was unnecessary.

On the contrary, the expression of penitence in its own right has tremendous value, just that it is not what motivates God to redeem His people. Malbim maintains a middle ground – God saves his people out of concern for His holy name, but the extent of the miracles that He performs on Israel's behalf is contingent on the nature of their repentance. Finally, Rabbi Hayyim Angel suggests that neither of the pleas is what ultimately moves God to act. Instead, God acts out of compassion, undeserved mercy. As such, states Angel:

> In this reading, verses 12–17 would reflect Joel's teaching of the
> proper religious response to adversity: repentance and petition

to God to avoid the desecration of His name. Verses 18–27 then present redemption as emanating from God's compassion and not being conditional on Joel's behavior.[1]

These verses contains several subunits. The first three verses describe how God will restore the land, including removing the invading army. Next, verses 21–24 present Joel's expectations of the people – they are to rejoice, in contrast to the commands to fear and tremble that marked this book's first half. Finally, in verses 25–27, God speaks again to reassure the people of His commitment to restoring the land and His Presence. As this section is a reversal of the curses that plagued the people in the first half of the book, it is not surprising to find numerous phrases in these verses that draw upon the previous negative portrayals.

The beginning of this section describes God's activity with four successive verbs (was zealous, had mercy, send [food], will not give [you over to the nations as a reproach]). This repetition establishes that God is responsible for all the positive changes that will occur. Joel speaks in the "prophetic past" – describing future events with such confidence and certainty as if they had already occurred. Joel begins with God's zealousness (K-N-A). This zealousness has a dual quality: On the one hand, God is not forgiving when the Jewish people are unfaithful and fail to worship God exclusively, as often expressed in connection to the prohibition against idolatry.[2] However, there is a second perspective to this zealousness in the Tanakh: God's passionate commitment to His people (Is. 9:7; Ezek. 39:25; Zech. 1:14). In Joel, God directs His zealousness towards the Land of Israel, and the second verb, "mercy," is for His people. Verse 19 introduces a short first-person divine speech. It begins with God promising to restore agricultural prosperity. with the words, "Behold – I will send to you." This phrase occurs mostly in prophetic literature and stresses

---

1. Angel, "The Uncertainty Principle," 156.
2. Cf. Ex. 20:3–5; 34:14; Deut. 4:24; 5:9; Josh. 24:19.

imminent action.[3] God will restore the three crops Joel mentioned when describing the devastation of the locust plague, "grain, and sweet wine, and young oil," staples of both the people's diet and the service in the Temple. Not only will God restore these crops, but they will also come in abundance. God then concludes by promising to remove the invading army from the Land of Israel.

Joel then switches to commanding the people for the last time in the book. Instead of scolding them and pleading with them, he has a simple goal. He wants them to consider what God has done and then to rejoice. Thus, Joel first addresses the land, followed by the animals, and finally the Jewish people. This progression encompasses everything that was devastated in Joel chapter 1 and demonstrates the completeness of God's restoration.

Joel begins by commanding the earth, "Fear not!" and then to "Rejoice! Be glad!" and concludes verse 21 by stating that God "has done great things." The phrase "great things" is a wordplay, reversing the "great things" of the locust horde in the previous verse. Joel continues to command, "Do not be afraid," this time to the animals, whose sufferings Joel details through vivid drought imagery. Joel replaces the earlier depictions of the desert with images of lush vegetation. The verb describing the appearance of vegetation (*dashu*) appears only one other time in the Tanakh – in Creation when God commands the earth to fill with greenery (Gen. 1:11). Again, this reverses 2:3, which told of the devastation of the Edenic landscape. Joel assures his listeners that the trees will produce fruit once more – explicitly mentioning fig trees and vines. This mention alludes to the devastation Joel described in 1:7: "It has laid My vines to waste and splintered My fig trees." Once again, the Jewish people can enjoy the traditional biblical formulation of prosperity – "each man under his vine and his fig tree" (I Kings 5:5; Mic. 4:4). He describes the fruits as abundant, using the Hebrew word *ḥeilam*. This word typically connotes military strength in the Tanakh,[4] and the

---

3. Cf. I Sam. 25:19; II Sam. 12:11; 1 Kings 5:19, 11:31; Jer. 1:15, 2:35, 6:21, 35: 17; Ezek. 4:16, 11:3; 22:19, 23:22; Hos. 2:8; Amos 6:14, 7:8.
4. Cf. Judges 6:12, 11:1; I Sam. 1:9, 16:18; I Kings 11:28; II Kings 5:1; Jer. 32:2, 34:1; Ezek. 17:17, 27:10.

previous appearance of this word referred to the army that God led against Zion (2:11). Again, Joel uses what was once a word indicating a threat to Judah to announce blessing instead.

Having called upon the land and the animals, Joel now turns to the Jewish people. Like the land and animals, Joel calls upon them to cheer and rejoice. He lists what God will give them – "the first rain (*moreh*) out of generosity (lit., for righteousness), He will rain down for you the first and last rain as it was in the beginning." There is much discussion about the meaning of the word *moreh*.[5] First, it can refer to a teacher or instructor (Deut. 11:30; Judges 7:1; Is. 30:20). This understanding appears in early translations like the Aramaic Targum and the Latin Vulgate. With this understanding, Rashi interprets *moreh* as "Your prophets who teach you."

However, we prefer to understand *moreh* not as teacher or prophets, but as rainfall, probably the early autumn rains that prepared the ground for plowing and sowing.[6] This phrasing is rare – Psalms 84:7 is the only other passage that uses *moreh* in this manner. The most substantial reason to consider this as the correct interpretation is the context of the remainder of the verse, which states, "He brought down for you rain (*geshem*), the first rain (*moreh*) and the last rain (*malkosh*) as in the beginning." This sequence is an example of merismus, where the general word *geshem* refers to the entire rainy season, followed by the particulars, the early autumn rainfalls to the final spring showers.[7] In the Tanakh, the gift of rain represents blessing (Lev. 26:3–4; Deut. 11:13–14), while lack of rain represents divine displeasure (Lev. 26:18–20; Deut. 28:23–24; I Kings 8:35–36). The rain mentioned here is the reversal of the drought described at the end of chapter 1. Additionally, Since Joel focuses on rebuilding the relationship between God and His people, the restoration of the rain plays a critical role in this process.

---

5. The Septuagint has a different reading here, τὰ βρώματα (food), based on the earlier promises of verses 21–22. Either the translator had a different version of the original Hebrew in his possession, or he is attempting to interpret a difficult passage by offering a more contextually appropriate reading.

6. Leslie C. Allen, *The Books of Joel, Obadiah, Jonah, and Micah* (Grand Rapids, MI: Eerdmans, 1976), 92–93.

7. See J. Barker, 261.

Verse 24 concludes Joel's depictions of the restoration of Israel's agricultural bounty. It refers again to God providing grain, new wine, and oil – this time, in the place of their manufacture. Produce will grow, and the people will enjoy it (as opposed to the biblical curse that what one person plants, another person will enjoy [Deut. 28:30, 33]). This trio of crops effectively creates an *inclusio* with verse 19, which also contains grain, wine, and oil, bringing Joel's descriptions of God's goodness to an end.

God assumes the role of speaker for the chapter's final three verses. He commits to repaying the Jewish people for all the devastation caused by the locust invasion, mentioning all the synonyms for locusts that appeared in Joel 1:4. Joel describes the locusts as God's army, alluding to Joel 2:11, which described God at the head of the invading army. God then tells the people to "eat, eat and be sated," leading them to praise "the name of the Lord, your God." Chapter 2 concludes with a declaration that the Jewish people will know that God resides among them. This formula frequently appears in Ezekiel and Zechariah, signifying the renewal of the bond between God and His people after a crisis (the destruction of the First Temple and the exile to Babylon in Ezekiel's time, the challenging return to Zion before the Second Temple was completed in Zechariah's time). The declaration continues that there is no other deity or power, emphasizing the exclusive nature of the bond between God and the Jewish people. It concludes by repeating the previous verse's assertion that "My people will never be ashamed," Joel's answer to the rhetorical question "where is their God?" that concluded the previous unit (2:17).[8]

PROPHECY FOR ALL (JOEL 3:1–5)

Afterward, this is what will be: I will pour My spirit out over humankind: your sons and your daughters will speak prophecy, your elders will dream dreams, your young men will see visions. In those days, even over the slaves and bondswomen I will pour My spirit out.

---

8. Repetition of a clause, or similar clauses, at the end of successive phrases is a literary device known as epiphora. It is often used to demarcate the end of a literary unit, and was employed by Joel at the end of chapter 1.

I will turn the skies and land into omens: blood and fire and plumes of smoke. The sun will go dark, the moon bloody, before the coming great and terrifying day of the Lord.

And all those who call on the name of the Lord will escape, for there will be a remnant on Mount Zion and in Jerusalem as the Lord has said; even among the survivors called by the Lord there will be a remnant. (3:1–5)

Chapters 3–4 signify a new beginning in content. Gone are discussions of locust hordes and invading armies. Instead, these chapters discuss nothing less than an outpouring of the divine spirit on humanity, darkness, judgment, and world wars, culminating with the restoration of a victorious Judah. These chapters announce the advent of the "day of the Lord, the great and awesome day." The first two chapters depict an imminent crisis facing the people. Chapters 3–4 point to the future (possibly quite distant). No longer is Joel concentrating on persuading the people to call to God and restore their relationship with him. Instead, chapters 3–4 depict a situation where God's commitment to the Jewish people is unquestioned. Yet, these final chapters are a logical continuation to the end of chapter 2. Indeed, chapter 3 begins with the temporal marker "after this."[9] God restored Judah after the invasion. The land filled with luscious vegetation, trees produced fruits, streams flowed with water. Most importantly, God promised that due to His actions, everyone would know Him.[10] The Jewish people became aware of his

---

9. Some early critical scholars posited that the two halves of Joel were originally two separate books. However, given the frequent and significant literary and thematic parallels between the two halves (of which we shall bring several examples in our commentary), the dominant trend in modern scholarship is to view the book of Joel as a unified whole.

10. The connection between the knowledge of God's presence in the land (v. 27) and the overflow of prophecy and the divine spirit, as described in the last verse of chapter 2 and the first verse of chapter 3, is made explicit in the final two verses of Ezekiel's apocalyptic vision of the war of Gog and Magog: "They will know that I the Lord am their God because I exiled them among the nations and then collected them back to their land, leaving none of them behind. I will not hide My face from them again, for I have poured out My spirit upon the House of Israel, declares the Lord God" (Ezek. 39:28–29).

power when He redeemed them from the invasion – now Joel describes how God will make His power known to all of creation.

This short chapter contains three subunits, and begins and ends with similar phrasing – "I will pour My spirit out over *all* humankind [lit., flesh]" and "And *all* those who call on the name of the Lord." The first two verses describe the outpouring of God's spirit, beginning and ending with the phrase "I will pour out My spirit" (serving as an *inclusio*). The following two verses describe the cosmological ramifications of the outpouring of the divine spirit, specifically directing it towards Zion. Joel resumes speaking in the final section and begins to outline for the people how they should respond in order to survive "the day of the Lord."

Verses 1–2 begin "Afterward, this is what will be," namely, after the deliverance from the invasion.[11] God guaranteed material restoration in Joel 2:18–27; now God promises spiritual redemption. God promises to pour out His spirit on everyone, with no distinction between gender, age, class, or position. The blessing will fall upon "humankind (lit., all flesh)" equally, enjoying the blessings of the divine spirit.[12] Emphasizing total equality, Joel mentions that He then lists all the subgroups within the community: "your sons" and "your daughters," "your elders" and "your young men," even male and female servants. This blessing is universal.[13] Only verse 5 limits the recipients of this blessing to "those

---

11. This is the only appearance of the words "And it will be" (*vehaya*) followed by "after this" (*aharei khen*) in Tanakh. Scholarship debates whether this phrase is intended to create a temporal connection (sequential) between chapters 2 and 3, or a logical connection: Only when the Jewish people are fully restored physically can the spiritual rebuilding begin (J. Barker, *Joel*, 283).

12. Rashi appears to limit the blessing to those who are worthy; however, the midrash expands it to include even animals and fowl: "This includes people, beasts, and birds. I would only know of people, but 'and also' expands it to all" (Avot DeRabbi Natan II:43).

13. In Tanakh, the term "all flesh" generally refers to all humanity, without any ethnic or geographical restrictions (Deut. 5:26; Is. 49:26, 66:16; Job 12:10), but sometimes this term refers to all living beings (Gen. 6:12, 13; 7:21; Num. 18:15). This expansive understanding is found in the Midrash (Avot DeRabbi Natan II:43):

"And it shall come to pass after this that I will pour out My spirit upon all flesh, and your sons and daughters will prophesy." And so it is written, "And even

who call upon the name of the Lord." Only those who profess loyalty to God are worthy of this great blessing.

Joel lists several examples of prophetic actions that reflect the outpouring of the divine spirit: prophesying, dreaming dreams, and seeing visions. Given the difficulties and tribulations faced by the Jewish people at the beginning of the book, the sudden outburst of prophetic activity is a clear indication of divine favor.[14] A parallel prophecy is found in Ezekiel 39:29: "I will not hide My face from them again, *for I have poured out My spirit* upon the House of Israel, declares the Lord God."[15] Assis suggests expanding the literary parallels between Joel and Ezekiel. Joel spoke of a physical restoration in the land in chapter 2, followed by a spiritual revival in chapter 3. To Assis, Joel's usage of the phrase "all flesh" (Heb., כל בשר) alludes to Ezekiel's vision of the Dry Bones in chapter 37, where God transforms skeletal remains into living beings through the addition of flesh: "the transformation of the bodies to living beings ...

---

upon the slaves and the maidservants." *This includes people, beasts, and birds.* I would know [that the promise applies] only to people, but "and even" expands it to all living beings.

Rashi limits this spirituality to humanity, those who are receptive to the divine message – "Upon one whose heart is made soft like flesh, as in (Ezek. 36:26), 'And I will give you a heart of flesh.'"

Radak limits this further, claiming that only the Jewish people will receive this blessing. Here, too, "all flesh" refers to Israel, who are fit to experience divine inspiration.

Abrabanel attempts to create a middle ground between Rashi and Radak: All mankind will achieve a clear and unfiltered awareness of God, but only the Jewish people will reach the level of prophecy.

14. Similarly, a lack of prophetic activity is considered to be a sign of divine displeasure. For example, after a prophecy against the moral and spiritual corruption of Eli's household (I Sam. 2:27–36), chapter 3 begins with the statement "In those days, the Lord's word was scarce; visions were far from common." Similarly, Amos lists a dearth of the divine word as one of the punishments that awaits Israel for its waywardness: "Yes, days are coming – the Lord God has spoken – I will cast hunger over the land: not hunger for bread nor thirst for water, but hunger to hear the words of the Lord. They will wander from sea to sea and from the north to the east to seek the word of the Lord, but they will not find it" (Amos 8:11–12; cf. Jer. 18:18; Ezek. 7:26; Mic. 3:6–7).

15. Cf. Is. 32:15, 44:3, 59:21; Zech. 12:10.

accomplished through the giving of the spirit to them…understood to mean the removal of the people from their exile."[16]

Most importantly, these verses allude to one of the pivotal episodes in the formation of the Jewish people in the desert. In Numbers 11, God responds to Moses's request for relief by endowing seventy of the nation's elders with the divine spirit. While these elders prophesy at the Tent of Meeting, Eldad and Medad begin to prophesy elsewhere in the camp. Joshua is alarmed, worried that they pose a potential threat to Moses's authority. Joshua demands their imprisonment. Moses's response is stunning. He brushes aside Joshua's concerns. Instead, Moses avers, "Are you jealous for me? Would that all the Lord's people were prophets, that the Lord would put His spirit upon them all!" (Num. 11:29). This democratic attitude that every person can achieve the highest levels of communion with God represents one of the radical ideas that Judaism brought to the world.

What will the impact of the outpouring of the divine spirit be? According to Joel, nothing less than cosmological upheaval. Once the people can understand a larger measure of God's power, God is willing to reveal more power. In verses 3–4, God announces that He will perform signs and wonders. There will be blood, fire, pillars of smoke. Heavenly bodies will change colors.[17] The term "omens" [Heb., *moftim*] is significant, as it alludes to the plagues that God visited upon Egypt to liberate His people (blood and fiery hail being two of the plagues that destroyed Egypt [Ex. 7:17; 9:23–24], the pillars of smoke may allude to the pillars that miraculously led the people out to freedom [Ex. 13:21]). In chapter 1, the locust invasion represents a reversal of the Exodus by having God strike the Jewish people. Now, God announces that He will overturn the natural order to redeem His people again. Specifically, the darkening of both the sun and the moon recalls the Exodus plague of darkness (Ex. 10:21), and it

---

16. Assis, *The Book of Joel*, 203.

17. While Radak here suggests that the darkening of the skies is meant to be understood poetically, symbolizing the war clouds that will gathering on the horizon, we prefer Ibn Ezra's approach, which views these verses as a literal description of what will occur, thus maintaining the parallels with Egypt.

reverses the descriptions of darkness that accompanied the invasion of Judah in chapter 2.

Finally, verse 4 concludes by stating these occurrences emanate from the "day of the Lord." Joel adds here the adjectives "great and terrifying," referring back to the invasion of Zion in 2:11. As noted earlier, the phrase "the day of the Lord" involves God acting in judgment. As such, there will be those who face punishments, while others will be saved. The frightening depictions of God's immense power should inspire fear and terror among Joel's listeners, invoking the urgent need to find sanctuary among them. These feelings lead to verse 5, the climax of this chapter.

Verse 5 promises escape on Mt. Zion and in Jerusalem (even among the survivors of previous sufferings – like those who escaped the troubles of the first two chapters).[18] This final verse of the unit contains a threefold repetition of God's divine name – likely to demonstrate the closure of this unit (cf. Hos. 1:9, 2:3, 25). Joel uses two Hebrew words to describe the survivors, *peleita* (refuge) and *seridim* (survivors). Ominously, the pair often appear together in the Tanakh in the negated form, generally after the complete defeat and destruction of an opposing populace in war (cf. Josh. 8:22; Jer. 42:17; 44:14). Now, there is security, specifically in Jerusalem, which Joel mentions here for the first time. Joel had previously referred to Zion (2:1, 15, 23), but as a clever reversal. He previously described how the invading army encountered little difficulty in overrunning Zion (2:1–11). However, Zion is also the place where the people gathered to call to God (2:15). This linkage helps reinforce Joel's message: Calling to God for deliverance in Zion activates God's promise of salvation, resulting in safety and security for those within it.

If Joel is prophesying at the time of Sennacherib's invasion of Judah in 701 BCE, as we tentatively suggested in the introduction, than verse 5's promise of salvation is an almost direct quotation of a similar promise Isaiah made at the exact same moment to Hezekiah, who

---

18. The words Zion and Jerusalem are often used interchangeably in the prophets. Amos Hakham comments that "[while the proper name Zion generally] refers to either the mountain or the fortress within the city's [Jerusalem] boundaries, in the majority of biblical texts, the name 'Zion' is a poetic name for the entire city" (*Daat Mikra*, Joel, commentary on 2:1).

prayed to God to save him and the people when the Assyrian forces were arrayed outside of Jerusalem's walls (Is. 37):

Joel 3:5	Isaiah 37:21, 32
And all those who *call on the name* of the Lord will escape, for there will be a *remnant on Mount Zion and in Jerusalem* as the Lord has said; even *among the survivors called by the Lord* there will be a remnant.	And Isaiah son of Amotz sent word to Hezekiah: "Thus says the Lord, God of Israel: *Because you prayed to Me* about Sennacherib, king of Assyria, this is the word the Lord has spoken of him:... *For a remnant will emerge from Jerusalem, survivors from Mount Zion;* the passion of the Lord of Hosts will bring all this to be.

There are several understandings of what calling to God entails. The simple meaning is to pray, an understanding strengthened by the parallel to Isaiah above. Rashi makes a different suggestion: that people recognize that you have been called in God's name:

> And where did He say it [that you will be saved]? [In Deut. 28:9–10:] "if you keep the Lord your God's commandments and walk in His ways. All the peoples of earth shall see that you are called by the Lord's name, and they shall hold you in awe." (*Mekhilta*, Ex. 12: 25)

Midrashic tradition provides a final approach (possibly intended by Rashi) that substantially reinterprets the meaning of "calling on God":

> How is it possible to call in God's name? Instead, just as God is called merciful (as it states, "The Lord is gracious and compassionate," Ps. 145:8), so should you be gracious.... Therefore, it says, "All who are called in the name of the Lord will escape." (*Sifrei* 49)

According to this approach, to call in God's name is to behave in a Godly manner. Only then is a person worthy of redemption. Thus, the fate of the unworthy is the subject of Joel's next section.

THE FINAL BATTLE (JOEL 4:1–17)

For it will be in those days and at that time that I will restore those held captive from Judah and Jerusalem. I will gather all the nations and bring them down to the Valley of Jehoshafat. There I will carry out judgment against them for the sake of My people – My possession Israel, whom they scattered among the nations – and for the sake of My land, which they divided among themselves. They cast lots for My nation and handed over young boys for the hire of a harlot, and sold young girls for wine, and they drank.

But what are you to Me, Tyre and Sidon, all the Philistine regions? Do you deign to retaliate against Me? And if you retaliate, how quickly and easily I will repay your deeds upon your head. You took My silver and gold and carried My precious things away to your temples. You sold the Judahites and Jerusalemites to the Ionians to cast them far from their borders. But I will rouse them from the place to which you sold them, and I will repay your deeds upon your head. I will sell your sons and daughters into the hands of the Judahites, who will sell them to the people of Sheba – a far-off nation. For the Lord has spoken.

Call this out to the nations: Declare a war! Stir the warriors! Let all the men of war approach, ascend. Beat your plowshares into swords and your pruning hooks into spears. Let the weak say, "I am mighty." Come swiftly, all you surrounding nations, and gather together there. O Lord, let Your warriors descend. Let the nations stir and go up to the Valley of Yehoshafat, for it is there that I will sit and judge all the surrounding nations. Hoist the sickle; the harvest is ripe. Come, trample; the winepress is full. The vats of wine overflow, so great is the evil they have done.

Masses upon masses in the Valley of Decision, for the day of the Lord is nigh in the Valley of Decision. The sun and moon go dark, and the stars draw in their light. The Lord roars from Zion; from Jerusalem He raises His voice. The heavens and the earth tremble. But the Lord will be a shelter for His people, a stronghold for the children of Israel. So you will know that I am the Lord, your God – the One who resides in Zion, My holy mountain. Jerusalem will be sacred; strangers will pass through her no longer. (4:1–17)

Joel's final chapter describes the "great and terrible day of the Lord," alternating between salvation for the Jewish people and judgment and punishment for the world's nations. Though Joel groups the nations together as a collective entity, he also highlights the offenses of specific nations. God does not judge the nations based on their ethnicity but their actions. Verses 1–17 consist of a series of directives that Joel issues to the enemy nations. In contrast, the final four verses vividly describe the restoration of Judah and Jerusalem.

There are three distinct sections in this chapter. Verses 1–3 are a general announcement that God intends to judge the nations for their crimes against the Jewish people. The next section has Joel directly address three of Judah's neighbors, Tyre, Sidon, and Philistia, and promise them a specifically tailored punishment for their transgressions. The final section returns to God, addressing all the nations of the world. He taunts them and summons them to battle in the Valley of Jehoshaphat. At the end of the section, the purpose of this summons becomes clear.

Chapter 4 focuses on the removal of Judah's external enemies. The subtext of Joel's message is that a physical threat to Judah presently exists (or will exist) against the Jewish people. The early verses suggest that nations have sold the inhabitants of Judah into slavery and have despoiled the land. Here Joel insists that God will act to reverse the balance of power dramatically. No longer will strangers maraud across the land, looting its treasures and capturing its inhabitants. When God stands to fight on Judah's behalf, no one can stand against him.

The chapter begins "in those days and at that time." This exact phrase occurs elsewhere only in Jeremiah, in a prophecy that also alternates between promises of redemption for Judah and Jerusalem and punishments and suffering for God's enemies (cf. Jer. 33:15; 50:4, 20). This introduction also alludes to chapter 3's introduction, the beginning of this process of ultimate redemption.[19] God promises to restore the captives

---

19. Most of the medieval commentators (except Ibn Ezra) date the final two chapters to the Messianic Era. Radak writes:

of Judah and Jerusalem. Variations of the wording "return the captivity" (*shuv shevut*) appear twenty-seven times in the Tanakh, generally in the context of a reversal of divine judgment and restoration to the land.[20] The first occurrence of this wording is in Deuteronomy 30, perhaps the clearest outline of redemption and restoration in the entire Torah:

> When all these things have come upon you, the blessings and the curses I have set before you, and you – amidst all the nations where the Lord your God has driven you – take them to heart, and return, you and your children, to the Lord your God, obeying Him with all your heart and all your soul, just as I am commanding you today, then the Lord your God will bring your captives back (*ve-shav Hashem et shevutekha*) and show you compassion. He will bring you back together from all the nations among whom the Lord your God has scattered you. … The Lord your God will bring you into the land that belonged to your ancestors, and you will possess it. He will make you yet more prosperous and numerous than your ancestors were. (Deut. 30:1–5)

Joel then shifts focus from the Jewish people to the other nations. As part of the restoration process, God must exercise his dominion over the nations of the world, demonstrated by gathering them together in the Valley of Jehoshaphat for judgment. Some commentators suggest that the valley is named after King Jehoshaphat. The Radak speculates that King Jehoshaphat either built an important edifice there or performed an act there so significant that the valley was called in his name. The Ibn Ezra suggests that this is the Valley of Berakha where King Jehoshaphat led Judah to a great victory against a coalition of Moab, Ammon and Edom (II Chr. 20:26). If Joel's intent is to refer to this historical event,

---

This will be in the days and at the time when I will return the captivity of Judah and Jerusalem. These are the times of the Messiah. He mentioned Judah and Jerusalem despite the fact that all of Israel will return; he mentioned Judah because the Messiah will be from the tribe of Judah, and he mentioned Jerusalem because it is the head of the kingdom and because that will be the site of the war of Gog and Magog.

20. Cf. Jer. 30:3, 18; 31:23; 32:44; 33:7, 11.

his rhetorical intention is likely allusive as well. A multitude of nations gathered to wage war on Judah. After prayer and supplications, King Jehoshaphat received a prophetic message advising him:

> Listen, all of Judah and the people of Jerusalem and King Jehoshaphat: Thus says the Lord to you: Do not be frightened or dismayed in the face of this vast horde, for this battle is not yours, but God's. Tomorrow, charge down at them as they ascend the Ascent of the Blossom; you will encounter them at the end of the wadi before the wilderness of Jeruel. You will not need to fight this battle – take your positions and stand still, and you will see the Lord's victory among you, Judah and Jerusalem. Do not be frightened or dismayed; tomorrow, go out before them, and the Lord will be with you. (II Chr. 20:15–17)

Ultimately, God fought the battle on behalf of the Jewish people, without their involvement. By referring to that incident, Joel alludes to the fact that divine action alone will win the upcoming battle with the nations.

However, the more prevalent interpretation of this valley's name is that is it is a clever wordplay on judgment (SH-PH-T), precisely the action that God will perform on them.[21] In Tanakh, valleys are traditionally a location where major battles occur,[22] and within the prophetic literature, God's judgment and punishments of the nations takes place in a valley (cf. Is. 22:1–5; Ezek. 39:11; Zech. 14:4–5). All of these references come from sections that mention the "day of the Lord." Yechezkel

---

21. Developing this theme of judgment, several commentators state that God is answering the nations, who offer several claims in self-defense, including asserting that they were carrying out God's will in enslaving the Jewish people (cf. Malbim).
22. A partial list of battles that occur in a valley include the battle of the Four Kings vs. the Five Kings in "The Valley of Siddim" (Gen. 14: 8); Midian's armies encamp in Israel during the time of Gideon in "The Valley of Yizreel" (Judges 6:33); the showdown between the Philistines and Israel (and David and Goliath) takes place in the "Elah Valley" (I Sam. 17:2); the Philistines invade in King David's time through the "Valley of Rephaim"; and Jehoshaphat's battle with Ammon and Moab occurs in the "Valley of Berakha" (II Chr. 20:17, 26).

Kaufmann writes that Joel's vision, though drawing on other biblical descriptions of Divine battle, differs in one fundamental aspect:

> The image of the gathering of the nations to the land of Israel to performance the divine decree draws upon the visions of Isaiah and Micah, and in Zechariah…however Joel changes this imagery. In the other prophets, the nations ascend for war, and God is revealed through a decisive victory over them . But here, though they ascend for battle…the war is not a war. They do not ascend against Jerusalem as in the visions of Isaiah, Micah and Zechariah. Certainly, no similarity exists between Joel's vision and the vision of Gog and Magog in Ezekiel…. They do not besiege Jerusalem, they do not attack the cities of Judah. [Instead] they congregate at the Valley of Jehoshaphat, a place of visions, as though for war. A kind of spirit brings them to the "Valley of Jehoshaphat" – where God sits to judge them. This is Joel's new vision: God no longer appears as a military commander or a warrior on the day of battle [but as a judge].[23]

Joel's description of this event contains also several literary parallels with Ezekiel's description of the war of Gog and Magog in the Valley of Hamon (Ezek. 38–39). Specifically, they both use the same verb for divine judgment (*venishpateti* – Ezek. 38:22; Joel 4:2). The destruction of Gog in that verse refers to blood and fire, just like Joel (3:3, 4:20). Ezekiel identifies Gog as coming from the north, with Joel having made the identical identification in 2:20.

Having announced divine judgment, Joel then articulates the crimes committed by the nations. God unapologetically describes the Jewish people and the land of Judah as "My people and My inheritance." Earlier, Joel told the people to pray to God on behalf of "Your people" and "Your inheritance" (2:17); God's positive response was attributed to His zeal and pity "for His people" and "for His land" (2:18). Now, Joel presents the accusation to the nations. They have scattered God's people, claimed God's land for themselves, and engaged in slave trading.

---

23. Yechezkel Kauffmann, *Toldot haEmuna haYisraelit*, vol. 7 (Tel Aviv: Bialik, 1960), 345.

The first two offenses stated without detail are crime enough. However, Joel spares no quarter in detailing the final charge of enslavement. The culmination of the list of curses which Moses utters against those who break the covenant is being sold into slavery: "And the Lord will bring you back to Egypt in ships, through the way about which I had said to you, You will never see it again. And there, you will seek to be sold to your enemies for slaves and handmaids, but there will be no buyer" (Deut. 28:68).

Joel divides this crime into three offenses. First, they cast lots for the captives and then bartered for the sale of the boys and girls, respectively. The verb for casting lots appears in only two other locations in the Tanakh, each dealing with the humiliation of a fallen power (Ob. 1:11 [Edom]; Nahum 3:10 [Assyria]). After a military victory, the victors would sit and cast lots to divide the plunder and riches. That humans became subject to this procedure demonstrated the level of humiliation that befell them – they are no longer people, just property. This crime of dehumanization is heightened when Joel states that the foreigners would barter children for wine, then selling both young boys and girls into sexual slavery. These actions underlie God's angry accusations against the nations.

Having described the fate of unnamed nations who face judgment in general terms, the following several verses focus on the crimes of three specific countries – Tyre, Sidon, and Philistia – and detail the punishment God will mete out to them.[24] The Philistines are an ancient enemy, the prime antagonist of the nascent Jewish community in Israel during the era of the judges and the early monarchy (until their defeat by King David – see Judges 3:31, chs. 13–16, and I Sam. chs. 4 and 13–14). They disappear from biblical history for several generations but reappear as antagonists during the eighth and seventh century BCE (I Chr. 28 describes their exploitation of Judah during the Syro-Ephraimite invasion of 734–732 BCE). Tyre and Sidon are the capital cities of the Phoenician empire. They are portrayed as allies of David and Solomon

---

24. The appearance of these three nations for punishment, as well as Egypt and Edom at the end of the chapter, provide an argument in favor of those who suggest an earlier dating for Joel (see introduction).

(cf. II Sam. 5; I Kings 5), and Ahab marries the Sidonite princess Jezebel to strengthen his kingdom. However, in later years, prophets, including such as Amos and Ezekiel, recite oracles of punishment against them for their sins against God (cf. Ezek. 26–29; Amos 1:9–10). Interestingly, Amos places his oracle against Philistia and his oracle against Tyre and Sidon next to each other. He condemns both for slave trading, accusing them of selling Israelite captives to Edom (Amos 1:6–10).

Joel asks Tyre, Sidon, and Philistia two rhetorical questions in God's name. First, "What are you to Me?" Second, "Do you deign to retaliate against Me? (lit., Are you paying back a recompense [*gemul*] against Me?)" The word recompense appears three times within this verse, first in this rhetorical question and then twice more in God's answer. The implication is that the nations claim that they attacked Judah out of a sense of aggrieved justice. God insists that they will reap their just rewards instead. Other commentators suggest that the nations accuse God of wrongdoing, to which God challenges them to cite any instance in which that was true (Ibn Ezra, Radak, Malbim). *Daat Mikra* interprets the exchange as "Do you think that you are more powerful than Me – that I am impotent, incapable of striking back?" Rashi interprets the word *gemul* positively, "Is this how you repay Me for the kindness that I have shown you (in the time of Hiram of Tyre)?" Joel continues to enumerate the crimes that these nations committed. In addition to slave trading, they took God's silver and gold into their places of idol worship and adorned their buildings. Verse 6 returns to the subject of slave trading. These countries sold the children of Judah and Jerusalem into captivity, selling them to a land far away from Israel (customarily identified as Ionians or Greeks). Ezekiel also mentions this country in his oracle against Tyre as one who would exchange slaves for Tyre's produce (Ezek. 27:13; see also Zech. 9:1–13). Joel makes explicit the purpose of their slave trading – not for profit, but to remove the Jewish people from its land.

In verses 7–8, Joel announces the verdict against these nations. The word "recompense" appears for its fourth and final appearance, emphasizing the sense of justice in this decision. First, God will return the captives home, no matter how far they may be from Judah. Then, God will execute judgment on the nations by selling their children as slaves in faraway lands.[25] This section concludes with the declaration "that God has spoken," the second appearance of this phrase in the book. This phrase adds gravitas to the previous declaration of the verdict – it has been irreversibly sealed.

The final subunit of this section (vv. 9–17) contains God's summons to war against the nations.[26] It reverts to God speaking in the first-person (continuing verses 1–3, interrupted in verses 4–8). The rhythm is sharp, staccato – short phrases with a military beat. God pronounces: "Announce (*kiru*) this among the nations! Prepare (*kadshu*) [for] war! Stir the warriors!" Notably, the first two commands appear in the reverse order when Joel implored the people to "sanctify (*kadshu*) a fast! Announce (*kiru*) an assembly!" (1:14). The contrast could not be starker. God commands the Jewish people to sanctify themselves and turn to God in prayer. The nations (that oppose God) sanctify/prepare for war instead.

Verse 10 continues the call to war, with God commanding the nations to "beat your plowshares into swords, your pruning hooks into

---

25. This is a biblical example of *lex talonis* ("an eye for an eye") – that judgment is meted out in accordance with the crime. J. Barker quotes Miller approvingly: "Miller places Joel 4:4–8 in context with other passages that emphasize the correspondence between the offense and the divinely prescribed punishment (cf. Is. 3:9, 11; Jer. 50:16; Hos. 8:7; Ob. 1:15–16). He considers correspondence between sin and punishment in conjunction with punishment as a consequence of the stated sin, noting that the two criteria for determining punishment often tend to blur together" (P. D. Miller, *Sin and Judgment in the Prophets* [Society of Biblical Literature], 76, 122–32), quoted in J. Barker, *Joel*, 276, n. 53.

26. Barker makes a fascinating observation while comparing this summons to war with other examples in the prophetic literature:

> In a prophetic "call to war" there are typically three stages: i) statements about the call to arms and the army's advance; ii) statements concerning the preparation of weapons; and iii) statements about the war itself (cf. Jer. 6:4–6; 46:3–4; 50:14–15, 16, 21, 26–27, 29; Hos. 5:8; Mic. 4:13; Ob. 1). As the following analysis demonstrates, Joel 4:9–12 contains phrases that admirably fit the first two categories, but the third is notably absent.

He suggests that this lacuna reflects the message Joel is trying to convey. There will be no real battle – as no matter how powerful an army the nations may have, it is so miniscule and insignificant against God's might that it is as if the battle never occurred (J. Barker, *Joel*, 329).

spears!" Joel deliberately invokes and reverses the prophet's traditional affirmation of universal peace (Is. 2:2–4, Mic. 4:1–4). Similarly, instead of a universal pilgrimage to Mount Zion in Jerusalem to learn the ways of God, Joel depicts a pilgrimage by the nations – but this time, to a valley to be defeated militarily. Isaiah and Micah foresaw an idyllic future in which God's mountain of Zion becomes the tallest mountain in the world, where all those who chose to learn His ways gather (Mic. 4:2: "Many nations will come, saying: 'Come, let us go up to the mount of the Lord, to the House of Jacob's God; He will teach us of His ways; we will walk in His pathways' – for teaching will come forth from Zion, from Jerusalem the Lord's word"). By reversing the quote, Joel reminds his listeners that before that wonderful day arrives, there is still one more day that humanity must experience – the terrifying day of judgment, "the day of the Lord."

Joel continues, "The weak shall say 'I am mighty,'" which can be understood literally – the drafting of non-soldiers into military service. However, as the Alsheikh notes, this is more likely God mocking the nations. How can mere mortals (the weak) defeat the Almighty (the strong)? Verses 11 and 12 repeat the command for the countries to arouse themselves to gather every single soldier available. They are to come to the Valley of Jehoshaphat. Verse 9 was a summons to battle – verse 12 is a judgment of the vanquished, with no battle having occurred.

Verses 13–17 conclude with the results of the battle. Joel begins by inverting agricultural imagery to describe the confrontation – an echo of the call to turn "plowshares into swords." The nations are a field, and God issues the command to harvest. The countries are an overflowing vat – God commands to trample. These actions are both performed when the crops have achieved maturity. Joel's images parallel other prophetic descriptions that utilize harvest metaphors to indicate judgment.[27] Isaiah portrays God as a divine warrior, whose clothes are stained with His enemies' blood whom He trampled like grapes in a winepress. Joel describes the magnitude of the victory with the phrase "the vats overflow." Joel used this phrase earlier in 2:24 to express God's generosity to the Jewish people after the famine. So many

---

27. Cf. Is. 17:5; Jer. 24:2, 48:32; Hos. 2:9; Amos 8:1–2.

grapes will grow that the vats will overflow. Now, the vats overflow again, but this time due to the nations' guilt. Verse 14 repeats the word "Masses! Masses!" – suggesting it is impossible to count the countries who came to battle with God.

He then repeats the location where they gather, "the Valley of Decision."[28] There they assemble, and there they encounter judgment on the "day of the Lord." One can imagine the surprise of the nations. They came to make war. Instead, they face judgment for the violence they have committed, the proof of which are the very weapons they carry in their own hands. Joel continues to describe the effects of the "day of the Lord." The heavenly bodies darken (just like 2:10, 3:3). God roars, and heaven and earth convulse in fear.[29]

The description of "the day of the Lord" takes a surprising turn in the middle of verse 16. This fearful battle is motivated by God's desire to protect His people. God transforms suddenly from divine warrior to a shelter and a stronghold for His people. Even with the heavens dark and the earth trembling, the Jewish people enjoy salvation and security. The location also subtly shifts from the Valley of Jehoshaphat (judgment) to Jerusalem, where those who called on God's name find refuge.

Verses 15 and 16 are also a restatement of Joel's description of the legions that invaded the land of Judah in chapter 2, with one significant difference:

---

28. The Aramaic Targum translates both "the Valley of Jehoshaphat" and "the Valley of Decision" as מישר פילוג דינא, implying that the two valleys are one and the same.

29. The phrase "The Lord roars from Zion, and from Jerusalem he utters his voice" appears in Amos 1:2 as well. Both use this sentence to introduce a prophecy against nations, and the common portrayal of God roaring, evoking the image of a lion announcing its presence, serves to depict God announcing that He is King and is assuming authority. In Amos, the roar encompasses the entire land, from the shepherds' pastures to the top of the Carmel mountain. Joel's roar is louder, encompassing the heaven and the earth.

However, the two prophets use the divine roar for differing purposes. In Amos, this sentence begins a rhetorical trap that announces judgment on the nations – but then on Judah and Israel as well. In Joel, the divine roar reflects God's promise to protect the Jewish people from harm.

Joel 2:10–11	Joel 4:15–16
The earth trembles before Him, the skies thunder, the sun and the moon go dark, and the stars draw in their light. Then the Lord raises His voice before His troops – for His camp is vast…	*The sun and moon go dark, and the stars draw in their light. The Lord roars from Zion; from Jerusalem He raises His voice. The heavens and the earth tremble.*

In chapter 2, God was located at the head of the invading army, standing against the city of Jerusalem and its inhabitants. Now, in this prophecy of redemption, God is firmly within the city walls, standing squarely with His people.

Verse 17 concludes with the statement, "So you will *know* that I am the Lord your God." Once again, Joel refers to the Exodus tradition. This exact sentence appears at the beginning of the Exodus story (Ex. 6:7), where God promises Moses that the children of Israel will know that the Lord is their God because He will redeem the Jewish people from Egypt and provide for them in the desert. Joel concluded his description of the physical restoration after the locust invasion by declaring, "And you shall *know* that I am among Israel, and I am the Lord your God, there is no other" (2:27). After their spiritual salvation and physical redemption, Joel returns to the theme of knowledge of God as the ultimate objective that the people can achieve. Together, "the formulas of knowing God serve to resolve with glorious certainty the cautious question 'Who knows?' concerning God in 2:14."[30]

The section concludes with the statement that God dwells in Zion on the mountain of his holiness. We first encountered Zion as a target of invasion, whose walls will ultimately be breached (2:1–11). Now, with God present in Zion, "strangers will pass through Jerusalem no longer." Chapter 3 ended with the promise that those who call on God's name will find refuge in Jerusalem. This verse is the actualization of this promise.

---

30. J. Barker quoting Allen, 350.

THE END OF DAYS (JOEL 4:18–21)

> On that day, the mountains will drip with sweet wine, the
> hills will flow with milk, and all of Judah's rivers will flow,
> full of water. A spring will surge forth from the House of the
> Lord and irrigate the Valley of Acacias. Egypt will be deso-
> late, Edom a barren desert, because of the violence they have
> perpetrated against Judah – because of the innocent blood
> they spilled in their land. But Judah will be forever settled,
> Jerusalem to the end of time. Even though I pardon, I will
> not pardon the spilling of their blood, for the Lord resides
> in Zion. (4:18–21)

Joel's final section invites us into the idyllic future. When the "day
of the Lord" is over and the dust settles, what will Judah look like?
Locusts once ravaged the land. Now, Judah is filled with wine and
water, its deserts replaced by oases and vineyards. The Jewish people
once felt encircled, surrounded by adversaries. Now, no one is left
to threaten them. Assis suggests that these verses are indeed a fitting
conclusion to a literary masterpiece: verse 18 summarizes the agricultural restoration of 2:18–27, and verses 19–21 summarize Judah's
political redemption.[31] Instead, God will meticulously repay every
country that once dared to attack Israel for the violence they perpe-
trated on the Jewish people. Enemies are temporary – but Judah and
Jerusalem are eternal.

The section begins with the phrase "On that day," which recalls
the openings of chapters 3 and 4. Both chapters describe God's intervening in human history, whether to pour His spirit on humanity or to
hold accountable those nations who refuse to acknowledge God through
their actions. Joel continues to depict his vision of the new Judah. He
already promised the restoration of the land at the end of chapter 2, after
the locust invasion. However, these images go far beyond what chapter
2 presented. Miraculous abundance fills the land (cf. Is. 65: 17–25; Zech.
14:6–11), beginning with mountains dripping sweet wine (cf. Amos 9:13),
in contrast to one of Joel's earliest calls to the wine drinkers to mourn

---

31. Assis, *The Book of Joel*, 247–52.

the loss of this vintage (1:5).[32] Cattle will be able to graze freely due to the abundance of grass, producing endless milk, reversing the destruction of the beast's fodder in 1:18. Now, wine will drip from the mountains, and milk will flow from the hills, recalling the Torah's description of the Land of Israel as "flowing with milk and honey" (Ex. 3:8; Lev. 20:24).

Joel's images of copious liquids throughout the land continue with the promise that all the streams and brooks will flow with water in addition to the milk and wine[33] (again, reversing Joel 1:20 in which the streams dry up). For a land where water is not guaranteed (Deut. 11:12), an overflowing supply of water symbolizes divine approval and blessing. Many of Israel's wadis only flow with water for a few days a year, rainfall permitting. Not only are the lowlands to be blessed, but a spring will erupt from the Temple Mount. The image of water flowing from the Temple appears in several biblical descriptions of the Messianic future (cf. Ps. 46:5; Ezek. 47:1–12 and Zech. 14:8).[34] Warren Wiersbe notes how the vision of water flowing from Zion repairs an extraordinary

---

32. The Midrash is bothered by the abundance of wine – will excessive alcohol not lead to drunkenness, just as it did with Noah? It therefore declares that Joel's prophecy must refer to Messianic times:

> Wherever you find wine you find stumbling. Noah's failure was due to wine, as were the tribes who sat to eat bread and sold their brother Joseph. And so at the sin at Shittim (Num. 25)…and at the sin of the Golden Calf (Ex. 32)…. God declared: In this world, wine is created for stumbling; in the next world I will make wine as syrup, as it is written…"And it shall come to pass on that day that the mountains shall drip with wine." (Tanḥuma Noah 21)

33. This may be the source of the talmudic statement, regarding Messianic times, that even the water will be sweet: "R. Jeremiah sat before R. Zeira and said: In the future, God will produce a river from the Holy of Holies, on which will be all manners of delicacies" (Sanhedrin 100a).

34. The Talmud poetically describes how this blessing will come to fruition (Yoma 77b–78a):

> R. Pinhas cited R. Huna of Tzippori: The spring which will emerge from the Holy of Holies will resemble grasshoppers' antennae at first. When it reaches the entrance of the Sanctuary it will be like the warp thread. When it reaches the Entrance Hall it will be like the woof thread. When it reaches the entrance to the Courtyard it will be like the mouth of a small jug…. From there it will strengthen and increase until it reaches the entrance of the House of David, at which point it will be as a flooding river in which impure people immerse.

peculiarity about Jerusalem when compared to the other great cities of the ancient world:

> "Jerusalem is the only city of antiquity that wasn't built near a great river. Rome had the Tiber; Nineveh was built near the Tigris and Babylon on the Euphrates; and the great Egyptian cities were built near the Nile. But in the [future] ... Jerusalem will have a river that proceeds from the Temple of God."[35]

Most significantly, in the story of Creation, the Torah portrays the Garden of Eden as the source of all of the major currents of water in the world (Gen. 2:10). Now, God's house will become the life-giving center of the world. – with an allusion to the creation of a new Garden. In chapter 2, Joel described how the invading armies devastated the land, "The land, like Eden, before it; after it, a barren desert" (2:3). Now, Joel confidently predicts the creation of a new Garden of Eden, whose waters will reach even the driest areas. He concludes by stating that this stream of water will irrigate the Valley of Shittim. This location appears only here in the Tanakh. Shittim are acacia trees, which generally grow in an arid desert environment. Metaphorically, Joel portrays the Temple as providing life-giving waters to even the driest regions in the world. Rashi quotes a midrash that suggests that God will finally forgive the Jewish people totally for the sin they committed in Shittim (Num. 25). The mention of Shittim also recalls the Valley of Shittim, the last encampment of the Jewish people before their entry into the land of Israel (Numbers 25). This was the first generation after the Exodus from Egypt, another allusion to the redemption in Joel's imagery.

In verse 19, Joel returns to his judgment theme, alternating between blessing for Israel and punishment for the nations until the end of the book. For their crimes against the Jewish people, God will turn Egypt and Edom into a desert (a stark reversal of the blessing enjoyed

---

35. Warren W. Wiersbe, *Bible Exposition Commentary: Joel* (Colorado Springs, CO: Cook Communications Ministries; and Eastbourne, UK: Kingsway Communications Ltd., 2002), 340.

by fertile, lush Judah).[36] This curse is especially poignant, as the land of Egypt, with its guarantee of water from the Nile, is considered the foil of the Land of Israel, which has no natural sources of water and must always turn to heaven in prayer to receive rain. Joel does not specify which sin Egypt and Edom committed, though the word violence (*ḥamas*) may allude to Obadiah's censure of Edom for committing violence against "your brother Jacob" (Ob. 1:10).

Unlike Egypt and Edom, who have become uninhabitable, Judah and Jerusalem's prosperity have become enduring, and the Jewish people will always dwell within them. The effect of Joel's juxtaposing the two groups is to accentuate the contrast between God's people and God's enemies.

Joel's final verse appears at first read to be self-contradictory – "Even though I pardon, I will not pardon the spilling of their blood." The Hebrew for "to pardon" (*nikeiti*) is literally to clean, recalling verse 19, in which Joel censures Egypt and Edom for shedding Judah's innocent blood (*dam naki*), making clear why God refuses to forgive the nations. Rashi reads the text as "[Even if I wanted to] pardon them, I cannot hold them innocent [for they shed innocent blood in Judah]." Abrabanel reads the first clause as a rhetorical question. "Have I held them innocent? I have

---

36. Why does Joel single out Egypt and Edom? Rashi understands that since it was Egypt who ensured Edom's survival (I Kings 11:16–25), they are to share Edom's fate. Abrabanel and Malbim suggest that these two countries are, respectively, the first country to enslave the Jewish people and the final country to destroy the Second Temple. Radak suggests a typological answer with Messianic overtones, with Egypt representing the Arab/Muslim countries, and Edom representing Rome/Christianity:

It mentioned Edom and Egypt: Egypt because of the Ishmaelites and Edom because of the Roman empire. These two nations are the ones that have been mighty for many years, and they will be so until the time of redemption. These are the fourth beast in Daniel's visions. It mentioned Egypt for the Ishmaelites because Ishmael's wife was Egyptian... and his mother Hagar was Egyptian... and it mentioned Edom for Rome, as did Isaiah... because most of Rome's kingdom were Edomites. Although many other nations were mixed in, as many nations were also mixed among the Ishmaelites, they are identified by the central character. The Caesar was Edomite.... And this is stated regarding our exile, which is why it mentioned only Judah and not the ten tribes exiled by the Assyrian king. Those have not yet returned, and so they are not in the domain of these two nations. (Radak on Joel 4:19)

not! For they have shed blood." The Targum and Malbim translate the word *nikeiti* not as to pardon but to take retribution. They read the phrase as "I will exact retribution from those whom I have not yet exacted retribution." A final understanding comes from looking at the Greek translation in the Septuagint, which read ἐκδικήσω, "I will avenge, I will not hold innocent."[37] This closure (*venikeiti damam lo nikeiti*) also alludes to Joel's allusion to the thirteen attributes of mercy in the middle of chapter 2. God is merciful, but even that list in Exodus 33:6–7 concludes with the phrase *nakei lo yenakei* – God will ultimately not forget or forgive evil.

The book ends with Joel's emphatic declaration that God dwells in Zion. Rashi understands this as a temporal marker: When will God avenge His people? When He dwells in Zion. Ultimately, the nations' attack on Judah leads to their ultimate downfall, ironically guaranteeing peace and security for the Jewish people that dwell in Zion and Jerusalem.

---

37. Likely, their original text read *venakamti*, not *venikeiti* – with a *mem* instead of a *yud*.

Final Thoughts on Joel

When discussing the date when Joel prophesied, we noted that most scholars prefer to place him in the Second Temple period. Angel develops the theological consequences of this approach – arguing that Joel's book is not intended as prophecy but as a guide to the Jewish people on how to react to tragedy at a time when prophecy will no longer be available to them (prophecy disappears during the Second Temple era):

This point can be pushed further. Joel did not need to be a prophet in order to speak to the people as he did. Everyone witnessed the plague. Joel calls for a fast and repentance, which any religious leader can do with or without prophecy. Indeed, the Sages of the Talmud used Joel's prayer as a model for their own prayers during public fast days:

What is the order [of service] for fast days? ...The eldest member of them [the community] says to them reproof, for example: Our brothers, it is not stated with regard to the people of Nineveh: And God saw their sackcloth and their fasting. Rather, the verse says: "And God saw their deeds, that they had turned from their evil way" (Jonah 3:10). And in the Prophets it says:

"And rend your hearts and not your garments, and return to the Lord your God" (Joel 2:13). This teaches that prayer and fasting are insufficient, as one must also repent and amend his ways in practice. (Taanit 15a)[1]

As noted above, Angel credits his teacher, Rabbi Shalom Carmy, with observing that "the book of Joel is unique in prophetic literature in not identifying any sin as cause for a specific disaster nor as an impetus for repentance."[2] We suggested above that the purpose of this lacuna was to encourage the people to place their individual sufferings within a broader, national and historical perspective. Most importantly, however, is the following underlying principle. The book is one of optimism and hope. This may be why Joel is counted among the few successful prophets of the Bible. God is close and remains close, even during the most difficult, darkest, and trying times. The role of leadership is not to justify God to the people but to restore the people to God. God does not need public relations agents; what He wants is for people to desire to be close to Him and to seek His Presence at all times. Joel provides the formula to inspire the people. The proverbial ball remains in their court: Will they respond?

---

1. While Angel is undoubtedly correct regarding the "non-prophetic" nature of the first half of the book of Joel, we maintain strong reservations to his generalizing his approach to the entire book. Clearly the eschatological visions that dominate chapters 3–4 reflect prophecy, not sage advice. Similarly, other prophets emphasize that their message does not require divine revelation without removing them from the level of prophecy. Indeed, they complain that the people do not follow what they already know to be true: "He has told you, O man, what is good, and what the Lord demands of you; but to do justice, to love loving-kindness, and to walk discreetly with your God" (Mic. 6:8). For further development of Rabbi Angel's ideas, see his article "The Book of Joel: Anticipating a Post-Prophetic Age," in *Vision from the Prophets and Counsel from the Elders* (New York: OU Press, 2013), 22–30.
2. Ibid., 42–43.

Obadiah

Introduction

The fourth book of the Twelve Minor Prophets is also its shortest, with only twenty-one verses in one chapter. We know nothing about Obadiah the person, neither who he was nor when he lived. He delivered only one message – an extraordinary rebuke of Judah's southeastern neighbor, Edom. At first glance, this is not unusual. Israel's prophets never restricted their prophecies to the Jewish people. From Isaiah to Jeremiah and Ezekiel, from Amos to Zephaniah, the Jewish impulse towards a universal sense of morality and connectedness inspired them to speak out against moral wrongs committed by other nations.[1] However, the Tanakh always treats Edom differently. Obadiah is not the only prophet to single out Edom for punishment. Ten times do the prophets and writers vent their rage on the tiny desert kingdom and predict a horrible fate for Edom.[2] The only countries that received more anger than Edom were the reigning

---

1. Prophetic oracles against the gentile nations (known as OAN in biblical research) appear in Is. 13–23; Jer. 26–51; Ezek. 25–32; Amos 1–2; Zeph. 2:4–15. Apart from Obadiah, only Nahum and Jonah focus their prophecy on one country alone (Assyria). The three also share one other commonality in their message: because they focus on external threats, unlike most prophets, they do not demand repentance from the Jewish people.
2. Denunciations of Edom can be found in Is. 34:1–17, 63:1–6; Jer. 49:7–22; Ezek. 25:12–14, 35:1–15; Amos 4:21–22, 9:11–12; Joel 4:19–21; Mal. 1:2–5; and Ps. 137:7.

superpowers of the time. Obadiah's treatment of Edom differs from the other prophets. While Edom is his prophecy's focus, Obadiah transforms the divine treatment of Edom into a microcosm that allows us to understand how God's justice interacts with the entire world. To appreciate this and the impact of Obadiah's passionate attack on Edom, we must step back to understand why Edom deserved such attention.

FOREVER LINKED

What led to Obadiah's fierce anger against Edom? After all, many nations engaged in conflict with the Jewish people throughout the ages. The history of enmity between Edom and Judah[3] appears to be no different or significant than the enduring disputes with Ammon, Aram, Moab, the Philistines, or any of the nations that shared a border with Israel or Judah. Even Edom's betrayal of their alliance with Judah and embrace of the Babylonians during Judah's final days (Jeremiah 27), and their appropriation of southern sections of Judah during the Babylonian exile, do not appear to explain the depth of hatred displayed by the biblical prophets towards them. To understand the intensity of their anger, we must appreciate that from the Jewish perspective, the relationship with Edom stems from the close ties shared by their founders – the twin brothers Esau and Jacob. When their mother Rebecca was pregnant, she received a vague prophecy that would hang over her children like Damocles's sword:

> Two nations are in your womb, and two peoples will part from you, and one kingdom will become mightier than the other kingdom, and the elder will serve the younger. (Gen. 25:23)

The resulting rivalry between Jacob and Esau became one of the defining stories of Genesis. They competed in the womb, and while alive, their tumultuous relationship went far beyond the regular ups and downs experienced by competing brothers. Esau agreed to sell the firstborn rights for a mere bowl of soup, and Jacob employed deception to gain the blessings of the firstborn. Esau swore to kill his younger brother as soon as his father would pass away. Rebecca sent Jacob to Aram to hide,

---

3. See I Sam. 14:47; II Sam. 8:13–14; I Kings 11:14–22; II Kings 8:20–22, 14:7, 16:6.

hoping that Esau's anger would subside. Ultimately, Jacob returned to Israel for one final meeting with his older sibling. After decades of conflict, it appears that the two finally reconciled. Nevertheless, though they parted as brothers, the dramatic reunion did not clarify where the two stood towards each other, as evidenced by the following rabbinic debate:

Esau ran to meet him and embraced him. He threw his arms around his neck and kissed him, and they wept. (Gen. 33:4)

Rashi: And he kissed him (*veyishakeihu*) is dotted because he did not kiss him with all his heart. R. Shimon bar Yoḥai said: It is a known principle of law (*halakha*) that Esau hates Jacob, but at that moment, his mercy overturned his anger, and he kissed him with all his heart.

As Israel traveled through the desert to Canaan, they reached Edom's border. Requesting passage through the country, they appealed to their sibling bond. Though Edom rejected them, Israel continued to show them special deference,[4] and the fraternal link later guided Israel's behavior toward them upon settling the land.[5] Consequentially, when

---

4. Numbers 20:14–17; Moses sent messengers from Kadesh to the king of Edom:
   This is what *your brother Israel* says: "You know all the hardship we have encountered, how our ancestors went down to Egypt and lived in Egypt for a long time. And the Egyptians oppressed us and our forebears, and we cried out to the Lord. He heard our voice, sent a messenger, and He brought us out of Egypt. Now here we are in Kadesh, a town adjoining your border. Please, let us pass through your land. We will not pass through any field or vineyard, nor will we drink water from any well. We will go along the King's Highway and not turn from it to the right or the left until we have passed through your territory." Rabbi Yitzchak Etshalom notes in his studies on the book of Amos that the language that Moses uses in requesting passage parallels the language used by Jacob many generations earlier, when he told his brother that he was returning to the land of Israel: "Your servant Jacob says: I have been staying with Laban, and I have tarried until now" (Genesis 32:5). See https://etzion.org.il/en/tanakh/neviim/sefer-amos/prophecies-amos-oracles-against-nations-f.
5. As divinely prescribed twice in Deuteronomy:
   And command the people saying, "You are about to pass through the boundary *of your kinsmen, the children of Esau*, who dwell in Seir, and they will be afraid of you. Be very careful. You shall not provoke them, for I will not give you any of

Edom betrayed this sibling bond, the prophets respond with harsh words of judgment.

> Amos 1:11: So says the Lord: On account of Edom's three crimes and on account of the fourth, I will not forgive them: They have pursued *their brother* in war and suppressed their own mercy. They have allowed their anger to rage forever and nursed their wrath unending.

> Obadiah 1:10–12: For the violence you wrought against *your brother Jacob* shame will cover you, and you will be cut off forever. The day you stood aside, the day strangers took captive his forces, and foreigners entered his gates, casting lots for Jerusalem – you too were like one of them. Do not gloat over the day of *your brother's* destruction, the day he becomes a stranger. Do not rejoice over the children of Judah on the day of their destruction. Do not open your mouth on the day of trouble.

> Malachi 1:2–4: The Lord says, "I have loved you." But you say, "How have You loved us?" *Is Esau not a brother to Jacob?* So says the Lord: Yet I loved Jacob and hated Esau, so I made his mountains desolate and gave his inheritance over to desert jackals. Even should Edom say, "We have been destroyed, but we will return and rebuild the ruins," says the Lord of Hosts, they will build; I will destroy, and they will be called the territory of evil and the nation that suffers the Lord's wrath forever.

From the time Israel enters the land of Israel under Joshua and becomes a nation, Edom is a non-factor. The book of Judges does not mention them. Instead, they receive a fleeting mention in the list of wars that King Saul waged against Israel's neighbors, all of whom had taken advantage of the

---

their land, not so much as a foot step, because *I have given Mount Seir to Esau for an inheritance.*" (2:4–5)

Do not despise an Edomite, for he is your brother. Do not despise an Egyptian, for you lived as a stranger in his land. (23:8)

Philistine regional domination to chisel away at Israel's borders (I Sam.
14:47). Later, in the chapter that describes how King David eliminated
Israel's ancient adversaries from among its neighbors (sometimes per-
manently), including the Philistines, Aram, Ammon, and Moab, there
is another brief mention of Edom, in the context of Israel's occupation
of the southern region:

> King David devoted those [gifts], too, to the Lord, in addition to
> all the silver and gold he had devoted from all the nations he had
> conquered; from Aram, Moav, the Amonites, the Philistines, Ama-
> lek, and the spoil from Hadadezer son of Reḥov, King of Tzova.
> David made a name for himself when he returned from defeating
> the Arameans in the Valley of Salt – eighteen thousand of them. *He*
> *stationed governors in Edom – throughout Edom, he stationed gover-*
> *nors, and all of Edom became David's vassals.* And the Lord granted
> David victory wherever he went. David reigned over all of Israel,
> and David administered justice and righteousness. (II Sam. 8:11–15)

In the text, there is no criticism of David's behavior.[6] Indeed, it continues with a list of David's administration, starting with Joab, his general.[7]

---

6. Indeed, one version of the midrash justifies David's behavior, suggesting that this
   occupation was due to Edom's alliance with the hostile Arameans:
   "When he fought with Aram-Naharaim and with Aram-Zobah, and Joab returned
   and he struck Edom, twelve thousand men in the Valley of Salt" (Ps. 60:2). "And
   he struck Edom": It should say Aram, not Edom! When Joab came to battle
   Aram, the Edomites stood against him, saying: Did not God tell you, "Do not
   attack them"? [You are forbidden to attack us in order to get to Aram!] Joab
   replied: Did not God tell us, "You are traveling along the border of your brethren,
   the children of Esau – Let us pass. [All we are asking for is right of passage –
   if you prevent us, we are allowed to attack!]" They refused. (Tanḥuma Deut. 3)
   In a private correspondence, Rosh Yeshivat Har Etzion Rav Yaakov Medan argued
   that the description of the war against Aram, as described in Psalms 60, indicates that
   it was a much more pivotal and critical battle than what is described in the book of
   Samuel, to the extent that had David lost, it would have led to the extermination of
   the Jewish people. Therefore, he argued, the subsequent occupation of Edom was
   justified (if not Joab's acts of cruelty, as delineated later).
7. Rashi's comment on II Samuel 8:16 is informative and striking:
   "And David administered justice … and Joab the son of Zeruyah was the commander of his army" (vv. 15–16): David caused Joab to be successful over the

However, the story is retold differently in I Kings 11, with lasting and devastating consequences for the future:

> The Lord raised up an adversary for Solomon: Hadad the Edomite, who was of the royal line of Edom. When David had been in Edom, Joab had gone up to bury the slain, for he had struck down every male in Edom during the six months that Joab and all of Israel had stayed there, until they had wiped out every last male in Edom. (vv. 14–16)

Rabbinic thought sharply criticized Joab's cruelty.[8] The historical ramifications were severe: The two nations, if not former allies, were now sworn enemies, and history became a series of atrocities committed against each other.

During his reign, Solomon developed the port city of Etzion-Geber (present-day Eilat) near the Edomite border (I Kings 9:26–28). Unable to oppose Solomon directly, a member of the Edomite royal family named Hadad fled to the south and set up a government in exile

---

> host because he executed justice and charity, and Joab caused David to execute justice and charity because he would judge, and Joab would enforce and chastise for him. Also, because Joab was engaged in the battles, David was not busied with them, and was (lit., his heart was) left free to judge righteously.

8. The book of Kings places the responsibility for the massacre squarely on Joab's shoulders. In the Talmud (Bava Batra 21a–b), a tradition describes how Joab places the blame upon his elementary school teacher, who negligently mistaught him the relevant texts which led to Edom's near annihilation. As Rashi notes on I Kings 11:15, Joab's cruelty is contrasted with David's apparent kindness:

> This is what is referred to in the book of II Samuel 8:13: "And David made for himself a name when he returned from smiting the Edomites," for all were praising him as a kind man who buried his slain. And so Scripture says concerning the wars of Gog and Magog (Ezek. 39:13): "And they will bury all the people of the land, and it will be for them for a name." [However,] the Targum pseudo-Jonathan [translates]: to strip the slain, to take their clothing.

However, another stream in rabbinic interpretation holds David accountable for the atrocities that were committed during his administration: "'For Joab and all Israel camped there for six months' (I Kings 11:16): God said to him: I told you, 'Do not attack them,' and you tried to attack them. By your life, those months will not be counted for you" (Y. Rosh HaShana 1:1).

in Egypt (I Kings 11:14–17). However, Judah still maintained the stronger position. Several decades later, King Jehoshaphat posted a military governor in Edom (I Kings 22:47–48). At that time, there even seems to have been an alliance between the two countries as they fought a Moabite rebellion (II Kings 3). However, Edom gained its freedom from Judah in 845 BCE, rebelling against Jehoshaphat's son Jehoram (II Kings 8:20–22; II Chr. 21:8–10, 16–17). King Amaziah of Judah partially recaptured Edom between 790 and 770 BCE (II Kings 14:7). However, the cost of doing so far exceeded the value of his victories: "[Amaziah] captured ten thousand men alive, led them to the top of a cliff, and threw them down so that all were dashed to pieces" (II Chr. 25:12).

While this violence may "merely" reflect norms of ancient warfare, one midrashic source not only condemns it but identifies it as the cause of the exile:

> I smiled upon you in the days of Amaziah, as it is said: "And Amaziah took courage, and led forth his people to the Valley of Salt.... He captured ten thousand men alive, led them to the top of a cliff, and threw them down" (II Chr. 25:11–12). At that time, the Holy One, Blessed be He, said: I decreed death upon the descendants of Noah only by the sword, but these "threw them down, so that all were dashed to pieces,".... At that time, the Holy One, Blessed Be He, said, "Since they acted thus, they shall go into exile." (Lamentations Rabba 14)

King Uzziah of Judah retook the port of Etzion-Geber (II Kings 14:21–22), which Aram (Syria) would capture from his son Ahaz (II Kings 16:5–6). When Ahaz faced invasion from the north in 734–732 BCE, the Edomites revolted and attacked Judah from the south (II Chr. 28:17). A century later, they were ostensibly counted among Judah's allies when the region's nations formed a coalition to oppose the Babylonians; however, when King Nebuchadnezzar attacked, the Edomites stood with the Babylonians.[9] After the Babylonian exile, many of the Edomites

---

9. For additional denunciations of their behavior in Tanakh, see Jer. 49:7–22; Ezek. 25:12–14; 35:1–15; Ps. 137:7.

began to settle in the emptied southern regions of Judah. This migration intensified when the Nabatean Arabs invaded Edom, conquering the capital city of Sela (known today by its Greek name Petra) and forcing the remaining Edomites into southern Judah, where they settled. With Alexander the Great's conquest of Israel in 331 BCE, they named this area "Idumea" and its inhabitants Idumeans. When the Romans replaced the Greeks as the dominant power, they granted the Idumeans some sovereignty, appointing them to leadership positions over the Jewish population (for example, King Herod, born from an Idumean). This policy intensified Jewish resentment against the Idumeans and eventually contributed to the rabbinic identification of Edom as Rome.[10] As noted

---

10. Examples of this approach, ahistorical as it is, can be found in the words of the following commentators, who viewed the Roman empire either as evolving from the
Edomites, or as benefiting from Edomite assistance during the Jewish wars which
led to the destruction of the Second Temple. (Of interest is the idea found at the end
of Ibn Ezra that it was the Edomites who originally embraced Christianity, which in
325 CE became the official religion of the Roman Empire.)
Radak on Obadiah 1:1:
> The land of Edom does not belong to Edomites today, for the nations were con-
> fused and most of them are Christians or Muslims, and one cannot tell who is
> Edomite, Moabite, Ammonite, or of other nations. All of them were exiled and
> blended among the nations. But the Roman empire was originally mostly Edomite.
Ibn Ezra on Genesis 27:40:
> The sleeping who have not wakened think that we are in the Edomite exile.
> It is not so. Edom was under Judah's hand...Joab killed every male Edomite.
> Because they were under Judah's hand, they rejoiced upon our day of misfortune,
> telling the Babylonians, "Dig, dig until the foundation!" (Ps. 137:7). This shame
> was harsher for Israel, having Edom, in their evil, mock them. And so we have,
> "Rejoice, daughter of Edom" (Lam. 4:21).... Also during the time of Hyrcanus
> he made them guards of Jerusalem and he had them circumcised. In the day of
> Agrippas, when Jerusalem was conquered, Edomite legions came to help Judah,
> and the nation that exiled us was from the seed of the Kitim.... Few believed
> the new religion, and when they believed in the time of (Roman Emperor)
> Constantine, he created the whole religion anew, no one would observe this
> new Torah, aside from the Edomites.
For further reading, see Gerson D. Cohen, "Esau as Symbol in Early Medieval
Thought," in *Jewish Medieval and Renaissance Studies*, ed. Altmann (Cambridge, MA:
Harvard University Press, 1967), 19–48 (recommended by Rabbi Yitzchak Etshalom);
Elie Assis, "Why Edom? On the Hostility Towards Jacob's Brother in Prophetic
Sources," *Vetus Testamentum* 56:1 (2006): 1–20.

in the commentary, this heavily influenced the traditional commentators on Obadiah. Ibn Ezra interprets most of the chapter as referring to the destruction of Rome. Other commentators (Radak, Abrabanel, and Malbim) interpret most of Obadiah as referring to the End of Days but also introduce elements of the Roman Empire's destruction in their interpretations of Obadiah.

OBADIAH THE PERSON

Who was Obadiah? When did he live and prophesy? Tanakh does not tell us. In fact, a dozen people in Tanakh share his name, which can mean "servant of" or "worshipper of" God. Some even suggest that our Obadiah was not the name of an individual but a symbolic title of the writer (others make a similar suggestion regarding Malachi, "My messenger").[11] In II Kings 9:7 and (perhaps) 10:23, *eved Hashem* appears as a technical term for a prophet. Of the people who carry the name Obadiah in Tanakh, most appear in books dating from the Second Temple, with two noticeable exceptions.[12] The first is the Obadiah who serves as minister of Ahab's house and meets Elijah as they search desperately for water. The second is a near contemporary of the first. II Chronicles lists the servants that King Jehoshaphat of Judah sent to his cities to teach Torah: "And in the third year of his reign, he sent his officers, Ben Hail, Obadiah, Zechariah, Nethanel, and Micaiah, to teach in the cities of Judah" (17:7). Indeed, Rabbi Saadia Gaon identifies our prophet as Jehoshaphat's servant.

Traditional rabbinic thought identified Obadiah as Ahab's palace official. As a reward for faithfulness to God while serving the wicked Ahab, this Obadiah merited to receive the gift of prophecy:

> "And Ahab summoned Obadiah, who oversaw the house, and Obadiah was very God-fearing" (I Kings 18:3). What is this text saying? R. Yitzḥak explained: Ahab said to Obadiah: Regarding

---

11. Similarly, while most prophets are introduced with some pertinent identifying detail, generally the father's name, some of their ancestors, and/or their hometown, this descriptive information is absent in only two of the prophetical books: Obadiah and Malachi. See Beasley, *Nahum, Habakkuk, and Zephaniah*, 55.
12. The name also appears in the genealogical lists in I Chronicles (3:21; 7:3; 8:38; 9:16, 44; 12:9).

Jacob, it says, "I have been fortunate, and God has blessed me because of you" (Gen. 30:27). Regarding Joseph, it says, "And God blessed the house of the Egyptian because of Joseph" (Gen. 39:5). My household has not been blessed; perhaps you are not God-fearing! At which point, a voice emerged and said: Obadiah was very God-fearing, but Ahab's household is not deserving of blessing.[13]

... R. Yitzḥak said: Why did Obadiah merit prophecy? For he hid one hundred prophets in a cave [during the period of persecution when Jezebel attempted to murder all of the prophets of God after Elijah's victory at Mt. Carmel].

...Why was Obadiah the one to prophesy for Edom? R. Yitzḥak said: God said: Let Obadiah, who lived between two wicked ones [Ahab and Jezebel] and did not learn from their deeds, prophesy against wicked Esau who lived between two righteous people [Isaac and Rebekah] and did not learn from their deeds.

R. Meir's student, Efraim Makshaah, cited R. Meir as saying that Obadiah was an Edomite convert. As people say: From itself, the hatchet [made of wood] enters the tree. (Sanhedrin 39b)

Like most modern thinkers, both Radak and Ibn Ezra at the beginning of Obadiah argue that Obadiah's identity is unknown. In his commentary on verse 10, Ibn Ezra dates Obadiah to post-Temple destruction. He argues against the rabbinic identification of Obadiah as Ahab's minister since if he had been a prophet, the Tanakh would have identified him as such. Abrabanel rejects this, suggesting that Obadiah may not have yet received his prophecy when he first appears in the Tanakh. Abrabanel

---

13. It is fascinating that Ahab, the king who introduced the worship of foreign idols into the Northern Kingdom, would yet be concerned that his minister be a devout and religious Jew, if even as a good luck charm. However, a closer reading of the text reveals that Ahab is a much more complex character than first appears. See Hayyim Angel's article "Hopping Between Two Opinions: Understanding the Biblical Portrait of Ahab," *Jewish Bible Quarterly* 35:1 (2007): 3–10; reprinted in Angel, *Revealed Texts*, 107–16; Hayyim Angel, *Vision from the Prophet and Counsel from the Elders: A Survey of Nevi'im and Ketuvim* (New York: OU Press, 2013), 94–102.

himself strenuously defends the rabbinic identification, consistent with his approach, which interprets Obadiah as prophesying about the End of Days and not about contemporary events.

THE YEARS OF OBADIAH'S PROPHECY

Since we do not know who Obadiah was, it is tough to date this book.[14] There are three possible approaches to determining when the book was written and locating its author and his audience. First, by identifying the references to historical events in the book; second, by extrapolating from its placement among the books of the twelve minor prophets; finally, by identifying possible quotations or allusions to the writings of other prophets in Obadiah, and quotations or allusions to Obadiah in other books.

First, Obadiah refers to a time in the recent past when the Edomites gloated over (if not participated in) a successful foreign invasion of Jerusalem (vv. 10–14, 16). For this reason, most scholars place the book's writing at the time of the destruction of Jerusalem by the Babylonians in 586 BCE. As noted above, the conflict between Edom and the Jewish people continued well into the period of the Second Temple, as Edom occupied much of southern Judah. Additionally, Obadiah references the recovery of land to the north, pointing to a date after the exile of the Northern Kingdom in 722–721 BCE.[15] Edom had been in league with Judah before the Babylonian invasion (Jer. 27), making their betrayal even more devasting. Finally, much of the language in other Tanakh texts that describe the destruction of the Temple share similarities with Obadiah.

---

14. "This shortest book in the Old Testament, consisting of only twenty-one verses, bears the distinction of being the most difficult of all the prophecies to date." L. Archer Gleason Jr., *A Survey of Old Testament Introduction* (Chicago, IL: Moody Press, 2007), 299.

15. This is not conclusive, however. The Assyrians whittled down the Northern Kingdom gradually, as described in II Kings 15:29: "In the days of Pekah the king of Israel, Tiglath-Pileser the king of Assyria came and took Iyon, Abel-Beit-Maakha, Yanoah, Kedesh, Hazor, Gilead, and Galilee, the entire land of Naphtali; and he exiled them to Assyria."

Therefore, as Edom became Judah's primary adversary during the destruction of the Temple and the exiles' subsequent return several decades later, most scholars date Obadiah's prophecy to this period. However, this viewpoint is not without its difficulties. First, Obadiah mentions neither Babylonia nor the loss of the Temple. He only describes "the day strangers captured his wealth, and foreigners came into his gates" (v. 11). The mention of the house of Joseph (Samaria) in Obadiah's vision of the future working in tandem with the Southern Kingdom (v. 18) points towards dating the prophecy before 722–721 BCE. Amos's opening prophecy, dated to 762 BCE or earlier, refers several times to well-known crimes Edom committed against the Jewish people (Amos 1:6, 9, 11). Finally, at the end of the book, Obadiah mentions nations (the Philistines and the Canaanites) that would only be relevant to listeners from an earlier time. Though the destruction of 586 BCE was the greatest, Jerusalem had already faced invasion several times. The books of Kings and Chronicles record at least seven occasions when enemy forces attacked Jerusalem.[16] Of these past invasions and defeats, two that best seem to fit Obadiah's description of the Edomites' behavior are either: (a) the rebellion against King Jehoram's reign mentioned above (II Kings 8:20–22; II Chr. 21:8–10, 16–17; possibly referenced by Amos 1:6). This would make Obadiah a contemporary of Elijah and then Elisha, suggesting that Obadiah was one of the two servants/ministers mentioned above, either Jehoshaphat's or Ahab's;[17] (b) the terrifying invasion of Judah and Jerusalem by Aram and Israel in the time of King

---

16. Enemy invasions that reached Jerusalem include:
    1. during Rehoboam's reign (930–913 BCE: I Kings 14:25–26; II Chr. 12:2–9)
    2. during Jehoram's reign (853–841: II Kings 8:20–22; II Chr. 21:8–10, 16–17; cf. Amos 1:6)
    3. during Amaziah's reign (796–767: II Kings 14:13–14; II Chr. 25:23–24)
    4. during Ahaz's reign (732–715: II Chr. 28:16–18)
    5. during Jehoiakim's reign (609–598: II Kings 24:1–4; II Chr. 36:6–7)
    6. during Jehoiachin's reign (598–597: II Kings 24:10–16; II Chr. 36:10)
    7. during Zedekiah's reign (597–586: II Kings 25:3–7; II Chr. 36:15–20; cf. Lam. 4:21–22; Ps. 137:7).
17. Both the Targum on the book of Kings and Josephus identify Obadiah as the deceased righteous husband of the widow who pleads with Elisha for assistance (II Kings 4:1–7). The reference in Obadiah (v. 20) to the Israelite exiles in the Phoenician city

Ahaz (742–726 BCE), as described in the historical overview above and recorded in II Chronicles 28. This identification, preferred by this writer, has the advantage of placing Obadiah in the same period as the prophets whose books precede and succeed him in the Twelve Minor Prophets (Amos and Micah). For our purposes, two excerpts from this chapter in Chronicles stand out. First, the Israelite armies decide, after their military victories, to take tremendous numbers of the population captive until the prophet Oded rebukes them on their way back north, showing how despicable in God's eyes is taking innocent citizens captive to enslavement, a theme that will reappear in Obadiah:

> And the Israelites took 200,000 of their brothers captive – women, boys, and girls; they also seized vast amounts of spoil from them, and they brought the spoil to Shomron. But a prophet of the Lord by the name of Oded was there, and he went out before the army arriving at Shomron. "Behold!" he said to them. "In His wrath against Judah, the Lord, God of your ancestors, has

---

of Zarapheth, alludes to the Elijah episode when he was given shelter by a Zarapheth widow (I Kings 17).

In his thesis, "The Intertextual Impact of Obadiah on the Writing Prophets" (MA diss., The Master's College, Santa Clarita, California, 2014), Daniel Forbes also accepts the rabbinic identification of Obadiah as a contemporary of Elijah, for three reasons: (1) The plural verb "we have heard" in Obadiah verse 1 implies that "Obadiah was a member of a circle of prophets or at least part of a larger prophetic community. In this light it is interesting to find him interacting with a group of prophets in I Kings 18:3–4, whom he hides in a cave from Queen Jezebel's pogrom." (2) The fact that though "the conversation between Obadiah and Elijah prior to 'the battle of the gods' on Mount Carmel likely took place in 857 BCE," Elijah reappears "during the reign of King Jehoram (II Chr. 21:12–15), sandwiched between the Chronicler's account of Edom's uprising against Judah (21:8–10) and a small-time attack of the Philistines and Arabians on Jerusalem (21:16–17)." Forbes argues that "If the elderly Elijah lived another thirteen years until the fifth/sixth year of Jehoram, it is highly likely that Obadiah did as well. (3) Finally, he notes that "commentators recognize the importance of the theme of the remnant in Obadiah 10–18.... Although this concept appears early in the Old Testament (e.g., Gen. 7:23; 45:7; Ex. 14:21–31; Deut. 4:27; 28:62), it forms an integral role of Elijah's prophetic consciousness (I Kings 19:1–18).... It is possible, I would argue, that the prophecy of Obadiah was influenced by the traditions surrounding Elijah and the remnant of faithful worshippers he represented." Forbes, "Intertextual Impact," 11–12.

handed them over to you. But you have killed them in such anger that it has reached the heavens. Do you now intend to subjugate the people of Judah and Jerusalem as your own slaves and maidservants? Are you not guilty of an offense against the Lord your God yourselves? Now listen to me: send back those you took captive from among your brothers, for the Lord's wrath rages against you." (II Chr. 28:8–11)

Second, this chapter lists Jerusalem among the cities sacked and whose population was taken captive (II Chr. 28:10). Fortunately, several of Ephraim's tribal leaders hearken to Oded's words, clothe and feed the captive populations, and release them at Jericho. However, the text continues:

> Also, the Edomites had invaded once more, defeating Judah and taking captives, while the Philistines had raided the towns in the lowlands and the Negev of Judah. They captured Beit Shemesh, Ayalon, Gederot, Sokho with its villages, Timna with its villages, and Gimzo with its villages, and they settled there. (II Chr. 28: 17–18)

Unlike Aram and Israel, whose invasion of Judah was motivated by political reasons, Edom chooses to invade Judah at this time only because Judah was vulnerable. Unlike Israel to the north, they did not suffer pangs of conscience in taking Judah's population captive. The Philistines also took advantage of Judah's weakened state to encroach upon their borders. These ideas echo throughout Obadiah, suggesting that Obadiah prophesied against the Edomites during this period.

Another approach to identifying the date of Obadiah's prophecy is its placement within the Twelve Minor Prophets. As noted above, they appear in fundamentally chronological order (with exceptions).[18] Hosea

---

18. Hobart E. Freeman, *An Introduction to the Old Testament Prophets* ([Chicago: Moody Press, 1968], 135): "In the arrangement of The Twelve in the Hebrew Bible the chronological principle which seems to have determined the over-all order was as follows: (1) the prophets of the Assyrian period were placed first (Hosea to Nahum); (2) then followed those of the Babylonian period (Habakkuk and Zephaniah); (3) the series closed with the three prophets of the Persian period after the exile (Haggai,

leads off as it is the longest book of the pre-exilic minor prophets. Similar themes and words seem to have influenced the order since Joel, rather than Amos, the second-longest pre-exilic minor prophet, follows Hosea. Obadiah follows Amos, and some suggest that this is a commentary on Amos 9:12.[19] The placement leads to the conclusion that Obadiah was one of the earlier prophets.

A third approach to determine the date of Obadiah is to compare the book to similar contemporary texts. It is common for one prophet to use and develop themes and ideas that another prophet had previously uttered. There are similarities between Obadiah verses 9, 10, 14, 18, and 19 and Amos 1:2, 6, 11–12, and 9:12–14 (some scholars suggest that the placement of Obadiah after Amos is due to these links); and between Obadiah's first six verses and Jeremiah's prophecy against Edom in Jeremiah 49:9 and 14–17. There are also numerous similarities between Obadiah verses 10–18 and Joel 1:15; 2:1, 32; 3:3–4, 17, and 19.[20] Additionally, Obadiah's description of the Edomite's behavior during the invasion of Jerusalem parallels other descriptions found in prophetic texts that criticize Edom's behavior during the destruction of 586 BCE. (Ps. 137:7; Lam. 4:18–22; Ezra 25:12–14; 35:1–14).[21] However, these instances do not allow one to conclusively prove that Obadiah used and developed ideas and themes that originated with other prophets. It is feasible that the other prophets were referencing Obadiah instead, and a possibility exists that both depended on another common source that is unknown to us. Again, whether the sources are contemporary with Obadiah or not cannot be proven either way.

Zechariah and Malachi)." See also Greg Goswell, "The Order of the Books in the Hebrew Bible," *Journal of the Evangelical Theological Society* 51:4 (December 2008): 673–88.

19. Allen, *Books of Joel, Obadiah, Jonah, and Micah*, 129. Stuart suggests that Obadiah follows Amos because Obadiah used the name A-donai Elokim (v. 1), a rare name for God in the prophets, but also found in Ezekiel and Amos (D. Stuart, *Word Biblical Commentary* 31: *Hosea–Jonah*, 416).

20. Dating Joel's prophecies is also difficult. For a discussion of the date of the book of Joel, see introduction, "Who Was Joel? When Did He Live?" pp. 33–39.

21. The Apocrypha, I Esdras 4:45 assigns the actual burning of the Temple to the Edomites. Though this is historically doubtful, it reflects an ancient tradition that blames Edom.

Ultimately, like Radak and Ibn Ezra, we acknowledge that we do not have the ability to date the book with certainty. Our commentary reflects the belief that the episode of the Syro-Ephraimite invasion of Judah in 732 is the historical background for Obadiah's message. Fortunately, we are not dependent on the correct date of this prophecy to understand its message.

OBADIAH'S MESSAGE

But also with Judah the Lord has a dispute: He will visit upon Jacob as he deserves, *as he befits his deeds – He will repay him.* (Hosea 12:3)

For the day of the Lord draws near for all the nations. *What you have done shall be done to you; what you have wrought will return upon your head.* (Obadiah 1:15)

Throughout his prophecy, Obadiah delivers one clear message: Divine justice will be established. In the book's first two sections (vv. 1–15), Obadiah presents this message through the lens of Israel's specific historical experience of Edom's response to its defeat and exile. In the final section (vv. 16–21), Obadiah expands his scope to include all the nations and the upcoming day of the Lord, when God's justice becomes not only punishment of the wicked (of which Edom serves as the archetype), but also the Jewish people's redemption and vindication. Words of doom and destruction for Edom and the nations, first implicitly and then explicitly, affirm that justice will ultimately prevail, and the Jewish people will once again live free and unfettered in their land.

The fundamental principle that Obadiah uses to describe divine justice is the law of equivalent retribution (*lex talionis*; in Hebrew, *midda keneged midda*). The Torah established the principle that punishment should fit the crime, an eye for an eye, and a tooth for a tooth (Ex. 21:21–23; Lev. 24:19–20; Deut. 19:21).[22] Obadiah explicitly states

---

22. How this principle is applied in the legal and judicial frameworks is a matter for a separate discussion. The Oral Law is very clear that the verse "eye for an eye" refers to monetary compensation, as opposed to actual removal of the eye (as opposed to the Sadducees quoted approvingly by Josephus in *Antiquities of the Jews*, Book

this in verse 15: "For the day of the Lord over all the nations is close; *as you have done shall be done to you; your recompense shall be returned upon your head.*" Every sin Obadiah mentions shares this fate. Should a prideful person seek to ascend to the heavens, they will be brought low (vv. 2–4); should a person choose to mock others in their suffering, they too will be mocked (vv. 10, 13). Even the closing verses, focusing on Israel, are based on this principle. Nations that attempted to possess the land of Israel would themselves be dispossessed (vv. 17–21). Throughout the vision, God reverses the intentions of the perpetrators with the appropriate, corresponding punishment.

This principle is especially noteworthy because, as mentioned above, Obadiah presents it in the framework of the historical conflict not only between the two nations of Edom and Israel, but also between two brothers – Esau and Jacob. Though one could argue that the punishments reflect the specific crime of betraying a fraternal bond, the actions and their punishment represent not a nationalistic comeuppance, but the expression of a divine, universal morality and its natural consequences.

The history of Obadiah's vision is unclear. It begins at an undefined point, references specific historical events (vv. 1–14), but continues until the day of the Lord,[23] the End of Days (v. 15ff.). As such, Obadiah cleverly holds out hope and optimism for the future, which could arrive quickly or be delayed – but arrive, it will.

STYLE AND STRUCTURE

From a stylistic point of view, Obadiah demonstrates considerable literary talent. In his short prophecy, he employs dramatic imagery, rhetorical questions, irony, repetition, and various forms of parallelism, all

---

IV, 7:34, and in 4 Tammuz, *Megillat Taanit*). For development of this idea, see Rabbi Yaakov Medan, "An Eye for an Eye," available online at https://etzion.org.il/en/tanakh/torah/sefer-shemot/parashat-mishpatim/mishpatim-%E2%80%9C-eye-eye%E2%80%9D; Rabbi Meir Shpiegelman, "Two Concepts of Justice in the Torah's Laws of Damages," available online at https://etzion.org.il/en/tanakh/torah/sefer-shemot/parashat-mishpatim/mishpatim-two-concepts-justice-torahs-laws-damages; Rabbi Michael Hattin, "An Eye for an Eye," available online at https://www.etzion.org.il/en/eye-eye.

23. For more on the phrase "day of the Lord," see introduction, pp. 41–43.

of which we shall see in our commentary. Many scholars see parallels between Obadiah's message and the covenant-lawsuit form of address, familiar to the ancient Near East.[24] This format appears in many of the prophets and their messages and contains specific formulaic sections. These typically include addressing the defendant (including reproach based on an accusation and a statement that the accused has no defense), a pronouncement of guilt, and the sentence. Obadiah follows a similar form, with one major exception. In Obadiah, the verdict and punishment appear first, with the explanation which justifies them appearing afterward. Obadiah contains three large sections with several subsections. We suggest the following outline:

I. Edom's coming judgment, vv. 1–9

After introducing the oracle (v. 1), Obadiah describes how the enemy will breach Edom's defenses. The breach will occur despite the relatively high placements of Edom's fortresses (vv. 2–4). Once Edom's defenses fall, the enemy will thoroughly loot and plunder Edom's treasures (vv. 5–7) and destroy Edom's leadership (v. 8).

II. Esau's crimes against Jacob, vv. 10–15

Obadiah then states the charge against Edom, why they deserved the punishment described above (v. 10). Edom's (Esau's) crime is the betrayal of his brother, Jacob. Obadiah describes that this occurred both by passively standing to the side while the Jewish people were attacked and ultimately taking part in the devastation that afflicted Israel (v. 11–15).

III. The restoration of Israel's sovereignty, vv. 16–21

Obadiah concludes by describing the impending judgment against Edom and the nations (vv. 16–18), which will be all-encompassing and final. Ultimately, the exiles from Israel and Judah will return and occupy the land of Edom, and God will

---

24. See, for example, Herbert B. Huffmon, "The Covenant Lawsuit in the Prophets," *Journal of Biblical Literature* 78 (1959): 285–95.

reign sovereign over the entire world while being made known to all (vv. 19–21).

These three sections are of about equal size. However, as we will note, verses 8–9 straddle both the first and the second sections, linking them with a series of textual and thematic links. Scholars note that the same words recur towards the beginning and end of each section, forming *inclusios* around them: "deceived" (vv. 3, 7), "day" (vv. 8, 15), and "mountain" (vv. 16, 21).[25] Each section contains a different set of main actors: In vv. 1–7, Edom is alone against unnamed nations; in the middle section, verses 8–15 emphasize the brotherhood shared by Edom and Jacob, and the final section, verses 16–21, concludes again with discussions of the nations, featuring Edom and Judah. Each unit develops a different aspect of the book's theological message: God's universal justice is the theme of the first section. Obadiah accuses Edom of crimes that anyone could have done. The second section shifts to lambasting Edom's moral failings of indifference, an accusation that gains significance considering the fraternal relationship between Jacob and Esau's descendants.[26] The final section includes the future vindication and redemption of the Jewish people.

---

25. P. Jensen, *Obadiah, Jonah, Micah: A Theological Commentary* (New York: Bloomsbury Academic & Professional, 2008), 6.
26. This point is made by Rabbi Mosheh Lichtenstein:

> Ovadya's prophecy embraces both elements. It opens with passages that parallel the prophecy of Yirmiyahu, including the way he relates to Edom as one of the nations. Edom is defined as a nation that does not know its place, and instead of being small among the nations, it has pretensions of greatness. The problem, as stated above, is pride, and the issue is judged in the framework of Edom's status as a nation. This section…continues until verse 9, and it is very similar to Jeremiah's prophecy and approach.
>
> From verse 10 onwards, however, the [chapter] undergoes a complete change in direction. From now on, Ovadya rebukes Edom for denying Israel as a brother. The complaint about Edom's wrongdoing does not relate to the actions themselves, but to their ramifications for Yaakov as a brother. This point is sharpened in the coming verses, which speak not of the evil committed by Edom, but of Edom's indifference to the fate of a brother.

Available online at https://www.etzion.org.il/en/tanakh/torah/sefer-bereishit/parashat-vayishlach/esav-brother-esav-other.

Obadiah against Edom

EDOM'S END (OBADIAH 1–9)

The vision of Obadiah: So says the Lord God to Edom – we have heard tidings from the Lord: and an envoy has been sent among the nations, "Come, let us rise up in battle against her." Behold, I have made you small among nations; you are utterly scorned. The arrogance of your heart deceived you, you who dwell in the cliff's niches, your lofty abode, saying in your heart, "Who could bring me down to earth?" But even if you rise as high as an eagle, if you make your nest among the stars, I shall bring you down from there, declares the Lord.

If thieves come upon you, bandits in the night, do they not take only their fill? If grape gatherers come upon you, do they not leave gleanings? Yet how has Esau been ransacked, his hidden treasures laid bare. Your allies all have forced you to the borders; those with whom you had made peace all deceived you, defeated you. [Those with whom you broke] your bread laid a snare for you, bereft of awareness.

Behold, on that day, says the Lord, shall I not purge Edom of wise men, the mountains of Esau of awareness? Your warriors will be frightened, Teiman, for the mountains of Esau will be unmanned by slaughter. (vv. 1–9)

The first section of Obadiah's prophecy describes the imminent destruction and devastation that awaits Edom. Generally, an oracle of judgment sets out the reasons for the verdict and only then proclaims judgment. With Edom, the process is reversed. Though the first section alludes to the rationale for the punishment, the focus is on the gradual, almost clinical dismantling of everything that Edom held dear. In three distinct subsections, Obadiah methodically eliminates all possible means of escape from this upcoming punishment. He begins with Edom's geographical and strategic advantages (v. 3), the traditional sense of restraint occasionally exercised by enemy invaders (v. 5), and finally betrayal and abandonment by Edom's traditional allies (v. 7). Obadiah then lists Edom's human resources. Edom was famous for its wise men and their discernment, yet they too would prove to be of no help. Finally, Edomite society slowly collapses – their leaders (v. 8), their generals and, finally, the populace (v. 9).

The section's structure is as follows: Verse 1 is set off from verses 2–9 by the imperative and first-person plural verbs, which shift in verse 2 to first-person singular. Verses 2–4 begin with "behold," *hinneh*, and end with a divinely declarative sentence, "says the Lord," *ne'um Hashem*, which often functions as a "closing formula" in prophetic literature. Verses 5–7 are linked thematically with their description of Edom's utter destruction, bracketed by more occurrences of *ne'um Hashem*. Finally, verses 8–9 begin with "On that day," an additional temporal marker and a rhetorical question ("shall I not purge?").

Obadiah's opening, "The vision of Obadiah," is fitting – the shortest book in Tanakh should have the shortest opening. The word "vision" (*ḥazon*) occurs elsewhere in prophetic works – both Isaiah and Nahum's books begin with this word, and other prophetic works start with the verbal form *ḥaza*.[1] *Ḥazon* is not limited to visual imagery, but refers to the reception of a divine message. In Genesis 15:1, for example, we read: "The word of the Lord came unto Abram in a vision (*maḥazeh*)"; in Job 4:13–16, Eliphaz describes how "from the visions (*ḥezyonot*) of the night, when deep sleep falls on

---

1. See the first verses of Amos, Mica, and Habbakuk, and Daniel 8:1.

men…I heard a still voice." As the content here suggests, the word *ḥazon* generally refers to a prophecy that will occur in the future, not immediately.

Obadiah introduces his speech with "so said the Lord God concerning Edom," though God's actual words do not begin until the next verse. Starting in this manner helps Obadiah gain authenticity as a divinely authorized messenger. He begins poetically – "we have heard tidings" (the poetic alliteration is clearer in Hebrew – *shemua shamanu*).[2] Why the plural tense, "we"? If God is speaking, this can be interpreted as the royal, divine, we. Possibly, God is summoning other nations to act against Edom, probably through "natural" means (i.e., signaling that Edom is vulnerable to attack while stoking other nations' desire to defeat Edom and conquer its territory). Radak suggests that Obadiah is quoting the countries who confer among themselves, plotting Edom's demise. Ibn Ezra suggests that Obadiah is the speaker, and he is referencing other prophets who shared his message:

> We suggest that "we have heard tidings" refers to the prophet, and Jeremiah, Isaiah, and Amos (who prophesied regarding Edom), and so it says, "we have heard."

A final possible approach has Obadiah speaking on behalf of the entire Jewish people.

Obadiah continues poetically with another double verb. *Shemua shmanu* (we have heard a rumor) becomes *kumu venakuma* (arise, let us get up [to wage war]). The double repetition of the same root helps to highlight its urgency and importance.[3] Just as Joseph understood that the doubling of Pharaoh's dreams in Genesis 42 meant that the prophecy

---

2. Likely due to the difficulty of having the prophet speak in plural form, the Greek Septuagint amends the text to the singular ἤκουσα (I have heard); however, the plural form appears in all the other ancient manuscripts: Targum pseudo-Jonathan has *shemana,* and the Vulgate has *audivimus.*

3. As noted in the introduction, many interpret this book as referring to a war that would take place at the End of Days, the war of Gog and Magog. Abrabanel understands that it begins with an invasion of Egypt and Israel by Christian countries, only to be

therewithin would begin immediately, so too is the sentence about to be pronounced and punishment applied to Edom. Finally, there is a possible wordplay here. To describe the individual carrying the battle summons, Obadiah uses an uncommon word, *tzir*. This word may be a wordplay on *Se'ir*, which describes both Esau's physical appearance and one of the names of the mountain range where he settled (cf. Gen 27:11, 23; 36:8, 9).

Obadiah continues the first section of the declaration of punishment with God's assertion that "Behold I have made you small among the nations" in verse 2, ending in verse 4 with a divine confirmation ("so says the Lord"). The entire section focuses on the vertical dimension – appropriate for Edom, who were mountain dwellers and gained a sense of confidence and superiority accordingly. Height can be both physical, referring to their lofty dwellings that only the highest-flying birds can reach, and also a spiritual rebuke, height being a metaphor for pride. Isaiah declares, "For the Lord of Hosts has a day over everyone proud and high, and over everyone exalted, and he shall become humble."[4] Edom could look down upon the other nations from their mountain peaks, but they forgot to look upwards to the real Ruler.

Obadiah begins God's speech with what appears to be a gratuitous insult against Edom: "Behold I have made you small among the nations." The Talmud understands this phrase as referring to Edom's political instability and cultural insignificance:

> "Behold, I have made you small among the nations": They do not have a king who is a son of a king [instead, they kill each other for the right to rule]. "You are utterly scorned" – for they have neither script nor language. (Avoda Zara 10a)

Commentators like *Metzudat David* and Malbim suggest that this reminds the Edomites of their lowly beginnings. Unlike other great

---

met by a united effort among the Ishmaelites (Arab). The consultations in preparing for this war are what are being referenced here.

4. See also Ps. 138:6; Job 41:34; Ezra 31:10.

nations like the Egyptians, the Assyrians, or the Philistines, Edom was always a lowly outpost on the edge of the desert, never an essential player in international affairs.[5]

However, the word Obadiah uses, small (*katan*), the opposite of big (*gadol*), can also connote younger as opposed to older. Therefore, the Midrash understands these words as alluding to the original twins whose stories underlie Obadiah's prophecies – Jacob and Esau.

> His father [Isaac] called him "great": "And he called his older [*gadol* – great] son, Esau" (Gen. 27:1). His mother called him "great": "And Rebecca took the beloved garments of Esau, her older [*gadol* – great] son" (v. 15). So God said to them: He may be great in your eyes, but in My eyes, he is small. (Genesis Rabba 65:11)

Similarly, the Hebrew word that Obadiah uses to describes Edom as despised, *bazui*, alludes to Esau's despising his birthright when he sold it for lentil soup: *vayivez Esau et habekhora* (Gen. 25:34).

Verses 3–4 contain an interlocking set of parallelisms and thematic developments. Verse 3 begins with the heights in Edom's heart, emphasizes twice the lofty heights that Edom reaches, and concludes with a question that Edom asks – "who can bring me down?" Verse 4 provides the answer. From the question of "who can bring me down?" at the end of the previous verse, the verse again mentions height imagery twice again, and then God provides the answer to the question, "*I will bring you down.*"

Obadiah's height imagery also subtly changes from verses 3 to 4. The first verse alludes to "clefts of the rock, his high habitation." These are high places, but they remain physically connected to the earth.[6] The second verse lists the skies and the stars. Edom's

5. Unlike the previous commentators, Radak interprets this sentence as referring to the future, the eventual dissolution and disappearance of the Roman Empire, despite its previous grandeur.

6. Rashi prefers an allegorical understanding of the phrase "who dwell in the clefts of the rock." Instead of the literal meaning, referring to the mountain ranges where Edom is located, Rashi understands this as an allusion to the spiritual greatness of

pride has now transcended earthly boundaries and extended into the heavens, God's domain. Malbim suggests that this is deliberate; God is making known that He allowed Esau to reach abnormally lofty heights to increase the strength of the impact when Edom comes crashing down to earth.

The Hebrew word used here for pride (*zadon*) generally means to willingly act oppressively toward another. After the Exodus, Jethro says about God and the Egyptians, "Now I know that the Lord is greater than all the deities, for with the thing that they plotted (*zadu*), [He came] upon them" (Ex. 18:11). The word *zadon* is also etymologically similar to boiling liquid (*zid*). Obadiah imagines pride as slowly boiling water, building up in pressure like a closed pot on a fire. Not surprisingly, this same root word (z-d-h) appears three times in the first account in the Tanakh between Jacob and his brother Esau, who chose to squander his birthright for a bowl of lentil soup willingly (Gen. 25:27–34).

What was the cause of Edom's pride and ultimate downfall? Lying at the heart of Edom's self-deception was a false estimate of its geographical advantages:

> Edom's natural defenses were imposing…. This ridge exceeded 4,000 feet throughout its northern sector, and it rose in places to 5,700 feet in the south. Its height was rendered more inaccessible by the gorges radiating from it toward the Arabah on the west and the desert eastwards… In addition to these natural fortifications, Edom was strongly defended by a series of Iron Age fortresses, particularly on the eastern frontier, where the land descended more gradually to the desert.[7]

Esau's ancestors: "Who relies on the support of his ancestors, Abraham and Isaac, but they shall not avail him" (Rashi on v. 3).

7. Carl E. Armerding, "Obadiah," in *Daniel-Minor Prophets*, ed. Frank E. Gaebelein and Richard P. Polcyn. *The Expositor's Bible Commentary* VII (Grand Rapids: Zondervan Publishing House, 1985), 342–43.

The cliffs of Petra, as seen from the bottom of the cliff

From Judah's point of view, Edom did indeed dwell in the heights. They could fortify the passes that led to the fortresses quickly; during an emergency, the Edomites could find safety in caves. "Clefts in the rock" (Jer. 49:16; Song. 2:14) suggest inaccessible heights where only birds could live, anticipating the eagle imagery of the next verse. The eagle is both swift (II Sam. 1:23, "They were swifter than eagles, and mightier than lions"; cf. Jer. 4:13) and cunning, able to swoop down unexpectedly upon its prey. This metaphor captures Edom's military might as it charged down from the mountain, serving to increase the drama of the reversal of fortune. Furthermore, the mighty eagle provides a striking contrast to the vulture and hyena imagery that will appear in later verses – weak and cowardly animals who feast on the efforts of others.

Obadiah's descriptive imagery in the second subsection switches location from heaven to earth. His rhetorical style also changes. Obadiah now addresses Edom with various poetic techniques and rhetorical questions.[8] He uses a succession of protases ("if" statements), apodoses

---

8. While Abrabanel interprets most of Obadiah as a prophecy to take place in the end of days, he understands this subsection as describing calamitous events that occurred

("would not" statements), and exclamation statements ("how!"). These invite the listener to partake in the shock that the Edomites feel as their most precious places are invaded. In verse 5, Obadiah speaks to Edom/ Esau directly but reverts to the third person in verse 6 and climaxes with the anticipatory exclamation "how has Esau been ransacked!" This style of outburst appears in funeral laments (e.g., II Sam. 1:19; Jer. 9:19), but rather than striking a sympathetic note, here it takes on a savagely satirical context.[9]

Obadiah begins this subsection by describing two hypothetical events – the robbery and looting of a house of its treasures and harvesters raiding a vineyard of its grapes.[10] The plundering mocks the Edomites' feeling of security. Additionally, Obadiah uses these images to contrast human behavior with God's upcoming punishment. Thieves generally do not empty the house they raid; considerations of time, value, and the ability to carry the goods away are always present. Once God decrees something, however, the parameters change. As Obadiah makes clear, though human undertakings are partial and incomplete – treasures are left behind, grapes left on the vine – the upcoming divine judgment will be comprehensive and complete.

In the second image, the invaders reap the fruits of the hard work of the locals who grew the grapes. Grape-growing was tedious, labor-intensive work, as evidenced by Isaiah's usage of the vintager's efforts as the basis for his classic metaphor of God's treatment of Israel (Is. 5). Invariably, robbers would take only the most luxurious clusters and bunches, leaving behind those grapes that were unripe, rotten, or too small. This practice, ironically, is a commandment in the Torah: "When

---

in the past (either the destruction of biblical Edom, or alternatively, the Roman Empire).

9. Isaiah uses this style, the mock lament, for the king of Babylon, about to fall:
   Then you shall bear this parable to the king of Babylon; say: How could the oppressor be halted so, the city of gold be halted?!... How you have fallen from heaven now, shining one, son of the dawn light; how you are cut down to earth, you who decided nations' fates. (Is. 14:4, 12)

10. Edom was prime vineyard territory, as alluded to by Moses's promise to the king of Edom that the Jewish people would not "pass through fields or vineyards, nor will we drink well water. We will walk along the king's road, and we will turn neither to the right nor to the left until we have passed through your territory" (Num. 20:17).

you reap the harvest of your land, do not reap all the way to the edge of your field or gather the gleanings of your harvest. Do not harvest your vineyard bare or gather the grapes that have fallen there. Leave them for the poor and for the stranger" (Lev. 19:10; Deut. 24:21). However, even this consolation will be denied to the impoverished Edomites. While the first image of a house being robbed conjures up the shock of quick, sudden despoilment, the second image, of the reaping of the grapes, is even more startling, just for the systematic, almost leisurely manner, Edom would be ransacked. Unlike human robbers, who grab what they can in haste, preferring to escape with as much treasure as possible, and not risk being apprehended, the invaders feel no such fear. The punishment here is thus poetic justice for the looting that Edom carried out on Judah (v. 13). Again, Obadiah may be using subtle word-play, as the word for grape-gatherers, *botzrim*, is phonetically similar to *Botzra*, the capital of Edom.[11]

Finally, in verse 7, Obadiah describes how Edom would meet its allies, only to be unexpectedly betrayed. Again, this is the just reversal of their behavior towards Judah. First, Edom deceived itself regarding its physical security, believing itself to be impregnable (*zedon libekha hishi'ekha*, v. 3). Now, using the same exact root (*kol anshei veritekha hishi'ukha*, v. 7), Edom finds itself deceived concerning its political security and the faithfulness of its alliances. These terms describe those with whom Edom had made a treaty, who were on good terms with them. (The phrase *anshei shlomekha*, people of your peace, in this context means an alliance; see Jer. 38:22 where allies are similarly labeled *anshei shlomekha*). Whether or not these may even be the nations that Obadiah mentioned in verse 1, or are separate countries, is unclear.[12] The verbs here do not

---

11. Other prophets use Botzra as a metonym for the nation of Edom (the same way as Jerusalem can refer to all of Israel; see Is. 34:6, 63:1; Jer. 49:22; Amos 1:11–12).

12. Most commentators suggest that Edom's allies were guilty of the sin of abandonment to the enemies in verse 1. (See Rashi: "Those who promised to aid you, came with you and escorted you to the border of your land, to the boundary, whence the [other enemies] came upon you in war, and with this they enticed you and succeeded.") However, both Radak and Ibn Ezra understand that the people who broke the alliance are the people who attack Edom, and this reading seems to be a better reading of the text.

imply a military attack, but the usage of intelligent strategy ("deceived," "defeated," "laid a snare").[13] Ultimately, these nations did something considered reprehensible in ancient times – breaking a covenant with an ally.[14]

Obadiah's sudden mention of "your bread ([Those with whom you broke] your bread laid a snare for you)" is ambiguous. It may be a synonym for an ally; in Psalms, David decries, "Even my ally, in whom I trusted, *who eats my bread*, developed an ambush for me" (41:9). There is evidence that covenants are formed through ceremonial eating. Jacob and Laban make their covenant over bread: "So now, come, let us form a covenant, you and I, and may He be a witness between you and me... And Jacob slaughtered [food to be eaten] on the mountain, and he invited his friends to eat a meal, and they ate bread" (Gen. 31:44, 54). Eating also appears in the context of the giving of the Torah, when God and the Jewish people establish a covenant, "And he took the book of the covenant and read it within the hearing of the people, and they said, 'All that the Lord spoke we will do, and we will hear.'... and they perceived God, *and they ate and drank*" (Ex. 24:11).

Obadiah begins the final subsection , verses 8–9, with a description of the gradual decimation of the Edomites until their extinction. He starts with their leaders, whose role is to prevent harm from coming to their people, repeating the declaration from verse 4, "so says the Lord," emphasizing that everything that occurs ultimately comes from God's hand. The destruction in verse 8 could be either the physical undoing of Edom's wise men, for whom the nation was well known,[15] but also the undoing of their knowledge and understanding. They overestimated their physical security, and they chose to trust the wrong allies. Obadiah emphasizes that it will take place "on that day" – anticipating the "day of the Lord," the universal judgment that Obadiah will proclaim in verse 15. Malbim notes that in previous crises if some wise men survived, the

---

13. Grammatically, the prophet uses verbs in the past tense to refer to future events, commonly called the "prophetic past." B. K. Smith, "Obadiah," in Smith and Page, *Amos, Obadiah, Jonah* (Nashville, TN: Broadman and Holman, 1995), 186–87.
14. Amos castigates Tyre for the same transgression: "On account of Tyre's three crimes and on account of the fourth, I will not forgive them: they handed over an entire group of exiles to Edom and did not remember the brotherly covenant" (Amos 1:9).
15. Cf. I Kings 4:30; Jer. 49:7; Job 1:1, 2:11, 4:1; Lam. 4:21.

nation could rebuild and regenerate. To ensure that Edom's destruction was final, all of Edom's wise men had to be eliminated.[16]

The "mountain of Esau" (cf. v. 9) is Mount Seir, which God gave to Esau and his descendants to inherit (Deut. 2:5). The phrase "Mount Esau" is found only in Obadiah (vv. 8, 9, 19, 21), and it contrasts with Mount Zion (vv. 17, 21). The "mighty men" of Edom may be another term for Edom's wise men, or they could be their military leaders and warriors. Together, the two form the entirety of the leadership. Abrabanel notes that military success depends on excellent planning (wise men) and the physical strength and capability (mighty men) of the armies who had to carry out these plans. When the warriors were defeated, they would flee southwards.[17] Bereft of leadership, the downfall of the rest of the nation was assured.

WHAT HAPPENED? WHY? (OBADIAH 10–15)

> For the violence you wrought against your brother Jacob shame will cover you, and you will be cut off forever. The day you stood aside, the day strangers took captive his forces, and foreigners entered his gates, casting lots for Jerusalem – you too were like one of them. Do not look on the day of your brother's calamity. Do not rejoice over the children of Judah on the day of their destruction.
>
> Do not open your mouth on the day of trouble.
>
> Do not enter My people's gate on the day of their ruin.
>
> Do not gloat over its misfortune on the day of its ruin.
>
> Do not extend your hands to take its wealth on the day of his ruin.
>
> Do not stand at the crossroads to cut down his refugees.
>
> Do not surrender his survivors on the day of trouble.
>
> For the day of the Lord draws near for all the nations. What you have done shall be done to you; what you have wrought will return upon your head. (vv. 10–15)

---

16. A situation possibly alluded to by R. Yohanan ben Zakkai in his request of the Roman general: "Give me [the city of] Yavneh *and its wise men!*" If the Jewish people still had its Torah scholars, they could, and did, survive.

17. Commentators (Radak, Ibn Ezra) note that the Hebrew word for southwards – *teimana* – also alludes to Esau's grandson Teiman (Gen. 36:11, 15).

Obadiah now justifies the severity of the punishment that Edom would receive (namely, destruction). The accusation against Edom goes beyond pride to the twin crimes of betrayal and indifference. The opening verse 10 summarizes what verses 11–14 will detail, just as verse 1 relates to verses 2–9. He speaks in the divine voice (the reversal to his own voice in verse 15 is a common feature in prophetic texts, as the prophet and God often merge into one speaker).[18]

This section emphasizes a new message: Destruction is coming to Edom because of Edom's behavior toward his "brother," Israel. Until now, Edom's transgressions were universal failings – pride and over-confidence. Now, they reflect a betrayal of what should be humanity's most durable bond – brotherhood. As such, Edom's terrible fate is not arbitrary but the consequence of its behavior against Judah. After the introductory summary in verse 10, Obadiah accuses Edom of inaction (first part of v. 11), of participating in the plundering of Jerusalem (second part of v. 11), of gloating over Judah's misfortune (v. 12; cf. v. 2), and finally of entrapping the survivors (v. 14; cf. v. 7). These accusations consist of eight phrases with the same structure, each combining a warning ("do not...," *al...*) with an aspect of Judah's calamity. Almost all refer to what occurred "on the day of" (the seventh occurrence, referring what not to do to the refugees, being an exception). Obadiah formulates these phrases in a manner that generally refers to the present or future, but the section (bracketed by v. 11 and the second part of v. 15) clarifies that the disaster had already occurred. Some English translations reflect this by switching "you should not" to "you should not have...."

"Day" is a keyword in this section, occurring eleven times. They all refer to the attack on Jerusalem, except for the last occurrence. In this section, Obadiah provides a dramatic surprise in the upcoming "day of the Lord." In doing so, Obadiah gives universal significance to the particular crimes that Edom commits. Thus, Edom's transgressions become not just crimes against family but crimes against humanity. He concludes by reiterating the underlying basis for judgment – the principle of *lex*

---

18. See Ehud Ben Zvi, *A Historical-Critical Study of the Book of Obadiah* (Berlin: Walter de Gruyter, 1996), 172–74.

talionis (*midda keneged midda*): What will happen to them is a direct consequence of their actions.

Obadiah began by describing Edom's eventual downfall, but he refrained from explaining why it would occur. Verse 3 alluded to pride as the root of Edom's collapse, but deeper forces are at play. Now Obadiah begins to explain why Edom deserves annihilation. The mention of "Mount Esau" in verse 9 shifts the focus from nations to brothers. Obadiah's reference to "your brother Jacob" in verse 10 continues to strengthen and highlight the familial connection between them and begins to explain the severity of the judgment, which is intensified by the repetition of the root word K-R-T (to cut off entirely) in both verses 9 and 10.

Obadiah begins with the Hebrew word for "violence" (*ḥamas*).[19] Very few words carry a stronger connotation than this, which appears almost seventy times in the Tanakh. It can refer to both moral and physical wrongdoing. Ḥamas caused the world's destruction in the flood: "The earth also was corrupt before God, and the earth was filled with violence (*ḥamas*).... And God said unto Noah, The end of all flesh is come before Me, for the earth is filled with violence (*ḥamas*) through them; and, behold, I will destroy them with the earth"(Gen. 6:11, 13). Psalms declares, "the Lord examines righteous and wicked. He despises the lover of violence (*ḥamas*)" (11:5), describes evil-doers as "for false witnesses have risen against me, breathing *ḥamas*" (27:12), and encourages the Jewish people to look to their covenant, "Look to the covenant – for the land's dark crevasses are haunted with violence (*ḥamas*)" (74:20). Isaiah's vision of a peaceful future declares, "Violence (*ḥamas*) shall no more be heard in Your land, wasting nor destruction within Your borders; but thou shalt call Your walls salvation and Your gates praise" (Is. 60:18). In short, Edom is accused of the worst crime imaginable – compounded and especially despicable since it was against Edom's "brother, Jacob."

---

19. Joel 4:19 also uses the word *ḥamas* when he describes the eventual destruction of Edom: "Egypt will become a wasteland, and Edom will become a desolate wilderness, because of the violence (*ḥamas*) done to the sons of Judah, in whose land they have shed innocent blood."

Obadiah then begins to outline his specific accusations against Edom in verse 11, describing the looting of Jerusalem. The order in which the events occurred appears to be convoluted, yet makes good sense if the two pairs of lines of v. 11 represent an earlier and a later event, as follows (ACBD):[20] Edom (A) "stood aside," (C) "foreigners entered," (B) took the wealth, and then (D) "cast lots."[21] On the one hand, Obadiah is cautious in his phrasing. He does not explicitly associate the Edomites with those who "took captive his wealth," but instead attributes this action to "foreigners." Nevertheless, by standing aside, Edom took the part of a hostile observer rather than a brother and ally. Indeed, the phrase *amadekha mineged* – "standing aside" may also be translated as "standing against." The term "carried off" refers typically to taking people captive, so "wealth" (*hayil*) may include people as well as portable treasures, and allude to the capture and exile of some of Jerusalem's citizens (cf. II Kings 24:13–16). Afterward, we discover Edom casting lots with the invaders. The act of casting lots refers to some form of bargaining over the victor's spoils after ransacking a city (cf. Joel 4:3). Though ostensibly a passive observer, Edom's loyalties and betrayal were clear. After the structured parallelisms describing the actions of the enemies, Obadiah breaks the pattern and emphatically declares, "you too were like one of them."

Edom's treachery against Judah is now outlined in eight successive statements until the crescendo of Edom's guilt becomes too loud to bear. In the Hebrew they are phrased as commands for the future, though the actions had already occurred (a technique by which Obadiah conveys a moral message while describing history). Jensen notes, "The extraordinary degree of repetition helps to increase exponentially the reader's horror... [while] the inexorable progression increases the feeling of horrible inevitability."[22] There is also a clear progression in the guilt of Edom's actions. It begins with mere thoughts and words (v. 12).

---

20. P. R. Raabe, *Obadiah: A New Translation with Introduction and Commentary* (New Haven, CT: Yale University Press, 1996), 172.

21. Jensen, *Obadiah, Jonah, Micah*, 20.

22. Ibid. See also D. Baker, *Joel, Obadiah, Malachi* (Grand Rapids, MI: Zondervan, 2006), 181: "The author may use this form to express the immediacy of the horror to him, placing himself back directly into the time of the action and calling out, 'STOP!'"

However, Edom soon joins to assist Judah's enemies in their actions as Jerusalem is ravaged (v. 13). The climax is when they take aggressive and hostile actions on their own (v. 14).

Verse 12 begins, "Do not look on," which implies passivity when action was required (to defend Jerusalem and come to the aid of their brothers). Instead, Edom displayed its scorn for the Jewish people through their unrestrained joy at their suffering. There is a clever word-play here – Obadiah the prophet aligns the destruction (*nokhro*) that befell Judah with the foreigners (*nokhrim*). The word for calamity (*nokhro*) is rare, only here and in Job ("Isn't *calamity* reserved for the wicked, disaster for those who do evil?", 31:3).[23]

In verse 13, Edom follows the lead of the foreigners who had "entered the gate of my people" first. The Edomites peruse over the city's loot, deciding what they take for themselves. Obadiah returns to the theme he is developing that Edom has denied his brotherhood with Israel by saying, "you should not have joined." After using three different words to describe the disaster in verse 12, here Obadiah repeats the same phrase three times, "day of their ruin" – *eidam*. Again, this is clever wordplay, as the sound alludes to the enemy's name – Edom.

Finally, verse 14 describes how Edom actively harmed the fleeing Jews. As fugitives left the city, the Edomites met them at some fork in the road. Instead of proffering assistance and helping them escape, the Edomites either murdered them, handed them over to the invaders, or imprisoned them themselves, later exploiting them or selling them into slavery. The description in II Kings of the hapless King Zedekiah fleeing along passageways to Jericho, only to be intercepted at the crossroads (II Kings 25:4–5; Jer. 39:4–5) illustrates the kind of situation Obadiah portrays. Amos heavily castigates Edom (along with other nations) for taking part in slave trading (Amos 1:6, 9).

---

23. Forbes, "Intertextual Impact," 29. The commentators debate the exact translation of the word *nokhro*. We have translated it as destruction according to the Targum (also Mahari Kera). Radak and *Metzudat Tziyon* both translate it as estrangement. Rashi interprets it as deliverance: "On the day of his being delivered into the hands of the heathens. And so does Scripture state concerning Saul: 'He has delivered (*nikar*) him into my hand' (I Sam. 23:7)."

All the crimes listed by Obadiah here gain additional poignancy due to the violation of the fraternal relationship between Edom and Israel/Judah. However, they remain moral crimes and failings no matter who the participants involved are. It is this breach of universal morality that leads to Obadiah's startling conclusion in his words to Edom:

> For the day of the Lord over all the nations is close; as you have done shall be done to you; your recompense shall be returned upon your head. (v. 15)

Because of the "day" that Edom and the nations brought upon the Jewish people, God would have a "day" against Edom and the nations. Edom and "all the nations" are interchangeable – indeed, Edom is addressed once again in the second person singular in the second half of verse 15. In his work on biblical poetry, Robert Alter suggests that the prophet's movement "from the particular to the universal is a natural consequence of the progressive and intensifying character of prophetic poetry."[24] The previous description of Edom was a close-up, a snapshot. Now, Obadiah reveals a panoramic view: *yom Hashem* – "the day of the Lord," when the wicked will be punished, and Israel redeemed.[25]

Obadiah concludes with the simple statement that "As you have done, it shall be done to you," *lex talionis* or *midda keneged midda*. This principle is reflected through Obadiah's double usage of the same verb, first in the active form and then in the passive form (*asita – ye'aseh*). "This constitutes the core of Obadiah's prophecy, providing a theological framework for the preceding verses: the localized disasters befalling Edom and Jerusalem are not merely isolated incidents in a remote and insignificant theater of war, for they mark the footsteps of the

---

24. R. Alter, *The Art of Biblical Poetry* (New York: Basic Books, 1985), 146–62, cited in Jensen, *Obadiah, Jonah, Micah*, 22.
25. Cf. Is. 13:6–13; Amos 5:18–20; Joel 1:15, 3:14; Zeph. 1:7.

Lord himself, as he approaches to set up a 'kingdom that will never be destroyed' (Dan 2:44)."[26]

Malbim notes that Obadiah appears to use repetitious wording in describing the future retribution on the Edomites (and the nations). Nevertheless, he deduces from here an important principle regarding the nature of divine punishment. While precisely proportionate to the gravity of the crimes committed, divine punishment contains two aspects – as a recompense for the evil deeds themselves (*as you have done shall be done to you*); and also for the intensity and emotion with which the wrongdoer performed his evil deeds (*your recompense shall be returned upon your head*).

PUNISHMENT AND REDEMPTION (OBADIAH 16–21)

> What you drank on My holy mountain, all the nations will always drink. They will drink and they will swallow, and they will be as if they never were. There will be a remnant on Mount Zion, and it will be holy, and the House of Jacob will possess their inheritance. The House of Jacob will be fire, the House of Yosef, flame; the House of Esau, straw. They will blaze among them and consume them, and there will be no survivors of the House of Esau, for the Lord has spoken. They will take possession of the Negev, along with the mountains of Esau, and the Shefela, from the Philistines. And they will take possession of the land of Ephraim and the land of Shomron; and Benjamin, along with the Gilad – they, the exiled force of the children of Israel who are among the Canaanites as far as Tzarfat and the exiled of Jerusalem who are in Sepharad will take possession of the cities of the Negev. And saviors shall go up to Mount Zion to judge the mountains of Esau, and dominion shall be the Lord's. (vv. 16–21)

Obadiah shifts dramatically from castigating Edom to speaking about the Jewish people. The section is linked to the previous verse through the repetition of the opening word "for" – *ki*. The remainder of the speech is a thematic chiasm:

---

26. Armerding, "Obadiah," 353.

v. 16 and first part of v. 17: Mount Zion's fate and salvation
> second part of v. 17: the Jewish people will repossess their lands
>> v. 18: the victory of the house of Jacob over the house of Esau
> vv. 19–20: the Jewish people will repossess their lands
v. 21: Mount Zion will judge and rule over Mount Esau

Most of Obadiah's speech remains focused upon Edom. Still, as noted above, he directs his words at all the nations that took advantage of the Jewish people (Philistines, Canaanites, et al.) in their period of weakness. Moreover, he emphasizes that the issues here are more than mere national squabbles – they concern fundamental matters of morality that bind all humanity together.

Who is the subject of "what you drank on My holy mount"? Many commentators assume that it is Edom (Targum, Rashi, Radak). The drinking that Obadiah describes is feasting and reveling after the conquering and destruction of Jerusalem.[27] This approach continues the *lex talionis* theme from above: They drank to celebrate, but now they would drink from a different cup, one that would lead to their destruction and disappearance (the Targum calls it "the cup of punishment").

However, this description does not align with Obadiah's previous description; Edom was not inside the city with the invaders but was waiting outside the walls. Therefore, we prefer the second approach (found in Ibn Ezra, Alsheikh, *Metzudat David*, Abrabanel, and Malbim), that it was Judah who was forced to sip from the cup of divine wrath. Forced drinking is a common metaphor in the Tanakh. Drinking from the cup

---

27. An original approach is suggested by Marvin Sweeney. He interprets Edom as the drinkers, but not as celebrating the destruction or defeat of Jerusalem, but the opposite. As drinking wine together was a common manner through which treaties and alliances were sealed in the ancient world (quoting "The Vassal Treaties of Esarhaddon," J. B. Pritchard, ed., *Ancient Near Eastern Texts* [Princeton, NJ: Princeton University Press, 1969], 536–41, which lists "drinking from the cup" as one of the signs of a treaty's ratification), Sweeney argues that what is described here is the sealing of the pact between Judah and Edom, which Edom would later break (Sweeney, *The Twelve Prophets*, 294).

of divine wrath leads to effects best described as drunken-like - confusion, helplessness, and disgrace (Is. 51:17–22; Jer. 25:15–29).[28]

Obadiah now contrasts the fate of the nations (v. 16) to the fate of God's mountain and His people.[29] Again, Obadiah engages in word-play to convey a moral message. Edom (of whom there will be no survivors) stood at the crossroads to prevent the Jewish survivors (*pelitim*) from escaping (v. 14), yet there will be a remnant (*peleita*) at God's holy mountain. Unlike the nations that perished, there will always be a remnant of the Jewish people who will survive and return to Israel to dwell securely on Mount Zion (Radak).

Not only this, but the mountain will be holy. While many commentators understand this in a very technical sense (no one impure or uncircumcised will be allowed on it – Abrabanel), we prefer here to adopt the approach of Radak again: It is the Jewish people themselves who will become sanctified. They will reacquire the lands that they lost or their lost wealth (Rashi).

Obadiah then describes how the reunited Jewish people will strike the final blow against Edom. United for the first time since Solomon's reign, the houses of Jacob (Judah) and Joseph (Israel) act together.[30] It will be sudden and quick, as quickly as fire consumes straw (fire is often a tool of divine judgment in Tanakh) (cf. Deut. 28:24; 32:22).

If we suppose that Obadiah spoke this prophecy after the Assyrian exile of the Northern Kingdom in 722–721 BCE, his inclusion of Joseph (the Northern Kingdom) promises that the ten tribes would ultimately return from exile and play a crucial role in bringing about salvation (Malbim). Understanding the word Joseph here as limited to the tribe of Joseph, rabbinic tradition teaches that the descendants

---

28. For occurrences of the phrase "they would drink the cup of His wrath," see Is. 51:17–23; Jer. 25:17–26, 28–29; 49:12–13; Hab. 2:15–16; Ps. 60:3; 75:8.

29. Ibn Ezra comments that all the nations will be as if they had never existed, and none will escape, but on Har Zion there will be [Jews] who escaped. He cites Yefet who said that this prophecy will take place in the time of the Messiah; however, he also quotes Rabbi Moshe who said that it would take place during the times of Hezekiah, and Rabbi Yeshua who placed it in the time of the Second Temple.

30. For Joseph symbolizing the north, see Zech. 10:6; Ps. 77:15; cf. Is. 8:14; 46:3, as well as Radak on Amos 5:15.

of Esau will ultimately only succumb to the hands of a descendant of Joseph (Bava Batra 123b).

Obadiah closes this subsection with the formula *"for the Lord has spoken,"* emphasizing the certainty of the fulfillment of his vision.

Obadiah concludes in triumph – from the Negev desert, bounded by the Edomite mountain range in the south, to the Philistine plains on the western coast, to the captured Samaria in the north, and across the Jordan river to the Gilead heights in the east, the Jewish people will recover their land. Even those exiled into the farthest reaches will return home! Obadiah describes the reconquest geographically in a clockwise motion. First, he turns to the south (Edom) and then to the west against the Philistines, reclaiming the lowlands and the coast. Afterward, he turns to the north and the east – though who precisely will possess these areas is not clear. Finally, he specifies Benjamin, either as a metonym for all the northern tribes or as a description of how the land of Israel will expand in the future. Rashi suggests: And the children of Manasseh, whose territory was the land of Gilead, shall spread beyond the borders of the Land of Israel in the east.

This concluding subsection also has a framing phrase: "the mountain of Esau" (vv. 19, 21), setting up the contrast with the Lord's holy mountain, Mount Zion (vv. 16–17, 21).

The future redemption is not limited to the recovery of land. Obadiah predicts that Jews living in the most distant parts of the world will return. Zarephath, where Elijah receives assistance from a widow after the water in the valley of Kerit dried up (I Kings 17:9), is on the northern border of historical Israel, between Tyre and Sidon.[31] Scholars dispute the location of Sepharad, with suggestions locating it near Benghazi (ancient Berenice) in North Africa; Saparda in Southwest

---

31. Against Rashi, who states that "the exegetes claim that *Zarephat* is the kingdom called France in French," Radak brings a tradition that the people of modern-day Germany are the original Canaanites, who fled after the invasion of the land of Israel by Joshua and had to migrate northwards until they settled in the area of Germany [and France]. Therefore, contends Radak, when the Jews were dispersed across Europe after the Roman invasion and exile (70 CE), they found their way to those lands that had already been inhabited by descendants of the Canaanites. This theory, however, is vigorously refuted by Abrabanel.

Media, known from various Persian cuneiform inscriptions; and Sardis, the capital of Lydia in Asia Minor.[32]

Obadiah ends his prophecy with a fitting climax. As in the period of the judges, "saviors," will arise as officials of justice when exile ends, and will judge Mount Esau. Rashi calls them the "princes of Israel," Radak sees an allusion to Micah 5:4, who promises that seven shepherds and eight princes will stand to fight for Israel. *Metzudat David* concludes: "These are the Messiah and his officials."

But whom are they judging? Though Ibn Ezra suggests that a remnant of Edom would still remain, cowering in the mountain's crevices, verse 18 had already described how Edom was consumed. Therefore, Abrabanel suggests that the remaining nations would use the mountain of Edom as a gathering place to plan their final assault on the Jewish people, but to no avail.

Obadiah concludes with the simple statement: "the kingship will belong to the Lord." The *lamed* preposition connotes possession or ownership. As such, God owns kingship, namely, the right to rule. Obadiah's final statement describes the ideal future and summarizes everything that occurred in Obadiah's vision of two mountains. By judging the nations who performed evil, and by redeeming His people and bringing them back to their land, Israel, God proves His dominion over the entire earth.[33] As stated by Jensen: "The theological value of this little book lies in seeing the whole as an exposition of its last line."[34]

---

32. Here, the Targum's identification of *Sepharad* with modern day Spain (as quoted by Rashi) is unlikely, although it is shared by some modern scholars; see J. Gray, "The Diaspora of Israel and Judah in Obadiah 20," *Zeitschrift für die alttestamentliche Wissenschaft* 65 (1953): 53–59; David Neiman, "Sefarad: The Name of Spain," *Journal of Near Eastern Studies* 22:2 (1963): 128–32. The popular identification today is that it is the Persian city Sardis (e.g., E. Lipinski, "Obadiah 20," *Vetus Testamentum* 23 [1973]: 368–70). See also *Daat Mikra*.

33. Rashi comments that "this teaches you that His kingdom will not be complete until He exacts retribution from Amalek [Esau's grandson]" – an allusion to the first appearance of Amalek where God's name is written incomplete (as it were). The Midrash is more expansive: "'God reigns; may the land rejoice' (Ps. 97:1): This teaches you that there is no joy in the world as long as the monarchy of Edom endures, then the [divine] name is incomplete, and the [divine] throne is incomplete, as it is written (Ex. 17:17), 'For the hand is upon the throne of God'" (*Midrash Tehillim* 97:1). With only God ruling over the world (Radak), all mankind will ultimately accept His sovereignty (Abrabanel).

34. Jensen, *Obadiah, Jonah, Micah*, 27.

Final Thoughts on Obadiah

As noted, Obadiah is a prophecy against Edom, but not just Edom. Obadiah espouses the principles that reflect natural, universal justice; Edom's fate will ultimately become the fate of all the nations that stood against Jerusalem. However, the singling out of Edom is crucial. What began as the closest relationship between equals devolved into centuries of mistrust and hatred. Rabbinic thought has succinctly encapsulated the tricky relationship between the Jewish people and Edom in the well-known midrash, brought above, that attempts to explain a scribal anomaly in Genesis, describing the reunion of Esau and Jacob after decades of separation:

> "And Esau ran toward him [Jacob] and embraced him, and he fell on his neck, and he kissed him, and they wept" (Gen. 33:4). "And he kissed him" is dotted [in the Torah text, there is a dot over each letter] because he did not kiss him with all of his heart. So R. Shimon bar Yoḥai said: It is a known principle of law (*halakha*) that Esau hates Jacob, but at that moment, his mercy was overturned, and he kissed him with all of his heart.

For many, Esau's attitude reflects the attitude of other nations to the Jewish people in general. As Rabbi Moshe Lichtenstein has noted, rabbinic thought identified Edom with the Roman Empire. However, this identification was one-directional:

> Pagan Rome never had any pretensions about a special relationship with Israel, but rather it viewed Israel as a nation like all others. Augustus or Julius Ceasar and their heirs had no pretensions of coming in place of Israel, and their attitude towards us was not one of competition or rejoicing over our misfortune. Their attitude was characterized by great pride and a sense of unstoppable power.

However, history intervened, and suddenly a new entity appeared, which seemed to fit the criterion of Edom perfectly:

> However, the ascendancy of Christian Rome replaced this model with an entirely different one. Christianity claims to have replaced Israel and finds itself in constant competition with it. Its attitude toward us is one of happiness over our misfortune and the pretension of having replaced us as the chosen people who received special blessings. Our problem with Christianity is not the pride in and of itself, but the competition, its historical ascendancy being viewed as our replacement. Christianity is Edom, who claims to have inherited Israel's role and no longer recognizes Israel as the chosen people. This is Esau at the beginning of our *parashah*, and as may be understood from the prophets, this model was also viewed as a threat for future generations.[1]

For many, two millennia of exile consisted of nothing but animosity and misery, mainly in Christian Europe. To them, Obadiah's vision of a future in which the Edoms of the world will be decimated, Mount Seir destroyed, and Mount Zion raised, was a source of comfort and hope.

---

1. Rabbi Mosheh Lichtenstein, "Esav As Brother, Esav As Other," available online at https://www.etzion.org.il/en/tanakh/torah/sefer-bereishit/parashat-vayishlach/esav-brother-esav-other.

We can understand Obadiah differently, however. The Midrash above stated that "it is a known principle of law (*halakha*) that Esau hates Jacob," yet no law asserts that Jacob hates Esau. Animosity is not inevitable. Below the surface of Obadiah's vision, the rabbis saw that even Edom was worthy of respect and dignity:

> Although the prophecy here declares, "There shall be no remnant of the house of Esau" (v.18), R. [Yehuda Hanasi] interprets this as follows: "(This applies to) those who act like Esau." This teaching, which R. [Yehuda Hanasi] uttered in the presence of Antoninus, implies that an Edomite may still be redeemed from the fate of Esau. If he abandons the tradition of evil, then he no longer belongs to Esau's descendants. The close relations between Rebbe and Antoninus prove that not only is the hostility between Israel and Edom not a necessity – they are even able to recapture their brotherly relationship...This possibility is hinted at in God's words to Rebecca: "And God said to her, Two nations are in your womb." R. Yehuda commented on this, in the name of Rav: Do not read "nations" (*goyim*) but rather "lords" (*gayim*) – referring to Antoninus and R. [Yehuda Hanasi]. (Avoda Zara 10b–11a)[2]

---

2. Rabbi Yehuda Shaviv, "'And I Shall Walk Against You' (Sefer Ovadia)," available online at https://etzion.org.il/en/tanakh/torah/sefer-bereishit/parashat-vayishlach/vayishlach-and-i-shall-walk-against-you-sefer.

Micah

Introduction

[Jeremiah, speaking in the Temple]: This is what the Lord said: If you do not listen to Me to follow the teaching that I have placed before you, to obey the words of My servants the prophets, whom I have sent to you early and repeatedly – though you did not obey – I will make this House like Shilo, and this city I will turn into a curse for all the nations of the earth. (Jer. 26:4–6)

Some men from among the elders of the land stood up and said to all the assembled people, "Micah the Morashtite would prophesy in the days of Hezekiah, king of Judah. He addressed all the people of Judah, saying, 'This is what the Lord of Hosts said: Zion will be plowed over like a field, Jerusalem will come to be a mound of ruins, and the Temple Mount an overgrown hilltop shrine.' Did Hezekiah, king of Judah, and all of Judah put him to death? Did he not fear the Lord and beseech the Lord, so that the Lord reconsidered the evil that He had spoken concerning them? We would be bringing great evil upon ourselves." (Jer. 26:17–19)

While the Bible lauds very few prophets for their persuasive talents, Micah is a notable exception. Jeremiah 26 describes a clash between the prophet Jeremiah and the angry populace. They could not tolerate his prophecies of destruction; the mob demanded that he be put to death. They almost lynched him; instead, he was put on trial for blasphemy. During the proceedings, the elders reminded the people that Micah also uttered what could have been considered as sacrilegious words a century earlier, during Hezekiah's reign. He was the first prophet who dared to speak what had not yet been said: Should the people not mend their ways, God would not hesitate to destroy Jerusalem and the Temple. However, Micah not only avoided death, but he also managed to persuade the populace to change, averting disaster and saving Jerusalem from ruin.

When the moment of truth came, it was not the well-connected and politically savvy Isaiah, but the straight-speaking commoner from the coastlands whose message influenced the masses. Micah's voice became one that celebrates peace ("And they shall beat their swords into plowshares... nations shall not lift the sword against nation; neither shall they learn war anymore," 4:3), advocates for social justice, and insists that all God requires is to "do justice, to love loving-kindness, and to walk humbly with your God" (6:8). Nevertheless, because much of Micah's message appears to be similar to other prophets (especially Isaiah, with whom Micah shares at least fifteen passages with similar wording), many fail to recognize the unique message he conveyed and why he was singularly successful.

MICAH THE PERSON

The name Micah is a shortened form of Michaya, which means: "Who is like the Lord?" (Similar to the name Michael – "Who is like God"?) Many other biblical characters share this name[1] – one of whom, Michaya ben Imla, served as a prophet in the Northern Kingdom a century earlier during Ahab's reign in 874–853 BCE (I Kings 22:8–28; II Chr. 18:3–27).[2] The full name, Michaya, appears in the written form in the story of Jeremiah referenced above.[3] Significantly, Micah's question at the end of

---

1. Cf. Judges 17–18; I Kings 22:8; Neh. 10:11; I Chr. 5:5; 9:15; 23:20; II Chr. 34:20.
2. Micah shares more than a name with his earlier counterpart, but also common themes and wordings. See commentary for examples.
3. This is an example of the *qere/ketiv* phenomenon in the Tanakh. The written form in Jeremiah is Michaya; however, it is pronounced Micha. For brief summaries about the phenomenon, see M. Breuer, "Ketiv and Qere," in M. Bar-Asher, ed., *Hebrew*

the book, "Who is a God like you?", serves to reiterate this message of the uniqueness of the Lord reflected in his name.

Micah's hometown was Moreisha in Judah (1:1), located about 25 miles southwest of Jerusalem, generally identified as Tel el-Judeideh, 7 miles northeast of Lakhish. As his hometown was close to the Philistine town of Gath, Micah also calls it Moresheth-Gath (1:14). This region borders the low-lying coastlands and the foothills to the east of Jerusalem. The region occupies a critical military area, located on the vital passageway through which armies on the coast would have had to pass to reach Jerusalem. During his reign, Rehoboam built five fortified cities within a radius of ten kilometers of Moreisha, including Moreisha itself (II Chr. 11:5–12). That Micah comes from one of the outlying garrison towns is significant, and he returns to this theme repeatedly in his prophecy. He laments four of these towns in his first prophecy against Judah in 1:8–16 (Adullam, Gath, Mareshah [Moreisha], and Lakhish). Much of his message represents the voice of the countryside against the military policies of the capital of Jerusalem. The identification of Micah as coming from his home village[4] serves more than to fulfill our geographical curiosity or to explain his constant reliance on agricultural and natural metaphors.[5] Directing his words against the capital cities

Through the Ages: In Memory of Shoshanna Bahat (Jerusalem, 1997), 7–13 (Heb.); Y. Ofer, "Ketiv and Qere: The Phenomenon, Its Notation, and Its Reflection in Early Rabbinic Literature," *Leshonenu* 70 (2008): 55–73; Id. 71 (2009): 255–279 (Heb.); and A. Bazak, "*Nusach Ha-mikra* – Accuracy of the Biblical Text, part 4," available online at https://www.etzion.org.il/en/tanakh/studies-tanakh/core-studies-tanakh/nusach-ha-mikra-%E2%80%93-accuracy-biblical-text-4.

4. Usually, the Tanakh identifies a person by giving his father's name (Is. 1:1; Hos. 1:1). It is important to note, however, that some ancient translations translate Morashti as his family or clan name (Waltke, *Micah*, 35).

5. In the short seven chapters of his book, Micah uses agricultural and natural imagery of: the place for planting a vineyard as an open hilltop (1:6), the sounds of jackals and ostriches (1:8), the baldness of eagles (1:16), fields and houses (2:2–4), the plowing of fields (3:12), the hammering of swords into plowshares and spears into pruning hooks (4:3), vines and fig trees (4:4), the gathering of sheaves to the threshing floor (4:12), oxen threshing (4:13), a shepherd as deliverer/provider (5:4–6; 7:14), dew and rain on plants (5:7), sowing and reaping (6:15), treading olives and grapes (6:15), picking fruit (7:1), briars as hedges (7:4), and the moving of field boundary markers (7:11).

of Samaria and Jerusalem, the sense that Micah speaks from an outsider's perspective is glaringly apparent.[6] He references the existing social chasm between the wealthy, urban landowners, and the rural farming poor. Both his metaphors of destruction and redemption allude to the removal of city imagery and the return of the land to its agricultural roots ("And I will make Samaria into a heap in the field, into a place for planting vineyards; and I will cast its stones down into the valley, and its foundations I will uncover." [1:6]). A man of the country, he likely knew firsthand how the constant military buildups and conflicts affected the rural population in the coastlands and foothills. They bore the brunt of the invasions. The second half of his first chapter mourns the destruction that awaited these communities. To them, rearmament policies would likely have both entailed placing even higher taxes on their produce to finance the military buildup, and the conscription of young men who should have been working the fields.

WHEN DID MICAH PROPHESY?

The opening verse of the book of Micah places the prophet in the reign of Jotham, Ahaz, and Hezekiah, spanning the second half of the eighth century BCE. During this time, Judah fell dazzlingly quickly from the heights of political power and prosperity to the depths of poverty and powerlessness. Only the fortified city of Jerusalem survived among hilltops charred with burnt remains where villages and towns once stood. Micah likely witnessed the three major traumatic events that afflicted Judah during the closing decades of the eighth century BCE: first, the Syro-Ephraimite war in 734–732 BCE, which saw the two kingdoms to the north pillage the country and reach the gates of Jerusalem, and allowed the Edomites and Philistines to encroach upon a weakened

---

6. "While Isaiah chiefly satirizes [sic] the fashions of the town and the intrigues of the court, Micah scourges the avarice of the landowner and the injustice which oppresses the peasant…. Social wrongs are always felt most acutely, not in the town, but in the country…. Political discontent and religious heresy take their start among industrial and manufacturing centers, but the first springs of the social revolt are nearly always found among rural populations" (George Adam Smith, *The Book of the Twelve Prophets Commonly Called the Minor*, vol. 1 [London: Hodder and Stoughton, 1903], 386–87).

Judah; second, the fall of the Northern Kingdom to Assyria in 722–721 BCE, with the resulting displacement of many refugees to the south, which likely taxed Judah's resources to their limit. Hezekiah then had to pay Assyrian exactions of tribute to prevent further invasions, and the tax burdens probably fell on those who could least afford it. The third event occurred when Hezekiah chose to take advantage of Sargon's sudden death in 705 BCE to stop paying tribute, essentially declaring war on the Assyrian empire. Sennacherib and his forces arrived within a few short years, unleashing a deadly invasion of Judah that left dozens of cities ruined and tens of thousands sent to exile. Unfortunately, Micah does not date his prophecies to specific events. As such, we shall attempt to avoid speculative dating and instead try to present the general social and political background of each speech.

However, one consequence of determining the years in which Micah prophesied needs addressing: the relationship between Micah and Isaiah. There is a tendency to suggest that the two were not only contemporaries but colleagues. They both prophesied in Judah simultaneously, and they appear to share similar concerns and language. Because Isaiah began his prophetic career earlier than Micah (Isaiah began with Uzziah, while Micah started with his son and successor, Jotham), some even have suggested that Isaiah was Micah's teacher.[7] However, no evidence exists for this claim, which we categorically reject.

7. I have heard the teacher-student claim from Rabbi Yoel Bin-Nun orally several times. One can suggest that this claim is implied in Maimonides's Introduction to the Oral Law: "And Isaiah received from Amos and his court, and Micah received from Isaiah and his court" (translated by Ralph Lerner in *Maimonides' Empire of Light* [Chicago: University of Chicago Press, 2000], 134). However, what Maimonides is describing is the transfer of legal authority, which may entail, but does not necessarily mean, a teacher-student relationship.

We shall address similar visions and wordings when relevant. A full list of parallels (almost two dozen) between Micah's prophecies and Isaiah's (with varying degrees of verbal similarity) can be found in Richard L. Schultz, *The Search for Quotation: Verbal Parallels in the Prophets* (London: A&C Black, 1999), 307; Rick W. Byargeon, "The Relationship of Micah 4:1–3 and Isaiah 2:2–4: Implications for How We Understand the Prophetic Message," *Southwestern Journal of Theology* 46:1 (2006): 62–66; and Stansell Gary, *Micah and Isaiah: A Form and Tradition Historical Comparison* (Atlanta, GA: Scholars Press, 1988).

On the contrary, we shall demonstrate that Micah describes a future vision diametrically opposed to Isaiah's in several places. We shall tackle several of the literary parallels and differences in the commentary, but here we must address the fundamental difference between their two viewpoints. As harsh as Isaiah's visions could be, he could never envision the destruction of Jerusalem.[8] Even in his darkest prophecies, with the Judean countryside scarred and burnt, Isaiah foresaw Jerusalem surviving:

> Your land is laid waste; your cities burnt with fire. Your land – in your presence, strangers devour it, and it is desolate as that turned over to strangers. And the daughter of Zion [Jerusalem] shall be left like a hut in a vineyard, like a lodge in a cucumber field, like a city besieged. (Is. 1:8–9)

In contrast, Micah declared:

> And so because of you
> Zion will be plowed over like a field;
> Jerusalem will come to be a mound of ruins
> and the Temple Mount like the high places of a forest. (3:12)

MICAH'S BOLD MESSAGE

Micah's message appears to be very similar to his prophetic counterparts – Isaiah, Hosea, and Amos. He attacks idolatry, whether actual idolatry or as a metaphor for the political alliances. However, his focus is social injustice (2:1, 8–9; 3:11; 6:11). Commentators and scholars often call Micah "the prophet of the poor," or possibly, the prophet of the oppressed middle class.[9] However, his approach differs from his contemporaries. Although he also focuses on poverty and oppression, unlike in the books

---

8. We will discuss the full talmudic text of Shabbat 139a in our commentary on 3:9. However, it is instructive to note here that the talmudic rabbis contrasted Micah's prophecy as the source of punishment with the parallel verses from Isaiah as the source of redemption.

9. Bruce K. Waltke, "Micah," in *The Minor Prophets*, 594.

of Amos and Isaiah, the biblical words for poor people (*ani* and *evyon*) do not appear once in the book of Micah. Unlike the other two, his focus on social inequalities and injustice does not stem from a violated sense of compassion. Instead, Micah frames the issues in much starker terms – the injustices he describes are nothing less than fundamental violations of the covenant (*berit*) between God and the Jewish people.[10]

To him, the injured are invariably referred to as "my people" – a beautiful ambiguous wordplay, as it can mean that Micah identifies the Jewish people as his own, or if he is speaking in God's name, as "My people"! By framing the issue, Micah's underlying claim is that those people performing the injury are not part of (or have removed themselves from) the Jewish people. Micah attacks every segment of Judah's leadership – an act of bravery, if not folly, in ancient times. His conduct contrasts with Isaiah's behavior, who freely enters the royal palace, frequently interacting with Judah's leadership and often serving as royal advisor.[11] To attack the leadership so openly, Micah had to demonstrate pure fearlessness. He declares about himself, "But I, I am filled with the strength of the Lord's spirit of justice and courage to declare to Jacob his transgressions, to Israel his sins" (3:8). His wrath spared no sector of Judah's leadership – "Israel's leaders pronounce judgment for a bribe, her priests instruct for a price, and her prophets divine for money" (3:11). Micah identifies three types of leaders as corrupt: civil leadership (the princes), religious leadership (the priests), and moral leadership (the prophets). Judges judged, priests taught, and prophets gave prophecy, but it was all based on who paid them best, and they would tailor their messages accordingly.

---

10. Manfred P. Hedley's paper develops this idea thoroughly by comparing Micah with the "covenant section" of the book of Exodus. "Undoing Justice: Comparing Micah's Complaint with the Covenant Code in Exodus 21–23" (presented at the Society of Biblical Literature's International Meeting, Humboldt University, Berlin 2017), available online at https://www.academia.edu/34232066/Undoing_Justice_Comparing_Micahs_Complaint_with_the_Covenant_Code_in_Exodus_21–23.
11. This does not imply that Judah's kings were spared from criticism, and not only the evil kings like Ahaz, but even a king widely considered righteous like Hezekiah. What is clear, however, is that the rabbinic tradition that suggests that Isaiah ultimately became Hezekiah's father-in-law (Berakhot 10a) would never have been envisioned with Micah in Isaiah's stead.

Having framed his message not in terms of compassion but of the covenant, it is not surprising that Micah is the first prophet to dare predict the downfall and destruction of Jerusalem. Having denounced all aspects of the people's leadership, the climax of his message, that Jerusalem needs to be razed to the ground in order to be rebuilt, is its only logical conclusion. However, Micah continues with the hopeful message that Jerusalem will eventually be rebuilt and serve its ideal purpose – to be a guiding light for the nations.

Micah develops a new concept in prophetic eschatology: A remnant (*she'eirit*) of the Jewish people will always survive destruction. Wessels notes how the idea of the remnant thematically appears "in four strategic places in the book: 1:2–2:13; 3:1–4:8; 4:9–5:14 and 6:1–7:20. Each of these sections consists of a negative part followed by a positive section, which contains the idea of a remnant (cf. 2:12–13; 4:1–8; 5:1–14; 7:7–20)."[12] McComiskey writes:

> Micah's doctrine of the remnant is unique among the Prophets and is perhaps his most significant contribution to the prophetic theology of hope. The remnant is a force in the world, not simply a residue of people, as the word "remnant" (*she'eirit*) may seem to imply. It is a force that will ultimately conquer the world.[13]

STYLE AND STRUCTURE

Despite the relatively small size of Micah's seven chapters, the power of his poetry is undeniable.[14] Micah uses language like few other prophets,

12. W. Wessels, "YHWH, the God of new beginnings: Micah's testimony," *HTS Teologiese Studies / Theological Studies* 69:1, 2013, art. no. 1960, https://hts.org.za/index.php/hts/article/view/1960.
13. Thomas Edward McComiskey, "Micah," in *The Expositor's Bible Commentary*, vol. 7, ed. Frank E. Gaebelein and Richard P. Polcyn (Grand Rapids, MI: Zondervan, 1985), 399.
14. "Vividness and emphasis, lightning flashes of indignation at social wrongs, rapid transitions from threatening to mercy, vehement emotion and sympathetic tenderness, rhetorical force, cadence and rhythm at times elevated and sublime – these are among the prophet's outstanding literary characteristics. Micah wrote excellent Hebrew" (George L. Robinson, *The Twelve Minor Prophets* [Grand Rapids: Baker Book House, 1974], 104).

with many well-crafted sayings that reflect technique and craftsmanship.[15] He confidently moves between the usage of parallelism (possibly the defining characteristic of biblical Hebrew poetry), puns and wordplays, alliterations, and he cleverly utilizes ambiguous language for devastating rhetorical effect.

The structure of the book of Micah has been the topic of much discussion. Our approach is that the book is an anthology of speeches, with the following assumptions. First, Micah did not deliver these prophecies at once. Accordingly, this commentary identifies six addresses.[16] Second, we do not view the speeches as following a chronological order but attempt to identify thematic patterns instead. Finally, many suggest that the book is structured (though unevenly) on alternating messages of threats and hope.[17] However, we reject this understanding due to its

---

15. With Micah's poetic prowess comes a modern reader's difficulty in deciphering difficult verses, as we are unfamiliar with the intended literary rules Micah is using. Writing in their *Anchor Bible Commentary* about one verse (but one that could apply to several in the book), Andersen and Friedman state:

> The general content…is clear. When it comes to specific details, the passage is as obscure as any in the Hebrew Bible…the text is incoherent to the point of unintelligibility. Yet all the individual words are familiar…on the level of composition…the meaning eludes us. (Quoted in Norman Poderhatz, *The Prophets: Who They Were, What They Are* [Simon and Schuster, 2002], 158)

16. As is often his wont, David Dorsey claims to reveal a chiastic structure that girds the book, as follows (David A. Dorsey, *The Literary Structure of the Old Testament* [Grand Rapids, MI: Baker, 1999], 296):

A. Coming Defeat and Destruction (ch. 1).
B. Corruption of the People (ch. 2).
C. Corruption of the Leaders (ch. 3).
D. Future Restoration (chs. 4–5).
C'. Corruption of the City and Its Leaders (ch. 6).
B'. Corruption of the People (7:1–7).
A'. Future Reversal of Defeat and Destruction (7:8–20).

As his outline is based not on literary parallels between the sections, but thematic similarities so broad that they are almost meaningless (i.e., chapters 4 and 5 do discuss the future redemption, but also many of the contemporary issues facing Micah's listeners), we are not referencing it in our discussion.

17. For example, Allen (*Books of Joel, Obadiah, Jonah and Micah*, 257–61) outlines the book according to three cycles of doom and hope (namely, chapters 1–2, 3–5, 6–7), based on the summons to "hear" found at the beginning of each of these sections.

narrative unevenness. Instead, we identify six speeches, which we will explain as follows:

SPEECH 1 (Chapter 1): Micah against the Capital Cities
Micah pronounces judgment on Samaria and then laments the subsequent downfall of the cities of Judah.

SPEECH 2 (Chapter 2): Taking Land / Being Taken from the Land
Micah describes the cruel practice of a select elite that systematically oppresses the poor by seizing land (generally by abusing the legal system) and then argues with his opponents, likely false prophets, who insist that God will always protect them. He describes imminent destruction and exile, with a possible allusion to the future redemption.

SPEECH 3 (Chapter 3–4:7): Destroying Jerusalem to Rebuild
Micah attacks the leaders of Judah and declares that as a result of the total corruption that permeates the leadership, Jerusalem will be destroyed. Only afterward can the city be rebuilt as a shining light for all the nations.

SPEECH 4 (4:8–5:14): Grappling Towards Redemption
Micah engages in a pseudo-debate with his opponents regarding the correct policy that Judah should implement against the Assyrian invaders. He argues against the aggressive approach and counsels trusting in God to protect the people instead.

However, as noted in the text, this serves to equate the brief statement of hope (2:12–13) to the larger other two sections (sections of chapters 4–5; 7:8–20).

Other views include those of James L. Mays (*Micah, Old Testament Library* [Philadelphia: Westminster, 1976], 2–12) who suggests dividing the book into two sections (chs. 1–5, 6–7), as they both begin with the summons to "hear." He argues that the first five chapters address the entire earth, and only the last two chapters deal with Israel's sins. This viewpoint, however, does not acknowledge the repeated specific references to the sins of Samaria and Judah throughout the first section. For a full summary of the different views of how Micah is structured, see Kenneth H. Cuffey, *The Coherence of Micah: A Review of the Proposals and a New Interpretation* (Doctoral Thesis: Drew University, 1987); David G. Hagstrom, *The Coherence of the Book of Micah* (Atlanta: Scholars Press, 1988); and Mignon R. Jacobs, *The Conceptual Coherence of the Book of Micah* (Sheffield, UK: Sheffield Academic Press, 2001).

SPEECH 5 (Chapter 6): Judgment and Verdict
Micah creatively portrays a courtroom scene in which God sues the Jewish people for their sins. He describes a sense of ingratitude that Israel feels towards God, and he mocks the people's reliance on sacrifices to repair the relationship instead of improving their moral and ethical behavior. Finally, Micah describes the immorality that pervades Samaria and details their punishment and destruction.

SPEECH 6 (Chapter 7): A Prophet Alone, a People Redeemed
The final speech consists of two distinct halves. In the first, Micah speaks of the loneliness of the righteous person in a corrupt society. On behalf of the people, he acknowledges their failings before describing how God will eventually forgive and redeem the Jewish people due to His eternal covenant with the forefathers.

Speech 1 (1:1–16): Micah against the Capital Cities

THE SUPERSCRIPTION

> The word of the Lord that came to Micah the Morashtite in the days of Jotham, Ahaz, [and] Hezekiah, the kings of Judah, which he prophesied concerning Samaria and Jerusalem. (1:1)

Micah begins with a traditional opening to a book of prophecy – the prophet's identification details, dating him according to regnal reigns and establishing that what follows is indeed the divine word.[1] What is notable about this opening is that, unlike most other prophets, Micah addresses both the Southern and Northern Kingdom alike (despite being an inhabitant of Judah, not Israel). Instead of addressing the countries of Israel and Judah, Micah sets the tone by focusing on the capital cities of Samaria and Jerusalem. This focus is not mere synecdoche (the cities representing their respective nations); rather Micah launches the

---

1. The Midrash attempts to classify the forms of prophecy based on their opening words. While Rabbi Yohanan argues that the root D-B-R, "speech," introduces the harshest prophecies, Rabbi Eliezer argues that it is the word ḥazon, "vision," that symbolizes them (Genesis Rabba 44:6). For further discussion and comparison with the opening verses of the other prophets, see the commentary to Nahum's opening verse in Beasley, *Nahum, Habakkuk, and Zephaniah*, 39.

opening salvo of a full-barreled assault on the urban elite and the corruption of city life. The opening establishes the time in which he lived and explains many of the peculiarities of his message.

Micah does not mention the northern kings who reigned while he prophesied, even though he also spoke about Samaria. The commentaries differ as to why this is so. Abrabanel argues that this is an intentional snub, as southern prophets would not recognize the legitimacy of the northern monarchs. Possibly, the downfall of Jehu's dynasty and the resulting chaos during Samaria's final thirty years created a situation where none of the pretenders was worthy of recognition. *Metzudat David* argues that, unlike Hosea and Amos, Micah did not speak in Samaria, and therefore his prophecy does not mention their kings. However, the Northern Kingdom plays an integral part in Micah's message, as he repeatedly contrasts it with the Southern Kingdom. Furthermore, Micah does not spare Israel's citizens from criticism or prophecies of doom.

Micah's first speech, which we identify as the first chapter, uses various rhetorical approaches and genres to shock his listeners and intensify his message's force. It is hard to locate the exact time when he spoke these words. Because of the listing of cities in southern Judah in the second half of the chapter, many commentators and scholars assume that Micah uttered these words close to 701 BCE, the year when Sennacherib's force invaded Judah from the coast, devastating the countryside and destroying cities on their way to Jerusalem. This chapter, however, was spoken to both the north and the south, implying that the Northern Kingdom had not yet fallen (722–721 BCE) when Micah first uttered these words.

Not including the opening verse, we can divide the first chapter, Micah's first speech, into three sections:

1. God is coming to judge: Micah summons everyone to witness God's appearance to render judgment (without specifying who will be judged) (vv. 2–4).
2. The end of Samaria: Micah describes the imminent destruction of Samaria, the Northern Kingdom, followed by describing his personal reaction to the tragedy (vv. 5–8).

3. The destruction of Judah: Micah continues by describing the imminent destruction of Judah's cities, again followed by his personal reaction to and lament over the tragedy (vv. 9–16).

THE FIRST COURTROOM SCENE

> Hear ye, peoples, all of you; give heed, O earth and all its fullness. May the Lord God be a witness against you, the Lord from His holy Temple. For behold the Lord – He is coming out of His place; He will go down and tread upon the highest places of the earth. The mountains dissolve beneath Him, and the valleys split open like wax melting before fire, like waters surging down a steep slope. (1:2–4)

The first section of Micah's first speech begins with Micah announcing that God is coming: "Hear, ye peoples, all of you;[2] hearken, O land and the fullness thereof; and let the Lord God be a witness against you." His opening reminds us of the court clerk who announces to those gathered in the courtroom, "Pay attention to the testimony that will follow!" He then proclaims the entrance of the first (and only) witness – God Himself is coming out of "His holy Temple," apparently in the heavens, to present His testimony.[3] Thus, with simple imagery, Micah has transported his listeners (and readers) to the setting of a courtroom trial – the standard opening of the *riv* (the lawsuit) form, a rhetorical device that appears quite often in the Prophets.

But who is Micah preaching to? Is he speaking to the earth and heavenly bodies, to the Jewish people alone, or is he addressing all the nations of the world? Most traditional commentators assume that Micah is directly addressing a Jewish audience (*Metzudat David*, Rashi. Radak interprets "you peoples" as referring to the listeners and "all of them" as

---

2. The Hebrew that is translated as "all of you" is *kulam*, literally "all of them," but such grammatical incongruence is often found, not least in the close parallel of I Kings 22:28.
3. Both Rashi and Radak suggest that God's testimony is to support Micah's trustworthiness and authority (I prophesied to you in His name and warned you; Rashi on v. 2). We prefer to understand that the testimony is not yet revealed at this point, as per the developing metaphor from verses 2–4.

referring to those not present (thus explaining the discrepancy between the second and third person usages). Modern scholarship is more likely to suggest that Micah 1:2 is addressing a universal audience and not only the immediate Jewish listeners.[4]

We suggest that Micah deliberately intended to create ambiguity by not identifying his audience immediately, utilizing the ambiguity as a form of "rhetorical entrapment" (Amos uses the same tactic at the beginning of his addresses).[5] Micah's Jewish listeners hear the reference to the "peoples" and assume that God is preparing to render judgment against the world's nations. Assuming that Micah is delivering a positive message (they think that Micah will outline how God intends to destroy the enemies of the Jewish people), they would have flocked to hear him and pay attention. If God summons the world's nations to judgment, this likely entails redemption for the Jewish people. However, once Micah has his Jewish audience willing to listen to him, he then informs them, to their shock, that they (the inhabitants of Judah and Samaria) are the intended targets of divine justice.[6] This rhetorical entrapment causes

---

4. For example, D. Hillers writes: "It seems best to suppose that here, if only briefly, Micah touches on the idea of judgment against the heathen" (Hillers, *Micah: A Commentary on the Book of the Prophet Micah* [Minneapolis, MN: Fortress Press, 1988], 17). Similarly, James L. Mays opines that 1:2 must be viewed as reflecting the concern with the nations as a feature of Israel's future so evident in chapters 4–5 (Mays, *Micah*, 40).

5. See R. Alter, *The Art of Biblical Poetry* (New York: Basic Books, 1985), 144, for an expanded discussion of the usage of rhetorical entrapment in biblical prophecy and poetry.

6. Others have suggested analogous functions for the beginnings of Amos and Zephaniah, respectively. For Amos, John Barton suggests:

> Having won the people's sympathy [through his expression of moral outrage], he rounds on them by proclaiming judgment on Israel too. This technique has two obvious advantages... he has gained his audience's attention by flattering their feelings of superiority.... Secondly, it makes it much harder for them to exculpate themselves... since they have implicitly conceded that sin and judgment are rightly linked. (J. Barton, *Amos's Oracles against the Nations* [Cambridge: Cambridge University Press, 1980], 3)

Rudolph argues that the prophets' listeners shared a "universal expectation that the theophany brings disaster to all [of the Lord's] enemies... the shock for the listeners is that [the Lord] does not behave differently for Judah and Jerusalem" (W. Rudolph, *Kommentar zum Alten Testament: Micha-Nahum-Habakuk-Zephanja* [Gutersloher

the listener to expect a positive message and increases their willingness to listen to the speaker, only to continue with evil tidings. Additionally, Micah may ironically be imitating all the popular prophets who preached only the messages that their listeners wanted to hear (3:5).

Having gained his listeners' attention, Micah then announces that the star witness will be God Himself, coming out of His holy Temple, the *heikhal*, to give His testimony. What that testimony is, Micah has not yet revealed. Rashi and Radak suggest that God will testify on the prophet's behalf, that he [Micah] warned them in God's name.[7] Micah's usage of the name *Elokim* implies that the appearance is for judgment. Most commentators identify "His holy Temple" as a reference to God's heavenly Sanctuary.[8]

With God exiting His holy Sanctuary at the end of verse 2, verse 3 continues describing God's movement from the heavenly realm to the earthly one. The commentators explain this metaphor in differing manners. Both Rashi and *Metzudat David* interpret God's move as one from the "throne of mercy" to the "throne of judgment." In contrast, Radak

---

Verlagshaus, 1975], 265). Kapelrud notes that the same rhetorical strategy guides Amos, Zephaniah, and Micah:

> [Amos] wanted to arouse the interest of the people and he did not start straightway with words of doom over his audience [in his first address]. In the same way, Zephaniah opened his speech (or speeches) with a few general remarks, which made the people stop and listen. Then, when the audience was listening and waiting for more, he let go his harsh words against Jerusalem, the city where he was preaching. If we have a look at, e.g., Micah 1.2–4, we find the same pattern: first all peoples are threatened, then the prophet turns toward his own people, v. 5. (Kapelrud, *The Message of the Prophet Zephaniah: Morphology and Ideas* [Universitetsforlaget, 1975], 20)

7. The Midrash (*Sifrei Devarim* 306) brings several examples of God serving as a witness, including our text:

> How do we know that God is termed a "witness"? As it is written, "And I will draw close to you for justice, and I will be a hastening witness" (Mal. 3:5); "And I know and testify, this is the word of God" (Jer. 29:23); and "And the Lord God be a witness against you, the Lord from His holy Temple" (Mic. 1:2).

8. See Radak, Ibn Ezra; cf. Ps. 11:4; Is. 3:13–14; Hab. 2:20. See, however, the opposite view in Malbim ad loc., that the place of God's domicile is Jerusalem and the Temple. Abrabanel attempts to reconcile the two approaches: God is leaving earthly Jerusalem to ascend to his heavenly abode. However, the wording "*from* His holy Temple" implies the opposite.

explains that Micah is describing how heavenly decrees affect the world below. Malbim focuses on the element of God's personal involvement – just as during the Exodus, it was God and no other (in the words of the Haggadah liturgy: "God and not a messenger, God and not an angel") who punished the Egyptians and freed the Jewish people, here too God is personally involved in the sentencing of those who are facing judgment.

Micah's description of God's appearance is generally known as theophany in biblical literature. Theophanies typically contain three main sections: the coming and the manifestation of God on earth, the reaction of nature to God's appearance, and finally, how the divine image will affect humanity. In one of the most famous theophanies in the Bible in Psalms 18, God rides on clouds and angels, the mountains tremble, earthquakes rumble, and water, hail, and fire take flight from before Him. In Micah's vision, God will "tread upon the high places of the earth" (cf. Amos 4:13; Hab. 3:19). The Hebrew word tread *darakh* appears in the context of the trampling of grapes (Job 24:11), treading on the backs of enemies (Deut. 33:29), and the crushing of serpents (Ps. 91:13). We can understand the high places (*bamot*) in several ways. First, they can refer literally to the mountains. Hence God tramples them. Second, they may be the high places of worship, which were the scourge of most of the kings of Judah. Finally, they may refer metaphorically to the proud and haughty who face judgment (see Rashi 1:3, and Abrabanel who interprets it as referring to the nation's leadership).

The next verse continues the theophany, describing how nature responds to God's appearance. Mountains and valleys alike will disappear. Again, Micah uses direct parallelism for poetic purposes – both the mountains and the wax melt away, and both the valleys and the bodies of water will burst. At the end of the verse, there is beautiful alliteration – like water flowing down a slope, *kamayim mugarim bamorad*. All four parts contain liquid imagery (melted wax, the waters) and a clear geological progression (the mountains crumble into the valleys below, which then collapse as well, possibly into the coastlands). The image is powerful – all the world is being flattened and leveled under God's footsteps. The commentators attempt to interpret the imagery metaphorically. Radak understands the collapse of the mountains and the valleys as symbolizing the destruction of the two kingdoms Israel and

Judah – facing a sudden blow (Assyria) as powerful as the tremendous force of water falling from heights above. Ibn Ezra and *Metzudot* understand the water metaphor differently: Just as water scatters in all directions after hitting the ground, the Jewish people will scatter among the nations after receiving the blow. Until now, Micah has only provided the listeners with powerful and dramatic imagery, possibly entertaining them. Now, he gives them its interpretation, which will not be to their liking.

SAMARIA RECEIVES ITS VERDICT

> All this owing to Jacob's sins, to the wrongdoings of the House of Israel. What then is the sin of Jacob if not Samaria? Who is behind the hilltop shrines in Judah if not Jerusalem? I will turn Samaria into a mass of stones in the fields, a place for planting vineyards, and will hurl her ruins into the valley and bare her foundations. All her statues will be shattered; all her tainted payment will go up in flames; all her idols I will lay waste, for she amassed it all from harlot's payment, and to harlot's payment it will return. Over this I will wail and lament; I will walk barefoot, stripped bare, my grief the cry of jackals, my mourning like desert owls. (1:5–8)

Micah now springs his rhetorical trap. Against the expectations and hopes of his listeners, he announces the defendant's identity – none other than the listeners themselves. He identifies them as Jacob and Israel, the two names of the Jewish people's third forefather. Generally, when the two terms Jacob and Israel appear together, they are used to describe the entirety of the Jewish people. Later, after Samaria's destruction, either term can apply to the Southern Kingdom (see 3:1, 8, 9) since it was the only remaining representative of the Jewish people.

He then identifies the two causes behind the sins – Samaria and Jerusalem – the capitals of the two kingdoms. Cleverly, the parallelism in verse 5 is not complete, as we would have expected "the house of Judah" instead of "the house of Israel" in the first part of the verse. Like his rhetorical entrapment above, Micah uses ambiguity to entrap his listeners, most likely only southerners, into assuming that God was not addressing them. Only when Micah reveals that the objects of the parallel between Jacob and the house of Israel are both Samaria and

Judah/Jerusalem, will Micah's listeners begin to realize that he is not merely condemning the Northern Kingdom.

Reading closely, one will note that of the two words used for sin, the stronger word P-SH-A (rebel) is attached to the Northern Kingdom, while the lesser word H-T-A (sin) is attached to the Southern Kingdom. The Northern Kingdom worshipped at the golden calves set up by Jeroboam and, since the time of Ahab, worshipped Baal; the Southern Kingdom was generally faithful but would bring offerings to God both at the Temple and the high places (*bamot*) (see *Metzudot*, Malbim). These *bamot* were the bane of Judah's kings; people preferred to offer sacrifices on them, not in Jerusalem. Ultimately, they became identified with Baal worship and idolatry (II Kings 17:11, 21:3,11). Radak notes that Micah is not attacking the people but their leadership (perhaps commenting on the usage of the capital cities to represent the nation). Having identified the defendants, Micah then proceeds to pronounce God's judgment on each in turn.

Micah first turns his attention to Samaria, the capital of the Northern Kingdom. Reinforcing the imagery utilized above, Micah speaks in God's voice and declares that although the city stood proudly atop a mountain, God would both destroy and humiliate it. Its heights would be flattened, its building ransacked and razed. Its stones would "flow" into the valley below so that the region would appear flat, with mounds and heaps of rocks dotting the landscape. No longer would defensive slopes surround the city. Instead, the area would revert to its primary agricultural usage – the growing of grapes and vineyards on the terraced hills (Radak notes that the location of Samaria is prime land for viniculture). The devastation would be so complete, with Assyrian sappers digging deep into the earth to weaken the walls' support while their battering rams pound the heavy stones above. It is as if God is exposing the city's foundations. Micah's description of God's appearance alludes to the punishments facing Samaria. Just as "wax melts before fire (*esh*) and water is poured down (*muGARim*) the steep place" (v. 4), so too will Samaria's idols be burnt in fire (*esh*, v. 7), and the city's rocks will be cast down (*vehiGARti*, v. 6). In an apt demonstration of wordplay, the final clause of verse 6, "and I will expose its foundations," can also be read as "I will exile its establishments" (the members of Samaria's elite).

Micah then identifies the root cause of God's anger against the Northern Kingdom – idolatry.[9] He uses three separate words to describe the images worshipped by the Northern Kingdom that the invaders will either plunder or destroy – *pesilim, etnanim,* and *atzabim.* The word "all" precedes each of these three terms, creating the sense that the entire city overflows with idols. The destruction of the idols begins with passive verbs – "all the graven images will be smashed," "all the harlot wages will be burnt in the fire." The passive verbs emphasize the powerlessness of these idols to defend themselves, let alone the city's inhabitants. Finally, God announces that He will make the idols waste. Moses commanded the Jewish people to burn and destroy the Canaanite idols upon entering Israel (Deut. 7:5, 12:3); now God Himself comes to complete the job.

There are various suggestions to differentiate between the different forms of idols.[10] Rashi defines a *pesel* as any carved or sculptured image (Rashi on Ex. 20:4). The word *atzav* is derived from the Hebrew word *etzev* (worry, anger, sadness). *Metzudot* suggests that this word implies that even the worshipper of idols does not entirely trust them to provide salvation and deliverance. Malbim suggests that the *pesel* refers to the head idol, while the word *atzav* refers to idols subordinate to the *pesel.*

Possibly the harshest word in Micah's arsenal is the term used to describe the riches that the people in the capital had acquired. They are *etnan* – literally, harlot earnings.[11] Some commentators understand this literally – Micah is accusing the northerners of committing adultery with temple prostitutes during their idolatry worship. In the form of measure for measure, the Assyrians would confiscate these gifts from

---

9. See I Kings 16:32, 22:53, and especially II Kings 17:7–18. In this, Micah echoes Hosea, in contrast to Amos, who concentrates more on the social injustices present in Samaria.

10. Charles Shaw stands alone among commentators and scholars in his attempt to interpret these verses as an attack on the excessive riches and income gaps that existed between the capital city and the agrarian poor. He suggests that the words are to be interpreted as "hewn stones, riches, and elaborate stone-carvings" (*The Speeches of Micah: A Rhetorical Historical Analysis* [London: Bloomsbury T&T Clark, 1993], 48–50).

11. The first appearance of the word *etnan* is in Deut. 23:18: "You shall not bring the fee of a prostitute (*etnan*) or the wages of a dog into the house of the Lord your God in payment for any vow, for both are an abomination to the Lord your God."

the northern temples, ultimately using them either to satisfy their carnal desires or to offer them to the Assyrian idols.[12]

However, the term *etnan* appears as a metaphor in two significant passages in the Prophets. Isaiah rebukes Tyre for its excessive political and commercial allegiances with other nations (Is. 23:17–18). He declares that at the end of seventy years, the Lord will visit Tyre. She will return to her wage-earning (*etnan*) and prostituting herself with all the kingdoms of the world. More significantly, Ezekiel uses the term *etnan* repeatedly while he rebukes the Jewish people for their constant idolatry and worship of other gods (Ezek. 16:31, 34, 41):

> "How languid is your heart, declares the Lord God, to have done all these things, the acts of a brazen prostitute!…But you were not like a regular whore; you scorned payment (*etnan*), the adulterous wife who takes strangers instead of her husband. All prostitutes are given gifts, but you in your whoring gave gifts to all your lovers, bribing them on every side to come to you. You have been the opposite of other women – by whoring unsolicited, by paying [the prostitute's fee (*etnan*)] and not being paid a prostitute's fee (*etnan*)….
>
> "So, whore, hear the word of the Lord. So says the Lord God: Because your lust was poured out and your nakedness bared in your whoring with your lovers, and for all the idols of your abominations,…I will condemn you to the punishment of the adulterous woman and the murderess, give you over to bloody fury and passionate anger…I will give you over into their hands, and they will tear down your platforms, pull down your raised places…Thus will I put an end to your whoring; you will no longer pay a prostitute's fee (*etnan*) no more… (Ezek. 16:30–41)[13]

---

12. See Allen, *Books of Joel, Obadiah, Jonah and Micah*, 274: "The reference is probably to the gold and silver plating on the images, melted down from the dirty money handed over for the use of religious brothels. Invading soldiers are to tear it off as loot and spend it as currency for further prostitution, as soldiers will."
13. For fuller discussion of this metaphor in Ezekiel, see Tova Ganzel's article "He Speaks in Allegories" at https://etzion.org.il/en/tanakh/neviim/sefer-yechezkel/he-speaks-allegories-ch-15-16.

The word for prostitution, *liznot*, often refers to turning away from God (Ex. 34:15, Lev. 17:7, Judges 2:17). The metaphor of Israel as prostituting itself, seen in Ezekiel and others, is the outgrowth of the common prophetic metaphor that portrays the relationship between God and the Jewish people as equivalent to that of the marriage relationship between a husband and wife (Hos. 2:16; Jer. 2:2–3, 3:14; Ezek. 16:8). When the Jewish people looked to other gods or nations for gain, it was equivalent to hiring themselves out as a prostitute (Hos 9:1; 2:12; 8:9, 10). It was often the creation of commercial allegiances to other nations that led to the worship of other gods, and the newfound wealth from these trading relationships enabled them to purchase idols.

Micah concludes his announcement of the decree of the destruction of the Northern Kingdom with cries and laments. He no longer speaks in God's voice; instead, he reverts to his prophetic persona ("I") and shares with us his reaction to the divine judgment – he will wail and cry, bordering on insanity, and walk around in a state of undress.[14]

14. *Metzudot*, Malbim, and Daat Mikra suggest that the mourning that Micah describes here is only meant to refer to the second half of the chapter, which describes the upcoming destruction of Judah and Jerusalem. Malbim justifies this saying that, unlike the inhabitants of the Northern Kingdom who were habitual idolaters, the people of Judah rarely worshipped idols. However, Radak argues that Micah is describing his reaction to the destruction and exile of the Northern Kingdom. We adopt this approach because a careful study of the appearances of the words "for this" (*al zot*) in prophetic books reveals that it invariably refers to what preceded it:

Jer. 4:7–8: The Lion has come up from his lair. The Destroyer of Nations has set forth. He has departed from his place in order to lay waste to your land. Your cities will become desolate, with no inhabitant. For this reason (*al zot*), don sackcloth, lament, and wail…

Amos 7:2–3: And as they consumed the land's greenery completely, I said, "My Lord God, please forgive. How could Jacob survive this – he, who is so small?" And the Lord relented on this (*al zot*): "This shall not be," said the Lord. [Note similar usage in 7:6.]

Amos 8:4–8: Hear this, those who trample the poor, who would decimate the destitute of the land, those who say, "When will the New Moon pass so we can sell grain, and the Sabbath so we can open the storehouses, so we can diminish the weight of an ephah but enlarge the shekel, skew false scales, sell the needy for silver and the poor for the price of shoes? Let us sell chaff as grain."
The Lord swears by the pride of Jacob: I will forever remember what they have done. Would the earth not shudder for this and all its inhabitants mourn?

Some commentators are not comfortable with a prophet going naked. *Metzudot* suggests that Micah never intended to behave in this manner. Instead, the imagery is intentionally excessive and exaggerated to accentuate the level of despair and suffering that he felt. Radak and the Targum suggest that Micah is not describing himself but the exiles from Samaria, being dragged away naked, chained, and wailing. Many Assyrian reliefs portray rows of prisoners stripped of their clothing and dignity while being led into exile.[15] One can imagine Micah himself walking alongside the chained and fettered rows of captives, crying with them, wishing to share their burdens and their sufferings as they leave behind the Land of Israel for uncertain destinations.[16]

The description of Micah's mourning for the Northern Kingdom concludes with the sounds and cries that emanate from his mouth. They are the mournful sounds of the uninhabited desert wilderness – of jackals and desert owls – poetically describing how the Assyrians ransacked Samaria's once-lush hills.[17]

The earth will rise like the Nile, churn and sink like the Nile of Egypt. (*al zot*), and shall all its inhabitants [not] be destroyed?

Bernard Renaurd concludes, "*l'expression resume toujours ce qui preclude et tire les consequences d'une situation on d'un evenement precis* (my translation: the expression [*al zot*] always summarizes what precludes and describes the consequences of a situation or a specific event)" (*La Formation du livre de Michée* [Paris: J. Gabalda et Cie, 1977], 38–41).

15. J. B. Pritchard, *The Ancient Near East in Pictures Relating to the Old Testament* (Princeton, 1969), photos 332, 373.

16. This is how the Midrash describes Jeremiah's behavior during the destruction of the First Temple in 586 BCE:

He [Jeremiah, returning to Jerusalem and seeing the devastation] began to cry... "Which route have the sinners taken? By which route have the forsaken journeyed? I shall go and lose myself with them." He set out with them and saw the path drenched with blood, corpses everywhere. He placed his face against the ground and saw limbs, legs of infants and children who were taken into captivity, he laid upon the earth and kissed them, When he arrived in Babylonia, he embraced his people and kissed them and cried with them and they with him. He said to them, "my brethren, my people, my children, such a terrible thing has befallen you since you did not heed the words of my prophecy" (Petiḥta Rabbati 26)

17. While *Metzudot* here translates the word *tan* as a type of snake, the verse in Lamentations 4:3 discusses the *tan* as a mammal. Ramban (Ḥullin 62b) interprets the *bat yaana* as a form of ostrich, but he also notes that these birds do not make a sound.

MICAH LAMENTS JUDAH'S FATE

For she is mortally ill [from] her wounds, for it has come up to Judah; it has reached the gate of My people, even to Jerusalem.
Do not tell of this in Gat, weep, not at all. But within Beit Le'ofra immerse yourself in mourner's ashes. Go then, resident of Shafir, nakedness uncovered; the resident of Tzaanan could not go forth; [in] mourning in Beit HaEtzel, [the enemy] will snatch his support from you, for though the resident of Marot hoped for good, disaster came down from the Lord just to the gates of Jerusalem. Hitch the chariot to the horses, resident of Lakhish – inciter of sin for the daughter of Zion – the rebellious acts of Israel were first embraced in your midst. So, then, send your gifts to Moreshet Gat; the houses of Akhziv deceive, disappoint the kings of Israel. I will yet bring a (dis)possessor upon you, O residents of Mareisha; the esteemed men of Israel will flee even to Adulam. Shave your head; pull out your hair in mourning over the children of your delight. Make yourself bald like the vulture, for they are gone from you into exile. (1:9–16)

Having expressed lament over Samaria, who will soon perish, Micah now turns his concern towards Jerusalem. An evil that began in the north has quickly spread to the south. His opening words are both ambiguous and grammatically tricky at first glance: "For she is mortally ill [from] her wounds, for it has come up to Judah; it has reached the gate of My people, even to Jerusalem." Neither is the subject of "*she* is mortally ill" identified, nor is the identity of "it" in "*it* has come to Judah" and "*it* has reached the gate" made manifest. The word for mortally ill (*anusha*) is feminine singular; the word for her wounds (*makoteha*) is plural. Rashi suggests that the changes from singular to plural are descriptive: Samaria is mortally ill because of the various punishments. Radak suggests that the plural wounds refer to the multiple punishments that befell the Northern Kingdom – invasions, famines, and plagues. Radak continues by identifying the unknown "it" in the verse: The Assyrians that had mortally wounded Samaria were now coming into Judah, making their way to the gates of the capital city. Radak refers to Sennacherib's invasion of the south in 701 BCE, which devastated the coastal plains and the towns along the road as his armies marched uphill to Jerusa-lem.[18] Accordingly, the remaining verses describing and mourning the destruction of the southern towns must be understood as a prophetic lament for Judah, having been uttered either before or soon after the year 701 BCE. The identification of the word "it" as the Assyrian army under Sennacherib (and the subsequent dating to the invasion of 701 BCE) is the dominant view in modern scholarship.[19]

However, we adopt Malbim's interpretation of verse 9 here, with its ramifications for dating the text. Malbim identifies the unknown "it" that came into Judah not as the Assyrians (like Radak above), but as the Northern Kingdom (during the Syro-Ephraimite invasion of Judah in 734–732 BCE). As such, the verse would read, "For she [Samaria] is mortally ill [from] her wounds, because it [Samaria] has come up to Judah; it has reached the gate of My people." Malbim suggests that the moment Samaria chose to take up arms against its brother and invade Judah, the Northern Kingdom's fate was sealed. These armies reach "until" Jerusalem – until, but they do not penetrate the walls. Ultimately,

---

18. Both *Metzudot* and Abrabanel prefer to interpret Micah's words, which draw a parallel between the fates of Samaria and Jerusalem, in consideration of subsequent histori-cal events. "For she is mortally ill [from] her wounds" refers to the Assyrian exile of the Northern Kingdom; "it has come to Judah" refers to the Babylonian exile of the Southern Kingdom in 586 BCE. We have rejected this approach because we believe that the prophet's words must be understood at the basic level as addressing the audience in front of him, imparting information relevant to his listeners, and not referring to distant future events.

19. This approach is best summarized by Sieges:

The period directly following Sennacherib's campaign through the Judean Shephelah [coastal plain] supplies the most likely period for the formation of the lament song. Following the campaign, when the cities of the Shephelah lay in ruins, displaced residents would have needed an expression for their grief that the lament song could fulfill. Several pieces of internal evidence point to the lament's composition following Sennacherib's siege. First, the prophetic speaker engages in this mourning song as a fellow mourner who experienced the suffering brought by the Shephelah's destruction. Second, the prophetic speaker knows of the events he describes and refers to the region Sennacherib actually attacked. Third, the lament song assumes that the cities of the Judean Shephelah already lie in ruins. (A. Sieges, "The Formation of Mic 1–3: From the Eighth Century to the Exile" [PhD diss., Baylor University, 2016], 152)

the invasion failed to take the capital and overthrow King Ahaz. For the heinous crime of turning on a brother, the Northern Kingdom would be destroyed, but not before it inflicted tremendous damage and suffering on the towns in the south. We thereby date this lament to 734, during the time of Ahaz and not during Hezekiah's reign, as we shall explain below.

Micah continues with a lament for these cities, directly addressing town after town with a series of brilliant wordplays that do not detract from the poignancy and sense of the tragedy of the devastation that occurs. These puns (the technical literary-rhetorical term is paronomasia; in Hebrew, *lashon nofel al lashon*)[20] begin in verse 10 and continue until verse 15. Then, Micah switches to speaking in God's first-person voice to conclude the list of cities, followed by divine orders to mourn (paralleling Micah's actions in verse 8).[21]

---

20. Explaining the puns, Barry Bandstra writes:

> Paronomasia is a play on words, a verbal pun, that makes specialized use of alliteration. The poetry of prophecy contains examples of this device. Amos used it masterfully, as in the following line where Gilgal puns on "go into exile": *ki hagilgal galoh yigleh* – For Gilgal will surely go into exile (Amos 5:5). Also, when Amos saw a basket of summer fruit, *kayitz*, he took this as a sign that the end, *ketz*, was near (8:12). Paronomasia is used throughout the Hebrew Bible and is not restricted to poetry. For example, Genesis 2:7 says that God formed man, *adam*, out of the ground, *adamah*." (Barry L. Bandstra, *Reading the Old Testament: Introduction to the Hebrew Bible* [Boston: Cengage Learning, 2008], 378)

While modern readers might be offended or troubled by the prophet using "puns" to describe a tragedy, as Micah is doing here, it should be noted that in the Bible, the purpose of these plays on sound and sense are not for humor, but to draw attention to the text:

> This figure is not by any means what we call a pun. Far from it. But two things are emphasized, and our attention is called to this emphasis by the similarity of sound. Otherwise, we might read the passage and pass it by unnoticed; but the eye or the ear is at once attracted by the similarity of sound or appearance, and our attention is thus drawn to a solemn or important statement which would otherwise have been unheeded. Sometimes a great lesson is taught us by this figure; an interpretation is put upon the one word by the use of the other; or a reason is given in the one for what is referred to by the other. Sometimes a contrast is made; sometimes a thought is added. (E. W. Bullinger, *Figures of Speech Used in the Bible* [Michigan: Baker Books, 2003], 306–7)

21. "Interestingly Sennacherib too used wordplays when recording his conquests" (John A. Martin, "Micah," in *The Bible Knowledge Commentary: Old Testament* [Wheaton, IL: Victor Books, 1985], 1477).

The List of Cities, the Wordplays, and Their Meaning in Micah's Lament

Verse #	Hebrew transliteration	Meaning	Pun (best understood if read aloud)
10	*beGat, al tagidu*	Do not tell of it in Gat	The city *Gat* sounds like the Hebrew word for "tell" (*tagidu*).
10	*beVeit le'Ofra, afar hitpalashi*[22]	But within Beit Le'ofra immerse yourself in mourner's ashes.	*Beit Le'ofra* means "house of ashes" (ashes are *afar*).
11	*Ivri lakhem yoshevet Shafir, erya boshet*	Pass on (to exile), resident of Shafir, nakedness uncovered	The town name *Shafir*, which means "pleasant or beautiful," also means the placenta that leaves a woman.[23] There is also another wordplay: dweller (*yoshevet*) is phonetically similar and rhymes with nakedness (*boshet*).
11	*lo yatza yoshevet Tza'anan*	the resident of Tza'anan did not go forth	The city *Tza'anan* sounds like go forth (*yatza*).
11	*Mispad Beit HaEtzel, yikaḥ mikem emdato*	[in] mourning in Beit HaEtzel, [the enemy] will snatch his support from you.	*Beit Etzel* means the house of another – but the enemy will remove any support [they will stand alone].

22. Rashi and Daat Mikra suggest another pun hidden here: The Hebrew to wallow (*hitpalashi*) is phonetically similar to the Philistines (*Paleshet*), of which Gat was one of their major cities.

23. Rashi comments here that "[leaving with the] exposed private parts, [is] appropriate for a city called Shafir, the name of the aborted fetus that comes out of the woman's womb." Radak suggests that a different poetic device is at play here. At times, the Bible will use one word at the beginning of a clause and conclude with its opposite. He suggests that here, Micah is contrasting *shafir*, beauty, with revealed nakedness and ugliness.

Verse #	Hebrew transliteration	Meaning	Pun (best understood if read aloud)
12	*Ki ḥala latov yoshevet Marot*	for though the resident of Marot hoped for good,	Again, the city name *Marot* (bitterness) contrasts with the end of the clause, *tov* (good).[24]
13	*Retom hamerkava larekhesh yoshevet Lakhish*	Hitch the chariot to the horses, resident of Lakhish	The word for swift steeds, *rekhesh*, sounds like the city name *Lakhish*.[25]
14	*titni shiluḥim le-Moreshet Gat*	So, then, send your gifts to Moreshet Gat;	The Hebrew for gifts, *shiluḥim*, also means sending away/divorce (Deut. 23), while *Moreshet* sounds like *me'ureset* (engaged).
14	*batei Akhziv le'akhzav lemalkhei Yisrael*	the houses of Akhziv deceive, disappoint the kings of Israel;	There is a double word-play on the city name *Akhziv*. It sounds like the word for disappointment (*Akhzava*), as well as the word for a dried-up spring (*Akhzav*).
15	*Od hayoreish avi lakh yoshevet Mareisha*	I will yet bring an (dis)possessor upon you, O residents of Mareisha;	The (dis)possessor [lit., inheritor] *yoreish* sounds like the city name *Mareisha*
15	*ad Adulam yavo kavod Yisrael*	the esteemed men of Israel will flee even to Adulam.	*ad Adulam* – the esteemed men will flee to Adulam (an area with numerous caves – see below)

---

24. Most of the commentators understand *Marot* to be the name of a city (see Radak and *Metzudot*). However, Rashi understands the word to be a pun meaning rebellion: For the one dwelling in tranquility and disobeying the word of the prophets (*mamre* – rebelling against) hoped for good (Rashi on v. 12).

25. To accomplish this wordplay, Micah inverts the normal order, telling Lakhish to harness the chariot to the steeds, and not vice versa.

These six verses, lamenting the fall of the communities that lie southwest of Jerusalem, comprise one of the most poignant and poetic laments in the Bible. The commentators dispute the purpose of the lament. Rashi finds several examples of reward and punishment in the elegy:

> "[The] mourning of Beit Etzel": The lament you [Beit Etzel] caused those who were robbed, whom you deprived of their inheritance to draw one house to the other, one field to the other, will take its stand from you – the stand of the houses that you built and erected on the [stolen] inheritances (v. 11).

> "the resident of Marot": [Directed at the] one dwelling in tranquility who disobeyed the word of the prophets while hoping for good (v. 12).

> "Send gifts to Moreshet-Gat": Since you attempted to expel [a play on words of the Hebrew for gifts (*shiluḥim*), which can also mean expulsions] the lineage of King David, who gave you the possession of Gat, as it states (I Chr. 18:1): "And he took Gat and its cities out of the hands of the Philistines"; but you reject it, as it states (Is. 8:6): "Since this people has rejected the waters of the Shiloah that flow gently," [referring to the house of David], therefore, "the houses of Achzib" which were of the land of Judah and were drawn after [captured by] Pekah the son of Remaliah, shall ultimately be a "dried-up spring" for the kings of Israel – for Pekah the son of Remaliah will be assassinated, and all those who relied on him will be disappointed. This prophecy was prophesied during Ahaz's reign.

Radak understands the speech differently. To him, this is a lament, without Micah placing blame on the cities, and refers to the imminent destruction of the cities of Judah during the Assyrian invasion.[26] He suggests that only these cities are mentioned since, "though all of Israel

---

26. In his commentary, Ibn Ezra suggests that this is merely a prediction of disaster, and he is willing to consider the possibility that Micah is referring to the later Babylonian

would be in ruins, for these the prophet found paronomasia (*lashon nofel al lashon*) in a polished manner. It is the way of poets and mourners to speak in their laments…in a polished (poetic) manner" (Radak on 1:10).

Micah begins by quoting David's lament at the death of Saul, "Tell it not in Gat!" (II Samuel 1:20).[27] These words once symbolized the downfall of a king from the north; now they introduce the downfall of the entire Northern Kingdom. While Radak argues that Micah is engaged in poetic license, merely wishing that the Philistines who dwelt in Gath not rejoice at the downfall of Samaria and Jerusalem, Malbim suggests that Micah is making a practical suggestion. If the Philistines know you have been defeated, they too will attack. Therefore, Micah recommends removing themselves to a location farther away from Gat and only then mourn without alerting the Philistines.[28]

Micah continues with the phrase "weep, not at all." In Hebrew, the rhyme is noticeable: *BeGat, al tagidu, bekho, al tivku*. Finally, he urges the inhabitants of Beit Le'ofra to roll in the dust. Sitting in the dust is a traditional sign of mourning.[29] It is uncertain whether Micah refers to the city of Ofra in Manasseh's portion (Rashi on Judges 6:11) or the city in Benjamin's portion (Josh. 18:23, per Radak and Malbim). There is no mention of Shafir, the first city in the next verse, anywhere else in the Bible. The identity of the city of Za'anan in verse 11 is also unclear, but it may be the city of Zanon that Joshua 15 lists among the cities of Judah (Malbim). Both Radak and *Metzudot* suggest that Za'anan and Beit HaEtzel were neighbors. When Beit HaEtzel fell, the inhabitants

invasion (Ibn Ezra on 1:10). Since this occurred more than one hundred years later, we have not considered it as Micah's primary meaning.

27. Additional parallel between David's elegy for Saul and Jonathan and Micah's laments for the cities: Both emphasize feminine mourning and feminine mourning practices.

28. Though Gath was originally a Philistine city, ownership changed hands several times, having been conquered first by David in the tenth century BCE (II Sam. 8; I Chr. 18), and again by Uzziah at the beginning of the eighth century BCE (II Chr. 26). However, by Micah's time, the city apparently reverted to Philistine control.

29. See Lamentations 2:10. Rolling in the dust may be a more extreme form of mourning. For example, "O daughter of My people, gird yourself with sackcloth and *wallow in ashes*; make yourself…a bitter lamentation" (Jer. 6:26); "And they will cause their voice to be heard over you and cry out bitterly; they will cast up dust upon their heads; they will *wallow in ashes*" (Ezek. 27:30).

of Za'anan did not come out to console them or mourn them, as they preferred to wait in their houses for their impending doom. Verse 12 also begins with an unidentified city Marot, and the commentators wonder what the unknown city is doing. Most commentators, including Ibn Ezra, Radak, and *Metzudot,* understand the verb *ḥala* to mean "to writhe/to anguish" (Judges 3:25; Job 35:14), while Rashi understands it to be related to *yaḥel* – to hope (see Ps. 130:5–7). If so, they understand the conjunction, *ki,* between the first and the second half of the verse differently. Rashi translates the verse as "Marot hoped for good, *but* evil came down…"; other commentators understand it as "Marot anguished over [the lost] good *because* evil came down." Micah then contrasts between bitter (*Marot* means bitterness) and sweet/good. However, he concludes with the same threat of destruction as the end of verse 9 – evil will come to the gate of Jerusalem.

Micah turns his attention to what was then the second-largest city in Judah, Lakhish. Exhorting them to fasten their chariots to their swift steeds, he warns them to escape quickly before the enemy overtakes their city. However, now he explicitly justifies their destruction: "It is the beginning of sin for the daughter of Zion, for in you were found the transgressions of Israel." Some of the commentators suggest that this city was the first of the cities of Judah to engage in idolatry (Ibn Ezra, *Metzudot*). Radak advances a novel theory. Baal worship was introduced to the Northern Kingdom by Ahab and his wife, Jezebel. It did not enter the south until Amaziah's reign, the first king of Judah to engage in idol worship. He took refuge in Lakhish after his failed invasion of the Northern Kingdom, where he remained until his assassination (II Kings 14:8–20 tells of the failed attack on Israel; II Chr. 25:14 details the idolatry).[30] Some modern scholars also suggest that the sin involved

---

30. Malbim develops a novel theory that attempts to combine the various references to Amaziah with the exact wording of Micah's lament about Lakhish. He writes:
    They began to worship idols in Lakhish first.… In Jerusalem the [loyal] priests of God were outraged at Amaziah's idolatry, but Lakhish supported him, [which enabled him to] reign there for twelve years until the people of Jerusalem were able to overcome them [the citizens of Lakhish] and kill him [Amaziah]. II Kings 14 writes that "they carried him upon horses, and he was buried in Jerusalem."… The worshippers of idolatry (which was chiefly toward the sun, which they

was idolatry, based on a supposed chiasmus with the terms when they appeared previously in verse 5 referring to idolatry: *pesha/hata'ot* (v. 5) – *hatat/pesha'ot* (v. 13).[31]

We suggest a more likely alternative, based on what we know about Lakhish from the immediate context of the verse and other appearances of Lakhish in the Tanakh. During the rebellion by the Northern Kingdom, Rehoboam heavily fortified the city (II Chr. 11:9); by the mid-eighth century, Lakhish was the strongest garrison in Judah after Jerusalem. As such, we interpret Micah decrying what he believed was a misplaced sense of military confidence as Judah's sin. This verse joins the long tradition of prophets, beginning with Moses, who condemned reliance on military might instead of trusting God.[32] The fact that Amaziah found sanctuary in Lakhish after his ill-fated excursion against the Northern Kingdom may suggest that the inhabitants of Lakhish were prone to pursue a more aggressive policy than preferred by the leadership in Jerusalem. If Lakhish's transgression occurred during the Syro-Ephraimite invasion in 734 BCE, Lakhish would likely have supported the invaders who wished to punish Ahaz for this failure to join the military coalition against Assyria.

The emphasis on the word chariot (*merkavah*) and horses reminds us of the prohibition in Deut. 17 that a king may neither amass many horses nor cause the people to return to Egypt, whose symbol was "the chariot and its rider." Micah's contemporary, Isaiah, denounced

---

considered the monarch of the heavens) dedicated horses and a chariot to its service, such that when the sun rose they went to greet it, to the east, with a chariot and horses, as they imagined the path of the sun embarking upon its circuit, as is known from the history records.... And Amaziah, in Lakhish, had horses dedicated to sun worship, and so when [he was killed], his supporters carried his body upon the horses of sun worship.... *Rotem* wood was used to build the chariots of the sun, because this type of wood preserves the heat of fire for long periods of time, signifying the heat of the sun and its perpetual fire.... [Micah adjures] Don't bind it to the horses which are dedicated to the sun, but do it for *rekhesh*, horses that are swift in flight, so that they will be able to flee before the enemy.

31. F. I. Andersen and D. N. Freedman, *Micah: A New Translation with Introduction and Commentary* (New York: Doubleday, 2000), 230.

32. Cf. Deut. 17:16; II Sam. 24:1–10; Is. 2:7; Hos. 10:13–15; 14:4.

those who "go down to Egypt for help, who rely on horses, who trust in the multitude of their chariots and the great strength of their horsemen" (Is. 31:3; see also Is. 36:9). This verse is generally understood that Isaiah was arguing against a military alliance with Egypt. However, Isaiah also berated Judah earlier (likely under Uzziah's rule) that "his land became full of silver and gold, without end to his treasures; and his land became full of horses, without end to his chariots" (Is. 2:7) Recent excavations at Lakhish have discovered tremendous stockpiles of military equipment, including horse stalls.[33]

Whatever sin Lakhish committed, it is essential to note that Micah connects it to the daughter of Zion, the personification of Jerusalem. Though Micah has mentioned and will mention a litany of cities, the lament is framed by Jerusalem, with Jerusalem's sin prominently located in the lament's center.

Micah continues with several more cities before concluding his lament with another call for mourning. He starts by stating that either Lakhish or the daughter of Zion (Jerusalem) will have to send gifts to the Philistine city Moreshet-Gat. Radak understands this as an ironic rebuke to the people, "look what has happened to you, having to bribe the Philistines for protection." Another good reading of the verse is that "you will have to send gifts [to the Assyrians] due to the fall of Moreshet-Gat." Rashi, however, understands that the subject is the houses of Achzib, whom he accuses of defecting to the Northern Kingdom led by Pekah ben Remaliah.[34] Only later will they realize that Pekah was a "dried-spring," someone unable to save them. Radak interprets "the houses of Achzib" not as a location but as houses of idolatry (*kezeb* being another term for idols).

Most significantly, Micah concludes that these people will be a disappointment to the kings of Israel. Given the audience of Micah's time, Radak's assertion that the kings of Judah were also known as kings of Israel is extremely unlikely. This verse is one of the most persuasive

---

33. Simon J. De Vries, *Word Biblical Commentary: I Kings* (Waco, TX: Word Books, 1985), 73.
34. Achzib likely refers to either Chezib from the Judah and Tamar story (Gen. 38:5), or the Achzib in the list of cities taken by the tribe of Judah (Josh. 15:44).

arguments in favor of dating Micah's lament in chapter 1 before the fall of Samaria in 722–721 BCE.

In the final two verses, Micah transfers into the voice of God first person. God announces that he will bring a (dis)possessor against the city of Mareisha with the wordplay mentioned above between the conqueror and the city. Like Moreshet-Gat above, Mareisha also sounds like *me'ureset* – an engaged girl, or *morasha* – an inheritance. Therefore, a plausible interpretation is that Jerusalem's inheritance from God, its cities and its towns, must be given to another owner/husband (namely, the invaders). Micah concludes his listing of Judah's cities by announcing that Israel's glory (possibly a reference to the king) would go to Adulam. II Chronicles 7 lists Adulam among the fortified towns in Judah. Yet, the most significant biblical allusion involving Adullam comes from an early incident in David's career. Forced into hiding and being chased by the now mad king Saul, David is forced to find refuge in the caves near Adullam (I Sam. 22:1). In other words, a king from the north is chasing a southern one to the point of death – precisely the situation faced by Ahaz and Judah during the Syro-Ephraimite invasion of 734 BCE! Therefore, Micah prophesies that his latter-day descendants will also have to flee Jerusalem and come to Adulam in similar dire straits. Throughout Micah's laments, all the cities mentioned are in the lowlands (*shefela*) in Judah that border Philistine territory, all of which are areas where David lodged while on the run from Saul, as noted by a modern scholar:

> This section begins with words that recall David's dirge over the death of Saul and ends with the name of the cave where David hid from Saul. These dark moments in David's life form a gloomy backdrop to the description of the fall of the towns Micah spoke. Though he is never directly mentioned, the figure of David appears hauntingly in the tapestry of destruction – not a David standing tall in triumph, but a David bowed down by humiliation. It is as if Micah saw in the fall of each town and the eventual captivity of the two kingdoms the final dissolution of the Davidic monarchy. Like David, the glory of Israel would come to Adulam.[35]

35. McComiskey, "Micah," 408.

The lament concludes with God calling upon an unknown feminine person to make herself bald and pull out her hair in mourning for the loss of her precious children. Radak suggests that the addressee was one of the cities (or perhaps all of them, referring to the land of Judah), which had its inhabitants pulled out from it and became figuratively bald. However, we suggest that the addressee is Jerusalem/*Bat Tziyon* (daughter of Zion), who is forced to see her children taken away (both in 734 BCE and 701 BCE, numerous inhabitants of Judah were exiled). Despite being forbidden by the Torah (Deut. 14:1), cutting and removing hair remained a prominent feature of mourning in ancient cultures.[36] We understand the symbolism: Hair growth is characteristic of the living, so removing the hair allows the mourner to identify symbolically with the dead. In the Bible, the act of going into exile, away from one's homeland and God, was equivalent to death.[37] In Micah's metaphor, the mourning mother must perform three separate actions – shave, shear, and enlarge her baldness like that of a vulture. The shaving of Mother Jerusalem is an outward physical expression of deep inner sorrow, with the use of three verbs suggesting that her grief is escalating, not diminishing, with time.

Verse 16 compares Micah's mourning practices to wild desert animals (just like his behavior in verse 8), this time to the vulture (*nesher*). Sweeney remarks that "just as the [vulture] soars away, so the people of these cities and towns will be exiled or removed … away from their homes," but Micah is not comparing movements but appearances.[38] The griffon vulture, common in the Middle East, has a white down-covered head and a neck that looks like a bald pate.

With the conclusion of chapter 1, Micah has both assailed the behavior and mourned the eventual downfall of the two centers of Jewish existence, Samaria and Jerusalem. However, while he alluded to the sins of Samaria, he has yet to reveal what crimes Jerusalem committed. This is the focus of the following speeches of his book.

---

36. See Job 1:20, Jer. 7:29, 16:6; Ezek. 27:31.
37. Jensen, *Obadiah, Jonah, Micah*, 117.
38. Sweeney, *The Twelve Prophets*, 357. While many translations render *nesher* as eagle, according to G. J. Botterweck, *Theological Dictionary of the Old Testament* (Grand Rapids, MI: Eerdmans, 1973), s.v. *nesher*; zoological considerations reveal that this bird is most likely a carrion vulture.

Speech 2 (2:1–13): Taking Land – Being Taken from the Land

Micah's second speech is perhaps one of the most excellent examples of prophetic rhetoric in the Tanakh. He no longer threatens the kingdoms with destruction due to idolatrous behavior. Instead, in chapters 2 and 3 Micah outlines a litany of sins for which Judah and Jerusalem will be held responsible. These sins are primarily crimes of social injustices and abuses of power. They include the sins of pride and arrogance that prevent the people from meaningfully evaluating their behavior and making the necessary changes. This speech can be divided into two. In chapter 2 he addresses the people, and in chapter 3 he rebukes Judah's corrupt leadership in a speech that ends in the middle of chapter 4.

Micah divides his second speech into three distinct sections. In the first section (2:1–5), he describes the behavior of those who plot to commit evil and their recompenses; he then debates the people (vv. 6–11); finally, he concludes the chapter with an ambiguous description of redemption that will leave his listeners baffled. The first section has a symmetrical construction – the first two verses describe the sins, and the following three verses announce the punishment. The word "therefore" links the two. (A second "therefore" in verse 5 serves to extend the judgment and reinforce the severity of the punishment.) Several words repeat themselves: fields in verses 2 and 4; evil in 1 and 3. The most significant verbal repetitions are the actions of the evildoers and God – they devise and plot (*hoshev*) to perform evil, and God devises and plots (*hoshev*) their demise. This structure reflects the underlying lesson of *midda keneged midda* – *lex talionis* – at its finest. Those who seize fields will have others grab them, and those who seek evil against others less powerful will find that others more powerful than them will subject them to evil. The Land of Israel and its ownership plays a central role in Micah's rebuke. It is not only a question of economic security and independence for everyone. Leviticus concludes its discussion of the need to support those who have lost their ancestral fields due to financial difficulties with God's declaration, "For the children of Israel are servants to Me" (25:55). Thus, Leviticus links the Jewish people remaining in Israel with the question of whether the people provide each other with economic support or not.

WOE TO THE PLOTTERS

Woe to those who plan wicked deeds, doers of evil from their beds; come morning light they carry it out merely because they have the power. They covet others' fields and seize them, eye others' homes and take them as theirs; they exploit men and their households, both man and his estate.

Therefore, so says the Lord: I too plot evil against this tribe of people, for you will not be able to move your necks from there, nor will you walk with your heads held high, for the time of disaster has come. On that day you will be made an object of ridicule; a wailing with bitter lamentation will arise, and it will be said, "We are raided and ruined, our people's portion seized. How then does he take what is mine and divide up our fields?" So then you will have no one to cast the lots for dividing the land among the community of the Lord. (2:1–5)

Micah's critique of the people begins with the proclamation, woe (*hoy*). The word *hoy* was originally used in a funeral lament to express deep sorrow over the dead (I Kings 13:30; Jer. 22:18). However, the prophets use it to herald a description of a specific sin followed by inevitable punishment – the announcement of the guilty party's demise.[1] The two meanings do not contradict; as seen above, Micah has demonstrated deep sadness and mourning for his people's fate (1:8) while condemning their moral failings.

The targets of Micah's diatribe are those that "lie in their beds," plotting the evil that they will perform in the morning. Already, Micah provides us with a sense of the challenge and the pervasiveness of the wickedness he faces. The night is a time to sleep – yet while the wicked lie in bed, they devise new forms of evil for the next day.[2] Malbim notes that while in Jewish thought, God generally does not punish people for sinful thoughts alone, because these people could carry out their plans immediately, without hesitation and any obstacles in their path, they would be punished. A close reading reveals that Micah has cleverly switched the order of the words. The standard idioms are to "plan evil (*ḥoshev ra*)" (2:3; Hos. 7:14) and "do wickedness" (*po'el aven*) (Hos. 6:8), while in the first verse of this speech, we have "planners of wicked deeds" (*ḥoshvei aven*) and "doers of evil" (*po'alei ra*). This wording has poetic alliterative overtones; the phrase begins with *ḥoshev* and concludes with *mishkevotam*. The word "beds" also provides a transition to the morning lights. In Tanakh, the morning generally symbolizes a time for justice and divine help.[3] However, the plotters had the power (*el*)[4] to ensure that their designs would come to fruition. In modern English, we would say that they had the courts in the palms of their hands. We begin to

---

1. See Is. 3:9, 11; Jer. 13:27; Ezek. 13:3, 18; Hos. 7:13; Amos 5:18; Hab. 2:6; Zeph. 2:5.
2. Amos had a similar complaint – the corrupt of his generation could not wait. They would say: "When will the new month be finished, so that we will sell grain; and the sabbatical year [finished], so that we will open [our stores of] grain, to make the ephah smaller and to make the shekel larger, and to pervert deceitful scales" (8:5).
3. See II Sam. 15:1–2; Jer. 21:12; Hos. 6:3, 5; Zeph. 3:5, Ps. 37:6; 73:14; 90:14; 143:8; Job 7:18.
4. While most appearances of the word *el* are divine in nature, here, the secular root of the word, power, is intended (Ibn Ezra here; see Gen. 31:29; Deut. 28:32).

appreciate the level of corruption that Micah faced. While a common thief works at night, afraid of detection, these individuals worked in broad daylight, shielded by a government, which provided the legal imprinter to their actions. It was not a few malicious individuals Micah stood against, but an entire system that was malevolent.

Micah then (v. 2) provides a detailed description of the plotters' actions and simultaneously condemns them with the steady repetition of short verbs that steadily build to a crescendo ("they covet…they seize…they take…they exploit").[5] Micah's first accusation is that they violate the tenth commandment, "do not covet" (H-M-D; see Ex. 20:17; Deut. 4:21). The Ten Commandments connect coveting to both fields and houses. Maimonides notes that a person who pressures another to sell an object that the buyer desires against the seller's will, even if the seller ultimately agrees and receives a high price, is guilty of coveting.[6] Radak suggests that the plotters would initially offer to buy the fields from the owners, but if the latter refused, they intended to seize it by force (force being through legal means). Radak continues that the plotters beat and sold to captivity those who persisted in their refusal. Micah makes two other subtle but significant changes in the second half of the verse. In the first half, he describes the damage and violence inflicted on fields and buildings. Now, the verse tells the effects suffered by "a man and his house." Not only was an individual hurt, but the plotters caused pain to his entire family. Micah uses the Hebrew word *gever* for "a man" – a term generally used for a person with rights, a citizen, yet helpless before the authorities.

---

5. Malbim understands the progression of verbs as follows:
   When they covet the field of another, they seize it by force…. [Malbim then notes the shift in the objects of desire, and suggests that] then they want houses, but houses are in the city and cannot be stolen so blatantly [neighbors would complain]. Therefore, "And they purchase [lit., take]," meaning that they take it through business means, trading the previously stolen fields for the houses…. [The next step in the progression is to] "cheat a man and his house" – after the trade, they do not relinquish possession of the house…and this is easy to perform while in the city. "And even a man and his portion [the fields they stole]," they will then take the person who had owned those fields as well. Because of his poverty, he will be sold to them as a slave.
6. Maimonides, *Hilkhot Geneva* 1:9.

The verse's conclusion emphasizes the depth of the plotters' sin. What they seize is not just land and house – it is the person's ancestral field (*naḥalato*). This is destined to be returned to a person when the jubilee year arrives. To appreciate the severity of this sin we need only remember the case of Naboth in I Kings. God condemned King Ahab for introducing the idolatrous Baal worship to the Northern Kingdom. However, God decreed to bring his dynasty to a bloody end only after the incident in which he and Jezebel fabricated a capital case against Naboth and then took possession of his ancestral land after Naboth initially refused to sell it to them:

> [Elijah pronounces punishment on Ahab:] "Because you have sold yourself to what is evil in the eyes of the Lord, I am about to bring evil upon you, and I will burn up every last trace of you. I will cut off every last male of Ahab in Israel, bond and free, and I will make your house like the house of Jeroboam son of Nebat and like the house of Basha son of Ahiya because of the anger you have provoked by leading Israel to sin. And the Lord has also spoken against Jezebel: The dogs will devour Jezebel within the bounds of Yizre'el. Those of Ahab's who die in the city will be devoured by dogs, and those of his who die in the field will be devoured by the birds of the sky." (I Kings 21:20–24)

Micah now pronounces the divine sentence. He begins (v. 3) with the transition word "therefore," and the standard messenger formula to emphasize Micah's reliability and authority – "so says the Lord," and then switches to the divine first person, "now I" (*hineni*) and declares that God is now thinking evil towards them. While *Daat Sofrim* interprets this as a sign of God's mercy, this is more likely Micah emphasizing the principle of *midda keneged midda* – that the punishment mirrors the crime. Not only will God cause their actions to boomerang against them, but He will even imitate their thought process. The plotters thought about committing evil; now, God thinks evil towards them. Micah does not specify what punishment God intends, but he does introduce the metaphor of a yoke and warns of an "evil time approaching." Although, the imagery of the yoke often means political subjugation (Is. 10:27;

Jer. 27:8; 28), Micah's primary purpose for the metaphor is to place it upon the necks of those who used to "walk haughtily." In prophetic language, to walk tall is always associated with pride (Is. 2:11, 17). The final phrase re-emphasizes the upcoming punishment by repeating the word for evil, noting that bad times are coming. Malbim suggests that this is the gradual tightening of the noose. When times are peaceful, people maintain hope that they will avoid calamity; however, when times are bad, people realize that they will not escape unscathed.

In this section, Micah subtly and cleverly changes the people who God intends to punish. First, he refers to the evil plotters as a family – possibly as a parallel to the family made to suffer in verse 2.[7] Given that they had taken a familial inheritance (*naḥala*), it makes sense to label the evildoers as family.[8] Second, Micah employs an even more intelligent form of rhetorical entrapment in the middle of the verse. For the first two and a half verses, Micah speaks of the evildoers in third-person language. They plot, they covet, they steal, they oppress. Again, one can imagine his audience becoming indignant and irate against these wicked people. Then, suddenly, in the middle of verse 3, Micah springs his trap. "You will not remove [the yoke] from your necks! You will not walk erect!" You cannot stand by quietly and serenely assume that only others are evil, and only they will suffer. Evil is coming for everyone.

In verse 4, Micah continues by describing the wailing and mourning that will follow the punishment in verse 3 before continuing to pronounce the punishment in verse 5. He starts the description with the words "on that day." While the phrase "on that day" in prophetic literature can refer to the distant future (Zech. 14:9), it can also describe a more imminent event (see Is. 22:8, 25; Hos. 1:5; Amos 8:13). Here, the

---

7. Many of the commentators assume that the family here actually refers to the entire Jewish people (Radak, *Metzudot*). See Amos 3:1, Jer. 10:25, and Zech. 14:18 for examples of this phenomenon.

8. The Torah details the land distribution in Numbers utilizing the family (*mishpaḥa*) as the unit by which an inheritance (*naḥala*) should be distributed: "You shall give the Land as an inheritance to your families by lot; to the large, you shall give a larger inheritance and to the small you shall give a smaller inheritance; wherever the lot falls shall be his; according to the tribes of your fathers, you shall inherit" (Num. 33:54).

mention of "that day" recalls the description of the evildoers plotting in verse 1. At night, they schemed; when the day came, they acted. So too, promises Micah, God will act on that day.

Micah then introduces the dirge using the Hebrew word *mashal*. While it can have the meaning of a satiric "taunt song" (see Num. 23:7; Is. 14:4; Hab. 2:6), the word is generally understood here as a lament. Radak suggests that the person performing the wailing is the false prophet who convinces the sinners that their way was just, for that was the way these false prophets spoke. However, given Micah's behavior in chapter 1, responding to every decree with mourning, it is not unfeasible that he laments how the entire people have been pillaged and plundered. In the second half of verse 4, the oppressed and ravaged people cry out as they watch their ancestral land being seized. Radak continues with his approach: It is the false prophet who assured his listeners that even if an enemy came, the troubles would be temporary, and now sees the conqueror dividing up the country among his people.

Micah's phrasing "wailing with bitter lamentation" is full of alliteration and assonance (*naha nehi nihya*), reflecting his love of wordplay again. Rashi understands the phrase as "he will lament, 'A lamentation has come about in the world…'" Ibn Ezra understands the words as a moaning sound that grows longer and louder. The wordplay continues with the cry, "we have been plundered!" – *shadod neshadunu*. It is unclear grammatically whether the second word is active or passive – "We have been robbed" or "they have robbed us." Rashi comments on this difficulty with a fascinating suggestion:

> Had [Micah] written *neshadonu* [using the passive voice], the expression would refer to the robbed and not to the robbers. Had he written *shadunu* [using the active voice], the word would refer to the robbers and not to the robbed. This way, it refers to both: we were given into the hand of those who robbed us.… [Another explanation]: *neshadonu* means we brought it upon ourselves that they robbed us.

Micah uses a word for "inheritance" (*ḥelek*) other than what he used in verse 2. However, the two synonyms for a parcel of land are frequently found together (Gen. 31:14; Deut. 10:9). The root Ḥ-L-K means "divide," and using it here in the sense of "inheritance" carries echoes of the original division of the land under Joshua to the families by tribe (Josh 15:13; 19:9). Now, strangers parcel out the land. The sudden shift in the lament to the exclamation, "how he (He?) removes it from me," strengthens the emotional impact Micah wishes to express.

Micah concludes this section by returning to address the plotters and the evildoers of verses 1 and 2 (Ibn Ezra, *Metzudot*; however, Radak suggests that in verse 4 Micah is addressing the false prophets who filled the people with false hopes[9]). The plotters who had removed inheritance rights from others would find themselves with no heirs who could receive a portion of land. Micah continues to use language that alludes to the original division of the land under Joshua as related in Joshua 14–21. The casting of rope (*ḥevel*) symbolized a method of measuring length or area (II Sam. 8:2, Zech. 2:1; see Mishna Bava Batra 7:2). The word *ḥevel* carries a double meaning, referring to both the rope and the parcel of land it delineated (see Josh. 17:5; 19:9). The other word Micah uses here to describe the sections of land is lot (*goral*). Again, this word appears throughout the book of Joshua to designate both the portions that the tribes received (17:14) and how it was distributed to them (by lottery – Num. 33:54; Josh. 18:6). This lottery was generally performed in front of or by the priest. Usage of a lottery was another form of acknowledging that God was ultimately the One who decides who shall dwell in the Land of Israel and that the Jewish people received the land from God as a gift.

The continued references to the book of Joshua suggest that Micah is trying to create for his listeners the sense that everything would be re-evaluated and distributed anew – in Jensen's words, "[this is a] repetition of the primeval division of land, from which the wicked are excluded from the 'assembly of the Lord.'"[10] The sense of *lex talonis*,

---

9. Radak's suggestion, in the context of verse 5's curse that they will have no descendants, recalls Jeremiah's prophecy about the false prophets at his time that would also not have any descendant who would merit seeing the redemption of the Jewish people from exile (29:30–32).

10. Jensen, *Obadiah, Jonah, Micah*, 123. Note that the concepts of having descendants and being a member of the "assembly of the Lord" are entwined in the following laws in Deuteronomy:

midda keneged midda, reaffirms our understanding of the nature of the crimes performed by the plotters. How the plotters enriched themselves legally suggests that victims lacked representation in the constitutional assembly when the land was divided and assigned. Here, the plotters were able to assert their power (2:2). Following "that day," fortunes reverse, and now it is the evildoers who lack representation in the assembly. Micah concludes this section and begins the next with a command not to prophecy, echoing how Amos ended his prophecy before declaring the destruction of the Northern Kingdom:

> And now, hearken to the word of the Lord. You say, *Do not prophesy concerning Israel and do not prophesy concerning the house of Isaac.* ... Therefore, says the Lord, your wife will sell herself in the city, your sons and daughters will be slaughtered by the sword, and your land will be divided by the surveyor's rope (*hevel*). And as for you, you will die in an impure land, and Israel will surely be exiled from their land. (Amos 7:16–17)

THE PEOPLE DISPUTE MICAH'S CLAIMS

Preach not, those who preach; they shall not preach to these; [for they will] not shrink back in shame. Is that what is said by the house of Jacob? Has the Lord's patience grown short? Can these truly be His deeds? Will My words not grant goodness to those who walk righteously?

But instead, My people arise as their own enemy; they strip fine outer garments from passersby; those who felt safe returning from war [become like hopeless men]. You drive out the wives of My people from their secure and joyful homes, from their young children; you forever remove the honor I gave them.

"No one whose testicles have been crushed or whose member is severed shall be admitted to the assembly of the Lord. No one born of an illicit union shall be admitted to the assembly of the Lord; even to the tenth generation, no descendant of such a union may be admitted to the assembly of the Lord." "No Ammonite or Moabite shall be admitted to the assembly of the Lord; even to the tenth generation, none of their descendants shall be admitted to the assembly of the Lord." (23:2–4)

So, get up and go! This is not your place to rest, for the defilement you brought will destroy; it will bring down a harsh line of destruction. If there were a man with a spirit of falsehood and lies who would preach toward drink and drunkenness, he would be welcomed as preacher of this people. (2:6–11)

Micah's strong words in verses 1–5 manage to arouse the ire and anger of his listeners. Their response to Micah begins the second section (vv. 6–7). Micah responds by mocking their misplaced confidence. He continues to describe their corrupt behavior: theft of land, oppressing the innocent, and removing them from their homes. Again, the targets are the corrupt, mighty, and powerful, who do this because they can. Micah begins and concludes this section targeting the false prophets[11] (see the repeated word for to preach [*lehatif*] in verses 6 and 11), and in verses 8–10, Micah criticizes the greedy and the corrupt in Judah. His literary technique, placing the attacks on the prophets around his attacks on the corrupt, cleverly reflects what was occurring in Judah. The wicked and the corrupt and the powers that be surrounded themselves with false prophets, who for the right price would justify and protect them.[12] His opponents demanded that he stop preaching in verse 6; and in verse 11, Micah concludes with an example of the only type of preaching that they would appreciate.

This section has traditionally been difficult to interpret because while it is a disputation between Micah and the false prophets, as the references and vocabulary associated with prophecy make clear, it is unclear who speaks which section. We find examples of a disputation between the lonely prophet against the religious establishment in several places in Tanakh: Micaiah vs. Ahab's prophets (I Kings 22), Amos vs. Amaziah (Amos 7), and Jeremiah vs. Hananiah (Jer. 28). Understanding the disputation here is challenging because Micah will often quote

---

11. While the false prophets are the obvious choice as Micah's disputants, and this is the approach we have followed in our commentary, they are not the only option. Micah could be quoting the responses of the people who refuse to listen, or the wealthy and corrupt themselves. Prophets (like rabbis) have no monopoly on speaking.
12. For a modern example, consider paid lobbyists for the tobacco industry arguing that smoking has health benefits.

his opponents without specifying where their words begin and end. We understand his disputants as having said all of verses 6 and 7 (although most commentators understand the final phrase of verse 7 as Micah's opening response to his disputants).

The preachers (the false prophets representing the establishment – see Micah 3:5–8; Amos 5:10, 7:10–17) demand that Micah stop preaching.[13] The verse contains three short negative statements: "Preach not!…They shall not preach!…they [we] will not shrink back in shame!"[14] With these brief statements, Micah's disputants confidently reject both Micah's message and the threat of any reckoning for their actions. The Hebrew for overtake, *yisag*, is phonetically similar to the statements made by Pharaoh and the Egyptian army as they chased Israel at the Red Sea: "The enemy said: I will chase, and I will overtake (*asig*) [the Jewish people]" (Ex. 15:9). The defiant prophets, speaking for the powerful, declare that just as Pharaoh's armies could not reach their ancestors, retribution would not reach them either.

The prophets continue in verse 7, explaining the source of their confidence: "Has the Lord's patience grown short? Can these truly be His deeds? Will My words not grant goodness to those who walk righteously?" Two simple questions reveal both the confidence of the wicked and the source of their errors. First, they accuse Micah of portraying God as not being merciful but rather unforgiving. Does Micah's God only punish? By claiming that God is loving and caring, they allow themselves to ignore the consequences of their actions, taking refuge in the traditional affirmation that the Lord is patient and slow to anger (*erekh apayim*, Ex. 34:6). The literal translation of their words "Is the Lord's patience exhausted" is "has the Lord's breath become short" – an idiom that Proverbs contrasts with the virtue of patience. "He who is slow to anger is of great understanding, but he who is quick-tempered

---

13. Ibn Ezra and Radak. Rashi suggests that Micah is speaking to other prophets, telling them to refrain from preaching, for the people are no longer listening.
14. Rashi and Radak interpret the phrase "they will not shrink back in shame" as the consequence of the beginning of the verse – if the prophets stop preaching, then disgrace [from the rebellious people] will not befall them.

(lit., short-breathed) chooses foolishness (14:29)." While Micah tries to warn his audience that punishment is coming and quickly, the false prophets assure them that God does not rush to punish. Even if they were to admit some level of guilt, God's ways and actions would never lead to the consequences that Micah threatened. The false prophets also carefully and cleverly craft their phrases. The wording with which the prophets accuse Micah: "Are these His deeds (*ma'alalav*)?" connotes the evil schemes and actions of humanity (see Micah 3:4 – "as they wrought evil with their deeds [*ma'alaleihem*]"). One can hear their righteous indignation: Of what, Micah, do you accuse God?

The final phrase of verse 7: "Will My words not grant goodness to those who walk righteously (lit., goes straight)?" is such an unblemished and immaculate declaration of God's justice and integrity that many commentators read these words as being Micah's words, his response to the false prophets. Rashi represents this approach, with God Himself rebuking Micah's disputants:

> I am not impatient – neither are these My deeds except to the wicked. With the person who goes the straight path, I perform goodness.

Philip Jensen adds similarly:

> We hear Micah's response in the final words. He adds a crucial qualification that his opponents have ignored, the issue of walking uprightly. God's attitude towards his people depends on the quality of their lives. Whether he will do good to them or does harm (Josh. 24:20; Is. 41:23; Zeph. 1:12) matches whether they walk in evil (v. 1) or walk uprightly.[15]

Though it is against the mainstream of interpretation, we wish to suggest that Micah's opponents could have spoken this phrase as well. They look at their situation. They do not see divine censure and disapproval for their actions. Instead, they look at their successes and affluence and

---

15. Jensen, *Obadiah, Jonah, Micah*, 125.

draw, what is to them, the only possible theological conclusion. If God did not desire or approve of our actions, we would not have prospered. The belief that a person can judge their level of divine approval by the level of their portfolio permeated the confident Northern Kingdom when they faced criticism from Amos, and the same was likely of Judah's elite in the south. To them, the statement "Will My words not grant goodness to those who walk righteously?" carried a logical corollary – if I am benefitting, the clear recipient of God's goodness, then that proves that I have acted righteously.[16]

In response, Micah then lambasts the greedy and corrupt for their behavior towards their people, listing additional sins that they performed. They would take the clothing of their fellow Israelites as payment for their debts, something the Torah expressly forbids (Ex. 22:26–27; Deut. 24:13–14). Amos also criticizes the wealthy of the Northern Kingdom for a similar crime ("They spread confiscated clothing beside every altar and drink wine bought with fines in the house of their gods" Amos 2:8). They treated travelers and the helpless as prisoners of war. Their aggressive land grabs served to evict women from their homes, devastating the poor not only economically but also destroying the family unit. The actual words in verse 8 are complicated. Who is the enemy; and who is threatened? Micah's usage of the phrase "My people" has always carried positive connotations – the prophet's sympathy and empathy for his people are unquestioned. Our suggested interpretation of the phrase "My people arose as an enemy" is that Micah presents the establishment's perspective, "My people [the ordinary people] arose as [became] an

---

16. One personal vignette that remains with me after several decades: A notable Jewish educational institution held its annual dinner, and rabbi after rabbi spoke praising the organization, with its many branches and its many charitable works. One of the speakers excitedly declared, "Look at our successes and how we've spread – clearly, this is the will of God (he said the Hebrew/Yiddish equivalent – *ratzon der Eibeshter*), or else how could we have been so successful!" That statement bothered me then; and several months later, it bothered me even more, when several of the heads of the institution, rabbis and trustees alike, were charged by the federal government with schemes for illegally receiving tax monies for non-extant students or programs. Sometimes, it behooves us to remember the quote often attributed to Abraham Lincoln, who was asked whether God supported the Union or the Confederacy. "It doesn't matter if God is on our side. What matters is that we are on God's side."

enemy [in the eyes of the wealthy establishment]." Both the rich land-owners and the system that supported and protected them turned their people into the enemy, justifying their continued abuse. Rashi treats it as a continuation of God's speech in verse 7 and renders the beginning of verse 8 as: "Though I am good and I perform good deeds, the matter for which My people make Me rise as an enemy to them." In this read-ing, it is as if it is God who is the enemy of the people. Ibn Ezra and Radak understand the verse differently, rendering it "[Since] yesterday, you were an enemy [to the poor], stripped off a garment, a robe...today you face a foreign enemy." Rashi suggests that the people of Israel would take advantage of well-dressed travelers. They would "strip the glorious raiment from all those who pass by on the road.... Instead of passing by securely, they [the travelers] became as if they were returning from war without clothing or food because their enemies took everything they had." If Rashi's interpretation is correct, it is one of Micah's most damn-ing indictments yet. Hospitality is among the highest values in the Bible. God does not reveal his desire to include Abraham in his thinking until He sees how Abraham educates his family in providing hospitality for the three passersby (Gen. 18). Sodom seals their fate when they fail to offer hospitality to the guests and attempt to assault them instead. Later, searching for an appropriate match for Isaac, Abraham's servant's test of Rebekah's character is not her looks or lineage, but whether she is willing to offer water to a thirsty and tired stranger (Gen. 24).[17] If the people of Micah's time were not only not performing hospitality but instead

---

17. The Talmud (Shabbat 127a), in a discussion of what kinds of "work" may be performed in order to properly receive a guest, records the following:

R. Yohanan said: Receiving guests is as great as rising early to attend the study hall.... And R. Dimi from Nehardea said: Welcoming guests is even greater than rising early to attend the study hall.... R. Yehuda said in the name of Rav: Welcoming guests is greater than greeting the Divine Presence, for it is written (Gen. 18:3): "And [Abraham] said: 'My Lord, if I have now found favor in Your eyes, please do not pass away from Your servant.'"

R. Yehuda lets us know that there are six mitzvot which, while providing some reward in this world, reach their real value in the world to come, and these six are: welcoming guests, visiting the sick, concentrating during prayer, rising early to attend the study hall, raising one's children to the study of Torah, and judging one's fellow favorably in a case of doubt.

taking advantage of their travelers, they had functionally repudiated the basis of the covenant God made with Abraham.

Radak offers two different interpretations of the evil. His first interpretation describes blatant muggings: If a rich person saw and coveted a beautiful garment on a poor person, he had no compulsion in removing it from him in public, without hesitation or fear of consequences. He then quotes an interpretation of his father, that the rich performed this robbery in a more "legal" and "respectable" manner. The wealthy would send tax collectors into the houses of the lower class. These collectors would then claim that the payments or collateral given were not enough and confiscate the clothing of the poor, leaving them as naked and as helpless as prisoners of war. Radak develops his father's interpretation into the next verse. After they had removed everything of value from the house, the collectors would then confiscate the house itself, even evacuating the women and their children from it.[18] Thus, the corrupt and greedy systematically dismantled the fundamental security of the Jewish family. The husbands are impoverished (possibly forced to leave their families to serve as forced labor to pay off debts).[19] Without their husbands present, the wives struggled to make ends meet, and ultimately they were also evicted from their house and the children expelled. The removal may have been physical, as evidenced by the widow's complaint to the prophet Elisha:

> Now a woman, of the wives of the disciples of the prophets, cried out to Elisha, saying, "Your servant, my husband, has died, and you know that your servant did fear the Lord, and the creditor has come to take my two children for himself as slaves." (II Kings 4:1)

Since Micah describes "My glory" as being removed, Rashi suggests that the object of the removal is financial – by impoverishing the parents, the

---

18. The Targum pseudo-Jonathan interprets this metaphorically, so that the wife who is being evicted from her home represents the Jewish people being evicted from the Land of Israel.
19. Rashi's two poignant interpretations complement each other: "For you slay their husbands, and they sit as widows. Alternatively: Since you take their husbands' money, and they (the husbands) sit and grieve and do not bring joy to their wives."

children, the gifts (and accompanying opportunities) that God intended to bestow upon them. Jensen notes that "The portion of land due to an orphaned child would be the only hope of escape from poverty and slavery. However, the land grabbers remove the possibility of farming forever or working the land, even when the child grows up."[20]

Radak interprets "from her infants you take away My glory forever" in a fascinating manner. He suggests: "What is the divine glory that is being taken? It is the marital relationship between husbands and wives." When families are torn apart, when couples can no longer bring children into the world, God's glory is also absent.

Verse 10 concludes Micah's condemnation of the corrupt and greedy landowners: Get up and go! This is not your place to rest! Leave this land! Having become defiled, it is no longer the land of tranquility, *menuḥa*.[21] Telling them to leave their land reiterates the theme of *midda keneged midda – lex talonis* that Micah has emphasized throughout this speech. One can imagine the wealthy landowners using the same words to the impoverished farmers they were evicting that Micah now speaks to them: Get up! Leave! They denied others a secure home; now they were being told that they would be leaving their home to an insecure exile. Additionally, Micah accuses them of defiling the Land of Israel through their evil deeds. The word impure (*tamei*) generally refers to ritual forms of uncleanliness. The Torah does not hesitate to state that immoral behavior will negatively impact the very land itself (Lev. 18:24–28; Num. 35:33; Deut. 21:23). Micah concludes his admonition to the corrupt that "it will destroy you."[22] Being in the Land of Israel while behaving in an immoral manner is not merely foolhardy; it is suicidal.

---

20. See Jensen, *Obadiah, Jonah, Micah*, 127.
21. See Deuteronomy 12:9 where the Land of Israel is called *menuḥa venaḥala*. Rashi does not understand *menuḥa*, tranquility, here as the name of the Land of Israel, but instead interprets "this is not the tranquility" as "for it was not for this purpose that I gave it to you for tranquility."
22. We have translated the phrase *teḥabel veḥevel nimratz* as "it will absolutely destroy you" like Radak and Ibn Ezra, who interpret *ḥabel/ḥevel* from the root Ḥ-B-L, to destroy (see Eccl. 5:5). *Metzudot* similarly interprets: it is the Land of Israel, having been defiled, that will be the source of destruction. Rashi has a unique understanding. He interprets Ḥ-B-L as meaning bands, referring us to I Samuel 10:5: "a band of prophets," and Psalms 119:61: "bands of wicked men." He thereby punctuates the verse differently:

Micah concludes this speech's section by returning to the topic he began – the false prophets. The word to preach (*lehatif*), which appeared three times in verse 6, reappears here twice more. Now he mockingly describes what qualified a person to join the prophets of the regime. It was these charlatans, whose self-serving prophecies served to prop up the establishment, who had attempted to silence him. However, as Micah acknowledges, anyone who preaches prosperity would have an easier time finding a receptive audience. Those who held up a mirror to the unflattering side of society and foresaw doom and despair would not be popular.

Micah describes the false prophets first through three separate descriptions of their falsehoods – they are "empty wind" (*ruaḥ*), lies (*sheker*), and deception (*kazav*).[23] These words appear in various permutations throughout the Bible when describing false prophets (see I Kings 22:22, Is. 41:29; Jer. 5:13). They may be there for emphasis, though Malbim differentiates between *sheker* as readily known to be false, while *kazav* is something that will only be revealed as false later. Next, Micah tells his listeners how they became popular preachers – by telling the listeners to drink more wine and liquor![24] That, he ruefully concludes, is how to win the hearts and minds of men.

A PROMISE OF PROTECTION – OR EXILE!

Assemble, I will assemble all of you, O Jacob; Collect, I will surely collect the remnant of Israel; together I will make them as sheep in a fold, as a flock within its stall shall they stir, a commotion of men. The breaker has risen before them; they broke and passed through a gate and went out through it; and their king passed before them, and the Lord was at their head. (2:12–13)

"In order to contaminate it [the Land of Israel], [the people] form bands of groups of wicked men.... And at the time of their banding together, they took counsel among themselves and clarified for which purpose they were uniting together."

23. In Micah's words, the word for deception is in its verb form, *kizev*, deceive.

24. This is Rashi's interpretation. However, Radak and *Metzudot* understand the Hebrew *atif leyayin* as meaning not "I will preach to [drink] wine," but "I will preach for wine" – in exchange for a good vintage, the prophet assures his listeners that they will receive a good prophecy.

Most commentators understand the final two verses of the second speech as Micah attempting to provide consolation. Having promised judgment and exile for the crimes outlined above, Micah is trying to express a measure of hope and consolation. For a remnant of the people, there will be salvation, and God Himself will lead it.[25] The optimistic interpretation blends in well with Micah's overall strategy – one common throughout the Tanakh – of combining both threats of judgment and destruction (should the people continue to sin) with promises of salvation and hope. Punishment is meted through the people's relationship with the Land of Israel. Disobedience leads to the severing of the ties between the people of Israel and the Land of Israel. Even exile, however, is not permanent. There will be a return from exile as well (Deut. 4:25–31; 29:17–30:5).

However, not all the commentators view verses 12–13 as describing a future redemption. Malbim understands them as positive but interprets them as a continuation of the words of the false prophets above.[26] This debate reminds us that Jeremiah had to contend with

---

25. Here we start to see the stark contrast between Isaiah and Micah. Micah assumes that Jerusalem will be destroyed, unlike Isaiah who cannot imagine that possibility. History would indeed prove Isaiah right in 701 BCE, when Sennacherib's siege of the city was broken due to a miracle (II Kings 19). However, it is Micah who later generations would credit with influencing Hezekiah and saving the city (Jer. 26:18). Because these verses assume a state of exile, many secular scholars automatically assume that they are later additions from after the destruction of the First Temple in 586 BCE. However, this is not only false, but it is unnecessary, both for historical reasons and because it is based on a misunderstanding of prophecy. Historically, even if Micah had been speaking to a Judean audience, they would have been clearly aware of the possibility of exile. Already in Pekah's reign in the north, Assyria had begun to exile the populations of the northern and eastern regions of the Northern Kingdom (II Kings 15:29). Most crucially, these scholars maintain faulty assumptions about the nature of biblical prophecy. In the Tanakh, prophecies are not absolute, but are related to specific situations and context, and if the people use their free will to change their attitudes and behavior, they can affect a prophetic judgment for good or bad. Indeed, as Jeremiah 26:17–18 proves, the people trusted the veracity of Micah's message, even though the predicted destruction did not come to pass. Instead, they attributed its suspension to the repentance undertaken by Hezekiah.

26. Since the false prophets denied the possibility of exile, this approach seems unlikely.

the same phenomenon one hundred years later when Nebuchadne-zzar exiled King Jeconiah and the elite of Jerusalem to Babylonia in 597 BCE. Even after the first exile, false prophets like Hananiah son of Azzur told the people that this was only a temporary lapse; in two years, God would break the yoke of Babylon and return the exiles speedily (see Jer. 28–29). Radak is perhaps most sensitive to the nega-tive connotations of many of the words in these verses. He interprets them as a continuation of the punishments that the people will face, not their deliverance.

Micah begins with two parallel phrases of doubled verbs (*asof e'esof / kabetz akabetz*) that describe that God will gather His people. The verb doublets are in the emphatic construction (absolute infinitive + imperfect) mode. Close synonyms serve to reinforce and emphasize the certainty of the promise of redemption that God is making to the Jewish people scattered by exile.[27] He continues with one of the most prominent metaphors for the relationship between God and the Jewish people – that of shepherd and sheep. The shepherd is God (Ps. 23:1) or the leadership (II Sam. 5:2), and the Jewish people are the sheep. This metaphor portrays the Jewish people's enemies as predators, who scatter them over the mountains (I Kings 22:17), and it is the good shepherd who will gather them (Jer. 23:1–4; Ezek. 34:12–13). Rashi understands Micah's prophecy to mean that just as a good shepherd gathers his sheep into the safety of the pen, so too God gathers the Jewish people into the safe and secure Land of Israel. The formerly desolate land will once again be filled with so many people that the cities will quickly fill up with bustle and noise.

---

27. See similar usages of these verses in Is. 40:11; Jer. 23:3; Ezek. 11:17. As is his wont, Malbim distinguishes between the two Hebrew terms for gathering: *asof* and *kabetz*. Malbim argues that *asof* connotes moving items that are gathered from one area and then placed in one place in a second area. *Kabetz* connotes gathering items that had been scattered all about into one specific place. Therefore, suggests Malbim, the word used to describe the gathering of the Northern Kingdom is *asof*, as they were exiled to one specific area (see Malbim on Is. 11:12), while the word used to describe the gathering of the Southern Kingdom is *kabetz*, as they were scattered to the four corners of the globe.

The next verse continues with this optimistic portrayal of the incoming of the exiles. Micah uses an interesting phrase to describe the person who will save them: the breaker (*haporetz*). Rashi poetically depicts him as the one who breaks down the obstacles to the return: who breaks the fences of thorns and the hedges of briers to straighten out the road before them. Rabbi Eliezer of Beaugency identifies the breaker as the angel God sends before the Jewish people; *Metzudot* suggests that the reference is to Elijah the prophet, who will break down the spiritual barriers that exist, both between generations and between the people and God (Mal. 3:24); and the Mahari Kara suggests that the breaker is none other than the Messiah himself.

However, Radak did not view these final two verses positively. We suggest this is because many of the phrases in verses 12–13 generally carry negative connotations in the Tanakh. For example, the doublet to gather, *asof e'esof*, appears in Jeremiah 8:13 and Zephaniah 1:2. In both those texts, God gathers to destroy (in Zephaniah, people; in Jeremiah, grapes), not to save. The verb for the breaker in verse 13, *haporetz*, also generally carries negative tones when it appears, referring to the destruction of walls (II Kings 14:13, Neh. 3:35), fences (Is. 5:5, Ps. 80:13), or the breaking out of violence (II Sam. 5:20, Hos. 4:2).

To appreciate what Micah is saying, we must pay close attention to the metaphor. No one in Micah's audience would ever envision sheep leaving the pen's safety into the wilderness as a positive message. Combining the two verses, we understand the metaphor not as one of deliverance, but as preparation for exile, as follows: Micah describes a situation where sheep have been gathered in a sheep pen, only to have someone break down the barriers and force the flock to leave, with their leaders at their heads. However, the image is eerily similar to that found on Assyrian reliefs that brag about their conquests of foreign cities. After breaking down the city's protective walls, the Assyrians would lead the captured populace outside into exile, generally with their captured leaders forced to lead the procession. In ancient times, country dwellers ran to the cities for shelter from invading armies. If Micah is describing what would happen to Jerusalem (using the destruction of the Northern Kingdom as his paradigm), the situation would be made even worse for King Hezekiah due to the influx of refugees from the Northern Kingdom that he had to absorb.[28] Therefore, throughout these verses, Radak interprets them as part of the punishment. The sheep being led into the folds were the people fleeing the advancing enemy, looking for security in the cities. He makes an interesting suggestion for the identity of the breaker. Radak identifies him as Zedekiah, the last king of Judah, and notes that right before Jerusalem fell before the Babylonians, Zedekiah tried to abandon the city and flee with his guard by breaching the city walls and breaking through the Babylonian siege to escape (II Kings 25:1–12; Jer. 39:1–10). Hence, their king (Zedekiah) passed before them (the trapped populace). He understands the final phrase "with God at their head" as meaning that God's presence had abandoned the city long before this.[29] This understanding turns this final phrase into words of comfort: despite being led into exile, God will accompany His people.

---

28. Isaiah describes King Hezekiah's building programs in Jerusalem (22:9–10): "You have seen also the breaches of the city of David, that they are many; and you gathered together the waters of the lower pool. And you have numbered the houses of Jerusalem and the houses have you broken down to fortify the wall." During the 1970s, archaeologists identified the defensive walls that King Hezekiah built to encompass the engorged city of Jerusalem, which was teeming with refugees from the Northern Kingdom after its downfall, augmented by survivors of the Assyrian invasion in the lowlands (the *shefela*). The wall, of which sections are visible in the Old City today, was eventually called "the Broad Wall" later in the Bible (Neh. 3:8). For further discussion, see M. Broshi, "The Expansion of Jerusalem in the Reigns of Hezekiah and Manasseh," *Israel Exploration Journal* 24:1 (1974): 21–26.

29. The theme of God's leaving of Jerusalem is common in prophetic literature (e.g., Isaiah's vision of the Divine Throne hovering over the Temple [6:2] as understood by Rav Yoel bin Nun [see https://etzion.org.il/en/tanakh/neviim/sefer-amos/period-yarovam-uziyahu-pekach-and-achaz-1]; Ezekiel's vision of God's chariot leaving Jerusalem in chapter 1).

Speech 3 (3:1–4:7): Destroying Jerusalem to Rebuild

Micah harshly condemned the greed and avarice of the wealthy in chapter 2, whose insatiable desire to enrich themselves led to the abuse and exploitation of the landed farmers. Traditional Israelite society rested on families that lived on their traditional ancestral holdings, worked the land, and produced what they needed. It maintained a relative level of equality between the various groups with added social/ religious mechanisms to prevent a state of perpetual poverty.[1] Now, the influx of trade and commerce into the capital cities led to an unbalanced concentration of wealth, which encouraged absentee landowners to buy lands at high rates in a manner that transformed Israel and Judah's farmers from independent landowners to indebted workers on their ancestral lands. The avarice and lack of concern of these landowners were the targets of Micah's anger and prophecies in chapter 2.

---

1. See the laws of Jubilee et al. in Leviticus 25.

Micah's third speech begins with chapter 3, which appears to be a continuation and a recapitulation of Micah's thoughts from chapter 2,[2] While several literary similarities link the two chapters,[3] the overriding themes, however, are notably different. Chapter 2 was fundamentally an attack on the worse vices of human nature. Yet, greed and selfishness will exist in every era, no matter the economic system people establish. We tried to demonstrate in chapter 2 that the ability of those people motivated by avarice and greed could not have succeeded without either the encouragement of the authorities responsible for maintaining the social order or, at least, the willingness of the same leaders to turn a blind eye to the corruption. Now Micah turns his fury towards the authorities which enabled the crimes outlined in chapter 2. No longer does Micah attack human nature; instead, he raises the question of whether the system and society had become so corrupt that it enabled corruption to prosper maintained its right to exist.

Chapter 3 contains three short speeches of judgment, each four verses long. In the judgment sections, Micah makes his general accusation (3:1, 5, 9) and follows it with the relative pronoun ("you" in 3:2, 6, 12) to directly attack the wicked. The third section combines the targets of the first two – Israel's political leaders (compare verses 1 and 9) and the false prophets (compare verses 5–6 and 11). Micah includes the

---

2. Malbim also views chapter 3 as a direct continuation of chapter 2. He suggests that the purpose of this chapter is to answer the complaints of the people in 2:7 who argued that God was too compassionate to the Jewish people to even contemplate allowing the punishments and horrors that Micah prophesied from ever coming to pass. To them, according to Malbim, Micah returns to describe in greater detail and horror the actions of the wicked and corrupt leadership. If they show no compassion, then neither will God.

3. The literary similarities go beyond the general thematic parallels (beginning with social injustices, continuing with attacks on the false prophets, and the resulting condemnation and prediction of destruction and exile). Similar metaphors (primarily a corrupt sacrificial system – see commentary) and several words also tie the two chapters together. Both the rulers of 3:1 and the evildoers of 2:2 do the same thing – both tear/seize (*gozel*). The rulers flay their victims (*hifshitu*), the same wording Micah used to describe the evil-doers stripping (*tafshitun*) the victims' clothing. Similar parallels exist between the sections that attack the false prophets – the emphasis on food for prophesying, and the argument over the "spirit of God" – whether it is forgiving (the false claim of 2:7) or whether it fills Micah with indignation (3:8).

corruption of the religious leaders and reprises both the justice system and rampant bribery but emphasizes what he considers their underlying fault: their misunderstanding of what God wants from them. He then predicts that Jerusalem will suffer the same fate as Samaria (compare 1:7 with 3:12).

However, as dramatic as chapter 3's call for the obliteration of the evil system is, it is neither the end nor the purpose of the speech. Micah does not desire destruction. He looks forward to a rebuilt Jerusalem, a place of justice and peace, where all the nations will serve God. The beginning of chapter 4, which describes Micah's ideals and aspirations for the rebuilt city, is the only possible conclusion to the speech in chapter 3, which calls for destruction. In the commentary, we will demonstrate the many connections, both literary and thematic, that link the sections. His full speech is structured as follows:

a) Attack on political leadership (3:1–4)
b) Attack on religious leadership (3:5–8)
c) Decree of Jerusalem's destruction (3:9–12)
d) Promise of Jerusalem's rebuilding and restoration (4:1–7)

A FAILURE OF LEADERSHIP

> And I say: Hear me, heads of Jacob, rulers of the House of Israel: Is it not for you to know what is just? Haters of good, lovers of evil, you rip off their skin, the flesh from their very bones, you who feasted on the flesh of my people, who stripped off their skins and cracked their bones, carving them like pieces into a pot like meat in a caldron. Then they will call out to the Lord, but He will not answer. He will hide His face from them at that time, for they have ingrained evil in their ways. (3:1–4)

Micah begins his third speech by declaring its fundamental theme, "Shouldn't the leaders of the people know what justice is?" By beginning, "And I say," Micah connects us to the previous chapter, which protested the injustices committed; but now he delineates a new line of argument: Granted that evil exists, whose responsibility is it to control, to prevent its pernicious effects from preventing society from functioning properly?[4] Therefore, states Radak, Micah is turning specifically to the leadership. Their responsibility is to know, enforce the law, and return to the poor what the corrupt seized from them. Abrabanel adds that even if they pleaded ignorance of what had occurred, the leadership was still responsible for ensuring that injustices did not occur under their watch, and for administering social justice.

Micah addresses his audience with the doublet Jacob/Israel for the third time (1:5, 2:12). As noted, when this word pair occurs, the term Jacob refers to the Northern Kingdom of Israel, and Israel refers to the Southern Kingdom of Judah. The leaders are known as the "heads of Jacob and rulers [officers] of the house of Israel." Malbim suggests that since the legitimate dynasty of David ruled over Judah, the word rulers (officers) appears with them.

Elsewhere in Tanakh, the term "heads" (*rashei*) refers to the tribal leaders who had either judicial obligations (Ex. 18:25) or military/ administrative responsibilities (Josh. 14:1), while the word for rulers/ officers can mean both military leadership (Josh. 10:24) or anyone in a position of power (Is. 3:6–7). In the eighth century BCE, with its constant military challenges and invasions, with their grim accompanying effects on the rural populations, an appearance of *ketzinim* here as army officers is quite relevant and in keeping with Micah's anti-war theme.[5] Whatever the technical definition of these positions, the premise of Micah's claim is that these leaders are not performing their fundamental duty – the performance of justice. We cannot overstate the importance

---

4. Malbim suggests that the introduction "And I say" was Micah's response to the people's complaints (according to Malbim's interpretation of 2:7) that the threatened punishments were much too strict for the sins they committed. Therefore, Micah was answering them: Then judge yourselves!

5. Throughout his book, Micah never mentions the king. Of course, this makes precise dating of his prophecies difficult (only from Jeremiah 26 do we know that chapter 3, or at least the chapter's final section, was uttered during the reign of Hezekiah). It may be that Micah wishes to accuse only those who are directly responsible for the administering of justice, those functionaries who are lower down in the official hierarchy. However, given the breadth of the threatened punishment, the destruction of the country and Jerusalem, it is difficult to suggest that Micah was ignoring the king in his attack. Clearly, the king is included in the accusation, for it is his ultimate responsibility to maintain justice in his kingdom.

of this charge. God chose Abraham because he would instruct his family in the way of justice (Gen. 18:17). Abraham, in return, turned to God and challenged, "Shall not the Judge of all the earth do justice?" (Gen. 18:25). Justice is not an abstract concept for the Jewish people; it is how they envision God – a God of justice.[6] It became the framework of the covenant between God and the Jewish people, allowing them to adopt God's concern for justice: "The Lord loves righteousness and justice. The earth is full of his loving-kindness" (Ps. 33:5). In Tanakh, justice is as much a call for action as it is a principle of evaluation (cf. Is. 58:6; Job 29:16; Jer. 21:12).[7] Micah is warning the people: If you slacken in administering justice, God, the ultimate guardian of justice, will act to maintain it ("I know that the Lord will uphold justice for the lowly, the cause of the needy," Ps. 140:13).

Like the other two accusatory sections of this speech, Micah makes a general accusation (3:1, 5, 9) and follows it with a direct address to the wicked (3:2, 6, 12). He begins with echoes of his predecessor Amos, who demanded that the people "Hate evil, and love good, and establish justice in the gate" (Amos 5:15). Micah here describes the leadership's corruption with a double reversal – they love evil and hate good.[8] Radak notes here that this is a second accusation: Not only are the leaders failing to perform goodness, but they are the active committers of injustice towards the weak. Micah's phrasing cleverly combines both legal terminology "good/evil" as well as the strongest of human emotions, "love/hate," serving to emphasize that even the most impersonal of societal standards ultimately reflects individual passions. The leadership of

---

6. C. J. Wright's formulation is beautiful: "It was rooted in the character of the LORD, their God; it flowed from his action in history; it was demanded by his covenant relationship with Israel; it would ultimately be established on earth only by his sovereign power" (C. J. Wright, *Old Testament Ethics for the People of God* [Leicester, UK: Inter-Varsity Press, 2006], 254).

7. Blessing Onoriode Boloje, "Micah's Theory of the Justice of Judgement (Micah 3:1–12)," *Journal of Semitics* 26/2 (2017): 689.

8. Micah's contemporary Isaiah also describes the behavior of the corrupt with the metaphor of basic human values: "Woe to those who say of evil, 'good'; of good, 'evil'; those who call darkness light and light darkness; who consider sweetness bitter and bitter things sweet" (Is. 5:20).

Micah's time rejected legal norms and the fundamental moral values that govern society. That society must be overthrown.

Micah continues with powerful and gruesome metaphoric imagery, describing how his people have become prey for the wealthy, whom he portrays as carnivores (Judges 14:6, Ezek. 34:5).[9] *Metzudot* suggests that the exaggerated metaphor represents the extent of their thievery from the poor. In contrast, Radak indicates that the imagery of skin and bones is to describe how emaciated the victims have become. Micah is here cleverly engaging in wordplay – the word for tearing skin, (*gazal*), has been used before in 2:2, as well as by other prophets to describe the act of the judicial system robbing the poor.[10] In verse 3, Micah continues the carnivore imagery (in a chiastic pattern: skin – flesh – flesh – skin) but switches to the past tense (from "those who rob" to "you have feasted on the flesh of my people, who stripped off their skins and cracked their bones"). He identifies the unnamed victims of verse 2 as "my [My] people" and adds a uniquely human element to the bestial carnivore metaphor – cooking. Micah uses two phrases to describe the initial preparation of the food (dealing with the skin and bones) and then adds another two to describe the cooking process (cutting up the meat, then cooking it in a cauldron). The leadership not only behaves like wild predators that hunt prey – but they are also human as well, taking the time to prepare and season their catch, which will be cooked and devoured at their leisure. Again, Micah engages in clever wordplay – the root of the word used for the flaying of the skin (*hiFSHiT* – causative form) is the same used to describe how the rich would strip the clothing off the poor (*taFSHiTun*) above (2:8). More strikingly, the Hebrew word for cauldron, *kalaḥat*, only appears one other time in the Tanakh. In describing the corruption of the priests

---

9. The people as food metaphor can be found in Psalms 14:4 ("Have they no knowledge, all those evildoers, who devour My people as if devouring bread, who do not call out to the Lord?") and Proverbs 30:14 ("A generation whose teeth are swords and whose jaws are knives, ready to devour the poor from the earth…"). Literal cannibalism is found in the Tanakh only during extreme situations of siege (see the curses in Deut. 28:52–57; and its fulfillment in II Kings 6:26–29).

10. See Isaiah 10:2 – "who turn justice away from the needy, stealing (*gazal*) the judgments of My people's poor, making widows their plunder and orphans their spoils"; see also Ezekiel 18:12.

when Eli was the high priest in the Tabernacle, the Tanakh writes how the priests would take whatever piece of meat that caught their fancy from the sacrifices, whether or not it had been adequately prepared or offered to God already or not:

> Eli's sons were depraved men who would not acknowledge the Lord. This was how the priests would deal with the people: Whenever someone offered a sacrifice, the priest's boy would come along as the meat was boiling, a three-pronged fork in his hand. He would stab it into the cauldron (*kalaḥat*), kettle, pot, or vat, and the priest would snatch whatever came up on the fork. This was how they treated every Israelite who came there to Shiloh. (I Sam. 2:13–14)

Micah's usage of this rare word causes the listener to recall the imagery of the corruption surrounding Eli's reign as the high priest in Shiloh. The debauchery led not only to his family's destruction but to the destruction of the Tabernacle as well. In doing so, Micah may be foreshadowing what he will declare to be Jerusalem and the Temple's ultimate fate (3:12).

Micah uses the conjunction "then" (v. 4) to switch the time frame to the future when the punishment for their actions arrives.[11] Their punishment is not the onset of hard times. Micah does not specify the specific nature of the tribulations that will provoke the wicked and corrupt to pray. Instead, he chooses to leave it to his listeners' imagination what sufferings await Israel's evil and corrupt leaders. However, the actual punishment is not the difficulties they will face but rather God's refusal to assist them by hiding His face when they call for help. The Hebrew word for calling for help, *za'ak*, generally appears when a person calls God for assistance and salvation.[12] However, the word appears in Tanakh when calling for help from a human leader also (e.g., Neh. 5:6).

---

11. Rashi here suggests that the leadership crying out will occur when Israel is already in exile and God comes to redeem them (2:12). Due to their sins, they will not be saved. Since the word to cry out, *za'ak*, is generally used when the caller is in immediate danger, we have adopted the understanding of Radak and *Metzudot* that it is an imminent threat that provokes the cries.

12. Cf. Judges 6:7; Hos. 7:14; Neh. 5:20, 9:9; Ps. 22:6, 142:6.

Again, Micah may be demonstrating measure for measure. Radak and Abrabanel both write that just as the wicked and corrupt ignored their victims' cries, so will God ignore their cries as well. In addition, Micah has cleverly reversed the expected chronological order. Instead of listing the sin and then the punishment, Micah first describes the punishment "He will not answer them," and only at the end does he return to why God is hiding His face – because of their evil deeds. By doing so, he creates a sense of helplessness for those calling out for help – a sharp contrast to the portrayal of the previous verses, when they acted as if they were omnipotent, answerable to no one, and reliant only on themselves.

PROPHETIC FAILURES

> So says the Lord: As to those prophets who mislead My people, who call for peace while sinking in their teeth but declare war on those who do not feed them their fill, thus night will come to end your vision; darkness will fall upon your divination; the sun will set on the prophets, and their day will darken upon them. The seers will be ashamed, the diviners disgraced; they will veil their mouths, every one – God does not answer.
>
> But I, I am filled with the strength of the Lord's spirit of justice and courage to declare to Jacob his transgressions, to Israel his sins. (3:5–8)

Micah begins his second section, a full-fledged attack on the false prophets, with a traditional prophetic formula "So says the Lord" – possibly to emphasize the contrast between Micah's genuine prophecies and the false messages from charlatans, who offered predictions for payment and forecasts for fees. The role that these fakers played in undermining the social fabric is immense. Within the political structure, the role of God's prophets is to hold the political leaders accountable. The prophet's position does not change this, neither when he is a court prophet like Nathan, who fearlessly confronted David after his misdeed with Bathsheba (II Sam. 12), nor when he is a societal outsider like Elijah, who stormed into Ahab's garden to accuse him: "Have you also murdered and also inherited?" (I Kings 21:21), those who speak for God must have the courage to confront wealth and power when abused.

The prophets in Micah's time did not do this. Instead, these impostors misled the people for money, ultimately leading the generation astray. The Hebrew root for mislead (T-A-H) alludes to both Hagar and Joseph wandering lost in the desert (Gen. 21:14; 37:15), or a misplaced meandering donkey found without its owner (Ex. 23:4). A century later, Micah's broadside would echo in the prophecy of Jeremiah, who faced his fair share of struggles with the false prophets of his generation: "Behold I am against those who prophesy with false dreams, says the Lord, and they tell them and mislead My people (*vayaTE'U*) with their falsehoods and with their bewilderment, but I neither sent them nor commanded them" (Jer. 23:32). The prophets of Micah's time would only offer optimism "when they have something to eat." The Hebrew is literally "who bite with their teeth." The verb to bite (N-SH-KH) is used to describe the bite of poisonous snakes (Num. 21:9; Jer. 8:17; Amos 5:19) and continues the imagery of the corrupt feasting on the weak. However, the verb has another meaning – the extortion of interest.[13] Though traditionally, there was a custom to bring a gift to the prophet (I Sam. 9:7; I Kings 14:3), the seers' dependence on their king or a wealthy patron ultimately compromised their message. A true prophet had to be prepared to suffer unpopularity, oppose the powerful, and risk rejection, imprisonment (and possible execution).[14] This corruption of the position of the prophet may explain why Micah, like Amos before him (7:14), never describes himself as a prophet – rather as someone to whom the Lord has spoken to deliver a message to the people. Micah is not attacking the institution of prophecy – but the motivations of those who became prophets for profit.

---

13. See Ex. 22:24; Lev. 25:36; Deut. 23:20; Ezek. 18:17.
14. While God's opening words to Jeremiah when He appoints him a prophet can be seen as reassurance, there is clearly ominous foreshadowing of Jeremiah's unpleasant future lot as well:

> As for you, be courageous; stand up and speak to them as I will instruct you. Do not break down because of them lest I break you down before them. I have made you today a fortress city, an iron column, and walls of bronze against the entire land – against the kings of Judah, its princes, its priests, and the people of the land. They will wage battle against you, but they will not prevail, for I am with you," declares the Lord, "to rescue you." (Jer. 1:17–19)

The false prophets' corruption consisted of two crimes. First, they demanded the most exquisite delicacies from the people, "the flesh of fattened animals," as Rashi expresses it in verse 5. Radak reminds us of Micah's complaint above – "I will preach to you for wine and strong drink" (2:11). Once satiated, in return for services rendered, the prophets would "foresee" a pleasant, peaceful future. However, should a person decide not to submit to their extortion, they declared war. According to Metzudot, the war meant the external troubles and tribulations that would befall the listener. However, Radak presents a different interpretation: The prophets would band together, and once united, declare war against the person who refused to feed them! Each of the prophets would speak out against this individual, blacklisting him until that person submitted to their blackmail. Ironically, the Hebrew word used to declare war is *kidshu*, sanctify. This word appears in various permutations in several places in the Tanakh to describe preparing for battle (Josh. 7:13; Is. 13:3; Jer. 6:4; Joel 4:9). Here, the prophets declare holy war on the one who does not surrender to their blackmail. Abrabanel concludes that Micah demonstrates that the prophets are false prophets through the clear linkage between the value of the gift offered and the value of the oracle received in return.

Micah describes the punishments that await the false prophets in eight brief phrases. The first two directly address the prophets, describing their inability to attain future prophecy. The remaining phrases address the nation and describe the false prophets' humiliation. Finally, Micah refers to the false prophets using three different Hebrew roots, in the following order:

(v. 6) Ḥ-Z-H (vision) ... K-S-M (divination) ... N-B-A (prophets) ...

(v. 7) Ḥ-Z-H (seers) ... K-S-M (diviners) ... _____

With clever wordplay, by not repeating "prophets," Micah has literally removed these impostors from their office.

Another way in which Micah demonstrates their illegitimacy is by placing the word "divination," a forbidden act, between the other two terms in verse 6, hence equating them. The word for diviners (*kosmim*) often implies attempting to read meaning into signs. For example, Ezekiel describes how the king of Babylon read signs into order to decide whether to attack Ammon or Jerusalem:

> And the word of the Lord came to me: "And you, Man, mark out two roads for the sword of the king of Babylon to advance upon, both exiting from the same land, and clear space for a sign at the beginning of the road leading to each city; clear space. Mark out a road for the sword to advance upon – to Raba of the Amonites and to Judah in fortified Jerusalem. For the king of Babylon stands at the fork in the road, at the beginning of the two roads, to perform a divination (*liksom kesem*); shaking arrows, inquiring of household gods, scrutinizing the liver. In his right hand is the omen that signals Jerusalem: to post battering rams, to demand slaughter, to shout out war cries; to post battering rams at the gates, to throw up earthworks, to build a siege wall. It will be seen as a false divination in their eyes – for they have had reassuring oaths sworn to them which recall the sin for which they will be seized. (Ezek. 21:24–27)

The act of divination is fiercely condemned as an abomination (Deut. 18:10–12). It is compared to idolatry by Samuel when he rebuked Saul ("For rebellion is as the sin of divination, and stubbornness is as idolatry and *teraphim*," I Sam. 15:23).

Not surprisingly, Micah describes their loss of power through the metaphor of darkness. Malbim suggests an elaborate parallel between the forms of prophecy and how the removal of their abilities will occur.

Category	Form of Prophecy	Form of Punishment
Seer	Received visions at night	Visions become night
Diviner	Practiced divinations in darkened places	Divinations become darkness
False Prophets	Prophesied by day	The sun will set on them, and the day will be blackened

As a result of the people understanding that the optimistic predictions did not materialize and were nothing more than fabrications and falsehood, they will also realize the "prophets" were nothing more than charlatans. No longer will they be looked upon as sources of knowledge and enlightenment – just derision and humiliation. Without the public believing in their "divine" channels, the false prophets would lose both status and subsistence. They will cover their upper lip in mourning (see Lev. 13:45; Ezek. 24:17, 22; Maimonides, *Hilkhot Evel* 5:19). Their mourning is either a sign of their social humiliation (Radak) or their loss of "prophecy." Micah concludes: "*Ki* (for/because) they had no word of God." Once again, measure for measure – they took advantage of others who searched for God's word; now they find that God refuses to answer them.

However, Micah reminds the people that there is true prophecy. Confidently, he explains why he trusts the authenticity of his message and, in doing so, he encourages the people to trust in his integrity. Having demolished the fictitious spirituality of the false prophets, he declares: "But as for me!"[15] Micah describes himself as a container, "filled by the spirit of God" with strength/courage, justice, and power.[16] Isaiah expands on Micah's brief self-description of being filled with divine inspiration in his portrayal of the redeemer: "And the spirit of the Lord shall rest upon him; a spirit of wisdom and understanding, a spirit of counsel and courage.... And he shall judge the poor justly" (Is. 11:2–5).

THE DESTRUCTION OF JERUSALEM

And I say: Hear me now, heads of Jacob, leaders of the House of Israel who abhor justice and pervert all that is straight – who build Zion with bloodshed, Jerusalem with iniquity. Her leaders arbitrate for bribes, her priests will teach for a price, and her prophets for dividends will divine, yet they rely upon the Lord, saying, "Surely the Lord is in our midst! No calamity can befall us."

---

15. This phrase appears in the middle of speeches providing contrast between the preceding section and what follows. See Num. 14:21; I Kings 20:23.
16. Jeremiah will later apply the same metaphor to himself, that he has been filled with fury to speak against evil and injustice (Jer. 6:11; 15:17).

> And so because of you Zion shall be plowed like a field, and Jerusalem shall become heaps of rubble, and the Temple Mount like the high places of the forest. (3:9–12)

In verses 9–12, Micah begins his summary attack on his day's political and religious leaders, including a new group for condemnation – the priests (v. 11). He amplifies his previous attack. Not only do they hate good and love evil, now these despise justice and twist all that is straight. Finally, he mocks them with their own words: "Behold, the Lord is in our midst! No calamity can come upon us," and then delivers the sentence: Due to the overwhelming guilt of the leadership, Jerusalem will suffer the same punishment as Samaria – total and utter destruction. The Talmud learns from here the power and influence that the judges have on the state of the nation and the world:

> R. Yosei ben Elisha says: If you see a generation upon which many troubles come, go and examine the deeds of the judges in the Jewish courts, because misfortune come to the world only on account of corrupt judges in Israel, as it is written (Micah 3:9–11): "Listen, now, you heads of the house of Jacob, and rulers of the house of Israel, who loathe justice and pervert all equity; who build up Zion with blood, and Jerusalem with iniquity. Their heads judge for bribes and their priests teach for hire, and their prophets divine for money; yet they lean upon the Lord and say: Is the Lord not among us? No evil can come upon us!"
>
> They are wicked evildoers, yet they placed their trust in the Creator. Therefore the Lord brings upon them three types of suffering, according to the three sins of their hands as it is written (Micah 3:12): "Therefore, because of you, Zion shall be plowed like a field, and Jerusalem shall become heaps of rubble, and the Temple Mount like the high places of the forest." (Shabbat 139a)[17]

---

17. Interestingly, while our Sages understood that it was Micah's role to deliver the decree of punishment, they turned to Isaiah for the parallel prophecies of redemption, as the citation from the Talmud above continues:

Micah begins the final section by recalling the "heads of the house of Jacob, the officers of the house of Israel." He describes how they abhor justice. The root for abhorring, T-A-V, appears in both religious (Deut. 7:26) and ethical (Amos 5:10) contexts.[18] Similarly, the heads and officers "pervert all that is straight." Under these circumstances, when the foundations of basic morality are under attack, Micah argues that cosmetic repairs will not be enough. Only the complete removal of the entire edifice will allow the erection of a newer, sturdier structure.

Micah then turns to attack the builders. They built Zion with blood, and Jerusalem with iniquity. The sentence begins with the singular form – one who builds Zion. Radak and others explain the singular form as referring to each type of individual leader mentioned in verse 9. However, the Mahari Kara interprets "the one who builds Zion" as referring to God. He understands the verse as a rhetorical question: Do they think that God will build Zion while there is still blood [on their hands]?

Metzudot takes the accusation of blood literally. He opines that Micah is condemning those who murder and then use their victims' profits to build homes in Zion. Radak understands, however, that blood (*damim*) metaphorically means money. He suggests that stealing from the poor is akin to murdering them, as they have no way to sustain themselves. One can easily imagine other potential victims – the poor

---

And the Holy One, Blessed be He, will not cause His Divine Presence to rest on Israel until the evil judges and authorities cease to exist within Israel, as it is stated (Is. 1:25–27): "And I will turn my hand upon you, and smelt away your dross as with lye, and take away all your base alloy; and I will restore your judges as at the first, and your counselors as at the beginning; afterward you shall be called: the city of righteousness, the faithful city. Zion shall be redeemed with judgment, and those who return to her with righteousness."

18. The Torah describes several prohibitions using the same root as *to'eiva*, abominations: homosexual relations (Lev. 18:22), idolatry (Deut. 7:26; 13:15), prohibited foods (Deut. 14:3), defective sacrifices (Deut. 17:1), the prohibition of wearing clothes of the opposite gender (Deut. 22:5), the prohibition of bringing immoral earnings, or the price of sale of a dog, as a sacrifice (Deut. 23:19), and cheating in measuring, counting, or weighing (Deut. 25:16). Targum pseudo-Jonathan translates the term *to'eiva* into the Aramaic as *merḥaka*, meaning distance, possibly from the natural order. Rashi on the verse discussing dishonest judges (Lev. 19:15), comments: "For the judge who distorts judgment is called ... *to'eiva*, for distortion is called *to'eiva*, as it says 'for the *to'eiva* of God ... all those who commit distortion'" (Deut. 25:16).

whose land was expropriated, the underpaid workers, or the farmers who overworked themselves as their sons were conscripted for duty. The Midrash on the Tower of Babel describes that during the construction of the tower, if a person fell off the tower and died, no one reacted – while if a brick fell and cracked, everyone present would stop to mourn the lost brick (Pirkei DeRabi Eliezer, 24). Combining this with the Radak's interpretation, we can understand Micah as bemoaning a society which valued technology and construction over human life and dignity.

It is uncertain which building projects drew Micah's ire. Amos already condemned the luxury homes that the wealthy Samaritans built while ignoring the needs of the poor (e.g., Amos 6:4–6). Isaiah likewise directed many of his first prophecies (chapters 2–5) at the excesses of the golden age that occurred under Uzziah in the first half of the eighth century BCE. In Micah's time, only one brief period saw large-scale building – in the reign of Hezekiah during the decade of relative quiet and tranquility that followed the downfall of Samaria and the exile of the northern tribes. The Tanakh describes both periods as periods of wealth and prosperity, distinguished by large-scale building projects:

UZZIAH: And [it was Uzziah's custom] to seek God in the days of Zechariah, who understood the visions of God, and as long as he sought the Lord, God caused him to prosper…. He went out to fight against the Philistines and breached the walls of Gat, Yavneh, and Ashdod, and he built cities in Ashdod and among the Philistines… his fame reached all the way to the border of Egypt, for he grew very powerful. Uzziah built towers in Jerusalem… He built towers in the wilderness and dug many cisterns because he had a wealth of livestock in the lowlands and on the plain… And his fame spread far and wide, for he had been miraculously helped until he grew powerful. (II Chr. 26:4–15)

HEZEKIAH: Determined, he repaired all the breaches in the wall, raised up towers over it, and built another wall outside it. He reinforced the Milo in the City of David, and he commissioned weapons and shields in abundance.

Hezekiah had great riches and honor, and he made himself treasuries for silver, gold, gems, spices, decorative shields, and all kinds of precious objects, as well as storehouses for produce of grain, wine, and oil, stalls for all kinds of animals, and stables for livestock. And he acquired cities and vast flocks of sheep and cattle, for God had endowed him with a wealth of possessions. (II Chr. 32:5, 27–30)

If Micah is preaching regarding specific public building programs, then the expansions of Jerusalem that served to enhance the capital during Hezekiah's reign are likely candidates. Alternatively, we suggest that much of Hezekiah's building spree was not to beautify the capital but to serve a different purpose entirely – to prepare for war (specifically, a potential Assyrian invasion, i.e., II Chr. 32:5 above). One can imagine everyone being asked "to play their part" in the war effort. Massive fortifications were built, taxes were enforced, and work details drafted. But, asks Micah, was the war necessary? If not, then all the construction was for naught and responsible for additional and unnecessary suffering.

Finally, this verse echoes in rhythm one of Isaiah's most famous prophecies, while delivering the exact opposite message:

Micah 3:10	Isaiah 1:27
Boneh Tziyon bedamim, Yerushalayim be'avla.	*Tziyon bemishpat tipadeh, veshaveha bitzedaka.*
The one who builds Zion with blood, and Jerusalem with injustice.	Zion will be redeemed by justice, and by righteousness – those who return to her.

As noted above, Micah again presents a darker, more negative prophecy than Isaiah.[19]

19. While we are trying to avoid speculation, most date the first chapter of Isaiah to after the Assyrian invasion in 701 BCE (the description of Jerusalem alone in the burnt countryside in verse 8 being the marker). Therefore, we confidently suggest

Micah concludes by condemning the entire fabric of Judah's leadership – the political/legal, the ritual, and the spiritual. The verbs are all in imperfect form, which suggests continued and persistent conduct. The judges (lit., the heads) give rulings based on bribes (prohibited in Ex. 23:8; Deut. 16:19; see Prov. 17:8). The priests received several tasks: to serve in the Temple, to teach (Lev. 10:11; Deut. 33:10; Hos. 4:6; Mal. 2:7), and to rule on ritual issues (i.e., Lev. 14:5–7; 22:20). Malachi describes the phenomenon of the priests and the people offering blemished sacrifices (Mal. 1:8). One can imagine that as an unblemished animal was likely more expensive, a discreet bribe to the priest to ignore specific blemishes could be a profitable transaction for both parties. Finally, Micah returns to his accusations above that the prophets were nothing more than diviners for profit.

What caused this corruption? Micah points to one fundamentally flawed belief – their absolute trust that God would never abandon them or Jerusalem. Micah uses the metaphor of the people leaning on God as if He were an immovable object. Isaiah uses the same analogy to describe Hezekiah's mistaken reliance on the Egyptian for military assistance, with disastrous results:

> Because you have despised this word to place your trust in oppression and strayed *and leaned upon that [Egypt];* because of this, this sin shall be like the crack lengthening, ready to bring down your exalted wall – the breaking of which will come so very suddenly. (Is. 30:12–13)

Nevertheless, the people argue: "Is not the Lord in our midst?!" God's abode, the Holy Temple, was in Jerusalem. As the psalmist declares: "God is in its [Jerusalem's] midst; it will not collapse!" (Ps. 46:6). Amos previously had to describe the end of Israel as being caused by "the sinful of My people perish, those who say, 'The evil shall not soon come upon us'" (Amos 9:10). Jeremiah would confront the same mistaken confidence a century later, in his desperate attempts to persuade the

---

that Micah was the original speaker, and that Isaiah spoke his verse later, cleverly paraphrasing Micah's line to offer hope after the destruction.

people of Judah to repent before Jerusalem was destroyed: "Do not rely upon words of false assurance that say: This is the Temple of the Lord, the Temple of the Lord, the Temple of the Lord" (Jer. 7:4).[20] However, as the Talmud points out, Judah's leadership sinned so grievously that destruction had to follow.

Micah begins his declaration of punishment with the word "therefore" (v. 12), just as he did in verse 6. Just as with the false prophets above, the punishment fits the crimes of Judah's leadership. All of his metaphors invoke images of destruction – plowed fields and heaps of rubble. For a city situated on a mountain, the imagery of a leveled field implies devastation.[21] All of the building projects alluded to in verse 10 will be utterly demolished. All the land taken from the indigent rural populace will return to its farming roots – as Zion will be "plowed over like a field." The walls of Jerusalem, God's abode, will be demolished, leaving mounds of rock and rubble. The Temple, built from expensive marble and the cedars of Lebanon, will now become heaps of stone in a forest. As Judah behaved like the northern neighbor Samaria, the end will be the same. The prophecy is so powerful that a century later, elders will quote it authoritatively in defense of Jeremiah during the reign of King Jehoiakim:[22]

> Some men from among the elders of the land stood up and said to all the assembled people, "Micah the Morashtite would prophesy in the days of Hezekiah, king of Judah. He addressed all the people of Judah, saying, '*This is what the Lord of Hosts said: Zion will be plowed over like a field, Jerusalem will come to be a mound*

---

20. Tragically, one could suggest that the miraculous victory over Sennacherib's army in 701 BCE only served to embed this mistaken belief even more firmly among much of the populace.
21. J. D. Nogalski, *The Book of the Twelve: Micah-Malachi* (Macon, GA: Smyth & Helwys Publishing, 2011), 549.
22. The elders make one subtle yet significant addition to Micah's words: "So said the Lord of Hosts." Clearly, with the passage of time, the impression had been made on the people that Micah truly spoke in God's name. Also significant is the fact that the elders attribute Hezekiah's repentance as stemming from Micah's message, not Isaiah's, even though it was Isaiah who served more in the role of royal advisor.

of ruins, and the Temple Mount an overgrown hilltop shrine.' Did Hezekiah, king of Judah, and all of Judah put him to death? Did he not fear the Lord and beseech the Lord, so that the Lord reconsidered the evil that He had spoken concerning them? We would be bringing great evil upon ourselves." (Jer. 26:17–19)

As history demonstrated, Micah's negative prophecy was suspended with Hezekiah's repentance, but not revoked. The failure of the people to repent despite Jeremiah's (and Josiah's) efforts ultimately led to its tragic fulfillment in 586 BCE: "O God! Nations have come into Your heritage; they have defiled Your Holy Temple; they have made Jerusalem into heaps" (Ps. 79:1).

Micah's prophecy of destruction began with the outer regions – Zion and Jerusalem – progressively going inwards until breaching the Temple Mount. Usually, the name of God is added to the house (*beit Hashem*), as appears in the very next verse (4:1). It is possible that Micah deliberately avoided using the divine name here, signaling to his listeners that God had already abandoned his dwelling place (Ezek. 10:9; 11:23). The prophecy ends with Judaism's most holy city becoming its most unclean place. However, all is not lost. Despite the destruction, Micah alludes to redemption as well. After the devastation, the fields will be plowed, the soil tilled, and the rubble piled up. Once again, Jerusalem will be suitable land for growing. Ultimately, this leads to the climax of his vision – a newly rebuilt Jerusalem.

JERUSALEM REBUILT

This will be in days to come: The mountain of the Lord's House will be rooted firm, the highest of mountains, raised high above all hills, and all the peoples will stream to it. Many nations will come, saying: "Come, let us go up to the mount of the Lord, to the House of Jacob's God; He will teach us of His ways; we will walk in His pathways" – for teaching will come forth from Zion, from Jerusalem the Lord's word. He will judge among peoples and arbitrate for mighty nations, far away; they shall beat their swords into plowshares, their spears into pruning hooks. Nation shall not raise sword against nation; no more will they learn to make war. Every man will sit beneath his grapevine, under his fig tree with none to trouble him, for the Lord of Hosts has spoken. For all peoples follow, each the call of his god; we will follow the Lord our God, His call, for ever and ever.

On that day, so says the Lord: I will gather the lame, draw close those driven away and any I have afflicted. I will set the lame as the remnant and her who was far removed as a great nation, and the Lord will reign over them in Mount Zion from then and forever. (4:1–7)

The conclusion of Micah's third speech begins with one of the Bible's most optimistic descriptions of the future. It is very similar to the prophecy at the beginning of Isaiah 2. Most attribute the vision to Isaiah, not Micah [we shall compare and contrast how the two prophets deliver their vision in the commentary]. Micah begins with an image of the resplendent rebuilt Temple (v. 1), which has become the center for the world's nations to make a pilgrimage to learn the Torah of God. The result of this is an outbreak of justice; causes are judged, conflicts are resolved. With the end of wars, peace will break forth, and weapons will disappear, transformed into useful implements. Micah promises that every individual will enjoy both prosperity and security – for this is the divine promise. The people will respond with a declaration of faith. Micah concludes the speech with a description of the ingathering and the healing transformation of the Jewish people from exiles to a proud, sovereign nation.

This section begins with the words "in the days to come (lit., at the end of days)" causing many to view chapter 4 as a separate section (as is reflected in the chapter division).[23] The understanding is that

---

23. That chapter 4 introduces a separate section is an almost universally accepted axiom in biblical scholarship. Early German Bible critics even argued that only the first three chapters were authentic Micah, as they felt that the prophet could only deliver a negative message of destruction and therefore the later optimistic chapters were later additions. More recent scholars reject these assumptions as unfounded – it makes no sense to maintain that prophets cannot offer hope along with rebuke. Indeed, how would a prophet motivate his listeners to repent if destruction was inevitable, with no expectation of improving their situation. However, for reasons which we will explain below, Bible critics still view chapter 4 as a separate entity from chapter 3.

chapter 4 begins a new subject – an eschatological survey of a glorious Messianic future. Indeed, this is the dominant approach of traditional commentators, who eagerly awaited the fulfillment of Micah's vision. Most of them could not conceptualize Micah referring to an earlier time since such a time never really happened in biblical history (or beyond).[24] However, we argue that Micah never intended the beginning of chapter 4 to describe a distant future vision. Instead, Micah directed these words at his listeners in the time of Hezekiah, and he intended to provide comfort and direction to the Jews of Judah.[25] As such, his placement

---

Most do so because they view chapter 4 as a new subject, dealing with the distant future as opposed to the immediate present of Micah's context. A few scholars attempt to demonstrate the connectiveness between the beginning of chapter 4 with the rest of the chapter, and chapter 5 as well. There are several linguistic markers that create a sense of coherence within chapters 4–5. For example, the key opening words or phrases, including "On that day, says God" (4:6; 5:10), "now" (4:9, 11; 5:1) "and shall be" (5:5, 7, 10). Bernard Renaud suggests a chiastic structure for chapters 4–5:

    A. 4:1–5: In the last days: pilgrimage of the nations

        B. 4:6–7: The remnant transformed into a strong nation

            C. 4:8–13: To Jerusalem: promise of victory

            C'. 4:14–5:2: To Bethlehem: establishment of the Messianic Era

        B'. 5:3–8: The remnant supreme in the Messianic Era

    A'. 5:9–14: In the last days: purification of the nations and destruction of idols

However, these thematic titles are too general and ignore many other repetitions within the text. For reasons we will expound upon, we interpret the first verses of chapter 4 as the natural conclusion of the speech that begins in chapter 3, and that 4:8 begins a new discourse. Interestingly, one of the first and few scholars to claim that the beginning of chapter 4 is a natural continuation of chapter 3 was Charles Shaw, who investigated the book of Micah as a series of persuasive speeches, and discovered many linking connections between the two units, which we will describe.

24. As noted by Radak, *Metzudot*, and others. Ibn Ezra eloquently represents this approach, with a fascinating (and possibly anti-Christological) proof:

    There is no doubt that this prophecy is for the future, and so it says, "In the days to come." Because he mentioned that the Temple Mount would become "as the high places of the forest," he returned to comfort Israel that the glory of the Temple would return.… [Proof that these days have not yet occurred is that] until today, no generation has passed without war. If one place is quiet, another is not. And it says, "Nation will not raise up sword against nation." (Ibn Ezra on 4:1, 3)

25. The rabbis in the Talmud also pointed to the time of Hezekiah as containing tremendous (and sadly unfulfilled) Messianic potential:

of these verses after serve a specific rhetorical purpose. Micah tells his listeners – to arrive at a better future (4:1–7), we have to destroy the corrupt society that we've built now (3:1–12).

This concluding section opens with a dramatic announcement. Though Jerusalem and Zion face destruction, this is only temporary. Sometime in the future, Jerusalem will transform from a small provincial capital, where the corrupt Judean elite designed futile military strategies, to the most central significant location globally, focusing on justice, peace, and reconciliation. Indeed, the leadership that Micah castigated in chapter 3 will have completely disappeared, and instead, God will fulfill their functions (judging, teaching, guaranteeing the people's physical and economic security). While many interpret chapter 4 as the beginning of a new speech, dedicated to the distant future, the beginning of chapter 4 shares many words and themes with the concluding verses of chapter 3, including head (*rosh*), house (*beit*), war (*milḥama*), judgment (root: SH-F-T), instruction/ teaching/ruling (root: H-R-H), Jacob and Israel, Jerusalem and the Temple Mount. Micah contrasts the Jerusalem of his day, worthy of condemnation, with his vision of a transcendent Jerusalem of the future.

Micah 3:9–12	Micah 4:1–5
Jerusalem is a city where leaders and judges detested justice and perverted the law for bribes: (3:9) *hameta'avim miSHPaT* (3:11) *rosheha beshoḥad yiSHPoTu*	Jerusalem will be a center of justice for nations: (4:3) *veSHaFaT bein amim rabim*

God wished to make Hezekiah the Messiah, and Sennacherib, Gog and Magog, but the Attribute of Justice protested before God: "Master of the Universe! David, king of Israel, sang many praises before You – and You did not make him the Messiah. You performed all of these miracles for Hezekiah and he did not sing before You – will You make him the Messiah?" (Sanhedrin 94a)

The dual nature of certain prophecies, that they can refer to both present listeners and later generations (should the prophecy not be fulfilled) is labelled the "Malbim Principle" by Rabbi Hayyim Angel, based on Malbim's interpretation of Isaiah 11 (see also Malbim's introduction to Haggai). Rabbi Angel develops this idea fully in "Prophecy as Potential: The Consolations of Isaiah 1–12 in Context," *Jewish Bible Quarterly* 37:1 (2009): 3–10.

Micah 3:9–12	Micah 4:1–5
Jerusalem's teachers (the priests) only instruct for a fee (possibly referring to bribes): (3:11) *veKohaneha bimechir YORu*	People will stream to Jerusalem for instruction in the ways of God: (4:2) *veYORenu midrakhav*
Jerusalem was a city of blood (3:10)	Jerusalem will be the inspiration to end war (4:3)
God is no longer present in Jerusalem (3:11–12): *vehar habayit lebamot ya'ar*	God will dwell in the Jerusalem of the future (4:1–2): **har beit** Hashem ... **har** Hashem

Perhaps most strikingly, Micah's vision goes far beyond repairing the specific faults of Judah. Micah's image extends beyond borders to include all the peoples of the world. Temple Mount, formerly flattened and plowed over, is now higher, dwarfing other mountains and hills. Symbolically, Jensen suggests that the exaggerated height makes it visible from the ends of the earth and, like a magnet, draws the peoples and nations to it for instruction, justice, and reconciliation.[26] For this reason, these words are plastered on the Isaiah Wall across from the United Nations.[27] Micah's promise of universal justice does not compromise the faith of the Jewish people. The world's nations come to learn from the God of Jacob, His Torah, in God's chosen city (v. 2). Indeed, the Jewish people exclaim a powerful declaration of faith and trust in the middle before Micah concludes with the ingathering of the exiles.

---

26. Jensen, *Obadiah, Jonah, Micah*, 144–45.
27. Though many think that the quotation is on the wall of the United Nations building itself, the history of the Isaiah Wall is (as always) more interesting. From the Blog of the European Journal of International Law:

    However, the wall with the words from Isaiah is not part of the UN complex. It was built in 1948 alongside some steps leading up to a housing development across the road from the site of the UN building, and the inscription was only added in September 1975 when the park was dedicated to Ralph Bunche. The quote was engraved without an attribution, a fact which so incensed one New York citizen that he lobbied the office of the mayor for ten years to have the word "Isaiah" added to it. His wish was duly granted by Ed Koch in 1985 and it is now known as the "Isaiah Wall."

When would Micah's vision occur? Though the phrase *beaḥarit hayamim* is generally translated as the "end of days" or "in days to come," the phrase does not always refer to the distant future, but rather to an indefinite period in the future.[28] More importantly, if Micah intended to refer to a distant future, this would reduce the effect of Micah's vision since it would not include any present ethical imperative.[29] *Daat Mikra*

"Let Us Beat Our Swords into Plowshares" – statue in the UN garden

There is also a statue in the UN garden entitled "Let Us Beat Our Swords into Plowshares." It was donated to the UN by the Soviet government in 1959 after being originally displayed at the 1958 World's Fair in Brussels. Needless to say, the Soviet records do not attribute the statue's title to either Isaiah or Micah. See https://www.ejiltalk.org/isaiahs-echo-progress-prophecy-and-the-un-charter/

28. See for example, Gen. 49:1, Num. 24:14, Dan. 2:28. *Theological Dictionary of the Old Testament*, s.v. *aḥarit hayamim*.

29. Daniel Smith-Christopher summarizes the issue succinctly: "It becomes more fantasy than vision, a false hope as opposed to a real hope or even a moral statement that

suggests that Micah is saying to his listeners: This vision is achievable today if you so desire.

As noted above, both Micah and Isaiah received the same prophecy:

Isaiah 2:1–5	Micah 4:1–5
1. The vision that Isaiah, son of Amoz, prophesied concerning Judah and Jerusalem.	1. *This will be in days to come: The mountain of the Lord's House will be rooted firm, the highest of mountains, raised high above all hills, and all the peoples will stream to it.*
2. *This will be in days to come: The mountain of the Lord's House will be rooted firm, the highest of mountains, raised high above all hills, and* all the nations *will stream to it.*	2. *Many* nations *will come, saying: "Come, let us go up to the mount of the Lord, to the House of Jacob's God; He will teach us of His ways; we will walk in His pathways" – for teaching will come forth from Zion, from Jerusalem the Lord's word.*
3. *Many* peoples *will come, saying: "Come, let us go up to the mount of the Lord, to the House of Jacob's God; He will teach us of His ways; we will walk in His pathways" – for teaching will come forth from Zion, from Jerusalem, the Lord's word.*	3. *And He shall judge between* many peoples *and reprove* mighty nations afar off; *and they shall beat their swords into plowshares, and their spears into pruning hooks; nations shall not lift the sword against nation; neither shall they learn war anymore.*
4. *He will judge among* nations *and arbitrate for* many peoples; *they shall beat their swords into plowshares, their spears into pruning hooks. Nation shall not raise sword against nation; no more will they learn to make war.*	4. Every man will sit beneath his grapevine, under his fig tree with none to trouble him, for the Lord of Hosts has spoken.
5. House of Jacob, *come, let us walk by the light of the Lord.*	5. For all peoples follow, each the call of his god; *we will follow the Lord our God, His call, for ever and ever.*

could guide contemporary action!" (*Micah: A Commentary*, Old Testament Library Commentary Series [Louisville, KY: Westminster John Knox, 2015], 30).

Why did Micah and Isaiah prophesy what is essentially the same vision?[30] Abrabanel suggests that both saw the same vision, and therefore Micah chose to use Isaiah's wording since the people were already familiar with it. The commentators generally explain the slight differences between the texts as reflecting the talmudic principle that while two prophets may both see the same vision, the exact formulation will vary (Sanhedrin 89a). Most assume that Isaiah's prophecy predates Micah, who had not yet begun his prophetic career. However, even though Micah utters nearly the same words as Isaiah, he intends to produce a very different effect. In Isaiah, this vision is likely Isaiah's first prophecy.[31] The context of Isaiah 2 is a period of great prosperity,[32] one that almost definitely

---

30. Scholarship traditionally suggests three options: (1) Isaiah took from Micah's oracles and incorporated it into his own; (2) Micah took from Isaiah's oracles and incorporated it into his own; (3) both were drawing upon a pre-existing oracle that was known to the people that each adapted for their purpose.
31. Rabbi Yoel bin-Nun argues that chapter 2 of Isaiah, with clear references to the wealth and grandeur accumulated by Uzziah, is the earliest of the prophecies in the book of Isaiah. See his series "Prophets Against Superpowers," https://www.etzion.org.il/he, and his article *"Kalbei Hashemira shel Hazehihut"* [The guard dogs of arrogance] at https://www.929.org.il/page/336/post/8663.
32. Isaiah 2–5 contains the following descriptions of the opulence and luxuries that led to the haughtiness and pride of Uzziah's era:
    * Their land is filled with silver and gold, there is no end to their treasures; their land is filled with horses, there is no end to their chariots. (2:7–8)
    * It is the day of the Lord of Hosts for each exalted, each proud man, for each man who is raised – to be brought down. For all the cedars of Lebanon, high and exalted... for all the ships of Tarshish and all coveted floors. Man's arrogance will be thrown down, the pride of men brought low.... On that day, man will throw down his gods of silver, gods of gold.... (2:11–20)
    * The Lord says: Because the daughters of Zion are proud, walking with their heads poised, casting their eyes around them, walking their dainty walk, their feet ringing with anklets.... On that day, the Lord will pull off the glory of those anklets, those headbands and moon pendants, earrings and bangles and scarves, those headdresses, silver bands, and sashes, the perfume boxes and amulets, all those finger rings and nose rings, the fine robes, the mantles, the stoles and the purses, the mirrors and shawls, the turbans and veils. (3:16–23)
    * Woe to those who rise early to chase ale, whom wine lights up through the night, who feast on lute and harp music, on timbrel, flutes, and wine, never once turning to look at the Lord's workings, never once noticing the work of His hands. (5:11–12)

could only refer to the reign of Uzziah during the first half of the eighth century BCE. During these decades, when both Judah under Uzziah, and Israel under Jeroboam II lived in peace and were unaffected by external threats, Isaiah chooses to begin his prophetic message with an inspirational vision of what the Jewish people could accomplish should they admit that God is behind their success. If they acknowledged God and thanked him, they could inspire the rest of humanity to do the same. As a result, Jerusalem would transform into the world's spiritual capital, nations would learn from God's ways, justice would sprout forth, and the world would live in peace.

Micah shares Isaiah's vision of justice, peace, and the transformation of Jerusalem with one caveat. The old Jerusalem must be destroyed. This is the real significance of Micah's placement of this utopian vision here, after the vision of destruction that concludes chapter 3. The corrupt and crooked city must be plowed over to grow a place of peace and prosperity.

Micah's first image of the possibilities of the new age is the raising of the Temple Mount to become the highest among the mountains, so prominent that people will stream to it. The geographical reality is that the Temple Mount is relatively low and surrounded by higher hills (such as the Mount of Olives). Radak immediately notes the metaphoric nature of Micah's imagery. Mount Moriah's physical height will not change. Instead, this symbolically asserts the Temple Mount's new status as the pre-eminent spiritual capital in the world.

Similarly, when Psalms describes Mount Zion as incomparable in height (Ps. 48:2–3; 78:69; cf. 68: 16–19), the intention is that the God who dwells there was incomparable to any other deity. Rashi interprets the mountain imagery as symbolic of the various miracles performed for the Jewish people. At Mount Sinai, God gave them the Torah (Ex. 19–20); at Mount Tabor, the tribes under Deborah and Barak miraculously defeated Sisera's chariots (Judges 4); and at Mount Carmel, Elijah brought fire down from heaven and restored the people's faith in God (I Kings 18). According to Rashi's interpretation, the miracle of the restoration of Jerusalem and the Temple will surpass anything yet seen in Jewish history.

Modern scholars have noted that for ancient peoples, mountains contained special significance. For example, Israel's pagan neighbors long built temples for their pantheons on mountains. They understood their deities as dwelling in these high sanctuaries, and the higher the mountain, the more powerful or prominent the deity was said to have been. Othmar Keel lists three theological notions that temple mountains had in ancient Near Eastern religions: they represented access to heaven, symbolized a god's victory over chaos, and provided a symbol of a god's presence (his house on a mountain on earth).[33] Now, says Micah, all the ancient religions will vanish. Instead, God's presence will be visible and known to all, and with this recognition, people from all over the earth will journey to God's Temple, with so many people making this pilgrimage that Micah and Isaiah describe it as a river of people that paradoxically "flows" uphill.

In verse 2, Micah reveals why everyone is streaming towards Jerusalem and the Temple – to learn from God and His Torah. Micah repeats the verb to go (H-L-KH) three times. It is understood literally in the first two instances, as it describes the physical movement of the nations (each nation encouraging the other – *Metzudot*) as they ascend to Jerusalem. In the third and final usage, to go refers to living according to God's dictates and commandments.

Micah labels the Temple as the "house of the God of Jacob." Rashi (Is. 2:3) explains that while Abraham and Isaac gave names to Mount Moriah according to their various experiences (Abraham called it "the mountain of God" – Gen. 22:14; Isaac called it a "field" – Gen. 24:63), only Jacob envisioned it as the place for a home when he called it Beth-El.

The teacher's identity in verse 2 – "*He (he?) will teach us of His ways*" – is disputed. Since the previous clause described the Lord's mount and God's house, *Metzudot* understands the teacher as referring to God (through his Torah scholars). Radak, however, suggests that this is a

---

33. O. Keel, *The Symbolism of the Biblical World: Ancient Near Eastern Iconography and the Book of Psalms* (New York: Seabury Press, 1978), 113, quoted in Wilhelm Wessels, "YHWH, the God of New Beginnings: Micah's Testimony," *HTS Teologiese Studies* 69:1 (Dec. 2012), 6, and available online at https://www.researchgate.net/publication/262438572_YHWH_the_God_of_new_beginnings_Micah's_testimony.

reference to the Messiah, who will teach the nations God's ways and arbitrate disputes between them. Malbim (on Is. 2:3) distinguishes between the ways of God, which will be taught to the nations, and the paths of God, on which they will walk. He suggests that ways (*derakhav*) refer to main roads, and paths (*orḥotav*) refer to sideroads that branch off from the main artery. As such, the nations are saying that while God (or the teacher[s]) will teach us the main principles of the Torah, we shall then attempt to learn the details and ramifications on our own.

The verse concludes with the famous statement, "for teaching will come forth from Zion, from Jerusalem the Lord's word." Some commentators suggest that this alludes to the Sanhedrin, who sat in an antechamber (the *lishkat hagazit*) in the Temple, symbolically connecting service and law. The speaker of this statement is also unclear. Radak suggests that these are Micah's (Isaiah's?) words, explaining to his amazed listeners why the world's nations choose to come to Zion. Mahari Kara suggests that these words continue the nations' speech right before explaining their pilgrimage to Jerusalem.

Once the numerous nations and distant peoples arrive in Jerusalem, not only will they receive instruction, but they will receive an audience to judge them and settle their differences. That a king would be involved in the arbitration of disputes was not unexpected. It often occurred when the judicial system was unable to bring redress (see II Sam. 14:4, I Kings 3:16), and in such an event, the parties would acknowledge the wisdom of the king who sits before them. The judge's identity is left unclear, but given the above, Mahari Kara's suggestion that it is God Himself who will judge between them is not unfeasible. Abrabanel suggests that the Great Sanhedrin will serve as God's representative to judge the nations. As with the unknown identity in the previous verse, Radak identifies the judge as the Messiah (Ibn Ezra; *Metzudot*).

Radak also sees a cause and effect between the two halves of the verse, switching from justice to peace. He writes:

> If there are wars or grievances between the nations, they will come before the Messiah for justice, for he will be the ruler over all the nations. He will teach them, informing the crooked one that he must "straighten out that which is unjust for your adversary. As

a result, there will be no war between nations, for he will make peace between them, and they will not need weapons."

According to this, it is the absence of justice that prevents peace from taking root.

Micah then describes the peace that will break out. It will be so complete that all the world's peoples will begin to disarm themselves willingly. This is opposed to other prophetic visions of the future – others describe how it is God who shatters weaponry before peace (Ps. 46:9[10]; 76:3[4]; Ezek. 39:9; Hos 2:18[20]). Waltke suggests that "the images of sword and spear symbolize the ancient foot-soldiers entire arsenal (I Sam. 17:14). Therefore, the hammering of swords into hoes, and spears into pruning knives serve as comprehensive synecdoches for the transition from war to peace."[34] Smith-Christopher emphasizes the agricultural nature of the implements. Just as Jerusalem would be best served if it were torn down and turned into arable farming land, the technologies of war are best transformed into instruments towards the peaceful growing of food.[35]

Malbim interprets that as God will settle any differences, nations will no longer need to go to war against each other. In fact, due to the spread of monotheism, not only will the nations not wage war anymore, but they will not even need to learn how to wage war! Additionally, in the absence of aggressors, they will not even possess any weapons for defense. Indeed, the world's energies will be able to be focused solely on growth and prosperity. With the absence of destruction, construction can begin.

With war a memory, Micah turns to one of the classic images of prosperity in the Bible. He sketches what the ancient rural farmer would have declared to be "his middle-class dream" – to sit under his vine and fig tree. Micah is highlighting the economic implications of what will have occurred. With peace between nations and peoples, "freedom from the crippling economic burden of war leads to a vision of paradise in

---

34. Waltke, *Micah*, 201.
35. Smith-Christopher, *Micah*, 135.

the language of an agrarian economy."[36] Noting the switch, Malbim suggests that this verse reclaims the ideal situation destroyed in chapters 2 and 3. With economic justice (if not equality), peace can reign. Agricultural abundance is one of the primary promises that God made for the Land of Israel:

> For the Lord your God is bringing you into a good land, a land of streams and springs and deep waters gushing out to the valleys and the hills, a land of wheat and barley, vines, fig trees and pomegranates, a land of olive oil and honey, a land where bread will not be scarce, where you will lack nothing. (Deut. 8:7–9)

Perhaps it reflects Micah's rural roots (as opposed to the urban Jerusalemite Isaiah) that he includes this pastoral imagery in his vision of the ideal future. But whose imagery did Micah adopt? The idea of sitting securely under vines and fig trees as an expression of satiety and safety first appears in the description in the book of Kings of the idyllic situation that the Jewish people enjoyed under the reign of King Solomon: "All the days of Solomon, Judah and Israel from Dan to Beersheba dwelt in safety, each person beneath his grapevine and fig tree " (I Kings 4:25). Some scholars suggest that Micah was influenced by the vision of Solomon's grandeur and wealth.[37] However, another unlikely contemporary of Micah also uttered the phrase – Rabshakeh, Sennacherib's royal

---

36. Jensen, *Obadiah, Jonah, Micah*, 147.
37. R. Binyamin Lau, *Eight Prophets: With Bindings of Love* (Heb.) (Rishon LeZion: Yediot Publishing), 122; the English translation of his discussion of Micah is available as an appendix to his work on Isaiah, co-authored by R. Yoel Bin-Nun, *Isaiah: Prophet of Righteousness and Justice* (Jerusalem: Maggid Books, 2020), 263–280. R. Lau interprets Micah as representing the hawkish approach in Hezekiah's cabinet: "Micah prophesied about the need to become stronger; to become swift and aggressive.... [Micah] called for the enemy to penetrate the enemy's borders, to strike in the heat of the battle" (Lau, *Isaiah*, 167).

R. Lau interprets Micah as being motivated by the desire to restore old glories, based on the allusion to Solomon's reign ("every man under his vine and fig tree," Mic. 4:4, cf. I Kings 5:5). He also bases his interpretation on the apparently militaristic verses at the end of chapter 4 and the beginning of chapter 5. As we have conclusively shown, this approach is at odds with everything Micah has said or done and has no

messenger. Rabshakeh spoke directly to the people of Jerusalem: "Do not listen to Hezekiah, for thus says the king of Assyria: Make peace with me; come out to me, and each will eat from his own vine and his own fig tree, and each will drink from his own cistern" (II Kings 18:31).[38] Given the Assyrians' previous treatment of Judah's captives, it is unlikely that Rabshakeh's promises, like those of many politicians, were meant to be taken seriously. However, Micah strenuously opposed the military buildup and the beginning of hostilities with Assyria. Rabshakeh (whom the Tanakh tells us knew Hebrew) may have been quoting Micah cynically: Look what would have happened had you not decided to wage war against us. However, Micah here is claiming that this is the ultimate goal for Judah and all of humanity. Once Jerusalem is raised, it will elevate all the world's nations; everyone will enjoy the blessing. Ultimately, the fig tree and the vine and all the prosperity that it entails are left for the future ("On that day – the Lord of Hosts has spoken – you will call one to another: Come under the shade of the vine; come under the shade of the fig," Zech. 3:10).

Verses 4–5 conclude Micah's vision of the future before the gathering of the exiles. They continue to describe a level of peaceful coexistence, but surprisingly, one in which everyone maintains their worship of idols. Unlike verses 1–3, which describe how the nations of the world stream to Jerusalem to learn God's ways and to settle disputes between them, in verse 4, Micah declares, "For all peoples shall go, each one in the name of his god." Rashi brings the Targum pseudo-Jonathan, who says that this refers to the nations that did not go to Jerusalem to learn from God but chose to continue to follow their gods and that ultimately, they will be destroyed. Ibn Ezra suggests Micah is encouraging his listeners to continue to walk in God's ways. Radak also suggests that this verse refers to Micah's time – only in the Messianic era will the nations leave their idolatry and serve God. Finally, *Metzudot* understands Micah

---

basis in the text, and a close reading of the relevant verses from chapters 4–5 suggests that these words were uttered by Micah's opponents.

38. Smith-Christopher (*Micah*, 137) even suggests that what Micah is really doing is telling the people to accept Rabshakeh's surrender terms, an approach that, given the Assyrian reputation for brutality, is patently ludicrous.

as explaining to his listeners that the Jewish people will be worthy of the honor described above because of their faithfulness to God throughout the long years of the exile (see also Malbim). These may even be the words of the people who hear Micah's words: As long as the nations of the world are no longer threatening us, we will be satisfied.

Finally, Micah turns to figuratively address the remnant who survived the cataclysm of the destruction detailed in chapter 3.[39] He begins, "On that day," echoing the beginning of "the days to come" from the first verse, implying that this is a continuation of the description of the future. His vision also differs from most prophet visions of the future as here, the ingathering of the exiles precedes the reestablishment of the Temple and Jerusalem.

Speaking in God's name, Micah then (v. 6) promises, "I will gather the lame, draw close those driven away and any I have afflicted."[40] The root for lame (TZ-L-A) only appears in two other places in Tanakh – in Gen. 32:22 to describe the injured Jacob, and in a similar context of salvation in Zephaniah 3:19. The Jacob allusion may reflect that Jacob was exiled, made lame by God's angel, and then brought safely back to Israel, a ready model for the people facing dispersion from their land. It may also return to the sheep metaphor that Micah (and other prophets) often uses to describe the relationship between God and Israel.

After calamity strike the herd (with the Assyrians as the predators) and the sheep scatter in panic, the shepherd then hustles to restore his flock. First, he takes in the lame, the injured, who are unable to defend themselves. Once they are safe, the shepherd then ventures out looking for the healthier animals who managed to flee to farther locations. While *Metzudot* and Radak both read the two types of sheep as referring to all of Israel, both Abrabanel and Malbim interpret the wounded flock as referring to the Northern Kingdom and the healthy flock to the Southern Kingdom. God then acknowledges that He is responsible for the state of the nation, as He gathers "those whom I have afflicted" (this

---

39. The concept that a remnant of the Jewish people will always survive appears four times in his book – 2:12; 4:7; 5:6–7; 7:18.
40. The translation of *osfa* as assemble follows Radak. Both Rashi and the Mahari Kara interpret it as "heal" – God will heal the lame.

is likely a general statement that sums up those spoken of in the preceding clauses). The root word for afflicted is *ra*, evil, echoing the previous appearances of the word in Micah when God was the perpetrator of the destruction (2:3; 3:4, 11). Both Radak and *Metzudot* suggest that God's acknowledgment here is a promise – just as I caused things to regress for the Jewish people, so too now I will cause things to be successful and to flourish.

Micah continues (4:7) to describe the ingathering of the exiles. He repeats the word "lame" but replaces the words "driven away" with "cast off." The word *hanhala'ah* only appears here, possibly derived from the word *hala*, "far off." The remnant, formerly the few who graciously survive, now become a mighty nation.

The final line – "and God will reign over them at Mount Zion forever," brings us back to the beginning of chapter 4. When all is complete, everyone will acknowledge that God rules over Israel from the Temple.

Speech 4 (4:8–5:14): Grappling towards Redemption

Micah's fourth speech is one of the most difficult in prophetic literature. Some verses call for military action; others call for passivity and patience. Some address the present; others address an unknown future. However, like a complex but well-structured symphony, every word and verse move the reader invariably closer to its desired goal – redemption. There are repeated and contrasting themes throughout the speech. Micah deftly compares the present grim reality with an idyllic future, contrasting his vision with those of the impatient people around him, who yearn for immediate redemption. The words bounce off each other as the past, the present, and the future merges: "On that day, says…" (4:6; 5:10) melds with "now" (4:9, 11; 5:1) and into "and shall be" (5:5, 7, 10). The first half of the speech (united by the keywords "daughter of Zion" [4:8, 10, 13]) contrasts the present era of distress with the coming era of salvation. The second half focuses on the positive implications of the coming of the Messianic Age for Israel.

Most importantly, the time for accusation is over. Micah no longer dwells upon the past sins, orienting the listeners towards God's actions in the future instead. This speech is structured as follows:

A) Downfall, Renewal, and False Steps
    1. A call to Jerusalem to prepare for exile (4:8–10)
    2. Jerusalem responds to the attack (4:11–14)
    3. Two leaders, two solutions (5:1–5)

B) A Full Redemption
    1. The Identity of the Jewish people (5:6–8)
    2. God brings salvation (5:9–14)

PREPARE FOR EXILE

And now you, Migdal Eder, the rampart of the daughter of Zion to you will come; dominion will return as first it was, and sovereignty to the daughter of Jerusalem. Now then, why do you cry out loud? Have you no king among you? Is your advisor lost to you that your agony overcomes you like a woman in labor? Suffer and strain as a laboring woman, daughter of Zion, for now you will leave the city and dwell in the open field. You will go as far as Babylon; there you will be rescued. (4:8–10)

Micah begins his speech by directly addressing "daughter of Zion," a term for Jerusalem or the Jewish people, to whom he will return in verses 10 and 13.[1] He speaks to her in the here and now – the brief positive description of the future sets up the stark contrast with Jerusalem's pitiable condition in the present. Next, he establishes the restoration of the kingship and Jerusalem, setting up the theme of his speech and the grounds for conflict. This verse also acts to frame the outer axes of this section. The sheep metaphor appears here and in 5:5, the concluding

---

1. Due to its positive nature, as well as the continuation of the sheep metaphor from verse 7, some suggest that verse 8 is the proper conclusion to the section that ended in verse 7. However, not only does the sheep metaphor continue well into the next speech, the temporal shift – the return to the present tense – signifies a clear break from the previous verse describing the Messianic Age.

verse; a connection between city and king appears in both here and in 5:1. Micah does this to surround his negative predictions for the immediate and the upcoming dispute with his opponents with positive prophecies.

Micah calls Jerusalem *Migdal Eder* – literally, the tower of the flock. The medieval commentators all assume that it refers to either the Temple (Rashi, Mahari Kara), the Tower of David (Radak), or the city of Jerusalem (*Metzudot*, Ibn Ezra). Targum pseudo-Jonathan suggests that it refers to the city of Migdal Eder, close to Bethlehem in Judah (see Rashbam on Gen. 35:21), where, according to Targum pseudo-Jonathan, the Messiah will first reveal his identity.[2] The image of the watchtower next to the herds envisions a shepherd watching his flock, guarding against wild animals or thieves.[3] Ideally, from the towering Mount Zion that Micah described in 4:1, God will protect the people of Jerusalem. However, the sense from the rest of the verse is that while positive events (the return of the kingdom) will occur in the future, the present situation is less optimistic. Perhaps Micah wishes to portray an image of a herd of sheep that grazes around a tower that still stands among the rubble and ruins of Jerusalem.

The second description of Jerusalem is *ofel*, a rampart. It is the ridge south of the Temple, which links the Temple to the City of David.[4]

Micah then uses two synonyms for "come" – *teteh, uva'a* – in the middle of the verse, which divide the verse into two halves. The first refers to coming back to the city, while the second anticipates the coming of the original kingship. Next, he uses two synonyms for kingship – "dominion" and "sovereignty" (*memshala* and *mamlakha*). Micah will return to the verb form of "dominion" (*moshel*) in

---

2. Rabbeinu Bahya on Gen. 35:21 suggests that the Messiah will reveal himself at this location because it is here that Benjamin was born, and here the tribes first became complete – twelve in number. When the Jewish people are finally reunited and made whole again, then the Messiah will arrive.

3. See the juxtaposition between Uzziah's towers and his numerous flocks in II Chr. 26:9–10.

4. See II Chr. 27:3, 33:14, where Jotham first builds the *ofel*, which Manasseh then heavily reinforces. Note that Nehemiah also refers to a lofty tower near the *ofel* (3:25–27). Malbim views the different names as a progress – from a place where flocks can graze safely (*Migdal Eder*), to a tower of strength (*ofel*), and ultimately becoming the rebuilt capital of David's kingdom.

his description of the new ruler that will arise from Bethlehem (5:1). Rashi understands the phrase the "former kingdom" as "the kingdom in its original form" – the united kingdom of Judah and Israel. The second word, *mamlakha,* appears several times to describe the early monarchy before it split into the Northern and Southern Kingdoms (I Sam. 24:20; II Sam. 5:12; 7:12). Finally, Micah tells how God will bring back the scattered flocks – both Samaria and Jerusalem. However, if Jerusalem and Judah are still standing and a king is ruling over Jerusalem, what will be their fate?

Micah continues with three short prophecies that begin with the word "now" (4:9, 11, 14). In all of them, hostile nations gather against Israel, and the people search desperately for a means of salvation. The first two prophecies are commands addressed to the daughter of Zion (vv. 10, 13), and the third addresses a mysterious "daughter of a troop" (v. 14). Two very different voices alternate within the section, which will lead to either defeat and exile or an immediate and decisive victory. One voice advocates for a robust and firm response to the military threats against Jerusalem. The other voice advocates for a milder reaction and resistance. Building tension among his listeners, Micah only reveals God's preference in the second half of the speech (5:6–14). The competing voices are so discordant that commentators debate whether Micah should be classified as a pacifist or a militant, while others alternate the time about which Micah speaks between the present or the Messianic future.[5]

In the first short section, Micah speaks to the daughter of Zion, but his tone is less hopeful or sympathetic, almost mocking. The context of his speech indicates that Jerusalem is distressed due to an impending invasion. Micah inquires, "Now, why do you seek foreign alliances?"[6] Isaiah counseled Ahaz during the Syro-Eframitic invasion (734–732 BCE) not to seek allies – advice that Ahaz rejected when he

---

5. Binyamin Lau portrays Micah as the prototypical "religious Zionist" militant (*Shemoneh Nevi'im,* 122–27); Smith-Christopher sees him as the embodiment of Quaker pacifism (*Micah,* 2).

6. In Hebrew, the words read *tari'i re'a.* Our understanding followings the translation of Rashi and Mahari Kara. Rashi writes: The literal translation of *tari'i re'a* is to "befriend a friend." Ask yourself: Why do you need to seek friends and beloved ones (namely, kings of Egypt and kings of Assyria) for assistance? However, Radak derives

chose to assume vassal status to Assyria in exchange for protection. Isaiah also castigated Hezekiah for his reliance on the Egyptians and the Babylonians during his campaigns against Assyria (II Kings 20:16–19, Is. 30:2–3). In both cases, the prophets advised that Judah stay neutral, not attempt to interfere in international politics, a viewpoint Micah would have heartily endorsed. Micah continues, "Is there not a King in your midst?" – universally understood by the commentators as referring to God (with most interpreting the counselors as God's prophets – *Metzudot*). Radak understands Micah as trying to console Jerusalem as it goes into exile, commenting that "though God presently hides His face, He is still your King and Advisor, and He will redeem you from Babylonia."

Micah concludes verse 9 and begins verse 10 with a painful analogy: The daughter of Zion is now in labor, gripped with agonizing birth pains. Malbim suggests that this is analogous to the Land of Israel, preparing to expel the Jewish people from within it. If this allusion is a connection to the Migdal Eder reference above, this becomes portentous. Migdal Eder reminds the listener of Rachel's death in childbirth (being where Jacob traveled to and pitched his tent after he buried Rachel); recalling it here only adds to the feeling of dread that has overtaken the people. Micah commands the daughter of Zion "Be in pain! Groan, like a woman giving birth!" His harsh tone leads commentators to interpret this as a rebuke. Micah continues to describe the defeat that Judah will suffer. The exile will comprise three stages: First, a forced departure from the city and all that they valued; second, being forced to dwell in open fields;[7] finally, eliminating the possibility of escape and sealing an irrevocable punishment, they are sent to the farthest, most eastern reaches of the Assyrian Empire, to Babylon.[8]

---

the words from the Hebrew *teru'a*, "call out." Why, asks Micah, do you call out and mourn? Instead, look to the future and think of your upcoming salvation.

7. Cf. "Go not forth into the field, and on the road do not go, for the enemy has a sword; there is fear all around" (Jer. 6:25).

8. The Hebrew for "to Babylon" (*ad Bavel*) could also be read as "as far as Babylon." The sudden appearance here of Babylon as the destination of exile is puzzling, as its fulfillment with the Babylonian exile did not occur until 597 BCE (and then in 586 BCE), almost a century and a half later. Medieval commentators view this verse as an explicit prophesy towards that future. Some modern scholars suggest that this

However, Micah does not end this short section with the negative image of the Jews in exile. No matter how far away from Israel the Jewish people are, they will be saved. Micah emphasizes this by using two synonyms for save – to rescue (*tenatzeli*) and to redeem (*yigalekh*). The word "rescue" will play a crucial role in the following sections. The term "redeem" is also significant. The Torah describes how when fields or persons belonging to a family were sold to someone else (generally due to impoverishment), a member of that family, a *go'el* (kinsman-redeemer) was obligated to purchase the relative's freedoms and recover the fields.[9] According to this analogy, it is God Himself who is redeeming His family members, the Jewish people, from their exile and recovering the Land of Israel from those who dwell in it, and returning it to its rightful owners.

JERUSALEM RESPONDS TO THE ATTACK

And now, though many nations rally against you, saying: "Let her be defiled; we will watch and gawk at Zion." But they know nothing of the Lord's thoughts; they do not realize His design, for He has gathered them like sheaves on the threshing floor. Rise and thresh! daughter of Zion, for I will make your horns iron, your hoofs bronze. You will crush multitudes of peoples. You will dedicate their spoils to the Lord, their riches to the Master of all the earth. Now, warrior daughter, assemble the warriors! A siege is laid against us; with a scepter, they strike the judge of Israel upon the cheek. (4:11–14)

verse is a later addition, an approach that we reject as unnecessary. The Assyrians ruled over Babylon at the time, evidenced by the fact that they transferred people from Babylon to replace the exiled ten tribes in the Northern Kingdom in II Kings 17:24. The reference here is more likely that Babylon is a distant place of exile, and not the exiling power. If the context of Micah's speech is Hezekiah's flirtations with the Babylonian envoys (II Kings 20:12–19), who were seeking to draw Judah into an anti-Assyrian coalition to rebel against Sennacherib, then the reference is quite appropriate.

9. See Lev. 25:25, 47–49; Jer. 32:6–15; Ruth 4.

Micah continues to discuss the impending invasion, presenting options for how the besieged kingdom can react.[10] The focus shifts from the beleaguered people to the many marauding nations. They are not the reformed and repentant nations of the ideal future described above. Instead, they are many – and references to many nations are universally negative in Deuteronomy (see 7:1, 15:6., 28:12; also Ps. 135:10). In the prophets, the phrase "many nations" often refers to the peoples of the world watching the fate of the Jewish people with astonishment (Is. 52:15, Jer. 22:8, Ezek. 38:23). Psalms 89 depicts Jerusalem humiliated under the taunting gaze of the world: "All wayfarers have plundered him; he was a disgrace to his neighbors…. Remember, O Lord, the disgrace of Your servants, which I bear in my bosom, [the disgrace] of all great nations (Ps. 89:42, 51)." Against the many nations of the world, Israel stands alone.

Here Micah describes how they look forward to defiling the city. The specific word Micah uses for "defile" generally does not carry religious overtones. The root commonly used is T-M-A. Here, the root is Ḥ-N-F, used elsewhere to describe ungodliness and wickedness (Is. 9:17; 10:6). Micah claims that the people's crimes are not ritual, but rather in the realm of social injustice and corruption. Therefore, Zion receives the same fate. Rashi suggests as much when he translates "defiled" as guilty: "[Those who say:] Let Zion be guilty of her sins, and let her iniquity be visited upon her."

Micah then describes God as reversing the nations' intentions because the nations "know nothing of the Lord's thoughts; they do not realize His design." Psalms praises God for protecting the Jewish people using the same idea: "The Lord foils the plans of nations; He thwarts the intentions of peoples. The Lord's plans endure forever, His

---

10. Despite the verse beginning with "And now," most commentators (Radak, *Metzudot*, Ibn Ezra) interpret the following verses as referring to the future, because the positive outcome – the defeat of the gathered nations – did not occur in Micah's time. Therefore, Malbim interprets the "many nations" that are gathered against Jerusalem to include the Babylonians, the Greeks, the Romans, etc., all the way to Gog and Magog – every nation that oppressed the Jewish people. Most commentators present some variation of this approach. *Tosafot Rid* tries to maintain a historical relevant approach, suggesting that the many nations refer to the many different peoples that were conscripted in the Assyrian army.

heart's intents for all generations" (Ps. 33:10–11). Radak explains simply that the nations thought they should concentrate all their energy and efforts towards destroying Jerusalem, despite it not being a threat to their existence. They hoped to profit from the spoils; instead, God planned to despoil them.

Micah continues with the agricultural imagery that epitomizes his message. In his metaphor to describe the military obliteration of the invaders, he depicts the nations as harvested sheaves of wheat. Amos used sheaves as a metaphor for the punishment that the Northern Kingdom would face (2:13); Jeremiah did the same for the people of Judah (9:22). In this parallel, God is the Owner who gathers the sheaves into His threshing floor (the battlefield outside of Jerusalem); the daughter of Zion fulfills God's will by becoming the thresher. Micah continues the metaphor in verse 13 when, in God's name, he commands the daughter of Zion to "Rise and thresh!" Now, the Jewish people are the ox that will do God's threshing. God promises that He will make Israel's "horn into iron." In the Torah, the imagery of an ox's horns carries the symbolism of unbridled aggression. Exodus 21 lists the goring ox among the archetypes of damage that a person is responsible to prevent. Later, in his valedictory address, Moses blessed the tribe of Joseph as one whose "horns are the grand horns of a *re'em*. With them, he gores the peoples, all, to the ends of the earth" (Deut. 33:17). When trying to convince kings Ahab and Jehoshaphat to go to war, the false prophet Zedekiah son of Chanina "made himself iron horns, and he said, 'Thus says the Lord: "With these you shall gore Aram until their demise"'" (I Kings 22:11). Having gored the invading enemies, "Israel the ox" now crushes its enemies. Here, the metaphor of threshing is not for positive ends, describing how wheat is separated, but to describe the forceful and complete manner in which the kernels are shattered, leaving behind worthless chaff (Is. 41:15; Jer. 51:33; Amos 1:3).

Both the nations' riches and their wealth are given to God (v. 13). Rashi distinguishes between the two types of booty. Riches, *betza*, refers to the ill-gotten gains that the invading armies had forcefully taken from preceding conquests, while wealth, *ḥeil*, refers to their original possessions. In Tanakh, when the Jewish people fought existential battles, the spoils of war were dedicated to God as a reminder of who gave them victory, and of the significance of the victory. So too, with the gains here. They are placed under a "ban," *ḥerem* to either be destroyed (Deut. 7:26) or placed in permanent storage in the Temple treasury (Josh. 6:17–24). People cannot wage war for survival if some members concern themselves with their profit margins.[11]

To summarize verses 11–13: Micah summons the Jewish people to war, promising victory against the invading armies. As noted, because this triumph never happened in Micah's lifetime, most commentators interpret the verses as referring to the Messianic future. For example, Ibn Ezra writes that the Jewish people need to be compared to a wild ox because years of exile will have sapped Israel's strength. Therefore, they need the encouragement that God will give them the strength to fight their enemies. Had Micah concluded his prophecy here, it would have been a fitting climax – the total defeat of the enemies and the transformation of Israel from a helpless daughter to a mighty warrior.

However, something does not seem right in these verses. Until now, Micah has not advocated a confrontational and aggressive policy. Instead, both his message and imagery have indicated that Micah would have preferred to see Jerusalem assume a peaceful posture towards the aggressors. If the invaders were the Arameans and Israelites during the years 734–732, Micah likely supported Isaiah's policy of patient neutrality. He knew that the danger would soon pass (Isaiah describes the enemies as "two smoking stubs of firebrands," Is. 7:4). On the other hand, if Micah is referencing the Assyrian invasion of 701 BCE during Hezekiah's reign, he likely foresaw the folly in Hezekiah's actions and the devastation that these policies would bring upon the countryside and its populace.

Most peculiar is that when Micah presents the imagery of a strong, militant daughter of Zion in verses 11–13, he draws upon the imagery used by a false prophet! If a prophet wished to be believed and trusted,

---

11. Radak suggests the possibility that the Jewish people could in fact keep ownership over some of the riches captured as long as they donated a share to God, while Malbim suggests that since the Jewish people represent God on this earth, it is as if their ownership and God's are identical. We haven't brought these opinions in the commentary, as they diverge sharply from the apparent simple meaning of Micah's words.

it is difficult to imagine that he would use words known universally as
emanating from a charlatan and a fraud. Yet the wording Micah uses here,
with the horn imagery, is a clear allusion to the attempt by Zedekiah
son of Chanina to convince Ahab to go to war, promising that Heaven
guaranteed his success (I Kings 22:24). However, Ahab went to his death.
Micah's quoting Zedekiah would raise the suspicions of his listeners
about the integrity of his message – does he mean what he is saying?
Finally, demonstrating that Micah does not believe in the militant message he is preaching, he overturns his confidence that Judah will defeat
the nations with one verse – the final verse of chapter 4: "Now, warrior
daughter, assemble the warriors! A siege is laid against us; with a scepter,
they strike the judge of Israel upon the cheek."

The commentators sense the sudden change in tone and message.
They suggest that Micah is no longer describing a Messianic future but
suddenly switches to a grim present. The simple reading of the verse is
that though Micah is calling upon the Jewish forces to gather, they will
be defeated. Not willing to have the prophet responsible for leading
the people to ruin, several commentators interpret Micah as addressing the foreign invaders. Mahari Kara understands the references to
troops as Micah telling the Assyrian army to attack, since, at this time,
Israel will fail due to her sins. Rashi makes a similar suggestion, except
that he argues that Micah is directing his words to the Babylonian army
under Nebuchadnezzar, who successfully defeated Judah in 586 BCE.
Radak maintains the simple meaning that Micah is addresses the Judean
armies, but avoids the issue by interpreting this verse referring to the
temporary setbacks during the final Messianic battle (see Zech. 14:2)
until the Jewish people finally prevail. Some modern interpreters argue
that as many appearances of the root (G-D-D) appear in the context of
gashes a person made on themselves while mourning (forbidden in
Deut. 14:1; see also I Kings 18:28; Jer. 41:5), we should interpret the verse
as Micah speaking directly to Judah, telling them to prepare to mourn:
"Inflict on yourselves wounds of mourning, you that are full of wounds of
mourning."[12] The second half of the verse explains Jerusalem's hopeless

---

12. Jensen, et al., quoting the NJPS translation, 156. Jensen also notes two other
interpretations: Following the LXX, the NJB and REB both change the final D in

military situation, as exemplified by the phrase: "with a scepter, they strike the judge of Israel upon the cheek."[13] Striking a cheek is a sign that one party has total control over the other.[14] Once again, Micah uses imagery drawn from the false prophet Zedekiah, who advocated military action, who struck Micah's namesake Micaiah, the one prophet who spoke truthfully to Ahab and Jehoshaphat, recommending that they not go to war against the enemy. By switching to the plural form: "Now you shall gather yourself in troops, O daughter of troops; he has laid siege to *us*," Micah also subtly hints that his opponents, and not he, are the speakers of these words that encourage a militant resistance. If this is the case, then this verse allows us a glimpse of Micah's genuine opinion: He presented the side that called for a firm, militaristic response, using his opponents' own words – only to cleverly and subtly undermine their call, by drawing upon imagery first utilized by a false prophet a century before. Then, Zedekiah's optimism led the people to an ignominious defeat and humiliation before the armies of Aram. Should the people choose to take up arms again, Micah thus alludes that the outcome will be the same.

---

the root G-D-D (Heb., troops or gash) to an R, creating G-D-R (Heb., fence). This changes the meaning of the verse to "Now you are walled around with a wall" – the walls of Jerusalem now comprise a prison rather than a refuge. However, Jensen prefers not emending the text of the MT when it is sensible. Jensen prefers an approach that combines two translations of the word G-D-D: "Now you gash yourself with marks of mourning, daughter of a troop" (cf. Rudolph, *Kommentar*; Allen, *Books of Joel, Obadiah, Jonah and Micah*; Mays, *Micah*), which enhances Micah's sense of wordplay.

13. Noticeably, Micah does not refer to the leader as a king, but as a judge. Rashi tries to give a historical explanation:

> Who caused them (Babylon) to succeed? The Israelites deride their prophets and their judges and strike them on the cheek. So were they wont to do, and so we find in *Pesikta* [*DeRav Kahana*, 125b], and so does Isaiah say (Is. 50:6), "I gave my back to smiters."

R. L. Smith feels the use of "judge" was used "to call attention to the impotency of the present ruler... [while] earlier judges were charismatic deliverers or saviors. The present king could not even save himself" (*Word Biblical Commentary 32: Micah – Malachi* [Nashville: Thomas Nelson, 1984], 43).

14. See I Kings 22:14; Job 16:10; Ps. 3:8; Lam. 3:30; Is. 50:6.

TWO LEADERS, TWO SOLUTIONS

And you, Bethlehem Efrathah, minor among the clans of Judah –
from you, one will emerge to rule Israel for Me, one whose descent
is from an earlier time, from ancient days. So, then, He will give
them over until that time when a woman in childbirth will give
birth. Only then will the remaining brothers return to the children
of Israel. And he will rise up and lead his flock with the strength
of the Lord, with the majesty of the name of the Lord his God,
and they will reside in safety, for His greatness will be known to
the ends of the earth.

This, then, will be [will assure] peace: when [should]
Assyria comes to invade our land, to trample our fortresses; we
will set against him seven shepherds and eight commanders of
men. They will pound the land of Assyria by sword and the land of
Nimrod at its gateways, and he will deliver us from Assyria when
they invade our land and trample our borders. (5:1–5)

Micah continues to address the dire situation that Jerusalem finds itself
in – but with a surprise. A new ruler is coming – not the present king,
humiliatingly trapped in the capital, but from a lowly, country town. In
the context of Micah, both wars against Jerusalem have come to a sudden end. With a miracle ending Sennacherib's siege, there was indeed a
remarkable reversal (II Kings 18–19; Is. 36–37). However, Micah is hoping for more than mere survival. He views the crisis as an opportunity
to uproot the corruption that has taken root in Jerusalem and replace
the present government with ethical leadership.

As in 4:8, Micah begins by the word *ve'ata*, and you, directly
addressing a city. However, instead of Zion, Micah turns to the lowly
hamlet of Bethlehem-Efrathah.[15] In Micah's vision, the present situation

---

15. Bethlehem, at the time a smaller country village, is found 9 km south of Jerusalem
(today, it borders directly on the southern Jerusalem neighborhood of Gilo). Efrathah
could be used as an alternative name for the town (Ruth 4:11) since it was the dis-
trict in which it was located (I Sam. 17:20), and also the name of the Judahite clan
that lived there (Ruth 1:2; I Chr. 2:50). Elsewhere it is called Bethlehem of Judah
(Judges 17:7; I Sam. 17:12), to distinguish it from a Bethlehem in Zebulun (Josh.
9:15) (*Metzudot*). For a related discussion of the debate regarding the location of

is hopeless, and Jerusalem is doomed. To restore and rebuild the country, a new David must appear, born and nurtured in David's birthplace – a town too small to be worthy of honor, yet one that merited that Israel's greatest king came from there. The Hebrew word for small, *tza'ir*, also means young, and in Tanakh implies both inferior strength and lowly stature (Judges 6:15; Job 32:6). Radak understands that the word *tza'ir* applies to Bethlehem, the town. In contrast, Rashi understands it as referring to David's family:[16] "You [David's family] should have been the lowest of Judah's clans because of the stigma of Ruth the Moabitess in you." One can also understand the word "young" as referring to David himself. Despite being the youngest son, Samuel appoints him as king (I Sam. 16:1–13). The youngest son taking power over the eldest is among the most prominent biblical themes, especially in the formative narratives of the Jewish people in Genesis. This theme demonstrates "the reversal of worldly expectation, showing how God can choose those who are accounted little."[17] Micah does not, as some scholars suggest, aspire towards the replacement of the Davidic line. Nathan's guarantee of the eternal Davidic dynasty remains valid (II Sam. 7:8–16), but it needs a fresh start. Isaiah imagined the cutting down of the Davidic family tree (Is. 11:1), but also saw a new branch growing from the stump. The phrase Micah uses here, "but from you [he] will come forth [*yetzei*]," alludes to Nathan's promise to David of an eternal dynasty:

Rachel's tomb, presently believed to be located on the border between Jerusalem and Bethlehem, see Yitz Etshalom, *Between the Lines of the Bible* (Brooklyn: Yasher Books, 2006), 138–58.

16. *Metzudot* emphasizes here that the Bible never states that the Messiah actually has to be born in Bethlehem, just that he must be a descendant of the Davidic family line. Given the importance that Christian commentators placed on Jesus being born in Bethlehem, this comment carries serious theological weight. In fact, Matthew constantly stressed the Davidic character of Jesus's person and ministry (Matt. 1:1, 17, 20; 15:22), and it is no surprise that he paraphrases Micah to buttress his claim: "And you, Bethlehem, in the land of Judah… from you shall come a ruler who is to shepherd my people Israel" (Matt. 2:4). In this context, it is likely that *Metzudot*'s comment carries a very strong anti-Christological element.

17. Jensen, *Obadiah, Jonah, Micah*, 157.

> For when your [David] days are done and you lie with your ances-
> tors, then I will raise your seed that shall come forth (*yetzei*) from
> your body after you – and I will establish his kingdom. He will
> build a house in My name, and I will firmly establish his royal
> throne forever. (II Sam. 7:12–13)

Micah continues to subtly criticize the present kingship, describing Bethlehem as small among the clans (*alfei*) of Judah (5:1). The word "clans"
appears in Joshua and Judges, implying that Micah aspires to reset the
clock to before the establishment of kingship. Similarly, Micah describes
the new king as someone who will rule (*moshel*), not as a king (*melekh*).
Only God is described as king in the book of Micah (2:13; 4:7).

Despite the new king's humble roots, his origins are ancient. The
Talmud states:

> Seven entities were created before the world: Torah, repen-
> tance, the Garden of Eden, Gehinnom, the divine throne, the
> Temple, and the name of the Messiah.... As it is written, the
> Messiah's name is "Before the sun; his name is Yinon" (Ps.
> 72:17). (Pesaḥim 54a)[18]

Radak suggests a more straightforward interpretation: The ancient roots
of the new ruler come directly from King David himself.

Micah returns to his imagery of a woman in childbirth. While
earlier in 4:9–10, the imagery suggested danger and foreboding, now
Micah is clarifying that the present difficulties portend a definite
purpose – the [re]birth of the savior/nation. As such, the Jewish
people's suffering is no accident but a necessary part of God's plan.
The Mahari Kara writes that suffering is needed to cleanse the Jewish
people of their sins. Rashi avoids the reproving interpretation and
states that Micah is only describing how the present struggles will
lead to future salvation:

---

18. The Ran comments that these seven entities were created before the world, because
without them the world could not exist (commentary on Nedarim 39b).

> God shall deliver them into the hands of their enemies until
> the coming of the time when Zion will have…borne her chil-
> dren; Zion, seized by the labor pangs, is now called a woman in
> confinement.

This imagery, comparing the process of redemption to childbirth, is
found both in the Tanakh and in rabbinic literature.[19] Explaining the
phrase "a woman in childbirth will give birth," Radak, suggests that the
repetition (the short doublet – *yoleida yalada*) emphasizes how painful
the process of redemption will be. He quotes Daniel: "And there will
be a time of great trouble, the likes of which has not happened since
nations came to be until that time" (Dan. 12:1).

However, all the suffering will lead to the rebirth of the Jewish people and its reunification. Micah's promises that "the rest of his
brothers shall return" could refer to David's immediate family (David
was apparently estranged from his brothers – see I Sam. 17:28; Ps. 69:8),
or to the exiled Northern Kingdom (II Kings 17:6). Rashi and Radak
understand this verse as predicting the reunification of the two kingdoms. We suggest that Micah envisions the new ruler encouraging the
survivors of the destruction of the Northern Kingdom to return (see II
Chr. 30:6; also II Kings 23:19).

Micah describes the ideal new ruler with the shepherd metaphor
that we have seen earlier (2:12; 4:6). With an inattentive shepherd, the
people are defenseless and quickly destroyed.[20] When God made His
covenant with David to grant him an eternal dynasty, He began by questioning David's request to build Him a Temple. In doing so, he established the nature of the good leader – the shepherd. Samuel told David:

> But wherever I roamed, among all the Israelites, have I ever
> spoken a word to any of the rulers of Israel whom I charged to

---

19. Abrabanel writes that the talmudic Sages had a tradition handed down to them
    from the prophets that the final war against the nations would last for exactly nine
    months: "Rav taught: the Messiah will come only after the wicked kingdom [Rome]
    will extend its dominion over Israel for nine months" (Sanhedrin 98b).
20. Cf. I Kings 22:17; Nahum 3:18; Ezek. 34:1–10; Zech. 13:7.

> shepherd My people Israel, saying: Why have you not built Me
> a cedarwood palace? Now you shall say so to My servant David:
> Thus says the Lord of Hosts: I took you out of the pastures, from
> following the sheep, to be ruler over My people Israel. (II Sam.
> 7:7–8)[21]

The shepherd's strength and majesty (*beoz... begaon*) comes from God.[22] He will perform the necessary tasks: bringing the Jewish people back from exile (Targum pseudo-Jonathan, Rashi), and causing them to dwell in peace (Radak, *Metzudot*, Malbim). Micah concludes this vision with the wish that "they will settle in peace."[23]

Having described his ideal leader, Micah abruptly shifts tone as he addresses the present crisis. Suddenly, the idyllic description of peace disappears, replaced by the sounds of saber-rattling and conscription of Judah's citizenry prevail. As noted at the beginning, Micah appears to alternate between two approaches – fighting the invaders with every-thing that Judah can muster (4:11–14, and here in 5:4–5a), or accept-ing defeat, preparing for a better future (4:8–10; 5:1–3). Traditional commentators solve the problem by removing the militant approach to the far future (preceding Messianic times). However, we noted that even in his presentation of the first approach, Micah used an indirect method to indicate his disapproval – the inclusion of two images drawn from the false prophet Zedekiah, who also advocated for an aggressive response with disastrous results (I Kings 22). How does he express his disapproval here?

As in 4:14, Micah indicates that he is not the speaker of the words by switching to the plural form. He retains the singular form for his own view, and when he quotes his opponents (the militants who encouraged confrontation with Assyria), he switches to the plural:

---

21. See Ps. 78:70–72.
22. Malbim differentiates between "strength," which he suggests connotes physical, military strength, and "majesty" which describes a more spiritual, supernatural form of strength.
23. Rashi and Radak suggest that it is the name of the ruler who will become exalted, publicized around the world; while *Metzudot* suggests that through the leader, it is God's name that will be sanctified worldwide.

> This, then, will be [will assure] peace: when [should] Assyria
> comes to invade *our* land, to trample *our* fortresses; *we* will set
> against him seven shepherds and eight commanders of men. They
> will pound the land of Assyria by sword and the land of Nimrod
> at its gateways. (vv. 4–5)

The aggressive, defiant tone uttered by these leaders is evident. Not only
can Judah withstand any invasion, but they also boast that they can
turn the tables so entirely that they will carry the battle deep into the
enemy heartland, thousands of miles away. Indeed, the nation will raise
seven shepherds, no, eight princes, all of whom will lead the troops to a
resounding victory over the "land of Nimrod."[24] Who are these heroes?
Radak, consistent with the approach of the medieval commentators that
any description of military victory will only occur in a distant Messianic
future, understands them as referring to the officers and the generals of
the Messiah. Rashi alludes to a talmudic tradition that names them, but
he acknowledges that he does not know from where the Sages learned
of their identity.[25] Malbim tries to understand this phrase by looking at
the kings of Israel and Judah of the time:

> One could also say that this phrase hints at past events. From the
> time the enemy began to infringe upon the Jews, in the days of
> Jehoahaz son of Jehu, until the Assyrian king exiled them in the
> days of Hoshea ben Elah, there were eight princes – meaning,
> kings of the ten tribes: Jehoahaz, Joash, Jeroboam, Zechariah,
> Menahem, Pekahiah, Pekah, and Hoshea. [These are the eight

---

24. The numerical sequence of 7, 8 appears in Eccl. 11:2, and the sequence is associated
    with abundance and totality. As such, the verses should be read as Judah fighting
    Assyria to the last man, with every soldier they can muster. Nimrod is identified in
    the Tanakh as "the great hunter/warrior," founder of the great cities of Assyria and
    Babylon (Gen. 10:8–12).
25. "Who are the seven shepherds? David in the middle; Adam, Seth, and Methuselah
    to his right; Abraham, Jacob, and Moses to his left. Who are the eight princes? Adam,
    Jesse, Saul, Samuel, Amos, Zephaniah, King Zedekiah, Elijah, and the Messiah"
    (Sukka 52b). The theme of seven shepherds appears in the Ḥanukka liturgy, with
    the song *Maoz Tzur* concluding with the plea *hakem lanu ro'eh shiva* – establish for
    us the seven shepherds.

kings until the end of the Northern Kingdom, excluding Shallum, who was quickly killed and therefore not counted.] From this time [the destruction of the Northern Kingdom in 722–721 BCE], seven shepherds reigned over Judah: Hezekiah, Manasseh, Amon, Jehoahaz, Jehoiakim, Jeconiah, Zedekiah. [Josiah is omitted, for he is the only king that managed not only to halt but to reverse Judah's downward slide.]

One could also apply this to the future, according to Ezekiel's prophecy about the upcoming wars of Gog and Magog (Ezek. 32 and 38). As prophesied [regarding the war] in chapter 32, seven shepherds will come – Egypt, Elam, Meshech, Tuvan, Edom, princes of the north, Zidonim. In the war listed in chapter 38, there are eight princes: Gog – king of the land of Magog, Meshech, Tuval, Paras, Kush, Put, Gomer, Beit Togarmah. There I explained that one time they would come upon the land, and they will not enter Jerusalem. Concerning this he says, "When he comes into our land;" and one time they would come into Jerusalem, concerning which it says, "When he tramples our palaces" (5:4).

However, if Micah is describing the bleak present, Judah, at this time, could not stand up to the most powerful empire the world had ever seen until then. Therefore, if Micah is quoting his opponents, he speaks with an incredulous tone, and he likely uttered them with a voice that dripped with sarcasm. Mimicking the besieged Jews in Jerusalem, surrounded by the mighty Assyrian army, Micah encloses his opponents' words with the words "[Assyria will] come into our land" and "trample (our palaces/our borders)." Both verses 4 and 5 begin by describing entry into the land and then intensify with a depiction of forced entry and destruction of strongly fortified areas:

When [should] Assyria comes to invade *our land*, to trample *our palaces* (5:4)

They will pound *the land of Assyria* … and the land of Nimrod at *its gateways* (5:5)

The "tit for tat" nature of their threat is evident. Judah's leaders imagine a rapid defeat of the invading Assyrian armies, followed by a punitive expedition into the heart of Mesopotamia and even the complete capitulation of the region. Ironically, the description of their actions in "pounding" Assyrian land, *vera'u*, comes from the same root as the word shepherd (R-A-H).[26] Thus, one can imagine the leaders telling Micah, "Do you want to know what real leaders (shepherds) do? They go into the enemy lair and destroy." To this boasting, Micah has a simple response in the second half of verse 5 (shifting back into single form from the plural verbs): And *he* shall save [us] (*vehitzil*) from Assyria, who comes into our land, and who treads in our border. (5:5)

Micah tells them to be content with repulsing the invasion. We do not aspire to invade others, nor do we dream of inflicting on others what they inflict on us. Micah uses a word, to save (*vehitzil*), translated as to rescue, that recalls one of the earliest tales of King David as a youth (noticeably – fulfilling the role of a shepherd, but before he was appointed king):

> "Your servant has been tending the sheep for his father," David said to Sha'ul, "and whenever a lion and also a bear came and carried off a sheep from the flock, I went after it, struck it down, and rescued (*vehitzalti*) the sheep from its jaws. And if it charged at me, I seized its mane, struck it down, and killed it.... And David continued, "The Lord who has rescued (*hitzilani*) me from the lion and the bear will rescue (*yatzileini*) me from this Philistine." And Saul said to David: Go, and may the Lord be with you. (I Sam. 17:34–37)

The responsibility of Israel's leadership is clear. The shepherd's role is to tend his flock – to defend them if necessary. However, the shepherds do not have to chase the predators back to their lairs, only to strike them hard enough to ensure that they stay far away from the herds.

---

26. Rashi interprets the word רעה as "break": "*Vera'u* – And they shall break, similar to (Ps. 2:9) 'You shall break them (*tero'em*) with an iron rod.'"

WHO ARE WE?

> And the remnant of Jacob will be found amid many peoples as
> dew brought down from the Lord, as ample rains shower upon
> grass; they will not look to any man, nor place their hopes in
> humankind.
>
> The remnant of Jacob will be among nations, amid many
> peoples, like a lion among wild beasts of the forest, like a young
> lion among flocks of sheep whom, as they pass, he tramples and
> rips to pieces; there is no one to save them.
>
> Your hand shall be raised over your foes; your enemies
> will be cut down. (5:6–8)

Micah now frames the choice facing the people with two stark similes.
He no longer discusses the proper response to the current predicament,
nor does he dangle Messianic hopes before his listeners. Instead, he
bluntly declares that there will be a remnant – which means that there
will be preceding destruction. The question is what role the survivors
will play among the nations.[27] The first simile in verse 6 compares the
Jewish people to dew from heaven and raindrops that fall gently upon
the grass. In the second simile in verse 7, the Jewish people are lions that
rule the animals and prey on the sheep. Micah emphasizes the contrast
by his almost identical repetition of the first lines in v. 7 and v. 8. The two
similes draw from ancient blessings of Israel's forefathers. Isaac blessed
his children to be blessed with dew from heaven (Gen. 27:28–29), and
Jacob's tribal blessing to Judah was "You are a lion cub…you return
from the prey" (49:9).

It is possible to suggest that the two similes complement each
other, as we often find two views of the role of the Jewish people among
the nations (see Is. 25:6–11; 60:10–12; cf. Prov. 19:12). On the positive
side, the opening blessing that God gives to Abraham emphasizes that

---

27. Considering that the Jewish people are supposed to return to Israel in the time of
redemption, the question remains to be asked why they are still "in the midst of"
the nations of the world. One approach is to understand the phrase "in the midst
of" as "surrounded by," which removes the problem. Ibn Ezra and Malbim (on 5:6)
are both willing to consider the possibility that Jews will live among the nations of
the world even after the arrival of the Messiah.

the blessing was not for him or his descendants alone (Gen. 12:2–4). It was universal in scope, extending to all of humanity that so desired it. Micah's vision of the ideal times has the Jewish people at the center of humanity, sharing the blessings of justice and peace with all (Mic. 4:1–3). The simile points towards the positive effect that the Jewish people have on humanity. Dew and rain are valued not in and of themselves but in their benefits to nature and the world.[28] The Tanakh connects dew to blessing and fertility (Gen. 27:28; Hos. 14:5), while the showers usually refer to the early light rains in October-November, which prepare the soil for plowing and planting (Jer. 3:3; 14:22; Ps. 65:11). The Tanakh often uses rain showers metaphorically for either the king's presence or divine teachings (Deut. 32:2; Ps. 72:6). Micah's movement from dew to rain showers is an intensification both of quantity and significance. It reflects the biblical understanding that the Land of Israel, without any natural sources of water (unlike Egypt with the Nile or Assyria with the Euphrates/Tigris basin), is entirely reliant on God for its water supply (Deut. 10).

Another approach notes that the negative verse 7 applies both to "many peoples" and "many nations," while verse 6 only applies to "many peoples." Abrabanel suggests that while verse 6 applies to the good nations of the world who assisted the Jewish people during their long

---

28. Malbim looks at the metaphor from the opposite direction. While dew and rain benefit the earth and grass, they themselves do not benefit:

> They will also be like rain upon the vegetation, causing the grass to grow but not receiving benefit from that vegetation; similarly, they [the Jewish people] will provide good and kindness to the nations among whom they live, and they will not receive anything from them, for they will not yearn to receive good and kindness from any man. They will receive all their benefit from God, without an intermediary. (Malbim on 5:6)

There is a similar approach among some scholars that also does not look at the relationship between the Jewish people and the world, but suggests instead that Micah's intent is to emphasize the heavenly origin of the Jewish people's ability to survive its trials and exiles:

> It is independence of the human realm which the comparison emphasizes. The remnant will be like the dew of mysterious heavenly origin. The existence of the eschatological Jacob will be wholly the work of God, neither dependent upon nor vulnerable to mere human strength. (Mays, *Micah*, 122–23)

struggles, verse 7 points towards the arrogant nations who reject God and morality (Deut. 28:36, 50). He suggests Edom and Ishmael as the likely candidates. The metaphor in verse 7 is that of a marauding lion. In the ancient Near East, the comparison to lions, whether of gods or kings, was a common metaphor.[29] Micah transforms the Jewish people

---

29. In the Bible, the lion motif dominates the poetic texts as the strongest and fiercest of the animals. G. J. Botterwick describes how the lions are ravenously hungry (Ezek. 22:25), eager for prey (Prov. 17:12), wait in ambush (Lam. 3:10) in the thicket (Jer. 4:7, 25:28), lurk after their victims (Ps. 10:9, 17:12) (*Theological Dictionary of the Old Testament* 1:382). Isaiah depicts the Assyrian warriors as roaring lions (5:29), and God as a lion who will tear up His prey to carry it off to His lair (Hos. 5:14, 15; 13:7, 8). No man is safe from the lion's attack (Is. 15:9; Ezek. 19:6), no person does not shudder upon hearing them roar (Hos. 11:10; Amos 3:8) (Waltke, *Micah*, 318).

The lion also populates many of the accounts of the Assyrian kings. Ashurbanipal, for example, wrote that at the beginning of his reign, there was so much rain that there was a population explosion among the lions. As a result, there was a dramatic rise in attacks on herds of cattle, flocks of sheep, and people, until the king took charge of the lion hunts in order to control the lion population (D. D. Luckenbill, ed., *Ancient Records of Assyria and Babylonia*, reprint of 1926–27 ed. [London: Histories and Mysteries of Man, 1989], 2:392). For further discussion of the lion metaphor, see Beasley, *Nahum, Habakkuk, and Zephaniah*, 76; Wilhelm J. Wessels, "Subversion of Power: Exploring the Lion Metaphor in Nahum 2:12–14," *Old Testament Essays* 27:2 (2014): 703–21.

In modern Jewish thought, Rabbi Abraham Isaac Kook also appropriated the lion metaphor to describe the reawakening nationalism of the Jewish people in his poem "*Ha'aryeh Basogar*" ("The Lion in the Cage"), first published in Rabbi Moshe Zuriel's *Otzerot HaRayah* in 1990. His poem tells of an ancient lion, broken in spirit, living out his days within the confines of a cage. His cubs, who were born in captivity, know no better and find their surroundings most enjoyable. They can't understand why the old lion is miserable, until one day the old lion tells them:

There is a world full of light,
filled with freedom and liberty
…the forest's invigorating fragrance,
free animals abound.
When I was your age, children,
I ruled the forest with pride and might –
all the forest's warriors bowed before me.
If not for my pursuers
who shattered my bones,
if not for this cramped cage –
even now, I would still rule the forest.
And you too would be free and proud.

from defenseless sheep to raging lions. After graphically describing how the lions seize their prey, drag it underfoot, and then tear it for meat, Micah concludes that "there will be no rescuer" (*matzil*). In the context of the verse, Micah is referring to the nations of the world. However, given Micah's demonstrated affinity for comparing the Jewish people to a flock of sheep, and the repetition of the word to rescue (*hitzil*), we suggest the following reading:

> And the remnant of Jacob will be found amid many peoples as dew brought down from the Lord.

Or:

> [If] the remnant of Jacob will be among nations, amid many peoples, like a lion among wild beasts of the forest … there is no one to save them [the Jewish people].

Micah concludes with a direct appeal to God "Lift your hand over your adversaries, and all your enemies will be cut off."[30] The first phrase may portray God readying the blow, and the second details the consequences. The raised hand traditionally implies victory (see Ex. 17:11; Deut. 32:27; Ps. 89:14). Jensen notes that the iconography of the ancient Near East will often depict warriors with weapons in their raised right hand.[31] The root Micah uses for "to be cut off" (K-R-T) frequently appears in prophetic

---

The poem concludes with the young whelps breaking out of the cage, followed by the old lion, majestic and strong once again. (Translation is the author's; full translations of this poem are available online: Bezalel Naor, *Times of Israel*, The Blogs, https://blogs.timesofisrael.com/the-jackals-and-the-lion-animal-fables-of-kafka-and-rav-kook-2/, and Tzvi Fishman, *The Jewish Press* online, https://www.jewishpress.com/blogs/felafel-on-rye/rav-kooks-the-caged-lion/2013/02/04/.)

30. *Metzudot* interprets the verse as a continuation of the previous one, and thereby understands the subject of verse 8 as the Jewish people. He reads the beginning of the verse as "Then, your hand will be lifted up."

31. Jensen, *Obadiah, Jonah, Micah*, 162; quoting Keel (*The Symbolism of the Biblical World: Ancient Near East Iconography in the Book of the Psalms*, trans. T. J. Hallett [London: SPCK, 1978], 219–20, 291–97.

oracles against the nations and connotes destruction.[32] Micah prays that God will completely erase His enemies.

ONLY GOD IS TO DESTROY HIS ENEMIES

> And it shall come to pass on that day, so says the Lord:
> I will cut out the horses from among you, I will destroy your chariots;
> and I will cut down the fortified cities of your land and demolish all your fortresses.
> I will cut out all practice of witchcraft, and there will be no more fortune-tellers among you.
> I will cut down your idols, the worship pillars from your midst; no longer will you bow down to the craft of your hands. I will rip out the Asherah from your midst, and I will destroy your cities.
> I will lash out with My anger and wrath in vengeance against nations who did not heed My words. (5:9–14)

With the climax of this speech, Micah, speaking directly in God's name, describes how He will cut down His enemies, as the prayer of the previous verse concluded. The opening of v. 10, "And it shall come to pass on that day," *vehaya*, links this section of the speech with the above (see verses 4, 6). The following phrase ("On that day, says the Lord") brings us back to 4:6, Micah's vision of the ideal future.[33] What follows is a list of four consecutive verses where God

---

32. Cf. Is. 14:22; Joel 1:15, 16; Amos 1:5; Ob. 1:9,10 14, Nah. 2:1.
33. The traditional medieval commentators, who interpret this section as referring to Messianic times, explain the complete destruction of Judah's military capability not as a punishment but rather as reflecting the new utopic reality in which the Jewish people will live. As an example of this approach, we quote Radak, who writes:

> Because you will live in peace with the world after the war of Gog and Magog, you will have no need for war-horses and chariots…neither will you need to live in thick walls and fortified cities, for there will be no more conflict with other peoples, and peace will prevail.

Radak suggests that there is also another blessing contained within the verse, as he claims that living in unwalled cities is in fact healthier for the human constitution (Radak on 5:9–10).

details what He will personally cut off, each beginning, "and I will cut off [eliminate]." Micah began with a prayer to God – destroy Your enemies! To Micah's listeners' surprise, God's enemies are not who they think they are. God's anger is not directed at the nations of the world, but at the armed fortifications and defenses of Judah itself. The list is comprehensive, not sequential, and the effect of the repetition is to emphasize God's determination to thoroughly eliminate anything at all that may lead the Jewish people to trust in something or someone other than Him.[34] The critique that Micah makes of the kingdom of Judah here is very similar to Isaiah's critique of Judah during the reign of Uzziah:

Isaiah 2:6–8	Micah 5:9–13
For you have forsaken your people, the House of Jacob, full of what comes from the east [*witchcraft*], full of *soothsayers* like the Philistines… Their land is filled with silver and gold, there is no end to their treasures; their land is filled with *horses*, there is no end to their *chariots*. Their land is filled with *idols – they bow to the craft of their hands* – their own fingers formed them.	And it shall come to pass on that day, so says the Lord: I will cut out the *horses* from among you, I will destroy your *chariots*, and I will cut down the fortified cities of your land and demolish all your fortresses. I will cut out all practice of *witchcraft*, and there will be no more *fortune-tellers* among you. I will cut down *your idols*, the worship pillars from your midst; no longer will you *bow down to the craft of your hands*.

---

34. It is similar to Jeremiah's nine-fold repetition of the word "shatter" (root: N-P-TZ) in his description of God taking retribution against Babylonia:

You are a *shatterer* for Me, a weapon of war. With you I will *shatter* nations; with you I will destroy kingdoms. With you I will *shatter* horse and rider; with you I will *shatter* chariot and driver. With you I will *shatter* man and woman; with you I will *shatter* old and young; with you I will *shatter* lad and lass. With you I will *shatter* the shepherd and his flock; with you I will *shatter* the farmer and his team; with you I will *shatter* governors and deputies. I will repay Babylon and all the inhabitants of Chaldea for all the evil they did to Zion before your eyes, declares the Lord. (Jer. 51:20–24)

It is worth noting the change between the time of Uzziah (Isaiah 2) and Hezekiah (Micah 5). Gone is the wealth and prosperity that Uzziah acquired. He invested it in armaments and fortresses, (II Chr. 26:41–2), with a military buildup that continued to Hezekiah's time during the extensive preparations made due to his revolt against Assyria (II Kings 18:7). Micah promises first that God will destroy all their reliance on their military might (vv. 9–10), and then God will eradicate all the sources of temptation and apostasy that remained in the land.[35] Like Isaiah, Micah would have heartily encouraged and approved of the religious reformation that Hezekiah undertook in the first years of his reign (see II Chr. 29–31). However, Hezekiah did not accompany the religious revival with appropriate societal reforms that restored Judah's citizens' economic justice. Once Hezekiah decided upon the folly of engaging in revolt against Assyria, Micah, who recognized that the massive rearmament placed all the incumbent costs on the populace, would have likely soured on Hezekiah's administration.[36] As such, he would have aspired to see the symbols of military might disappear, along with all the remaining sorceries and idolatrous practices that remained. One could imagine him looking at the thick walls built to protect the people inside and wondering: "How much protection do these walls offer if the people inside them have nothing left to eat?" Micah concludes by stating that only once the Jewish people are purified will God act against the nations that harmed Israel and Judah.

The military targets of God's wrath include war-horses, chariots, walled cities, and fortresses. The horses and chariots are the ancient world's epitome of military power and the first object of fear (Deut. 20:1; II Kings 7:6) and pride (Ps. 20:8). Isaiah lambasted the kings for relying on them (Is. 31:1). Rashi suggests that the horses symbolized reliance on the Egyptians for help. Abrabanel suggests that the destruction of these weapons of war indicates that the ultimate victory comes from God alone. Micah then moves from offense to defense armaments – the

---

35. However, as Isaiah may have been trying to demonstrate by jumbling military and idolatrous imagery together in his list in chapter 2, the overreliance on one's military technology is of itself a dangerous form of idolatry.

36. This does not suggest that Hezekiah did not take Micah's message to heart. Jeremiah 26:18–19 credits Micah for causing Hezekiah to perform enough repentance to stave off Jerusalem's destruction.

walled cities and the fortresses. As Judah discovered first in 701 BCE when Sennacherib invaded (II Kings 18), and then in 586 BCE when Nebuchadnezzar invaded (II Kings 24), neither armies nor strong walls could prevail against an enemy if God decreed otherwise. Jeremiah said as much to the people decades before, but they refused to listen:

> He will devour your harvest and your bread; they will devour your sons and daughters. He will devour your flocks and your herds, your vine and your fig tree. *He will devastate your fortress cities – those in which you place such confidence –* by the sword. (Jer. 5:17)

Micah then turns to describe God's removal of various forms of sorceries and idolatries. The first two, witchcraft and divination, may also have served a military function. Generals and commanders from time immemorial attempted to gain an advantage in their strategies by foreseeing the future.[37] The physical representations of idolatrous worship were next. Micah already condemned Samaria's reliance on its images ("all her idols [*pesileha*] I will lay waste," 1:7); now he looks forward to the same happening in Judah. Indeed, the Tanakh praises Hezekiah for removing them (II Kings 18:4; cf. Josiah in 23:14), and Hosea reflects the same uncompromising stance (Hos. 3:4; 10:1). Micah pairs the images with the monumental pillars (*pesilekha umatzevotekha*), both features of local Canaanite places of idolatry (II Kings 17:10). He then encourages the people to no longer rely on their handiwork – a necessary step to properly renew their relationship with God. Finally, Micah describes the destruction of the *asheirim*[38] and all the idolatries in the cities. The

---

37. Cf. Saul's visit to the necromancer in I Sam. 28.
38. Jensen succinctly explains the *asheirim*:

> Asherah was the Canaanite mother-goddess, associated with fertility. In the Ugaritic texts she is the consort of El, the high god. References to Asherah are sometimes to the goddess (Judges 3:7; I Kings 18:19; II Kings 23:4), but more usually to the cult objects (sacred poles) representing her. Whereas the pillars were of stone and so should be broken (Ex. 23:14), the sacred poles were of wood (Judges 6:26) and were to be cut down and burned (I Kings 15:13; II Kings 23:14). (Jensen, *Obadiah, Jonah, Micah*, 165)

parallelism between the *asheirim* and the cities is not apparent. It may be a summary of the previous verses, describing the extent of the coming destruction, or it may reflect the extent of the corruption – idols that had been limited to temples and sacred spaces now stood publicly in town squares.

Whatever the exact definition of all these sorceries and idolatries, all native to the Canaanite culture that the Torah abhors, what they all had in common was a lack of reliance and trust in God. Conversely, a person who lives with faith in God will not need them. Moses makes this connection explicit:

> When you come into the land that the Lord your God is giving you, do not learn to partake in the abhorrent practices those nations carry out. Let no one be found among you who makes a son or daughter pass through fire, or who casts spells, or is an augur or diviner or soothsayer, or who practices sorcery, or consults ghosts or spirits, or seeks oracles from the dead. For anyone who does these things is abhorrent to the Lord; it is because of such abhorrent acts that the Lord your God is driving them out before you. You must be wholehearted to the Lord your God. The nations that you are driving out listen to augurs and to those who cast spells. But as for you – the Lord your God does not permit you these. (Deut. 18:9–13)

After the purification of the Jewish people, Micah rewards his listeners with what they expected to hear initially. Micah shifts his (God's) attention to the nations of the world – more precisely, those that refused to listen to him.[39] It may be that the world's nations were supposed to see what God did to the Jewish people and take heed to fix themselves before the same happened to them. If not, they now face God's vengeance and anger.[40] Unlike the Jewish people, who, even when punished by God, will always have a remnant remain, the rebellious nations of the world will be entirely obliterated.

---

39. In rabbinic thought, this verse is a prooftext that God first offered the Torah to the nations of the world, but they refused to accept it (*Sifrei Devarim* 33:2).
40. For a deeper discussion of the nature of God's vengeance, see Beasley, *Nahum, Habakkuk, and Zephaniah*, 49–53.

Speech 5 (6:1–16):
Judgment and Verdict

What does God want from us? Until now, the question has been irrelevant, as we (the people) have not been Micah's audience. Chapters 1–5 describe the prophet's battle with the powers that be in Jerusalem (and Samaria). He focuses on the corruption of the leaders and their exploitation of their subjects. In the first five chapters, Micah displays nothing but sympathy for the commoners, victims of the crooked rule of the corrupt. Suddenly, however, Micah expands his focus to include everyone. Micah understands that even if outstanding leadership arises, it cannot move a nation forward if the people do not share its vision.[1] Even when leadership is corrupt, it does not absolve the people if they also engage in immoral behavior. By directing his final speeches to the people, Micah understands that for real change to

---

1. I suggest that the prime case of this in the Bible would be Josiah's reign and ultimate downfall near the end of the kingdom of Judah. Rabbinic thought places the blame on the failure of the Jewish people in Josiah's times to fundamentally change their ways (Lamentations Rabba 1:53; Taanit 22b). For further development of this idea, see Beasley, *Nahum, Habakkuk, and Zephaniah*, 20, n. 22.

occur, the people must now take an active role and responsibility for shaping their future. To do that, they must recognize their mistakes as well. Therefore, Micah concludes by addressing the people of Judah (and possibly Samaria) directly with two dramatic and compelling speeches. The first speech uses the external form of a courtroom trial, which serves to indict and convict the Northern Kingdom. It draws heavily from one of the most famous speeches in Jewish history – Samuel's valedictory address to the people upon his replacement by Saul. The final speech is Micah's personal cry over the immorality and corruption of the society in which he lives, which he then follows with poetic expressions of faith in God, drawing upon past promises to provide hope for the future.

Micah's fifth speech is structured as follows:

- a) Announcement of the "courtroom lawsuit" (vv. 1–2)
- b) First accusation: ingratitude and lack of memory (vv. 3–5)
- c) The people's revealing response (vv. 6–7)
- d) God declares the charges (v. 8)
- e) Second accusation: examining the evidence (vv. 9–12)
- f) The verdict (vv. 13–16)

In the first eight verses, Micah moves with dizzying speed from creation (vv. 1–2) to history (vv. 4–5) to ritual (vv. 6–7), climaxing with a demand for ethical behavior (v. 8). To accomplish this, he draws upon a famous motif in the prophets. He describes an imaginary courtroom dispute between God and the Jewish people – termed a *riv*.[2] This motif first

---

2. Allen, *Books of Joel, Obadiah, Jonah, and Micah*, 263–64, refers to examples of the covenant lawsuit in Deuteronomy 32 and Psalm 50, suggesting that it consists of five parts:
   - a) An introduction in which heaven and earth are summoned to witness the proceedings
   - b) A statement of the case by God's counsel
   - c) An accusation and references to the benefits his people have received from God in the past
   - d) Rejection of recourse to sacrifice to God or other gods
   - e) A verdict or an urging to change.

   See Herbert B. Huffmon, "Covenant Lawsuit in the Prophets," *Journal of Biblical Literature* 78 (1959): 285, 295; Paul L. Watson, "Form Criticism and an Exegesis of Micah 6:1–8," *Restoration Quarterly* (1963): 64. For a counter viewpoint, that holds

appears in the Bible in Deut. 32, in Moses's valedictory address to the Jewish people, when he summons the heavens and earth as witnesses to judge whether Israel has kept their part in the covenant:

> Listen, heavens, I will speak; let the earth hear the words of my mouth.... When I call out the name of the Lord – come, praise the greatness of our God. The Rock, His work is whole, and all His ways are justice. A God of faith who does no wrong, just is He and upright. Did He act ruinously? No, with His children lies the fault, a warped and twisted generation. Is this how you repay the Lord, you foolish, unwise people? Is not He your Father, your Maker, who formed you and set you on your feet? (Deut. 32:1–6)

Hosea, a contemporary of Micah, used this genre in his disputation with the people of Samaria:

> Hear the word of the Lord, children of Israel, for the Lord has a dispute (*riv*) with the people of this land – for there is neither truthfulness nor kindness nor awareness of God in the land. (Hosea 4:1)

The similar language that Micah and Hosea reflects similar concerns regarding the Jewish people.

Finally, Micah's countryman Isaiah also used a clever variation of this form when rebuking the people of Judah. Isaiah began with what appeared to be a love song ("Let me sing a song for my friend – my beloved's vineyard song," Is. 5:1), an act that would immediately attract the interest of his listeners. After he describes the vineyard only producing sour berries despite the owner's loving care, the love song suddenly transforms into a call for judgment ("And now, dwellers of Jerusalem and men of Judah, judge between Me and My vineyard," 5:3), and Isaiah then reveals, using clever word play, that the

---

that the suggested format is anachronistic, see Michael De Roche, "Yahweh's *Rib* against Israel: A Reassessment of the So-called 'Prophetic Lawsuit' in the Pre-exilic Prophets," *Journal of Biblical Literature* 102 (1983): 564, 574.

dispute is actually between God and the Jewish people ("The Lord of Hosts' vineyard is the House of Israel, the people of Judah His planting of joy; He hoped for justice [*mishpat*], and, behold, there was injustice [*mispaḥ*]; for righteousness [*tzedaka*], and behold, an outcry [*tze'aka*]," 5:7).

We saw Micah utilize elements of the courtroom genre at the beginning of the book. Micah acted as the courtroom crier who announced God's arrival as a witness before the announcement transformed into a declaration of the upcoming punishment of the guilty. In our chapter, Micah develops the courtroom metaphor more fully. He introduces it with a summons to the Jewish people and the mountains. Micah then presents God's first accusation, using the rhetorical trick of asking what complaints the people have against him, followed by a recitation of God's continual saving of the Jewish people in history – whether from Egypt, from dangers in the desert, or in granting them the land. Micah leaves unstated exactly which part of the covenant Israel did not keep. When the Jewish people finally answer, they declare that they are more than ready to fulfill their responsibilities through sacrifices, implicitly denying the charges of ingratitude. God responds with perhaps the most famous verse in Micah – the essence of what God wants from humanity: justice, kindness, and humility. Linking the pieces of the dialogue together is the simple keyword (*leitwort*) "what" (м-н), appearing seven times in three sub-sections (v. 3, twice; v. 5, twice; v. 6; v. 8, twice), and nowhere else in the book of Micah. In verse 3, Micah uses the word to rebuke the people. *Meh* takes on a mood of sad rebuke in v. 3 and presents evidence against them in verse 5. The people punctuate their plea of innocence with their exclamation of "with what" (*bamah*) in verse 6, God finally reveals to them the source of their error in a cunning question/answer sequence in verse 8, each beginning with the words "what" (*mah*). Finally, the speech ends by carefully and dramatically presenting the evidence that proves the Jewish people's wickedness. In four powerful concluding verses, Micah announces a verdict of punishment and destruction.

Micah's message – the contrast between ritual performance and ethical behavior – is not unlike other prophets of his time. Amos famously declared:

For even if you proffer Me burnt offerings and your grain offerings, I will not desire them, and I will not look at your peace offerings of fat cows. Take away your clamoring songs; I will not hear your harp tunes. But let justice roll on like water and righteousness like a roaring river. Did you offer Me sacrifices and grain offerings all those forty years in the desert, House of Israel? (Amos 5:22–24)

Isaiah also begins his book with:

Why, says the Lord, would I want all these offerings? I am sated with burnt offerings, with rams and fleshy creatures' fat, the blood of bulls and sheep and goats – I do not want them. You come, appear before Me – Who asked all this of you, who asked you for all this: trampling My courtyards? Bring no more your empty gifts – they are foul incense to Me; New Moon and Sabbath, the feast days you proclaim – I cannot endure these sins and assemblies. Your New Moons and festivals – how I hate them; they have become a burden to Me; I am weary, I cannot bear them. When you spread your hands out skyward, I must turn My eyes away; when you pray with such verbosity, I am not listening – Your hands, they are covered in blood. (Is. 1:11–15)

However, unlike his contemporaries, Micah does not issue a call for change. Isaiah demands of his listeners, "Wash, cleanse yourselves, remove your terrible deeds from My sight; stop bringing about such evils. Learn to do good. Seek justice. Correct what is cruel. Rule justice for orphans. Fight the widows' cause" (Is. 1:16–7). In Micah, the final sentence is a verdict, not an appeal.[3] Chapter 6 concludes with punishment. Given the multiple references to the Northern Kingdom throughout chapter 6 (and chapter 7),[4] this chapter may serve as Micah's eulogy for

---

3. Wording first found in Jan Joosten, "YHWH's Farewell to Northern Israel," *Festschrift für die Alttestamentliche Wissenschaft* 125:3 (2013): 448–62.

4. The references to the Northern Kingdom in chapters 6 and 7 include (but are not limited to) linguistic peculiarities that are reminiscent of texts composed in northern Israel, and several historical and geographical references that pertain to the north: Omri and the house of Ahab (6:16); Gilgal (6:5); Carmel, Bashan, Gilead (7:14). As

the kingdom of Samaria and its inhabitants, which would soon fall under the Assyrian sword and disappear from history (722 BCE). Most of the inhabitants would go into exile, lost forever. Those few who remained in the land would soon find themselves overrun by the new inhabitants brought by the Assyrians to colonize this territory. What Micah is describing is a failed dialogue between God and Israel. Undoubtedly, Micah would mourn the loss of the ten tribes, as he described so vividly in chapter 1. His hope? His southerner listeners will hear his lament, internalize his message, change their ways, and hopefully avoid their fate.

COURT IN SESSION

> Hear now what the Lord says: Arise; argue your case before the mountains; let the hills hear your plea. Hear, O mountains, the Lord's dispute – you, earth's everlasting foundations. For the Lord has a dispute with His people; He will contend with Israel. (6:1–2)

Micah begins by calling the audience's attention to the unfolding drama – God speaks, announcing a lawsuit. The call to listen appears three times:

> Hear – what the Lord says
> Hear – let the hills hear your plea.
> Hear – the mountains

---

significant, unlike the first five chapters, Micah does not mention Zion, Judah, or Jerusalem. Additionally, Gary Rendsburg identifies four specific linguistic details that suggest that the prophecy of Micah 6–7 originated in the north of Israel. These include *hitpael* used with the passive sense, as in Aramaic in 6:16 (*veyishtamer ḥukot Omri* – and the statutes of Omri shall be observed); the rare particle of existence, *ha'ish* in Mic. 6:10; the indefinite noun and indefinite demonstrative pronoun in Mic. 7:12 (*yom hu* – it is a day); and the word *ḥedeq* (briar, thorn) in 7:4. Gary Rensburg identifies all these examples as reflective of a northern dialect (G. Rendsburg, "A Comprehensive Guide to Israelian Hebrew: Grammar and Lexicon," *Orient* 38 (2003): 5–35). Other scholars that have noted the northern slant of chapters 6–7 include A. S. van der Woude, "*Deutero-Micha, ein Prophet aus Nord-Israel?*" *NTT* 25 (1971): 365–78; H. L. Ginsberg, *The Israelian Heritage of Judaism* (New York: Jewish Theological Seminary of America, 1982), 25–31. While we strongly reject their conclusion that a different prophet uttered these words, there is no question that Micah here is employing very "northern" language and imagery.

Everyone is to rise – possibly alluding to a requirement to stand in court when presenting or speaking (Deut. 19:15–16). God invites the mountains and the hills to serve as witnesses (cf. Deut. 32:1; Is. 1:2). Some of the commentators understand this call literally. The mountains are ancient, they heard God giving the Torah at Sinai and testify to what He said (Radak). Ibn Ezra suggests that this is hyperbole: Shout so loudly when you publicize Israel's sins so that even the inanimate mountains and hills will hear. Malbim interprets it as having cynical undertones: Appoint the mountains as judges, as human judges are too corrupt. Some modern scholars note that references to large geological and cosmic bodies are standard in ancient Near-Eastern treaties and the Torah.[5] Based on Targum pseudo-Jonathan, Rashi suggests that the mountains and hills symbolize the forefathers and foremothers of the Jewish people. In the Midrash, we see God presenting his verdict to the past giants of Jewish history before punishing Israel. At the same time, Abraham, Isaac, Jacob, Sarah, Rebecca, Rachel, and Leah serve as the defense attorneys for the Jewish people.[6] Ultimately, God is both prosecutor and judge. As

---

5. Jensen, *Obadiah, Jonah, Micah,* 168 (e.g., "the mountains, the rivers, the springs, the great Sea, heaven and earth," *Ancient Near Eastern Texts,* 205; cf. "Heaven and earth" in Deut. 4:26; 30:19; 31:28).

6. The Midrash is found in Lamentations Rabba, *Petiḥta* 24, and paraphrased by Rashi on Jeremiah 31:15:

   [When the Temple was destroyed,] the Holy One, blessed be He, wept and said, "Woe is Me for My house! My children, where are you? My priests, where are you? My lovers, where are you? What shall I do with you, seeing that I warned you but you did not repent?"

   The Holy One, blessed be He, said to Jeremiah… "Go, summon Abraham, Isaac and Jacob, and Moses." [They came before Him and each one pleaded on behalf of Israel]…. Then the matriarch Rachel broke forth into speech before the Holy One, blessed be He, and said, "Sovereign of the Universe, it is revealed before You that Your servant Jacob loved me exceedingly and toiled for my father on my behalf seven years. When those seven years were completed and the time arrived for my marriage with my husband, my father planned to substitute another for me to wed my husband for the sake of my sister. It was very hard for me, because the plot was known to me and I disclosed it to my husband; and I gave him a sign whereby he could distinguish between me and my sister, so that my father should not be able to make the substitution.

   "After that I relented, suppressed my desire, and had pity upon my sister that she should not be exposed to shame. In the evening they substituted my sister

in chapter 1, Micah does not immediately identify who God's adversary will be. Only when Micah is sure that the people are listening does he instruct the Jewish people to rise – they are the defendants in the lawsuit.

GOD TESTIFIES

> My people! How have I wronged you? How have I wearied you? Testify against Me! for I brought you up from the land of Egypt; I redeemed you from the house of slavery; I sent Moses, Aaron, and Miriam to lead you. My people, remember now how Balak, king of Moab, schemed, and how Bilaam son of Beor responded; remember from Shitim to Gilgal so that you may come to realize the righteous ways of the Lord. (6:3–5)

Before outlining the people's crimes, God asks a simple question directly to the Jewish people: Why are they unhappy with Him? Already, the impression is that this is not a court case, with presentations of dry facts and impersonal evidence. Instead, the tone is almost sorrowful, like an

---

for me with my husband, and I delivered over to my sister all the signs which I had arranged with my husband so that he should think that she was Rachel. More than that, I went beneath the bed upon which he lay with my sister; and when he spoke to her she remained silent and I made all the replies in order that he should not recognize my sister's voice.

"I did her a kindness, was not jealous of her, and did not expose her to shame. And if I, a creature of flesh and blood, formed of dust and ashes, was not envious of my rival and did not expose her to shame and contempt, why should You, a King who lives eternally and are merciful, be jealous of idolatry in which there is no reality, and exile my children and let them be slain by the sword, and their enemies have done with them as they wished!"

At once the mercy of the Holy One, blessed be He, was stirred, and He said, "For your sake, Rachel, I will restore Israel to their place." And so it is written, "This is what the Lord said: A sound is heard in Ramah: wailing, bitter weeping. It is Rachel, weeping for her children. She refuses to be consoled for her children, for they are gone" (Jer. 31:14). This is followed by, "This is what the Lord said: Restrain your voice from crying and your eyes from tears, for there is a reward for your labor, declares the Lord, and they will return from the land of the enemy. This is what the Lord said: A sound is heard in Ramah: wailing, bitter weeping. It is Rachel, weeping for her children. She refuses to be consoled for her children, for they are gone" (ibid. 15–16).

estranged parent or husband, expressing, as it were, feelings of disbelief. God calls them "My people," as Micah has done until now. The issue at hand is not specific actions or misdeeds but the very tenor and nature of their entire relationship.

While Radak interprets the questions "How have I wronged you? How have I wearied you?" as factual questions, other commentators suggest that they are an implied accusation. Micah assumes that the Jews realize they act as if they were weary with their relationship with God. Rashi interprets the people's questions to mean, "can't you recognize all the goodness I have done for you?" The Chida suggests that the people are complaining about their present-day troubles, which we have shown to be formidable. Despite their complaints and accusations, God responds: "Do you not realize that the punishments could have, and should have, been a lot worse, except for the fact that God loves you?" The phrase "testify against Me" (v. 3) is ironic, as ultimately, it is God who is innocent and the people who are guilty.

In verse 4, Micah continues to strengthen his portrayal of God's love for His people and not of God's anger against them. He begins with another clever wordplay. Verse 3 ends with "how have I wearied you," *hel'eitikha*. Verse 4 begins with how God took them out of Egypt, *he'elitikha*. This usage of assonance (similar sounds) contrasts the people's assumption of God's indifference with the substantive historical proof of God's concern for them. God intervened in history to take the Jewish people out of Egyptian bondage. He provided them with three great leaders – Moses, Aaron, and Miriam. Moses and Aaron jointly confronted Pharaoh.[7] Exodus 15 alludes to Miriam's role as the spiritual leader of the women.[8]

---

7. See also Josh. 24; I Sam. 12; Ps. 77:21, 105:26.
8. Numbers 20:1 states: "The entire congregation of the children of Israel arrived at the desert of Zin in the first month, and the people settled in Kadesh. Miriam died there and was buried there. The congregation had no water; so they assembled against Moses and Aaron." The Talmud (Taanit 9a) discusses the verse's juxtaposition of the shortage of water and Miriam's death, and concludes that the water that was available to the people during the desert was in Miriam's merit. The Midrash states that all the three "gifts" that God granted the Jews in the desert – the well of water,

Micah continues to add to the list of God's saving deeds for his people. He recalls the circumstances of the encounter with Balak, the king of Moab (Num. 22–25), an episode also referred to by Joshua (Josh. 24) and Samuel (I Sam. 12). Numbers 22–24 describes how Balak, king of Moab, posed one of the final obstacles between the Jewish people and their entering the Land of Israel. Rather than waging war against them, Balak hired the renowned sorcerer Balaam to curse them. However, God intervened and caused Balaam to bless them instead. The Jewish people were utterly unaware of the danger they faced and the greatness of God's salvation until Moses recounted the events in the Torah. This mention is not the only allusion to the story of Balaam in the chapter. God's opening question to the Jewish people, "My people, how have I wronged you (*meh asiti lekha*)?" (Mic. 6:2), echoes the donkey's first words to Balaam: "What have I done to you (*meh asiti lekha*) to make you beat me these three times?" (Num. 22:28).

Micah continues by describing the crossing from Shittim to Gilgal. Shittim was the final stop for the Jewish people in the desert. The book of Joshua states that two Israelite spies were dispatched from Shittim into the land of Canaan to spy on Jericho (Josh. 2:1). On the western side of the Jordan River, Gilgal was Israel's first settlement upon entering the Land of Israel after crossing the Jordan. There, Joshua erected a memorial of twelve stones taken from the Jordan River, symbolic of the twelve tribes who would possess the land. The name Gilgal (related to Heb. *galal*,

---

the pillar of clouds and the manna – were in the merit of Miriam, Aaron and Moses, respectively:

The manna was in Moses's merit. Know that it is in Moses's merit, as when Moses passed away, "And the manna ceased the next day" (Josh. 5:12).

And the Clouds of Glory were in Aaron's merit, as when Aaron passed away, what does it say? "And the soul of the nation became impatient on the way" (Num. 21:4), for the sun beat down upon them.

And the well was in Miriam's merit, for what does it say? "And Miriam died there and was buried there" (Num. 20:1), and what does it say afterwards? "And there was no water for the congregation" (Num. 20:2). (Numbers Rabba 1)

For a fuller development of these ideas, see Rabbanit Sharon Rimon's article, "The Deaths of Miriam, Aaron, and Moses," available at https://www.etzion.org.il/en/tanakh/torah/sefer-bamidbar/parashat-chukat/chukat-deaths-miriam-aaron-and-moses.

to roll) comes from Joshua's pronouncement that in this place "I [God] have rolled away from you the disgrace of Egypt" (Joshua 5:9). Thus, the phrase "from Shittim to Gilgal" is likely a form of shorthand for all the miracles God performed to bring the Jewish people into the Land of Israel.

Micah concludes that as such, he expects the people to have "knowledge of the righteous deeds of the Lord." The same phrase, which states that the Jewish people are required to know God's righteous deeds, also appears in Deborah's song of triumph over Sisera (Judges 5:11) and in Samuel's valedictory speech (I Sam. 12:7). In his "lawsuit" (*riv*) with the people, Hosea's accusations focus on the people's lack of knowledge of God, which result in their evil, corrupt behavior:

> Hear the word of the Lord, children of Israel, for the Lord has a dispute with the people of this land – for there is neither truthfulness nor kindness and *nor knowledge of God* in the land. False swearing and lying, murder, thievery, and prostitution are rampant, raging, and bloodshed spills over into bloodshed…. My people were silenced for *lack of knowledge*; because you have *rejected knowledge,* I will also reject you from being a priest to Me; as you have forgotten the Law of your God, I too will forget your children. (Hos. 4:1, 2–6)

Micah thus concludes God's opening speech against His people – they have forgotten their past and therefore behave in a wearied manner towards Him.

God's words, however, also draw heavily upon one of the most famous speeches in all the Tanakh. Moshe Seidel draws attention to several literary parallels that allude to Samuel's valedictory speech to the Jewish people in I Samuel 12, including some phrasing that appears exclusively in the two passages.[9]

---

9. *Daat Mikra*, 1990, 51–52 [Hebrew]. Moshe Seidel's interest in how biblical texts quote each other led to the "Seidel Law" being named after him. The "Seidel Law" suggests that when later texts refer to an older text, they tend to invert the order of the components of the earlier text (Moshe Seidel, "Parallels Between the Book of Isaiah and the Book of Psalms" (Hebrew), *Sinai* 38 (1955–1956), adapted by Meir Weiss in

Rare/Unique Literary Parallels between Samuel's Farewell Address in I Samuel 12 and Micah's Case in 6[10]	
I Samuel 12	**Micah 6**
"Here I am – *testify against me*" (v. 3)[11]	"*Testify against me*" (v. 3)
"He *sent Moses and Aaron* and brought your ancestors out of *the land of Egypt*." (v. 6)[12]	"I brought you up from *the land of Egypt…I sent Moses and Aaron*." (v. 4)
"*All the righteous acts of God* that He has done for you and your ancestors" (v. 7)[13]	"Remember… so that you may come to realize *the righteous acts of the Lord*." (v. 5)
Thematic Parallels between I Samuel 12 and Micah 6	
a) The prophet engages in a lawsuit/challenge on God's behalf	
Now take your stand, and I will plead my case with you before the Lord: concerning all the righteous acts of God that He has done for you and your ancestors. (v. 7)	Hear, O mountains, the Lord's dispute – you, earth's everlasting foundations. For the Lord has a dispute with His people; He will contend with Israel…Testify against Me! (v. 2, 3)
b) In the course of the lawsuit he evokes God's mighty acts in history in similar words	
the Lord sent Moses and Aaron, and they brought your forefathers out of Egypt, and they made them dwell in this place. (v. 8)	I brought you up from the land of Egypt, and I sent before you Moses, Aaron, and Miriam. (v. 4)

The Bible From Within (Jerusalem: Magnes Press, Hebrew University, 1984), 95. We will see an example of this phenomenon in Micah 6:8.

10. To the list of literary parallels, we may also add the appearance of the place name Gilgal. Although we explained the appearance according to its immediate context, as part of a phrase meaning to enter the land, Gilgal was also the location where Samuel delivered his final address.

11. The imperative form of the root A-N-H followed by *bet* in the first person is unique to these two cases.

12. Only in Josh. 24:5; I Sam. 1:8; Mic. 6:4 does it mention God's sending Moses and Aaron to the people (Micah adds Miriam).

13. The expression "the righteous acts of God" is found only in three places: Judges 5:11; I Sam. 12:7 and Mic. 6:5.

I Samuel 12	Micah 6
c) Both passages present speakers: the prophet in Samuel, God in Micah – who protest their innocence.	
Testify against me! In front of the Lord and in front of His anointed – whose ox have I seized, and whose donkey have I seized? Whom have I cheated, and whom have I oppressed, and from whose hand have I taken a bribe and averted my eyes from him? Let me repay you. (v. 3)	My people! How have I wronged you? How have I worn you down? Testify against Me. (v. 3)

What purpose was Micah trying to accomplish by covertly placing within his courtroom scene allusions to the story of Samuel's retirement? The context of Samuel's speech and protestation of innocence before the Jewish people was Saul's coronation. Though Samuel had led them for an extended period, the people chose a different direction – to be ruled by a king and not by God's representative. Despite his misgivings, Samuel concurs. However, he marks his departure with a long speech, beginning with his protestation of innocence. As the phrase "Testify against me!" is unique to only these two texts, it is clear that Micah alludes to Samuel's speech. However, Micah makes two subtle changes with terrifying ramifications. First – Micah leaves out the mention of God bringing the Jewish people into the land of Israel. This omission foreshadows the punishment that awaits them after the conclusion of the court case – their expulsion from the land. Second, Micah's most significant change to Samuel's speech is its most subtle – the speaker's identity. Instead of Samuel protesting his innocence before the people and God, now it is God Himself who is, as it were, choosing to retire and to allow Israel to continue in its direction without Him. Understood in this manner, the words of verses 3–5 are not just part of the courtroom give-and-take; they are nothing less than God's announcement of His choice to leave His people.

THE PEOPLE RESPOND

What then can I offer the Lord when I bow low to the God Most High? Should I come before Him with burnt offerings, with year-old calves? Would the Lord want a thousand rams, tens of thousands of streams of oil? Should I offer my firstborn as payment for my crimes, the fruit of my womb for the sins of my being? (6:6–7)

Until now, Micah has served as God's representative in the courtroom drama. Now, having asked the people to answer God's challenges in verse 3, Micah assumes the role of the people's spokesman. Following the accusations that God has leveled against them, the people do not even try to contest the allegations or offer excuses. Instead, they enter a plea of *nolo contendere*. They want to know what sacrifices they need to offer to appease God. They offer a variety of suggestions. They start with bringing burnt offerings (v. 6) and conclude with their first-born children (v. 7). Their final recommendation is so grotesque and ridiculous that it calls into question the very nature of their response – are they sincere or engaging in ironic hyperbole.[14]

The verses begin with the Jewish people speaking in first-person singular, as they recognize the need for a unified response.[15] However, even in their answer, we already sense the distance between the people and God. They refer to God in third person and as the "God Most High," emphasizing their lack of personal communication with Him and the distance they sense exists between them and God.[16] Their answer reveals this disconnect – a total distortion and misunderstanding of God's basic aspirations for humanity. Unlike other prophets, Micah does not directly attack the sacrificial service.[17] However, the people's answer reveals that

14. Generally, the commentators treat the people's questions in verses 6 and 7 as sincere. Connecting to the previous verses, Ibn Ezra interprets the question as asking how the Jewish people, the recipients of so much goodness from God to their ancestors as outlined by Micah, can possibly be accepted now? *Metzudot* suggests that they are asking if offering sacrifices serves any purpose (but if it does, they would gladly offer them!) The simple meaning appears to be like Radak, who interprets Israel's question as, "Which sacrifice does God want?"

15. Kenneth L. Barker, *Micah, Nahum, Habakkuk, Zephaniah: An Exegetical and Theological Exposition of Holy Scripture* (Nashville, TN: B&H Publishing Group, 1998), 112.

16. Rabbeinu Yona Gerondi in *Shaarei Teshuva* uses this verse as the prooftext for the emotions a penitent should feel before God, specifically the sense of subordination and humility (1:25).

17. For comparison, see Is. 1:11–15; Hos. 6:1–6, 7:13; Jer. 6:19–20, 7:21, 14:11; and especially Amos 5:21–25:

their religious lives center around ritual. If they need to appease God to avoid the upcoming calamity, the people are willing to pay the price. If burnt offerings are enough, they will bring the best year-old calves (Abrabanel; see Lev. 9:3; 22:27). If that is not sufficient, then perhaps thousands of rams or tens of thousands of rivers of oil would do. The numbers "thousands" followed by "tens of thousands" represent the highest form of numerical intensification (I Sam. 18:7; Dan. 7:10).[18] Then, as quoted by Micah, the Israelite representative speaker escalates the stakes even further, from multiple but countable rams to almost unfathomable amounts of oil. Should even this not be enough, and quantity does not impress God, perhaps quality will instead. Finally, the speaker arrives at the logical conclusion – the sacrifice of their first-born children to atone for transgressions committed.[19] The large numbers followed by the mention of a forbidden rite imply that the people's suggestion can be understood as hyperbole or sarcasm. It may also reflect desperation (the desperate King of Moab sacrificed his son to deliver himself and his people from invasion – II Kings 3:27). The people claim that they offered all they could to God – no one can demand anything else.

Clear to the listeners is that the Jewish people, focusing on the bringing of sacrifices for atonement, have completely misunderstood the true nature of the obligations demanded by the covenantal relationship.

I have hated, I have loathed your holiday sacrifices, and I will not take in the scent of your festival offerings. For even if you proffer Me burnt offerings and your grain offerings, I will not desire them, and I will not look at your peace offerings of fat cows. Take away your clamoring songs; I will not hear your harp tunes. But let justice roll on like water and righteousness like a roaring river. Did you offer Me sacrifices and grain offerings all those forty years in the desert, House of Israel?

18. I Kings 3:4 describes Solomon as having offered a thousand burnt offerings.

19. Radak understands the people as asking a serious question. However, we suggest that hints of the people's rebelliousness are hard to miss – the Torah explicitly forbids child sacrifice (Lev. 18:21, 20:2–5; Deut. 12:31, 18:10), although the practice tragically reappears throughout the Tanakh (Judges 11:34, II Kings 3:27, 16:3, 21:6; Jer. 7:21, 19:5; Ezek. 16:20, 20:26; Is. 57:5). "It is cited hypothetically as the logical climax of sacrifice, the acme of religious zeal, to be prepared to give one's dearest possession to God. Here the purpose of this sacrifice is explicitly stated to be for sin and rebellion" (Leslie C. Allen, *The Books of Joel, Obadiah, Jonah, and Micah*, 370).

As a result of emphasizing the cultic and ceremonial aspects, their relationship with God has become formalistic, based on commodities. As a result, the sense of personal involvement and relationship with God has vanished. Unwittingly, they have verified God's accusation against them above – "How have I worn you down?" Given what the people envision as God's demands, it is no wonder that they feel burdened by His commandments.

Micah's literary allusions to Balaam and Samuel above become sharpened by the people's response as well. In Numbers 22, Balak hires Balaam to curse the Jewish people. In preparation, Balaam commanded Balak to prepare seven altars for him and to offer sacrifices, hoping that the offerings would allow him to curse Israel. When he fails the first time, Balaam repeats the process twice more, each time unsuccessfully. He does not internalize the lesson that no amount of sacrifices can buy God's favor. The people in Samuel's time repeat his error, believing that offering gifts and bringing the Holy Ark to battle would be enough to receive God's blessing. However, only when Samuel demanded that they improve their internal behavior – "If you mean to return to the Lord with all your heart, then remove the alien gods from among you, along with the Ashtarot, and direct your hearts to the Lord, and serve Him alone; then He will save you from the hand of the Philistines." (I Sam. 7:3) – were they successful in overcoming their enemies. Sadly, Samuel's replacement, Saul, would lapse into the old way of thinking. When Samuel dismisses him for disobedience after the battle with Amalek (I Sam. 15), he rebukes him as follows:

> Does the Lord delight in burnt offerings and sacrifices as much as obedience to the Lord's voice? Behold – obedience is better than sacrifice, and compliance than the fat of rams. For rebellion is as bad as the sin of divination, and presumption as corruption and idolatry. Because you rejected the word of the Lord, He has rejected you as king. (I Sam. 15:22–23)

Just like Balaam and Saul, the Jewish people in Micah's time, relying on sacrifices to gain divine favor, demonstrated their complete misunderstanding of their covenantal responsibilities and how to relate to God.

WHAT GOD WANTS

> He has told you, man, what is good, and what the Lord demands of you; only to do justice, love kindness, and walk humbly with your God. (6:8)

Micah responds to the people's claims in verses 6–7. Instead of their arrogant and misguided "what" demanding to know God's price (v. 6), he says "what" is good. Additionally, he scolds them for daring to ask what God wants of them – after all, God has already told them! The listeners (and we) expect Micah to pronounce God's verdict as a conclusion to the courtroom drama. Instead, Micah interrupts and speaks in his own voice, as if he cannot contain himself once he heard how the Jewish people visualize restoring their relationship with God. He stops speaking on God's behalf and rebukes them himself. He answers them "what" three things God desires of people who wish to have a relationship with him.

Micah begins with a statement, which he then follows with a question. He speaks not just to his listeners, but all of humanity, using the word *adam* (lit., humankind). This word choice is a clever allusion to the people's request to know God through sacrifices – the laws of sacrifices they value begins with what an *adam* brings (Lev. 1:2). His emphasis on the listeners' humanity helps to stress the contrast between the people's mistaken approach and what God wants of them. People tend to analyze their behavior as if it were a commodity – how much is it worth if I perform this action? What value does my doing this service add? Therefore, they come to treat their relationship with God in the same manner. What price do I need to pay to receive God's favor and blessing? How many sacrifices will it cost? Micah tries to teach them that God uses different calculations. He is not interested in how people treat Him, if people are incapable of treating each other ethically and morally. Moreover, when they do approach Him, God desires humility, not show.

Micah reiterates that what he is about to say has already been said before. He emphasizes that this what God requires (*doresh*). The same word in Tanakh also connotes to "seek" and often appears to describe people who search for God (Deut. 4:29; I Kings 22:5). This word may also suggest that this alludes to a level of universal morality that is known to all. Radak suggests that Micah refers to Samuel's directive to Saul as quoted above: God desires obedience, not offerings (I Sam. 15:22). We propose that Micah is going back even earlier, alluding to (if not paraphrasing) a command Moses gives the Jewish people after he describes the grievous sin of the golden calf:

Micah 6:8	Deuteronomy 10:12–13
He has told you, O man, what is good; and *what does the Lord require* (lit., demands – Heb. *doresh*) *of you* but A. to do justice, B. and *to love* kindness, C. and *to walk* humbly with your God?	And now, Israel, *what does the Lord your God ask* (Heb. *sho'el) of you,* but C'. to fear the Lord your God, *to walk* in all His ways, B'. *to love* Him, A'. to serve the Lord your God with all your heart and with all your soul, and to keep the commandments and statutes of the Lord, which I am commanding you today for your *good*?

Comparing the two texts, we note the following. Both Moses and Micah address their people after a grave failure as a nation. Moses's demand of the people comes after his recounting of one of their greatest failures – their building and worship of a golden calf after receiving the Torah at Sinai, and the ramifications that followed (Deut. 9:8–10:11). This leads to Moses's request "And now, Israel, what does the Lord your God require of you?" followed by commandments to fear God, walk in His ways, and to love Him. Micah cleverly adjusts this message in three subtle ways. Most noticeably, instead of concentrating on a person's relationship with God, Micah places the focus on a person's relationship with another, with the only 'religious' request being that a person walk humbly with God. Second, Moses and Micah phrase their requests with different verbs. Moses "*asks,*" while Micah "*demands.*" Finally, Moses addresses the people based on their identity – "And now, *Israel.*" Micah addresses his audience based on their humanity – "He has told you, *O man* (Heb., *adam*)." His listeners felt that to repair their relationship with God, they had to focus on the religious dimension – the bringing of numerous sacrifices. Micah teaches that before addressing their religious failings as Jews, they had to start by being better people!

We identify several progressions in the three requirements Micah lays out before his listeners. He begins with external behavior (do) and moves to internal feelings (love and humility); he starts with human relations and concludes with humanity's relationship with God; he moves from concrete demands that gradually become more abstract and general. The first two demands, justice and kindness, are relational and deal with how people interact (Hosea 12:6 reverses the terms). They should love justice, act justly, and see to it that justice is done and protected, while not forgetting to act with kindness and compassion as well. To do justice refers to the realms of legality and conduct (Amos 5:14, Is. 1:17, Jer. 7:5),[20] and Micah has only used the term during his condemnations of the unjust leadership (Mic. 3:1, 3:8, 3:9). Indeed, among the specific responsibilities under the king's purview is to perform justice.[21] Micah emphasizes here that justice is incumbent on every individual to perform.

Micah then demands that the people "love kindness," ḥesed. In Micah's understanding of kindness, just doing acts of kindness is not sufficient. First, as Radak points out, a person should always try to do more for another than what the recipient needs or requires. Second, the person who engages in acts of kindness is expected to do more than simply act. He is expected to feel love when performing kindnesses, love of the other (the recipient), and love of the action.[22] Significantly, the first two terms, "justice" and "kindness" that Micah demands are also attributes of God, which the above-quoted verse from Deuteronomy 10 – you shall walk in God's ways – commands the Jewish people to emulate (Sota 14a).

Finally, Micah calls upon the people to "walk humbly." Walking in the third phrase continues the movement towards the internalizing that began with doing and continues with love. Walking with God is a

---

20. Interestingly, Radak includes all the laws of interpersonal relations in this first category, including the laws of sexual immorality.

21. See II Sam. 8:15; I Kings 3:28, 10:9; Ps. 99:4; Jer. 22:3, 15.

22. See Ḥafetz Ḥayim (Rabbi Yisrael Meir Kagan), *Ahavat Ḥessed* 2:1.

metaphor reserved for the most righteous people.[23] It reflects the total involvement of every aspect of a person's existence with God. The root of the word "humbly," *hatzne'a*,[24] only appears in one other place in Tanakh – in Proverbs 10:12 ("When willful wickedness comes, then comes disgrace, but with the modest [*tzenu'im*] is wisdom.") *Metzudot* suggests that this is a command to perform commandments between man and God privately, without concern for honor. Returning to the theme of the progression towards the internal mentioned above, Radak expands the reach of this final directive as referring to intellectual and emotional commandments (knowledge of God's unity, love, and fear of God, etc.). Rashi suggests that what Micah is trying to teach the people is how to repent. God does not need public apologies – just a sincere personal and private confession (see Maimonides, *Hilkhot Teshuva* 2:5 for the parameters of this requirement).

How does Micah's final demand of the people relate to the first two? One can suggest that Micah understands that though God primarily desires that the people dramatically improve their interpersonal and social relationships, he does not want to downplay the importance of their relationship with God. Thus, his final statement, walk humbly, can be understood to answer the people's question of what sacrifices God desires. It is a rebuke and a rejection of their suggestion that they offer myriads of sacrifices. Instead, Micah may be teaching them that if the offering is given with a sincere and contrite heart, one offering is equal to a thousand in God's eyes.

Anderson and Friedman suggest another approach in their commentary that is worthy of note. Discussing the meaning of the word "humbly" (Heb., *hatzne'a*):

---

23. Adam in the Garden of Eden, Noah, Abraham (Gen. 3, 8; 6:9; 18:1); see also Lev. 26.
24. Peter Jensen notes that the word "humbly," *hatzne'a*, is technically a *hiphil* infinitive absolute, but the verb serves here as an adverb. The translation as "humbly" is conjecture, and is translated differently by many scholars (Jensen notes: "humbly" [NRSV, REB; Dawes 1988]; "modestly" [NJPS], "attentively" [Lescow 1966, 56], "wisely" [Hillers 1984, 75], and "prudently" [Stoebe 1959]). This rare Hebrew root appears four times in Ben Sira (Sir 16:23; 31:22; 32:3; 42:8) and the Dead Sea Scrolls (1QS 4:5; 5:4; 8:2), but in all the cases they refer to this verse. See Jensen, *Obadiah, Jonah, Micah,* 173–74.

Scholars have been so preoccupied with trying to find out the meaning of the word … that they have missed the simple part that is as clear as day. "Walk with your God," whether humble or circumspectly or wisely, however, is not the main point. Walk with your God by doing justice and loving mercy![25]

Rabbinic thought saw special significance in Micah's tripartite formulation as reflecting the essence of what the Torah requires:[26]

R. Simlai, when preaching, said: Six hundred and thirteen precepts were communicated to Moses, three hundred and sixty-five negative precepts, corresponding to the number of solar days [in the year], and two hundred and forty-eight positive precepts, corresponding to the number of the members of man's body. Said R. Hamnuna: What is the [authentic] text for this? It is "Moses commanded us the Torah, it is an inheritance for the congregation of Jacob" (Deut. 33:4), with "Torah" being in gematria (letter-number value) equal to six hundred and eleven. [The first two commandments] "I am the Lord your God" and "You shall have no other gods before Me" (Ex. 20:2, 3) [are not counted among the 611, because] we heard [them] from the mouth of the Almighty.

David came and reduced them to eleven [principles], as it is written (Ps. 15): Lord, who may dwell in Your tent? Who may live on Your holy mountain? [i] The one whose ways are blameless, [ii] who does what is right, [iii] who speaks truth from the heart; [iv] the one who has no malice on his tongue, [v] who does no wrong to his fellow, [vi]who does not cast a slur against his neighbor; [vii] the one who scorns those who are vile, [viii]who honors those who fear the Lord, [ix] who keeps an oath even when it hurts; [x] the one who does not loan money for interest,

25. Anderson and Freedman, *Micah*, 560.
26. Interestingly, this verse serves as the motto of the alcove of religion in the reading-room of the Congressional Library in Washington.

[xi] who does not take a bribe against the innocent – anyone who acts thus will never be shaken. *Isaiah came and reduced them to six [principles]*, as it is written (Is. 33:15–6): [i] One who walks in righteousness, [ii] speaks the truth, [iii] rejects oppression's profits, [iv] and shakes his hands clear of bolstering corruption, [v] blocks his ears from hearing violence, [vi] and closes his eyes to the allure of wrong; he will reside on high, sheltered in strongholds of the rocks. His bread is given to him; his water flows faithfully...

Micah came and reduced them to three [principles], as it is written (6:8): He has told you, man, what is good, and what the Lord demands of you: [i] only to do justice, [ii] love kindness, [iii] and walk humbly with your God. "To do justice," that is, maintaining justice; and "to love kindness," that is, performing every kind action, "and walking humbly before your God," that is, walking in funeral and bridal processions. And do not these facts warrant a fortiori conclusion that if in matters that are not generally performed in private, the Torah enjoins "walking humbly," is it not ever so much more requisite on the issues that usually call for modesty?

Again came Isaiah and reduced them to two [principles], as it is written (Is. 56:1): So says the Lord, [i] Keep justice and [ii] do righteousness. Amos came and reduced them to one [principle], as it is written (Amos 5:4): For so says the Lord to the house of Israel, seek Me and live. To this, R. Nahman b. Isaac demurred, saying: [Might it not be taken as,] seek Me by observing the whole Torah and live? However, it is Habakkuk who came and based them all on one [principle], as it is written (Hab. 2:4): But the righteous shall live by his faith. (Makkot 23b–24a)

REVIEWING THE EVIDENCE

Micah begins a new subsection with verse 9. Superficially, this section does not connect with the previous verses, and it shifts addressees from the people of Israel (6:2) to an unnamed city (6:9).[27] However, the second half of chapter 6 provides the long-awaited accusation expected from the courtroom-lawsuit drama of the chapter's first half. Until now, the prophet has only accused the Jewish people of ingratitude, forgetfulness, and misplaced priorities. Suddenly, Micah brings damning evidence of wrongdoing before his listeners. Structuring his speech in this manner allows them to contrast what God desires and what they do. He begins by summoning the unnamed city (v. 9), then accuses them of dishonesty and injustice (vv. 10–12) and concludes in the next section God sentencing the people with a series of harsh punishments drawn from the ancient words of the covenant in Deuteronomy (vv. 13–16).

> The Lord's voice cries out to the city; wise men will perceive Your name. Heed the staff and He who sanctioned it. Are storerooms of evil still found in the homes of the wicked? And the scant measure so detested by God? Shall I be found innocent while using false scales and a bag full of deceptive weights? Her wealthy are filled with corruption; her residents speak lies with tongues of deceit in their mouths. (6:9–12)

Even though Micah often uses the word "hear"/"listen" to indicate the beginning of a new section, Ibn Ezra points out that the emphasis on false weights and the rampant cheating in the following verses is a natural continuation of the above demand to perform justice. Now, God is going to present the evidence of Israel's wrongdoings and declare His verdict. This time, instead of the prophet speaking in God's name directly to the people, Micah calls upon them to listen to God's voice that is calling to the city. The city is not identified by name. Rashi, Radak, and *Metzudot* suggest that Micah is speaking to Jerusalem; however, we prefer the alternative offered by Ibn Ezra that Micah is talking about Samaria. The phrase "The Lord's voice" alludes to the revelation at

---

27. The commentators are divided as to the city Micah refers to. Most believe that Micah is speaking about Jerusalem; however, Ibn Ezra suggests that Micah is speaking about the destruction of Samaria, the approach that we have adopted in this commentary for reasons listed above.

Mount Sinai, the power and the thunder of God's voice, which reflects and emphasizes his authority (see Ps. 29:1–3). God's voice "cries" or "calls" to the city, just as Jonah was commanded to do to Nineveh before its destruction (Jonah 1:2). Moreover, Micah emphasizes that the wise person chooses to listen (lit., the [man of] wisdom recognizes Your name). If God's voice is not heard, and his listeners are not wise, Micah begs them to at least take heed of the punishments that are about to be meted out – "heed the staff, and He who sanctioned it."[28]

God then asks two rhetorical questions: Can a house built on unjust foundations survive (6:10)? Did the people expect God to acquit wickedness (6:11)? God next asks whether anyone in "the wicked house"[29] possessed "treasures (of wickedness)." (Radak understands the question as an exclamation: How could anyone continue to cheat despite God's warning?! and brings the Targum pseudo-Jonathan's interpretation: Would this house last a long time? Definitively not!) Micah then asks if they expect God to judge them favorably: Do you think that the divine scales of justice could use false weights? By no means. These crimes are not simple misdemeanors but fundamental violations and breaches of the covenant.

Micah describes the people's practice of short-changing customers through the fraudulent use of false weights, a practice the Torah

---

28. The commentators are divided as to the exact translation of this final phrase. We have interpreted it as "heed the staff and He who sanctioned it!" Rashi and Radak suggest that Micah is rhetorically asking, "Do you think that God is incapable of punishing you?" Some modern scholars interpret the phrase as "Hear, O tribe and assembly of the city!" which is a typical poetic movement towards greater precision. Abrabanel has an interesting translation "Listen, corrupt ones!" The Hebrew word *mateh*, which we have interpreted as meaning "staff" and others interpret as "tribe," can mean to twist or corrupt, as in Deuteronomy 16:19. As such, Micah is speaking to those who have failed to live up to the three basic requirements Micah specifies above.

29. Smith-Christopher (*Micah*, 200) suggests the "wicked house" refers to the Temple, which used weights and measures regularly. He claims that this section is an attack on the "greed of the central authorities." Unfortunately, his interpretation suffers both from an overtly Christian influence and total historical inaccuracy, as no prophet (Micah included) complained about Hezekiah's management of the Temple. Additionally, given that Micah here addresses the entire people with their failures, interpreting these verses as an attack on the authorities is mistaken.

explicitly forbids twice (Lev. 19:35–36; Deut. 25:13–16 describes it as a *to'eiva*, an abhorrent form of behavior). One can easily imagine how this form of dishonesty would lead to bitter division and hostility between the powerful town merchants and the simple country farmers. Micah uses terms to describe the measures and weights that are usually moral and personal qualities – the weights themselves are wicked/righteous. In God's eyes, the character of the utensil and the user are the same.

The actual cheating could occur in one of three ways:

(a) The ephah was a basket that held about 10–20 liters (six gallons) of dry products,[30] and by using a basket that was slightly smaller than the accepted standard, the seller would cheat the buyer of the produce that he was purchasing for the price of an ephah (see Amos 8:5). Micah calls these baskets "lean measures." Rashi explains that they are called lean because they cause the poor to "become lean," to starve.

(b) If the merchant wished to cheat while weighing the goods, several options were available. The scales would have two pans on which the money (a weighted amount of metal) was weighed. The "scales of wickedness (*resha*)" ("rigged scales") might have a slightly heavier scale bowl or a curved crossbeam. The opposite are "righteous," accurate, scales (Job 31:6).

(c) Finally, another method used by dishonest merchants to cheat their customers was to use different weights that would be kept in a bag (Deut. 25:13). The merchant would procure heavier stones than the standard for buying, and would sell using lighter stones, from which pieces had been chipped off (in contrast to whole or complete weights – see Prov. 11:1). Micah makes it clear that God never tolerates such deceitful practices.

---

30. While some variance was expected, the sellers abused this to steal. *The New Bible Dictionary*, s.v. "Weights and Measures."

Micah's condemnation of this practice echoes Amos's fervent condemnation of Israel a generation earlier. Then, the prophet described the zeal in which the cheating merchants would rush to swindle their unsuspecting customers.

Micah 6:10–11	Amos 8:4–6
Are storerooms of evil still found in the homes of the wicked? And the scant measure so detested by God? Shall I be found innocent while using false scales and a bag full of deceptive weights?	Hear this, those who trample the poor, who would decimate the destitute of the land, those who say, "When will the New Moon pass so we can sell grain, and the Sabbath so we can open the storehouses, so we can diminish the weight of an ephah but enlarge the shekel, skew false scales, sell the needy for silver and the poor for the price of shoes? Let us sell chaff as grain."

In verse 12, Micah summarizes God's findings by declaring that the condemned city's people commit violence, *hamas*. The linkage between dishonest trade and violence (*hamas*) is a significant accusation, one that Ezekiel would level a century later against Tyre (Ezek. 28:16). In the Bible, the word *hamas* is accompanied by terrifying overtones, as it was for this specific crime that God assessed humanity in the time of Noah, deciding that they were irredeemable, and drowning them in a flood.[31] The term *hamas* applies to actions for which people generally cannot be

---

31. In the discussion of the appearance of the phrase *hamas* in Habakkuk, I explained it as follows:

> *Hamas* describes the abuse of the weak by the powerful, who act without fear or restraint. Jeremiah uses this word when bemoaning the rampant violence in his time (Jer. 6:7, 20:8), and the sentiment is echoed by Ezekiel (Ezek. 45:9), while Zephaniah uses the word to describe how the corruption of the religious leadership in his day caused violence to the Torah itself (Zeph. 3:4). More ominously, the word *hamas* is reminiscent of its first appearance in Tanakh, in Genesis 6:11: *Vatimalei haaretz hamas*, "And the earth was filled with violence." There it is used to describe the state of the earth right before God destroyed it with the Flood. From this original appearance in Genesis, we learn that when *hamas* is left unchecked, and theft and murder go unpunished, God moves

prosecuted. No one can even administer justice for the condemned city, as everyone has become an habitual liar. Malbim notes the two types of lies that have permeated the conversation of the city's inhabitants. The simple talk is filled with blatant lies, *dibru sheker*; clever conversations contain slick distortions and half-truths, *leshonam remiya*. This situation cannot continue, and the end will surely follow.

THE VERDICT

> And so I too will strike you with sickness, ruin you for your sins. You will eat and never be sated; sickness will settle in your innards. You will conceive but bear no young, and what you do bring forth I will give over to the sword. You will plant but not reap, you will tread olives but have no oil to anoint, and you will crush grapes but drink no wine. For the laws of Omri are upheld, the conventions of Ahav's house kept; you follow their counsel. So then I will lay waste to you, turn the people of this land into objects of disdain; you will bear the shame of My people. (6:13–16)

It is now time to pass sentence on Israel. No longer are the sinners described in the third person (6:12); God (Micah) shifts to second-person direct speech (6:13). I [God, the judge] speak to you [the sinful listeners]. Instead of the expected "therefore" (Mic 2:3; 3:6) to introduce the verdict, Micah uses the particle "too" (*vegam*), emphasizing the direct correspondence between the crimes and the punishment. Ibn Ezra and Radak interpret *gam* as "*just as* you have committed the crimes above, I too will punish you"; the NJPS translates *gam* as "I, in turn." The next phrase "strike you with sickness" is translated literally from the Hebrew as "I have made sick the striking of you" (a prophetic perfect). Some of the early translations emend the verb "I have made sick" to "I have begun."[32] However, the Bible often links sickness and punishment together (e.g., Deut. 28:59; Jer. 10:19). Micah concludes that

---

quickly to punish the entire nation, not just the guilty. (*Nahum, Habakkuk, and Zephaniah*, 122)

32. See LXX, Vulg., Syr.

what is about to occur "because of your sins," reinforcing the moral and religious grounds for the verdict (cf. 1:5).

Micah then lists five punishments. What he describes is nothing less than the overturning of the natural order – a series of "futility curses"[33] drawn from the sections of the covenant as written in Leviticus and Deuteronomy that describe the consequences of Israel's failure to keep the commandments:

Micah 6:14–15	Leviticus 26:26 Deuteronomy 28:30–31, 38–40
You will eat and never be sated; sickness will settle in your innards. You will conceive but bear no young, and what you do bring forth I will give over to the sword. You will plant but not reap, you will tread olives but have no oil to anoint, and you will crush grapes but drink no wine.	When I cut off your supply of bread, ten women shall bake bread in a single oven. They will ration it out by weight, and you will eat but not be full. You will betroth a woman and some other man will lie with her. You will build a house, but will not live there. You will plant a vineyard, but not harvest its fruit. Your ox will be slaughtered before your eyes, but you will not eat of it.

33. "Futility curses," reflecting the collapse of the natural order due to the collapse of the moral order, are a common theme in the prophets:

> As the people so too the priests; I will punish each according to their ways, and each will get what they deserve. They will eat but not be satisfied; they will whore but no offspring will come forth, for they left the Lord and did not heed His laws. (Hos. 4:9–10)

> Therefore, because you trample the poor and confiscate their allotment of grain, you have built houses of hewn stone but will not live in them; you have planted choice vineyards but will not drink the wine. (Amos 5:11)

> Their wealth will be pillaged, their homes laid waste; they will build houses but not dwell in them, plant vineyards but not drink of their wine. (Zeph. 1:13)

> You have sown much and you bring in little. You eat without being satiated. You drink without getting your fill. You dress, and it has no warmth. And he who profits, profits into a bundle with holes. (Hag. 1:6)

Micah 6:14–15	Leviticus 26:26 Deuteronomy 28:30–31, 38–40
	You will carry much seed into the field but gather little, because locusts will eat it. You will plant vineyards and cultivate them, but you will not drink the wine or gather the grapes, because worms will devour them. You will have olive trees throughout your country, but you will have no oil for anointing, because the olives will fall away. You will bear sons and daughters, but they will not remain yours, for they will be taken into captivity.

Micah does not explain how the upcoming devastation will occur. It could be through famine (compare with II Kings 7), or more likely, the result of enemy invasion. It does not matter what the immediate cause is, as the prophet has identified the root cause of the suffering: The people abandoned the fundamental moral principles outlined in 6:8 and instead engaged in the cheating and deceitful behaviors described in 6:10–12. The verdict? For their corruption, God promises that he will make the Jewish people desolate. They would continue to eat, but without any resulting satisfaction. (Radak understands that they will be not become satisfied; Rashi understands that the food will make them physically ill.)

Micah continues that the people will attempt to save their children who were taken as captives of war, but to no avail – they will die before being rescued (Rashi). Several commentators understand the word for "save" (*taflit*) as referring to childbirth (see Job 21:10). Women will no longer be able to conceive children (Abrabanel); hence "you will come to labor, but not bring forth," meaning miscarriages (Radak, Ibn Ezra; see Deut. 28:18; Hos. 9:11). The children that are born will become captives, exiled to a foreign land (Deut. 28:41; cf. Hos. 9:12–13).

Additionally, no longer would the people see any blessing from the work of their hands. Allen poetically describes Micah's depiction of the farmer's marketplace in the town square: "The fresh food displayed so lavishly on the market stalls among which Micah prophesied would soon be a mocking memory."[34] Despite their hard work during the winter months in sowing and planting, nothing of the harvest would remain until spring. The grapes expected in summer would be absent, and the olives harvested in fall/winter would disappear. The people would transform the grapes and olives into wine and oil, but they would never drink from the wine or anoint themselves with the oils (*Metzudot*). In summary, whatever the people grew or made would become the property of others – a fair punishment for those who did not protect the property rights of their people.

Micah concludes by mentioning the two kings who led the Northern Kingdom astray – Omri and his son Ahab. Omri assumed the throne after Zimri's rebellion and lengthy civil war with Tibni. The book of Kings summarizes Omri's reign as follows: "Omri did what was evil in the eyes of the Lord; he was worse than all who came before him... leading Israel to sin, angering the Lord, God of Israel, with their worthless idols" (I Kings 16:25–6). Ahab is described in even worse terms, becoming the standard against which future kings were assessed for their evil behavior (see II Kings 8:18, 27):

> Ahab son of Omri did what was evil in the eyes of the Lord, more than all who came before him. Following in the footsteps of Jeravam son of Nevat was the slightest of his sins; he married Jezebel, daughter of King Etbaal of the Sidonians, and went and served Baal and worshipped him. He erected an altar for Baal in the temple of Baal he built in Samaria. And Ahab made a sacred tree; he did more to anger the Lord, God of Israel, than any of the kings of Israel before him. (I Kings 16:30–33)

However, even this harsh evaluation would not suffice. In addition to introducing idolatry to the Northern Kingdom, Ahab began to utilize the machinery of government to defraud innocent citizens, and ultimately use the courts to kill them.

I Kings 21 describes how Ahab and Jezebel expropriated the vineyards belonging to Naboth. Jezebel hired false witnesses, had Naboth

---

34. Allen, *Books of Joel, Obadiah, Jonah, and Micah*, 381.

executed on fraudulent charges, and annexed his lands to their own. (Appropriately, her children would die in the very same field [II Kings 9].) I Kings' final evaluation of Ahab states:

> Never again was there anyone like Ahab, who sold himself to what was evil in the eyes of the Lord, goaded on by Jezebel his wife. Deeply corrupt, he followed after idols just as the Amorites did, whom the Lord had dispossessed before the Israelites. (I Kings 21:25–6).

Thus, not only is Ahab guilty of the crime that Micah has railed against throughout his speeches – the abuse of the powerless by the powerful by confiscating their lands – his punishment concludes with the reminder that God expels people from the Land of Israel for these sins. Unfortunately, Micah's present listeners continued to act in the manner of Omri and Ahab. Even worse, they have turned these moral crimes into "statutes" and "laws." God requested that the people "walk humbly with the Lord your God," but instead, they chose to "walk in the counsels of the house of Ahab." Therefore, they will share the same end as Ahab.

Micah concludes this speech by mentioning that the Jewish people have become an astonishment in the eyes of the nations. Moses already warned the people that while God punished them:

> All the nations will ask, "Why did the Lord do this to the land? Why this great, blazing anger?" They will say, "It is because they abandoned the covenant of the Lord, God of their ancestors, which He made with them when He brought them out of Egypt. They went and served other gods and worshipped them, gods they did not know." (Deut. 29:23–25)

The listeners will become "an object of hissing," a phrase that generally refers to a city (Nineveh in Zeph. 2:15; Jerusalem in Jer. 19:8; and Babylon in Jer. 51:37). Seeing the once-proud metropolis reduced to rubble causes the onlookers to instinctively express their shock with a sharp whistling or hissing intake of breath. Finally, the people in exile become objects of pity and disgrace. The prophets assure us that God will remove this disgrace when the Jewish people return to their land. Isaiah promises:

> Do not fear – you will not be shamed; fear not, for none can disgrace you. You will forget your youthful abjection; the debasement of your widowhood...for your husband, He who made you – the Lord of Hosts is His name, and your redeemer....Can the young bride ever be rejected? says your God; for one small moment I left you; with infinite care shall I gather you back; in the flash of My fury I hid My face from you for just a moment, and in everlasting love will I care for you now. So speaks the Lord, your redeemer. (Is. 54:4–8)

Similarly, Ezekiel prophesies: "I will no longer allow the insults of the nations to be heard against you, you will no longer bear the reproaches of peoples, and you will not cause your own nations to stumble again, declares the Lord God" (Ezek. 36:15).

Speech 6 (7:1–20):
A Prophet Alone,
a People Redeemed

Micah's final speech, the seventh chapter of the book, is among the most poetic and passionate in prophetic literature.[1] Many scholars see in its disparate sections several smaller prophecies that have been joined artificially. However, the movement from personal lament to confession to an expression of hope for future redemption is frequent among prophecies and psalms. Therefore, we see in this chapter one unified address to the people, structured as follows:

---

1. The language in chapter seven is so poetic that many see in it a liturgical poem sung at ritual occasions. Indeed, many scholars interpret the shifts in tone, subject, and speaker as reflecting a compendium of different prayers (H. Gunkel, *What Remains of the Old Testament and Other Essays*, [Oxford University Press, 1928] 115; Reicke, "Liturgical Traditions in Micah 7," *HTR* 60 [1967]: 349–67). However, we will demonstrate that shifts between speakers and forms are common among prophetic and psalmic literature. While the final verses are used during the Rosh HaShana ceremony of *Tashlikh*, we see no need to assume that powerful poetry automatically equals ritual recitation, a linkage we suspect Micah would have surely disapproved of!

A. Micah Alone / Collapse of Society (vv. 1–7)

Micah begins with a personal lament (v. 1), [2] and continues by bemoaning the sorry state of the Jewish people. Specifically, he details the collapse of societal mores (vv. 2–4) and familial ties (vv. 5–6). However, he maintains his trust in God and hopes for redemption.

B. Confession and Hope (vv. 8–13)

Micah assumes the voice of the city. By associating his disappointment, desolation, and suffering with Israel's, and by bonding his fate with his people's fate, Micah hopes to guide them towards his belief in a better future. He acknowledges on their behalf the sins they have committed and justifies the punishments that they have received (vv. 8–10), but he warns the enemies of Israel that their rejoicing is premature, as God will not forsake His people forever (vv. 11–13).

C. Redemption and Promises Kept (vv. 14–20)

Micah continues to express his conviction that the remnant that survives will merit seeing a miraculous redemption, equivalent to past glories, as a fulfillment of God's eternal and unbreakable covenant with the forefathers.

MICAH ALONE

Woe is me! I am like the last of summer fruit, the gleanings of harvest. No cluster of grapes is left to eat, no first, ripe fig that my soul desires. (7:1)

---

2. Marvin Sweeney speculates that Micah utters these words while wandering the streets of Jerusalem, during the Assyrian attack in 701 BCE. While we don't accept the speculation, his words carry powerful emotional truths worth repeating:

> A siege with its attendant starvation tends to bring out the worst in people as they struggle, even against each other, to survive. A refugee such as Micah would likely find himself on the streets of the city scrounging for food and fighting off those with whom he was forced to compete. (*The Twelve Prophets*, 407)

Micah continues with the imagery of the denuded harvest that he fore-cast above in verses 14–15 of the previous chapter, and compares himself to a poor person, desperately searching for food after the pickers have finished their harvest. The Torah commands Jewish farmers to leave behind some of the produce for the poor to glean (Lev. 19:9–10; Deut. 24:19–21), but now, Micah wanders among empty fig trees and vines. Not even a single grape remains. Once again, Micah engages in clever wordplay. The Hebrew word "Woe is me," *alelai*, is phonetically similar to grape gleanings, *oleilot*. Micah lists the fruits in a chiastic manner: figs ("summer fruit"), grapes ("vintage"), grapes ("cluster"), and figs ("the first ripe fig," see Is. 28:4). Micah longs for the fruits that his "soul desires." This desire is not that of a rich man looking for delicacies. For a poor person gathering food for winter, empty fields and trees are a death sentence.

> The righteous man is gone from the land; no upright men remain; all lie in wait for blood, each snaring his brother in a net. They extend their hands with skill for evil; the official makes his request, the judge names his price, and the powerful man states his heart's evil wish; together they weave it. The best of them are only prickly shrubs, the most righteous worse than a thorn hedge. The day you awaited will be the day of your reckoning; now is your time of confusion. Do not put your faith in a friend nor place trust in a confidant; guard your words from her who lies in your bosom. For a son denigrates his father; daughter rises up against mother; women stand against their husbands' moth-ers; a man's own household are his enemies. (vv. 2–6)

Having decried the lack of food, Micah continues with the interpretation of this imagery. He has looked everywhere for righteous people among Israel, only to find no one, just as Micah could find nary a single grape on the vineyard. No good people nor godly people remain.[3] God told

---

3. Rashi on verse 1 suggests that Micah is bemoaning the poor quality of the righteous people that he encounters ("unripe fruits"), while *Metzudot* suggests that Micah is emphasizing the sparse number of remaining fruits on the tree.

them to "love kindness," *ḥesed*; now there was not even one righteous person, *ḥasid*, left. With no upright people among them, family ties have disappeared, and brothers hunt each other with nets. They would do away with each other as simply as catching birds or fish (cf. Ezek. 26:5; Hab. 1:15–17).

Micah's comparison of the Jewish people to a vineyard alludes to a famous comparison made by Micah's contemporary, Isaiah, in his scathing condemnation of the injustices that plagued Judah under Uzziah:

> Let me sing a song for my friend – my beloved's vineyard song: My beloved had a vineyard on the side of a rich hill. He fenced it round, He cleared it, He planted it with vines. He built a watch-tower in it and hewed a winepress there. He hoped it would yield grapes – it grew them rotten. "Now, men of Jerusalem, of Judah, judge between Me and My vineyard. What more could I do for My vineyard, what, that I have not done? Why did I hope to husband grapes where they grew rotten? I tell you here and now what I must do to My vineyard. [I will] Tear up the border hedge and leave it to be ravaged. [I will] Burst through the fence, to let them trample it. I must turn this into wasteland, never pruned or hoed; brambles and briars will take it over; I forbid the clouds ever to rain their rain upon it." *For the vineyard of the Lord of Hosts is the House of Israel, and the people of Judah are the plant of His joy, and He hoped for justice, and, behold, there was injustice; for righteousness, and behold, an outcry.* (Is. 5:1–7)

Micah continues to describe the convoluted world with which he strives. The people are skilled at performing evil (v. 3) – with the root of the word skilled, *heitiv*, derived from the root word for good, *tov*.[4] Micah poetically describes how talented the evildoers were – it appears that they could do evil equally well with either hand – ambidextrous sinners! The corruption begins at the top – Micah uses three different terms for leaders: the "official," the "judge," and the "great one" – but it has filtered down

---

4. Radak here understands the word *leheitiv*, "to be skilled," as "to intensify." Not only do they commit evil, but they demand bribes to do so!

to the lowest levels of society and into a person's inner sanctum – his marriage bed. Micah begins his description of society's corruption by portraying how by working together, the three officials weave a web of corruption.[5] Even the best (perhaps those unable or unwilling to pay the demanded bribes) are compared to a thorny briar patch, which causes pain as soon as it is touched (Radak, *Metzudot*). Rashi understands the briar patch metaphor differently: The people caught in the web of deceit find that extricating themselves from the corruption is as problematic as withdrawing one's hand from the thorns of the briar. Ultimately, the awaited day of punishment has arrived. Punishment for them is not an external enemy invasion, but the collapse of internal societal mores into anarchy. Having abandoned fundamental mores of justice and fairness, they have brought confusion upon themselves.[6]

If the description in verses 2–4 describing the downfall of a functioning society was not terrifying enough, Micah does not hesitate to extend the punishment further. What he portrays in verses 5–6 is the total and complete breakdown of the personal sphere. He signals the shift by transferring from a removed, third-person description of the leadership to a second-person direct address (anticipated in the "your" in the second half of verse 4), where Micah candidly warns his listeners of what awaited them. Judah's social networks were so frayed that the people could no longer trust their neighbors, friends, or wives.[7] Everyone only looked out for themselves, telling lies with ease to gain some

---

5. Rashi (v. 3) describes the process as follows:

   "The official makes his request" for a bribe, "and the judge," who judges the case, also "names his price," while the king "states" in the case "his heart's evil wish." [Together,] they made it into a rope of sin among the three of them. As the cart ropes, so is the sin, for a rope is braided of three strands.

6. Unlike our commentary, which views the convoluted situation as its own punishment, as foretold by the true prophets, many of the commentators suggest that the day that the leaders were expecting was the day of reward as foretold by their false prophets (Radak, *Metzudot*).

7. Perhaps no modern experience in the Western world parallels the situation that Micah describes more than the opening of the Stasi files after the reunification of Germany. The Stasi was the secret service of communist East Germany, responsible for both domestic political surveillance and foreign espionage. As described in *Encyclopedia Britannica*:

advantage with the authorities. The psychological cost of living in such a society is almost unimaginable. Most people rely on concentric circles of increasing closeness with whom they find trust and security. Micah slowly demolishes each of these circles – friends – a best friend – a wife. In Hebrew, the "friend," *rei'ah*, is the person whom we are to love as ourselves (Lev. 19:18). Even closer is the best friend/loved one, *aluf*, as described in Proverbs 16:28 and 17:9, and over whom David weeps due to his betrayal (Ps. 55:13).[8] Finally, the closest person and the most painful betrayal is the wife "who lies in your bosom," a phrase connoting sexual intimacy.[9] Ideally, if a person is to trust one other person in this world, the spouse who shares their bed should be that person. However, even that is not enough to prevent betrayal. With no one left to trust, a person must keep quiet or face betrayal. The metaphor "guard the doors of your mouth" describes the lips as the double doors that allow words to emerge.

If verse 5's portrayal of the total collapse of friendship and family in Judah was not enough. Micah continues by illustrating the breakdown of relationships between individuals of equal status; describing the breakdown of three other relationships, two within the family structure and one within the class structure. According to Torah law (although never practiced), a rebellious son deserves death (Deut. 21:18–21), reflecting

[Stasi] sought to infiltrate every institution of society and every aspect of daily life, including even intimate personal and familial relationships. It accomplished this…through a vast network of informants and unofficial collaborators (*inoffizielle Mitarbeiter*), who spied on and denounced colleagues, friends, neighbors, and even family members. By 1989 the Stasi relied on 500,000 to 2,000,000 collaborators as well as 100,000 regular employees, and it maintained files on approximately 6,000,000 East German citizens – more than one-third of the population. (https://www.britannica.com/topic/Stasi)

Upon East Germany's downfall, many citizens applied to discover what information the police state had accumulated upon them, only to discover that in many cases, close friends and family had informed on them, leaving an explosion of hurt and betrayal that lasted far beyond the communist regime. For further reading, see https://www.nytimes.com/1992/04/12/magazine/east-germans-face-their-accusers.html; and https://www.spiegel.de/international/germany/stasi-files-revisited-the-banalities-and-betrayals-of-life-in-east-germany-a-659708.html.

8. Radak interprets *aluf* as an older brother; see Prov. 2:17.
9. NJPS translates this as "shares your bed"; cf. Gen. 16:5; Deut. 13:7; 28:54; I Kings 1:2.

the gravity of the honor and respect that children were to have for their parents (Ex. 20:12; Lev 19:4). But in Micah's Judah, "the son treats the father with contempt." The verb to treat with contempt, *menabel,* may be related to the noun meaning "fool" or "boor," *naval* (I Sam. 25:25; Prov. 17:21). This phrasing may suggest that the son publicly describes his father as an idiot in public. Females were not immune to the breakdown in societal values. Disobedience within the household was as damaging as external insubordination, yet the close relationship between mother and daughter-in-law was not immune. In theory, a daughter-in-law was the outsider within the traditional family structure and owed respect to her mother-in-law. Finally, Micah laments how the "enemies of a man are the persons of his house." These men are likely a person's household servants. Even though they are on a lower level, they do not hesitate to disrespect their masters. The basic family structure has unraveled, reflecting the disintegration of society in general. In the Talmud, this verse symbolizes the spread of arrogance and the downfall of traditional moral values in the generation before the Messiah comes. Peter Jenson beautifully summarizes Micah's portrait as follows: "For a people whose identity, security, and happiness were found above all in relationships within the community, this is indeed a portrait of hell."[10]

> Yet I, I will look toward the Lord; I will await my God who will save me, my God who will hearken to me. (v. 7)

Despite everything, Micah remains determined not to succumb to pessimism and hate. To do so, Micah turns his focus from the flawed people around him to God above him.[11] He contrasts the people's despair with his optimism: "But as for me." The return to the first-person speech brings us back to the first verse of our chapter.[12] Despite everything,

---

10. Jensen, *Obadiah, Jonah, Micah,* 181.
11. Sudden shifts between lament and hope populate prophetic literature as well as the psalms. See Jer. 17:16; Hab. 3:18, Ps. 38:15; 40:17.
12. As understood by the Mahari Kara, who interprets this verse as Micah speaking to the people: Despite your sins, I will wait for the Lord. Radak views Micah as speaking here on the people's behalf (an approach we adopt only in the next verse): Although I (we) have been exiled, I (we) will wait for salvation from God.

living in a world where the foundations of society and family no longer exist, Micah is determined to wait patiently for God, because God will hear his prayers. As such, he sets the tone for the optimism that pervades the remainder of his speech.

HOPE FOR THE FUTURE

Micah begins the second section of his speech with a new tone. He levels no more accusations or threats against the Jewish people; instead, he becomes one with them, in word, fate, and deed. The situation remains dire, but Micah seems singularly untroubled. He acknowledges sin but expresses hope that they will judge them favorably. In Micah's courtroom, God has changed from being the accuser of His people to their defender.

> My enemy, do not revel over me; although I have fallen, I have risen; although I sit in darkness, the Lord is my light. I will bear the rage of the Lord's anger, for I have sinned against Him, until He upholds my case and favors my justice. He will bring me out into the light; I will behold His righteousness. When my enemy sees this, she will be covered with shame – she who once said to me, "Where is the Lord your God?" My eyes will behold her defeat, how she is now trampled like mud in the streets. (7:8–10)

Micah suddenly switches voices to the first-person feminine singular. He no longer speaks for himself; now, he assumes the city's voice, likely Jerusalem or daughter of Zion (1:13; 4:9–10 – in Hebrew, the word for city, "*ir*," is feminine). Micah describes facing defeat, probably due to a military invasion, yet the rancor and fear that characterized his previous prophecies have disappeared. Instead, he acknowledges the sins that led to their predicament but immediately expresses confidence that the situation will change for the better. Indeed, Micah portrays the reversal of fortunes between the Jewish people and their invaders through clever wordplay, using the two meanings of the Hebrew word *TZoFeH* – hope and look – to create a clever chiasm:

A. But as for me, *I will look* (Heb – *a-TZaFeH*) unto the Lord; I
will wait for the God of my salvation: *my God shall hearken to
me.* (v. 7)

   B. *My enemy*, do not revel over me; (v. 8)

      C. although I have fallen, I have risen; although I
sit in *darkness*, the Lord is my *light.*

         D. I will bear the rage of the Lord's anger,
for I have sinned against Him, until He
upholds my case and favors my justice.

      C.' He shall bring me out into *the light*; I shall
behold His righteousness. (v. 9)

   B.' And *my enemy* shall see,

A.' she will be covered with shame – she who once said to me,
"Where is the Lord your God?" My eyes will *behold* her defeat,
how she is now trampled like mud in the streets. (v. 10)

Verse 8 begins with the Jewish people acknowledging their desperate state. They may be in darkness, but this is only temporary.[13] As
long as the Jewish people have God, light will return. As such, Micah
warns their enemies not to rejoice at their present fleeting success. The
enemy is unnamed, likely either Syria-Israel against Judah in 734 BCE,
or Assyria against Jerusalem in 701 BCE (Rashi understands the enemy
to be Babylonia or Rome). Micah's confidence is palpable – he uses the
"prophetic future" – I have risen – for he sees the future so clearly that
it is as if it has already occurred (Radak). *Metzudot* interprets the usage
of the past tense differently: Micah looks back at Jewish history, with all
its defeats and dark moments, and realizes that any setback is temporary,
for though we went down to Egypt (and were exiled to Babylonia), God
intervened in history to return us to our land. Despite having "fallen,"
often used to describe a military defeat and the attendant slaughter of
the inhabitants (Is. 21:9), Micah (the city) intends to "rise" again, like a
miraculously restored nation (Hos. 6:2).

---

13. Cf. Lam. 3:6–23: "He has made me dwell in darkness like those who are forever dead.…
This, I reply to my heart; therefore, I have hope.… They [God's kindnesses] are new
every morning."

Verse 9 sees Micah turning inwards, away from the external enemy, and acknowledging responsibility for having caused the current state of affairs. Like Hosea in Samaria (Hos. 14:3 – "take for yourselves words"), Micah provides the words for the people to use to confess. Like Daniel later, Micah confesses on behalf of the people.[14] It is not the Assyrians who are responsible for their sorry state but they, themselves. The idea is substantial but liberating. Accepting responsibility allows them to control their futures as well. Micah returns to the courtroom metaphor, but this time he looks forward to the implementation of divine justice. God is no longer their accuser but their defender. Micah is confident that God will bring light to their darkness, taking up their case with

---

14. Cf. Dan. 9:5, 8, 11, 15. Greatness in leaders is often reflected by their willingness to assume the burdens and even the failings of their people. Daniel begins his description of the vision regarding the fulfillment of Jeremiah's prophecy as follows:

I turned my face unto the Lord God to petition Him with prayer and entreaties, with fasting, sackcloth, and ashes. I prayed to the Lord my God and I confessed, saying, "O Lord, the great and awesome God, who keeps the covenant and the love with those who love Him and keep His commandments. *We have sinned, offended, done evil, and rebelled,* straying from Your commandments and Your laws. We did not obey Your servants, the prophets, who spoke in Your name to our kings, our princes, and our fathers and to all the people of the land. Justice is Yours, O Lord, *and ours is shamefacedness, even unto this day* .... Lord! *Shamefacedness is ours,* belonging to our kings, our princes, and our fathers because we have sinned against You." To the Lord our God belong mercy and pardon, *even though we have rebelled against Him and did not heed the voice of our Lord God* to walk according to His teachings ... the curse of breaking the oath that was written in the teaching of Moshe, servant of God, *was poured out upon us* because we sinned against Him. He fulfilled His word, that which He had spoken *regarding us and our judges who judged us, to bring upon us* a great evil the likes of which has never been done beneath all the heavens as it was done in Jerusalem. And I prayed to the Lord my God, and I confessed, and I said: "Please, O Lord, O great and awesome God, Who keeps the covenant and the loving-kindness to those who love Him and keep His commandments. *We have sinned and have dealt iniquitously; we have dealt wickedly and have rebelled,* turning away from Your commandments and from Your ordinances. *And we have not obeyed Your servants,* the prophets, who spoke in Your name.... To the Lord our God are the mercies and the pardons, *for we have rebelled against Him.... And all Israel have transgressed Your teaching,* turning away, not heeding Your voice, and the curse and the oath, which are written in the Law of Moses, the servant of God, have befallen us, *for we have sinned against Him.*" (Dan. 9:3–11)

the enemy on His people's behalf and their own. That knowledge gives Micah the strength to endure "the fury of the Lord." Until now, God's anger, *za'af*, has raged against the evil committed, as Micah described in the previous chapters (just as God "raged" in the storm against Jonah – Jonah 1:15), but it too will subside like the storm at sea.

The section concludes by describing how the unnamed enemy arrogantly bragged and mocked Israel, "Where is your God?" (see II Kings 18:19–26). They understood that the defeat of the Jewish people meant that God was defeated as well. Micah responds that God will have the final say. Measure for measure, just as the enemy looked upon the downfall and humiliation of the Jewish people, so too the Jewish people will look similarly upon their enemies' defeat. Upon seeing Israel's victory, the nations will be shamed for having dared to question and taunt God (Radak, *Metzudot*). Malbim suggests that what the nations will comprehend (see) is that all of the humiliations suffered by the Jewish people ultimately left them stronger and that God had never left them. The nations are pictured as being trampled on the ground like mud in the streets.[15]

> The day for mending your walls, that day is far away. There will be a day when they will come to you from Assyria and the cities of Egypt, and from Egypt to the river, from sea to sea and from mountain to mountain. And their lands will be devastated along with their people; this is the fruit of their actions. (vv. 11–13)

After Micah acknowledges and confesses the people's sins, he switches from speaking on their behalf to speaking to them in God's name with new, hopeful promises of restoration.[16] He mentions three days that they look forward to celebrating. The first day is a day of rebuilding walls. The breaching of Jerusalem's walls was so significant that the fast day of

---

15. Josh. 10:24 describes how Joshua placed his foot on the necks of the five Canaanite kings that attacked Israel. David prays to God, "Wait for My right hand until I make your enemies a footstool at your feet" (Ps. 110:1).

16. However, Radak understands Micah as addressing Israel's enemies, interpreting the verse as stating that the day that you expected to arrive, when you would build fences and establish a permanent presence in the Land of Israel will not arrive.

the seventeenth of Tammuz was established to commemorate it, representing the finality of the kingdom's downfall ("Why have You broken through its walls so that any passerby can pluck its fruit?" Ps. 80:13). In focusing on the rebuilding of the fences, Micah echoes Amos's final prophecy, also one of redemption: "On that day, I will lift up David's fallen tabernacle, repair its breaches, and lift up its ruins, rebuild it as it was in days of yore" (Amos 9:11).

Micah uses a word in verse 11, describing the city walls to be rebuilt, *gederayikh*, which is typically used to describe agricultural enclosures, sheep pens (Num. 32:16), and fences for vineyards (Num. 22:24; Is. 5:5), and not the fortified walls of a city.[17] In this manner, Micah cleverly returns to the two dominant metaphors he uses to describe the Jewish people. They are God's flock, and they are God's vineyard, both evoked by Micah's original language.

The second day that Micah announces will bring happiness describes the expansion of the country's boundaries.[18] The city's security allows its inhabitants to spread out in the countryside, expanding the nation's boundaries. In a similar vision, Isaiah describes Jerusalem's redemption as being followed by the growth of Israel's borders:

> On that day, this song will be sung in the land of Judah: How mighty – this our city: He has turned wall and bulwark to salvation. Open wide the gates; let a righteous nation in that kept its faith.… You have added to this people, Lord; You have added to the people; You are glorified; You have pushed back all the borders of the land. (Is. 26:1–15)[19]

---

17. Some see in this another demonstration of Micah's preference for the countryside over the city. However, it has been noted that Psalm 89:41 refers to city walls using the same Hebrew word.
18. We have interpreted the word *ḥok* as boundary above. However, other commentators differ – *Metzudot* suggests that this refers to the taxes foreign rulers imposed on Israel's inhabitants.
19. See also Ezek. 47:13–23 and Ob. 1:19–20 for similar prophecies of the growth of Israel's borders.

The final day of salvation that the people have to look forward to is a mass return to Jerusalem, with Jews returning from the far reaches of the known ancient Near East, returning from Assyria to Egypt, from Egypt to the Euphrates, from sea to sea, from mountain to mountain.[20] In this, Micah echoes his contemporary, Isaiah:

> And it shall come to pass on that day, that the Lord shall gather from the flood of the river to the stream of Egypt, and you shall be gathered one by one, O children of Israel. And it shall come to pass on that day, that a great shofar shall be sounded, and those lost in the land of Assyria and those exiled in the land of Egypt shall come, and they shall prostrate themselves before the Lord on the holy mount in Jerusalem. (Is. 27:12–13)

The word for Egypt is an unusual one (*matzor*), although Micah may have chosen it because it can also mean "stronghold" (parallel to "towns" of the previous phrase). In ancient cosmogony, the sea and the mountains mark the outer limits of the world. However, in contrast to Jerusalem, the rest of the earth will become desolate because of their actions. Throughout history, the Land of Israel was unique in that it spat out its inhabitants for its sins (see Lev. 18:25; Num. 35:33). Now, the entire world will achieve that level of sanctity – the ability to reject inhabitants because of their moral failings. In the future, the Land of Israel, populated by its righteous remnant, will be like an oasis in a desolate world.

FUTURE REDEMPTION FROM THE PAST

> Shepherd Your people with Your staff, the flock of Your legacy; they will dwell safely in lush forest lands, pasture in Bashan and Gilad as in ancient days. As in the days when you came out of Egypt, I will show My wonders. Nations will see and be shamed by the might they wielded; they will place their hands over their

---

20. Our interpretation follows the Targum pseudo-Jonathan and Malbim. Many commentators, including Rashi and Radak, provide an alternative reading, in which the enemy above is faced with his own invaders, who will come to devastate Assyria and Egypt in turn.

mouths; their ears will be deafened. Like snakes they will lick the dust, like slithering creatures of earth; they will come quivering out from their holes in terror; they will come before the Lord our God, and they will fear You.

Who is a God like You, Who forgives iniquity and passes over the transgression of the remnant of His own people? He does not maintain His anger forever, for He desires loving-kindness. He shall again grant us compassion; He shall hide our iniquities, and You shall cast into the depths of the sea all their sins.

You shall give truth to Jacob, loving-kindness to Abraham, as You swore to our forefathers from the earliest days. (vv. 14–20)

Micah concludes with a dramatic prayer that expresses complete hope and anticipation regarding the fantastic future that awaits the remnant of the Jewish people. The first two verses invoke God to return to His role as Israel's shepherd and redeem them in the same way that God saved them from Egypt. The following two verses focus on how Israel's redemption will affect the nations of the world. The final three verses describe the renewal of the covenant with the forefathers and the final removal of the real enemy of the Jewish people.

The image of God as Israel's shepherd is familiar– it generally expresses trust and hope (Ps. 80:1). What Micah adds in this prayer is that now the people are taking the initiative. They turn to God in prayer and ask Him to be their shepherd. At this moment, they choose Him and acknowledge Him as their king. Additionally, they describe themselves as His inheritance. Through this, they attach themselves to the past generations. Since they are His eternal possession, it becomes Him to answer when they call upon Him for protection and guidance. Radak interprets this prayer as referring to God leading them back to Israel, while Abrabanel emphasizes the aspect of security that a shepherd provides for His flock.

Micah continues to describe the Jewish people. They are alone, as a flock living in a forest, *ya'ar*. For grazing animals, this habitat is unnatural. Generally, these animals only head for the woods to take shelter when danger lurks in the fields. Micah had earlier (3:12) predicted that the Temple Mount would become like stone heaps in the forest, and an area populated by wild predators (5:8). The Jewish people express the hope that God, their shepherd, will return them to the ample pastures of Bashan and Gilead, that they have enjoyed before. Bashan and Gilead are considered the ultimate lands for grazing (Deut. 32:14; Jer. 50:19). Located on the plains on the eastern side of the Jordan, Moses granted them to the tribes of Reuben, Gad, and the half-tribe of Manasseh, and they represent the beginning of the nation's conquest and settlement of the land (Num. 32; Josh. 22). Historically, these fertile areas were the border between Israel and Aram. In Micah's time, they were also the first region conquered and exiled by Assyria (II Kings 15:29), making his plea to return to these lands more than symbolic.

To this prayer, Micah delivers God's simple response. Just as the people claim God's protection as their shepherd based on their history, God also draws upon history in his response. He had saved them before, and He would save them again. God delivered plagues on Egypt to free His people from oppression, and He would do the same to release His remnant.[21] God's first rescue of His people remained the foundation of Israel's hope for a future reversal of their fortunes.[22]

Micah turns his focus to the reaction of the nations of the world. For the Jewish people, bolstered by their belief in the God who acts in history, they could confidently envision what the future would ultimately bring. In chapter 4, Micah described how upon the building of the Temple and the cessation of all conflict, the nations of the world would willingly engage in pilgrimage to Jerusalem to learn from God's ways, and they would choose to eliminate warfare and competition forever. However, that moment would be preceded by an earlier moment – the nations' reaction upon witnessing God's return to history and His active salvation of the Jewish people.[23] They would see His wonders, and sit silently in shame

---

21. The Midrash learns from this verse that just as the original redemption took place in the month of Nisan, so too will the future redemption take place in the month of Nisan (Exodus Rabba 15:12).
22. God's mighty acts during the Exodus are an essential basis for the appeal to God in the laments of the Psalms (Ps. 78:12; 81:10; 106:7).
23. Dealing with the sharp contrast between Micah's portrayal of the nations' reactions in chapters 4 and chapters 7, many commentators (Radak, Abrabanel) suggests that the nations mentioned here refer to the nations that will come to destroy Israel during the final battle of Gog and Magog.

and fear. They had acted as victors, but God's eventual victory would be so immense that they would recognize how puny and miniscule their display of strength ultimately was in comparison to the divine might. In disbelief, and speechless, they can only cover their mouths with their hands.[24] Malbim understands this action symbolically – people will be unable to find the words to describe the extent of the miracle that occurred. Similarly, the nations will hope to be deaf, as if their deafness could prevent them from continuing to hear about Israel's ascendancy and God's greatness (*Metzudot*). They had mocked Jerusalem and its inhabitants; now they are humiliated, licking the dust like a snake (cf. Is. 49:23; Ps. 72:9).

Micah concludes his prophecy with a final praise of God. No longer concerned with the nations' reaction, Micah is more concerned with establishing the parameters of Israel's new relationship with God after redemption.[25] Micah turns to two historical pillars to create a new relationship between God and His people. Verses 18 and 19 represent the first pillar: God's forgiveness of his people. Micah's opening question "Who is a God like You?" is not only another rhetorical question,[26] but is a play on Micah's name (which means, "Who is like the Lord?"). He praises God for his uniqueness, but not in power or strength (as we would have expected, based on Ex. 15:11 and Deut. 3:24). Micah finds God's uniqueness in His ability to forgive the rebellious sins of the surviving "remnant of His people." This concept of forgiveness appears in seven different forms in these final verses. The repetition can reflect a need to reassure the people that despite all their failings and misdeeds, God will redeem them. The concluding verses form the basis of the *Tashlikh* ceremony on Rosh HaShana afternoon. In it, Jews gather together, generally around a fresh water source, and symbolically separate themselves from their sins by "casting them into the sea," and petitioning God for

---

24. Judges 18:19 describes how others force a person to be silenced by covering their mouths; Job demands silence of his listeners with the same gesture – 21:5; 29:9; 40:4.

25. Bruce Waltke correctly notes: "The rising crescendo of salvation oracles [in Micah] climaxes surprisingly in praising the Lord as a forgiving God, not as a Warrior as in Moses's Song of the Sea with which it has striking intertextual links. The change is profoundly insightful" (Waltke, *Micah*, 450).

26. Cf. Ex. 15:11; Ps. 35:10; 71:19; 77:13; 89:6; 113:5.

forgiveness.[27] Micah describes God as one who "bears sins," patiently waiting not to punish immediately but instead hoping for a person to repent (Malbim). He also "passes over transgressions," as if it did not exist (*Metzudot*). Even when man's failings lead God to anger (as it were), God's loving-kindness ultimately overcomes His anger (Radak).

These final verses, with their various descriptions of God's kindness and mercies, contain several allusions and paraphrases from the Thirteen Attributes of Mercy of Exodus 34:[28]

Exodus 34:6–7	Micah 7:18–20
1) Lord, Lord, benevolent God (*El*),	1) Who is a God (*El*) like you
2) Who is compassionate (*RaHuM*) and gracious	2) Who forgives rebellion (*PESHA*) ...
3) Slow to anger (*APayim*)	3) He does not maintain His anger (*APo*) forever
4) and abundant in loving-kindness (*hesed*) and truth (*emmet*)	4) for He desires loving-kindness (*hesed*)
5) preserving loving-kindness (*hesed*) for thousands	5) He shall return and grant us compassion (*yeRaHaMeinu*); He shall hide our iniquities (*AVONoteinu*), and You shall cast into the depths of the sea all their sins (*HATOTAM*).
6) forgiving iniquity (*AVON*) and rebellion (*PESHA*) and sin (*HATA'AH*)	6) You shall give the truth (*emmet*) of Jacob,
7) Nevertheless, He does not clear completely [of sin] [those who do not repent].	7) loving-kindness of Abraham (*hesed*)

---

27. Indeed, the very name *Tashlikh* comes from Micah's description of how God will cast (*tashlikh*) the sins of the Jewish people into the sea (7:19) – see Rema, *Orah Hayim* 583:2.

28. Accordingly, Michael Fishbane observes regarding this passage, "There can be little doubt that in vv. 18–19 the prophet Micah has readapted the language of Exodus 34:6–7 into a catena of hope and thanksgiving. The aggadic reapplication of an old guarantee that [God] would be compassionate and forgiving thus provides a new warrant of hope in a later time" (Michael Fishbane, *Biblical Interpretation in Ancient Israel* (Oxford, UK: Clarendon Press, 1985), 349. For a discussion of how the listing of the divine attributes of mercy in Exodus 34 are a fundamental restatement of the divine attributes of justice listed in the Ten Commandments, see Rabbi Menachem Leibtag's essay "Two Sins, Two Covenants," in *Torah MiEtzion: New Readings in Tanakh – Shemot* (Jerusalem: Maggid Books, 2012), 463–80.

Micah's usage of this text alludes to the Jewish people's first critical mistake – the creation of the Golden Calf (Ex. 32). It was thought that due the betrayal of the covenant forged at Sinai, the relationship between God and His people was irreversibly ruptured. Instead, God chose to present Moses with a new paradigm for their relationship based on forgiveness, as formulated in the Thirteen Attributes of Mercy. These are the attributes alluded to by Micah: He will not stay angry forever (Ex. 34:6) but instead desires kindness (*ḥesed* – 34:6). Micah engages in clever ambiguity by mentioning kindness; he does not specify who is performing the kindness. The verse's simple understanding is that God desires to be able to perform kindness. Nevertheless, given that loving-kindness is one of the three fundamental demands God asks of humanity, we can understand the verse as meaning that God desires for us to be deserving by our performing acts of kindness.

Micah continues with more specific praise of God, but instead of praising God directly, he turns to the Jewish people and describes God's future actions for them. He promises that God will "again have compassion" (*raḥamim*) on the Jewish people, just He had had so often in their history,[29] and because of this, they will be pardoned (Malbim). In verses 18 and 19, Micah uses the three significant synonyms for sin (rebellious act[s], *pesha*; iniquities, *avon*; and sin, *ḥet*) to describe the comprehensiveness of God's forgiveness. Most importantly, he confidently declares that God would conquer [hide] their transgressions[30] (Malbim, *Metzudot*) and cast their sins into the sea – an image that alludes to an act of deliverance similar to God's deliverance of Israel from their Egyptian pursuers at the Red Sea (Ex. 15:4–5), the parallels of which we explore below. The poetic image of God casting "all their sins into the depths of the sea" means that they no longer affect the Jewish people, guaranteeing that the sins will never again reappear to haunt their relationship with God. Micah subtly but significantly switches from the second person to the third person to emphasize the distance between the person and his former sins. *"our iniquities"* become *"their sins."*

---

29. Cf. Hos. 14:4; Zech. 10:6; Ps. 102:14; 103:4, 13; 116:5; 119:156.
30. Radak understands the Hebrew word for conquer (K-V-SH) can also by translated as "tread...under foot," which is usually used to describe the subjugation of nations (II Sam. 8:11) or people (Jer. 34:11; Est. 7:8).

Micah concludes with the second pillar of the relationship that the saved remnant of the Jewish people will have with God. In addition to forgiveness, Micah reveals the basis of his confidence in the ultimate redemption. God will always remain true to His promises to Jacob and Abraham. God promised the Land of Israel to the forefathers for posterity, for their descendants, who would enjoy a special relationship with God. Since the promise and covenant remain active, they continue to guide God's behavior, as they have "from days of old."

Jacob is mentioned here first. Of all the forefathers, Jacob was fated to spend most of his life in exile, awaiting redemption. Therefore, it was to Jacob that God swore never to forsake him or his descendants (Gen. 28:15). Abrabanel adds that Jacob received the vision of the trials and tribulations that awaited the Jewish people in his vision of the ascending and descending angels at Beth-El. Micah omits Isaac. Ibn Ezra suggests that this is due to his having fathered Esau. Abrabanel expands on this, saying that the omission is because Esau's descendants will not accept the peaceful world of the future. Radak suggests that the promise to Abraham included all three fathers, as Abraham was blessed that "I shall surely bless you *and your offspring*" (Gen. 22:18). The connection Micah makes between kindness (*ḥesed*) and Abraham is not accidental. It was due not only to Abraham's performance of kindness, but his ability to pass it on to his children that God chose to cast His lot with Abraham: "For I have chosen him so that he may direct his children and his household after him to keep the way of the Lord by doing what is right and just" (Gen. 18:19).[31] Ultimately, though the promises to the fathers have not yet been fully realized, God's faithfulness guarantees their eventual fulfillment.

Micah's conclusion, proclaiming God's abundant kindness, forgiveness, and mercy, serves to overshadow and eclipse the previous verses' presentation of the redemption as a conflict between Israel and

---

31. However, several of the commentaries emphasize that against the popular understanding that God had a special relationship with Abraham due to his commitment to performing kindnesses, and with Jacob due to Jacob's fealty to the truth, the simple meaning of the verse is that it is God who showed kindness to Abraham and truth to Jacob.

the nations. This conclusion is despite Micah's reference to the Exodus
from Egypt as the model for the present redemption: "As in the days
when you came out of the land of Egypt, I will show them wonders"
(v. 16); similarly, Micah declares that God will "*again* have compassion on
us" (v. 19). Nevertheless, the final verses ignore the nations with whom
the Jewish people have struggled. As we shall see, both the parallels
with Egypt and its subsequent disappearance are a brilliant rhetorical
tactic that Micah utilizes to convince his listeners of the fundamental
point of his message.

Several of the significant parallels between the Exodus narrative, in particular, the Song of the Sea in Ex. 15, and Micah's final prayer
appear in the following chart:

Micah 7	Exodus 15
Micah begins his prayer with the declaration: Who is a God like You? (v. 18)	Who is like you, O Lord, among the gods? (v. 18)
Israel is God's inheritance: Shepherd your people with your staff, the flock of your inheritance. (v. 14) Passing over transgression for the remnant of his inheritance. (v. 18)	You will bring them, You will plant them on the mountain, Your inheritance – the place, Lord, that You made for Your dwelling, the Sanctuary, Lord, that Your hands established. (v. 17)
God will perform wonders (*peleh*): I will show them wonders. (v. 15)	God performed wonders: [Who is like you] doing wonders? (v. 11)
The reaction of Israel's enemies is fear (*paḥad*) and trembling (*ragaz*): They shall tremble out of their strong-holds…they shall be in terror and awe of you. (v. 17)	The reaction of Israel's enemies is fear and trembling: The people have heard; they tremble. (v. 14) Terror and awe fell upon them. (v. 16)
The depths of the sea (*metzulot*) become the resting place for Israel's sins: You will cast all our sins into the depths of the sea. (v. 19)	The depths of the sea (*metzulot*) become the resting place for the Egyptians: The deep waters covered them; they sank to the depths like a stone.. (v. 5)

Micah 7	Exodus 15
God desires kindness (*ḥesed*): For he delights in kindness (v. 18)	**God took Israel out of Israel with kindness:** You have led in your kindness the people whom you have redeemed. (v. 13)

What is Micah attempting to accomplish with all these references to the Song of the Sea? I believe that Micah is intentionally adopting the language and metaphors of the Exodus to describe the future redemption in a manner that would inspire belief in his listeners: Hasn't God kept His promises once already? It also emphasizes the fundamental message of his prophecy. For most of the book, Micah has portrayed God as the shepherd of His nation, the Jewish people. He leads them, and He builds them pens and fences to protect them from the predators that lie in wait. Then, suddenly, Micah portrays God differently, as a warrior. As the Song at the Sea says explicitly: "God is a man of war!" God not only protects His people but also fights in combat on their behalf. He makes war on Egypt, and He conquers them in the depths of the sea.

Micah adopts this metaphor for God, as he vividly describes how the enemies of the Jewish people will tremble dumbfounded in fear as redemption occurs. Suddenly, at the end of verse 17, Micah appears to forsake the battle with the nations. Instead, he praises God for his loving-kindness and forgiveness to the Jewish people. Has Micah abandoned portraying God as a warrior? Here, Micah's final allusion to the Song of the Sea in verse 19 attains its full impact and power. Micah returns to the metaphor of God casting Israel's enemies into the sea, to exist no more – but they are not the Assyrians (or Babylonians, or Edomites, or Arameans, etc.). Israel's real enemies are their sins.[32] The correspondence between internal failings and external enemies is an apt conclusion to the message that Micah has been preaching from the beginning. If Israel and Judah had

---

32. An approach best formulated by cartoonist Walt Kelly's Pogo the possum, who famously uttered: "We have met the enemy, and he is us." For how this phrase evolved, see https://humorinamerica.wordpress.com/2014/05/19/the-morphology-of-a-humorous-phrase/.

built societies modeled on the moral principles outlined in the Torah, had its prosperous practiced compassion and not corruption, had its leadership acted from kindness and not avarice, then no country in the world, even a superpower as strong as Assyria, could have hurt Israel in any manner.

Final Thoughts on Micah

I have struggled to conclude this volume on an optimistic note. I would love to believe that our fictional characters in the prologue of the book, Israelite and Judean alike, can avoid the terrors and destruction that befall most of their neighbors. God miraculously saved Jerusalem from the Assyrians in 701. Yet, standing in the British Museum, we can still see the Assyrian reliefs of the siege and capture of Lakhish, the second largest fortified city in Judah, and the symbol of the populace at large outside of Jerusalem's walls. In their horrific glory, the stone carvings taken from Sennacherib's throne room in Nineveh describe in painful detail the horrific fates that awaited Judah's inhabitants – heroic defenders impaled on spikes, lines of naked and broken captives paraded before the Assyrian tyrant before being led into exile forever. No doubt, they despaired of relief and salvation. Yet, our prophets never did. Joel, in the midst of a natural disaster that threatened the nation, not only proffered hope to his listeners of immediate relief but portrayed for them a vision of the greater salvation that the Jewish people. Obadiah foresaw the downfall of one of Israel's most ancient enemies and transformed it into a message of both morality and hope. Finally, Micah, well aware of the grim state faced by the Jewish people while he lived, and never losing sight of the moral crimes that led to their downfall, never despaired that no matter how desperate and dire the situation, a remnant of God's chosen people would always survive. As such, despite the darkness that descended on Judah at the end of the eighth century BCE, ultimately, it is the optimism of our prophets which remain with us until these days. Though power may appear to govern our world, ultimately, lasting goodness, kindness, and morality would prevail for the betterment of not only the Jewish people but for all of humanity. May we be privileged to see their vision come true in our days.

Appendix

Determining the Chronology of the Kings of Israel and Judah[1]

Over 120 separate verses in the books of Kings and Chronicles date the kings of Israel and Judah, many presenting contradictory information. The problems have been known for generations; efforts to resolve them began in the second century CE when R. Yose bar Harlafta composed the midrashic work *Seder Olam Rabba*. They continued through the medieval commentators and into modern-day scholarship, which attempts to account for newly discovered Assyrian (and other) records when reconciling the

---

1. In this appendix, which attempts only to summarize the issues involved and not provide a universal solution, we have consulted many resources, based mostly on (but not limited to) the following works: E. R. Thiele, *The Mysterious Numbers of the Hebrew Kings* (Grand Rapids, MI: Zondervan, 1983); Gershon Galil, *The Chronology of the Kings of Israel and Judah* (Leiden: E. J. Brill, 1996); M. Christine Tetley, The Reconstructed Chronology of the Divided Kingdom (Winona Lake, IN: Eisenbrauns, 2005); as well as the following articles: Jeremy Goldberg, "Two Assyrian Campaigns against Hezekiah and Later Eighth Century Biblical Chronology," *Biblica* 80:3 (1999): 3603–90; K. Lawson Younger, Jr., "The Fall of Samaria in Light of Recent Research," *The Catholic Biblical Quarterly* 61:3 (July 1999): 4614–82.

various discrepancies. In his introduction to his magnum opus on biblical chronology, Edwin Thiele acknowledges the immense difficulty of the task:

> For more than two thousand years, Hebrew chronology has been a serious problem for Old Testament scholars. Every effort to weave the chronological data of the kings of Israel and Judah into some sort of harmonious scheme seemed doomed to failure.[2]

In this appendix, we shall focus on the challenges of organizing the chronology of the later divided kingdom, specifically the beginning of the reign of Jehu in 842 BCE until the destruction of Samaria in the North in 722 BCE and Sennacherib's invasion of Jerusalem in 701 BCE. The difficulties are both internal (contradictions within the books of Kings and Chronicles), as well as external (difficulties with synchronizing the biblical chronology with external sources – specifically the numerous Assyrian that have been recently discovered). Because of the challenge of the task, we shall limit ourselves to dealing with the period beginning with Jehu's ascension to the throne in the north, to the end of Hezekiah's in Judah almost one hundred and fifty years later.[3] Specifically, we will examine

---

2. Thiele, *Mysterious Numbers*, 15.
3. Therefore, we will not attempt to solve the question of the "missing 166 years" here. Most of the discussions on this issue focus on the discrepancy between conventional chronology and the midrashic dating system, due to the "missing" 166 years of Persian rule not listed in *Seder Olam*. Conventional chronology states that the Second Temple existed for 586 years (built in the year 516 BCE, and destroyed by the Romans in 70 CE), which includes approximately 210 years of Persian rule over Judea. However, the midrashic dating system (found in the work *Seder Olam*) assumes that the Second Temple existed for only 420 years (and was rebuilt only in the year 351 BCE; *Seder Olam*, ch. 29, Avoda Zara 9a). This tradition posits that the Persians only ruled for thirty-four years before the Greek conquest, as opposed to the 207 years historians attribute to Persian rule. Mitchell First (*Jewish History in Conflict: A Study of the Major Discrepancy Between Rabbinic and Conventional Chronology* [Northvale, NJ: Jason Aronson, 1997]) provides a comprehensive account of over one hundred different Jewish responses (!) to explain the missing years, and an excellent summary of the various approaches in rabbinic thought is available online at https://www.etzion.org.il/en/shiur-02-missing-years.

   Most attempts to reconcile the two dating systems focus on creatively reinterpreting the Persian records to shorten the time period to maintain the validity of the midrashic chronology. For example, Chaim Heifetz argued that the Greek historians did not understand that the various names listed in the Persian chronicles were

four cases: the reigns of Amaziah and Uzziah, the list of kings that reigned in Israel after the fall of Jehu's dynasty, the reigns of Uzziah and Jotham, and understanding the difficulties regarding dating the reign of Hezekiah. We shall point out the difficulties that exist in establishing fixed dates for these kings, and suggest several approaches used by the commentators and scholars to reconcile them. As an introduction to understanding the difficulties involved, we present the list of kings that ruled in each kingdom from the time Jehu ascended to the throne in Samaria until the fall of the Northern Kingdom, as based on Tanakh sources only:

Kings of Israel		Kings of Judah	
Name	Years Reigned	Name	Years Reigned
Jehu	28 years Jehu had reigned over Israel for twenty-eight years in Samaria. (II Kings 10:36)	Athaliah	7 years He stayed with her in the House of the Lord, hiding for six years, while Ataliah reigned over the land. (II Kings 11:3)

---

co-titles for the same person, and not names of separate individuals (available online in the journal *Megadim* in Hebrew, at www.herzog.ac.il/main/megadim/14hfz1.html; a translation of his ideas is online at https://www.simpletoremember.com/other/History166.htm), and an excellent summary and critique of his ideas appears at www.talkreason.org/articles/fixing1.cfm. Similarly, Rabbi Alexander Hool suggested a massive Greek conspiracy to rewrite history in his work *The Bible, The Greeks and The Missing 168 Years*. He argues that Alexander the Great defeated not Darius III but Darius the Great; however, they did not completely defeat the Persians, which allowed the surviving Persian empire, vastly weakened, to rule Judah under their supervision. To accomplish this rewrite of history, Hool suggests that the Greeks carried out a vast campaign to revise all the official records to make it appear that Alexander the Great conquered the entire Persian empire.

To date, no serious or accredited historian has provided any proof to support either of the theories postulated above. The main reason for this is that neither addresses the main issue, which is not the discrepancy with the Persian records, but the independent, exact, and accurate Assyrian and Babylonian records which have been uncovered in the past two centuries, which underlie all modern understandings of Ancient Near Eastern chronology, as we will demonstrate. As difficult as it is to contradict a midrashic tradition (even one not universally accepted), these findings force any honest and neutral observer to conclude that the historical dating of the destruction of the First Temple to 587/6 BCE is correct.

Kings of Israel		Kings of Judah	
Name	**Years Reigned**	**Name**	**Years Reigned**
Jehoahaz	17 years In the twenty-third year of Jehoash son of Ahaziah, king of Judah, Jehoahaz son of Jehu became king over Israel in Samaria for seventeen years. (II Kings 13:1)	Joash	40 years Jehoash became king in the seventh year of Jehu, and for forty years, he reigned in Jerusalem. (II Kings 12:2)
Jehoash	16 years In the thirty-seventh year of Joash, king of Judah, Jehoash son of Jehoahaz became king over Israel in Samaria for sixteen years. (II Kings 13:10)	Amaziah	29 years In the second year of King Joash son of Jehoahaz of Israel, Amaziah son of Joash, king of Judah, became king. He was twenty-five years old when he became king, and for twenty-nine years he reigned in Jerusalem. (II Kings 14:1,2)
Jeroboam	41 years In the fifteenth year of Amaziah son of Joash, king of Judah, Jeroboam son of Joash, king of Israel, became king in Samaria for forty-one years. (II Kings 14:23)	Azariah	52 years In the twenty-seventh year of Jeroboam king of Israel, In the twenty-seventh year of Jeroboam, king of Israel, Azariah son of Amaziah, king of Judah, became king. He was sixteen years old when he became king, and for fifty-two years he reigned in Jerusalem (II Kings 15:1–2)
Zechariah	6 months In the thirty-eighth year of Azariah, king of Judah, Zechariah son of Jeroboam became king over Israel in Samaria for six months. (*II Kings 15:8*)		

Kings of Israel		Kings of Judah	
Name	**Years Reigned**	**Name**	**Years Reigned**
Shallum	1 month Shallum son of Yavesh became king in the thirty-ninth year of Uzziah, king of Judah, and for one month, he reigned in Samaria. (II Kings 15:13)		
Menahem	10 years In the thirty-ninth year of Azariah king of Judah, Menahem son of Gadi began to reign over Israel and reigned ten years in Samaria. (II Kings 15:17)		
Pekahiah	2 years In the thirty-ninth year of Azariah, king of Judah, Menahem son of Gadi became king over Israel, for ten years in Samaria. (II Kings 15:23)	Jotham	16 years In the second year of Pekah son of Remaliah, king of Israel, Jotham son of Uzziah, king of Judah, became king. He was twenty-five years old when he became king, and for sixteen years he reigned in Jerusalem. (II Kings 15:32–33)
Pekah	20 years In the fifty-second year of Azariah, king of Judah, Pekah son of Remaliah became king over Israel in Samaria for twenty years. (II Kings 15:27)	Ahaz	16 years In the seventeenth year of Pekah son of Remaliah, Ahaz son of Jotham, king of Judah, became king. (II Kings 16:1)

Kings of Israel		Kings of Judah	
Name	Years Reigned	Name	Years Reigned
Hoshea	9 years In the twelfth year of Ahaz, king of Judah, Hoshea son of Ela became king over Israel in Samaria for nine years. (II Kings 17:1)	Heze-kiah	29 years In the third year of Hoshea son of Ela, king of Israel, Hezekiah son of Ahaz, king of Judah, became king. He was twenty-five years old when he became king, and for twenty-nine years he reigned in Jerusalem. (II Kings 18:2)
Samaria's downfall	In the fourth year of King Hezekiah – which was the seventh year of Hoshea son of Ela, king of Israel – Shalmaneser, king of Assyria, marched up against Samaria and besieged it. He captured it three years later during the sixth year of Hezekiah; it was during the ninth year of Hoshea, king of Israel, that Samaria was captured. (II Kings 18:9–10)		The downfall of Samaria is dated … He captured it three years later during the sixth year of Hezekiah; it was during the ninth year of Hoshea, king of Israel, that Samaria was captured. (II Kings 18:10)
Total years from the beginning of Jehu's reign until the fall of Samaria	143 years, 7 months		166 years

We already see the first major discrepancy – from the time Jehu assumes the throne in the north (synchronized with Athaliah's ascension in Judah) until the fall of Samaria, there is a 22-year gap between the two kingdoms, with additional years added to Judah's list. This is an internal contradiction, and reflects the difficulty in creating an orderly system of dates stems from the Tanakh's usage of relative chronology (dating one event in relation to another, as opposed to absolute chronology, which uses a fixed historical point as a reference point).[4] However, there is an external difficulty as well, as Assyrian sources suggest that the length of time from Jehu's ascension to the fall of Samaria was even less – approximately 120 years (as we shall explain below), meaning that the southern list contains an additional 44 years, and that the northern total is also inflated by over 20 years. We shall quickly discuss the Assyrian records, and then suggest an approach to reconciling the discrepancies by investigating the four kings varying dates suggested for each king.

RELIANCE ON ASSYRIAN RECORDS

At the beginning of the nineteenth century, excavators in Iraq led by Sir Henry Rawlinson discovered *limmu* lists, which record the various officials who held the office of *limmu* (eponyms in Greek), for that year.[5] These lists contained the names of the official and the important events that

---

4. I Kings 6:1, which states that the building of the Temple in the fourth year of King Solomon's reign, took place 480 years after the Exodus from Egypt, may be considered an exception.

5. The significance of this discovery cannot be overstated. Dr. O. T. Allis, who includes a full discussion of the subject in his book *The Old Testament: Its Claims and Its Critics* (Phillipsburg, NJ: Presbyterian & Reformed Pub. Co, 1972), 398, writes:

   Among the early results of excavation in Assyria was the discovery and publication by Rawlinson a century ago of tablets containing the Eponym Canon. These tablets recorded the names of the kings and high officials who, like the archons at Athens and the consuls at Rome, gave their names in succession, each to a year, thereby establishing the chronological sequence. While the system of dating by eponyms began centuries earlier, these lists cover a period of about 250 years, beginning about 900 B.C. A gratifying result of the discovery of these lists lies in the fact that they connect with and overlap for about a century the Ptolemaic Canon, which had been known and used for centuries.... It was quickly discovered that the two canons were in agreement for the periods which they both covered; and thus the year 722 B.C. for the fall of Samaria, as given

occurred in that year, and became the central evidence scholars relied upon to recreate the Assyrian chronology. As more annals of the Assyrian kings were independently found, it was possible to date them (or the campaigns mentioned in them) by the officials who figured in the eponym lists. Additionally, some of the Assyrian kings were also kings of Babylonia, and as such were included in Ptolemy's Canon of Babylonian kings.[6] By the beginning of the twentieth century, the full sequence of eponyms was known from 910 BCE to 647 BCE (from the second year of king Adad-nerari II to the 20th year of Assurbanipal) was firmly established,[7] and historians were able to reconstructed the entire Assyrian chronology.[8]

What gives the Assyrian evidence additional strength, however, is that the Assyrians recorded astronomical events such as eclipses of the sun in their chronicles. This feature allows for an absolute chronology – once one year is fixed, all the other years can be safely dated as well. The Eponym Canon lists a solar eclipse which provides a fixed reference point that will enable us to confidently date many biblical events. According to this list, in the month of Simanu (the 3rd month, covering parts of May and June) in the eponymy of Bur-Saggilê, who held the office in the tenth year of king Ashur-dan III, a solar eclipse occurred. Modern astronomers

---

by Ussher on the basis of the Ptolemaic Canon, served to anchor the Eponym Canon for the Assyrian chronology.

6. Ptolemy (full Latin name, Claudius Ptolemaeus), born approx. in 100 CE, was an Alexandrian scholar who excelled in astronomy, mathematics, and geography. He compiled a thirteen-volume work on astronomy, which was the basic textbook of astronomy for some 1,400 years and is considered one of the most influential scientific works in history. Ptolemy also wrote a treatise that included a chronological table of fifty-three kings and the length of their reigns (with two interregna) from the Babylonian, Persian, Greek, Ptolemaic (Egyptian), and Roman eras, beginning in 747 BCE, which became known as Ptolemy's Canon.

7. The information contained in the *limmu* lists was corroborated by the discovery in the past century of five separate lists of the Assyrian kings, of which the three primary ones are the "Nassouhi List," the "Khorsabad List," and the "SDAS List."

8. The Assyrians also did not count years, but instead they named them after the king, high officials, and provincial governors (hence the Greek term eponym). The year names have been collected in the Assyrian eponym lists and chronicles, copies of which were excavated in Nineveh, Assur, and Šibaniba (modern Sultantepe near Urfa). The texts were edited by Alan Millard, and can be found in A. R. Millard, *The Eponyms of the Assyrian Empire 9106–12 B.C.* (State Archives of Assyria Studies 2), Helsinki 1994.

have identified this eclipse with the above-mentioned eclipse of June 15, 763 BCE, in the Julian calendar. This date sets a fixed astronomical anchor upon which we can date biblical events.[9] This is unlike the Tanakh, which almost invariably does not provide an absolute date for any events, sufficing for relative chronology (the building of the Temple is 480 years after the Exodus, or "in the twenty-sixth year of King Asa of Judah, Elah son of Baasha became king over Israel, at Tirzah" [1 Kings 16:8]).

For our purposes, the following list of events, based on Assyrian records, are crucial to our understanding of the events of the book of Kings:

Event	Date	Description
Battle of Qarqar	853 BCE	A coalition of twelve kingdoms repulsed an Assyrian invasion under Shalmaneser III (859 BCE – 824 BCE) into northern Syria. This battle is recorded on the Kurkh monolith, and most scholars believe that the name of Ahab of Israel appears as a prominent member of the coalition.[10]

---

9. While some researchers have suggested different dates for this eclipse, the alternatives offered do not survive scrutiny of the evidence. For a full discussion, see Professor Hermann Hunger's article, *"Zur Datierung der neuassyrischen Eponymenliste,"* *Altorientalische Forschungen* 35:2 (2008): 323–25; translated as "About the Dating of the Neo-Assyrian Eponym List" and available online at http://www.kristenfrihet.se/kf4/dating.htm. Although the Assyrian lists have been independently verified by other discovered texts (e.g., the Babylonian Chronicle, the Assyrian King Lists), the importance of the Bur-Sagale eponomy cannot be overstated. Thiele writes as follows:

> Now on the basis of Ptolemy's canon we are able to provide dates to all the other eponymies on the Assyrian lists, and we thus secure 763 for the eponymy of Bur-Sagale – the same date as was secured for that eponymy by the evidence of the solar eclipse that took place that year in the month Simanu. So the date 763 for the eponymy of Bur-Sagale has been established not only by the astronomical evidence of Assyria but also by that of Ptolemy's canon. *We thus have complete assurance that 763 is the correct date for Bur-Sagale and that the other dates of the eponym lists, whether reckoned backward or forward from that date, are likewise correct.* (*Mysterious Numbers*, 71–72)

10. The Kurkh Monolith, a large stone stela found at Kurkh by J. E. Taylor in 1861, describes the coalition arrayed against Shalmaneser III:

Event	Date	Description
Jehu pays trib-ute to Assyria	841 BCE	The Black Obelisk of Shalmaneser III depicts his triumphs over several Syrian kingdoms.[11] In one panel in the second row, a bearded Semite named Jehu, son of Omri (a name by which all Israelite kings were identified, whether of the Omride dynasty or not) bows before the king while his servants present gifts. The event occurred in the year 841 BCE, twelve years after Ahab's death, exactly parallel to the biblical numbers.[12]

I razed, destroyed, and burned the city of Qarqar, the royal city. 1,200 chariots, 1,200 cavalry, and 20,000 troops of Hadad-Ezer ("Arad-idri") of Damascus; 700 chariots, 700 cavalry, and 10,000 troops of Irhuleni, the Hamathite; 2,000 chariots and 10,000 troops of **Ahab, the Israelite**; 500 troops of Byblos; 1,000 troops of Sumur; 10 chariots and 10,000 troops of the land of Irqanatu; 200 troops of Matinu-Ba'al of the city of Arvad; 200 troops of the land of Usanat; 30 chariots of Adon-Ba'al of the land of Šianu; 1,000 dromedaries of Gindibu of Arabia; I fought with them. I decisively defeated them from the city of Qarqar to the city of Gilzau. I felt with the sword 14,000 troops, their fighting men.... In the midst of the battle I took away from them chariots, cavalry, and teams of horses. (emphasis added; http://www.livius.org/articles/battle/qarqar-853-bce/)

Despite the typical Assyrian boasting, the historical reality was probably quite different, as reasonable doubt exists whether the Assyrians really overcame their enemies and defeated them. Reading their annals carefully reveals that they were actually on the defensive for many years. Ultimately, they reached Damascus in 841, and king Jehu of Israel offered tribute. (We have discussed the ramifications of this change of foreign policy above in the introduction: "A Brief History of Israel and Judah.) The battle of Qarqar may not have been the decisive battle Shalmaneser claims it had been, but it may have marked the beginning of the end of independent Syria (Aram), though Aram would afflict the Northern Kingdom for the next several decades.

11. Jehu's payment of tribute is mentioned in several inscriptions comprising Shalmaneser III's annals, but the event is most famously recorded in the Black Obelisk, which was discovered by Henry Layard at Calah in 1846. It contains the annals of Shalmaneser III's reign, from his accession to his 31st year. On one panel, a short, bearded figure bows before the Assyrian king, accompanied by an epigraph which reads "I received tribute from Jehu (*Iaua*) of the house of Omri: silver, gold, a gold bowl, a gold tureen, gold vessels, gold pails, tin, the staffs of the king's hand, (and) spears." Jehu is ironically referred to as of the "house of Omri," which is the Assyrian geopolitical designation for Israel, even though Jehu had wiped out all of Omri's descendants.
12. That both the biblical and the Assyrian records list a twelve-year period between the two events (Ahab's death and Jehu's ascension) caused Thiele to fix the two dates

Event	Date	Description
Fall of Samaria	722 BCE	Mentioned in two separate sources: the Babylonian Chronicle (I i28), attributed to Shalmaneser V, and in eight different inscriptions belonging to Sargon. The transfer of power (possibly a coup) occurred during the city's downfall.
Sennacherib's Invasion of Judah	701 BCE	The description of Sennacherib's invasion of Judah in 701 BCE can be found on one of the earliest and still most famous discoveries of modern archaeology – the Taylor Prism. Discovered among the ruins of Nineveh, it contains the Annals of Sennacherib himself, listing eight of the king's military campaigns. On the prism, Sennacherib brags that he shut up "Hezekiah the Judahite" within Jerusalem, his royal city, "like a caged bird."[13] The prism is located at the Oriental Institute in Chicago.

as a synchronism around which other dates could be fixed. It should be noted that Thiele assumes that Israel used non-accession year dating for Israel; however, if Israel was using accession year dating at the time, the intervening reigns of Ahaziah and Joram would span an interval of fourteen years (Thiele, *Mysterious Numbers*, 72–76).

13. Here is the relevant text from the Taylor Prism:

As for Hezekiah the Judahite, who did not submit to my yoke: forty-six of his strong, walled cities, as well as the small towns in their area, which were without number, by levelling with battering-rams and by bringing up siege-engines, and by attacking and storming on foot, by mines, tunnels, and breeches, I besieged and took them. 200,150 people, great and small, male and female, horses, mules, asses, camels, cattle and sheep without number, I brought away from them and counted as spoil. (Hezekiah) himself, like a caged bird I shut up in Jerusalem, his royal city. I threw up earthworks against him, the one coming out of the city-gate, I turned back to his misery. His cities, which I had despoiled, I cut off from his land, and to Mitinti, king of Ashdod, Padi, king of Ekron, and Silli-b?l, king of Gaza, I gave (them). And thus I diminished his land. I added to the former tribute, and I laid upon him the surrender of their land and gifts for my majesty. As for Hezekiah, the terrifying splendor of my majesty overcame him, and the Arabs and his mercenary troops which he had brought in to strengthen Jerusalem, his royal city, deserted him. In addition to the thirty talents of gold and eight hundred talents of silver, gems, antimony, jewels, large carnelians,

It is the mention of King Ahab of Israel at the battle of Qarqar in 853 BCE, and the subsequent appearance of Jehu paying tribute to Shalmaneser III on the Black Obelisk a mere 12 years after the death of Ahab, that creates the additional pressure upon the biblical chronology. In addition to the internal discrepancy of almost 23 years between the northern and southern kingdoms, an external discrepancy of another two decades appears, between the Tanakh's dates (which suggest minimally a period of 143 years between Jehu's offering tribute to the Assyrians to the final destruction of the Northern Kingdom), and the much shorter period of 122 years according to the Assyrian sources.

Several approaches have been offered to bridge these gaps. As noted above, we shall not attempt to explain the midrashic chronology here (what we shall call the traditionalist approach).[14] Our approach

---

ivory-inlaid couches, ivory-inlaid chairs, elephant hides, elephant tusks, ebony, boxwood, all kinds of valuable treasures, as well as his daughters, his harem, his male and female musicians, which he had brought after me to Nineveh, my royal city… (online at https://www.bible-history.com/empires/prism.html).

14. Orthodox Rabbi Berel Wein eloquently attempted to defend the traditionalist viewpoint:

I have nothing new to add to the debate regarding this problem. I accept the traditional Jewish system of dating the events of this period, and thus in this book, the First Temple's destruction is dated not 586 BCE but 423 BCE…. It is the combination of my faith in the collective memory of the Jewish people…. History, unlike mathematics and other exact sciences, always contains a bit of error, bias, misinformation, disinformation and selective reporting…. The existence of some discrepancies or conflicting evidence, therefore, is a "problem," but it does not refute the entire structure. So too in the traditional Jewish chronology. (Berel Wein, *Echoes of Glory* [New York: Mesorah Publications, 1995], x–xi.

However, as noted above, the issues and proofs against blanket acceptance of the traditionalist approach, specifically the almost ironclad dating of the Assyrian system, are so thorough and convincing that even a firm traditionalist like Rabbi Shimon Schwab was willing to contemplate that for reasons unknown to us, possibly to obscure the date of the Messiah's arrival, the rabbis were willing to erase 165 years from the calendar ("Comparative Jewish Chronology," Selected Speeches, available online at https://www.yutorah.org/_cdn/_materials/Rabbi-Shimon-Schwab-Comparative-Jewish-Chronology-Original-Version-526681.pdf).

Rabbi Menachem Leibtag adopts the approach that the chronology in *Seder Olam* is not meant to be a historical record. Instead, he explains it as a midrash on the biblical text, and he has argued that the missing 165 years can be explained as follows:

argues that it is possible to reconcile the discrepancy between the southern and northern chronologies, as well as the Assyrian and biblical dates, by understanding the principles of biblical chronology. We will not attempt to "stretch" Israel's data to fit the Judean chronology as some scholars suggest,[15] but compress Judah's data to fit the Israel's chronology, and then readjust both to correspond with the external Assyrian dates. We shall present various approaches to deal with the specific issues, but first, we shall establish three critical principles that underlie how the Tanakh presents royal dates.

1. Coregencies were a common feature in the ancient Near East. Several of them are explicitly mentioned in the Tanakh (II Kings 15:5), others are alluded to (the appointment of Solomon as king while David is still alive), while others may be assumed, as we will demonstrate below.[16]

Another apparent justification for *Seder Olam*'s skipping over 165 years is the assumption that years without Jewish progress, particularly in the context of the second Beit HaMikdash, are effectively removed from Jewish history.... For thematic reasons, the book of Ezra closes the gap on these years in which there was no progress. *Seder Olam* takes the next step and makes it that these years never existed.... *Seder Olam*'s goal may not be primarily to give a comprehensive and precise history of all time, but rather to use history as a tool for teaching. (https://sabbahillel.blogspot.com/2015/05/rabbi-leibtag-shiurim-hebrew-calendar.html)

More recently, Sheldon Epstein, Bernard Dickman and Yonah Wilamowsky suggest a pedagogic purpose for the removal of the missing years – a rabbinic attempt to situate the publication of the Mishna at the beginning of the fifth millennium, which tradition suggests ends the two thousand–year era of Torah and begins the two thousand–year era of the Messianic age (their ideas are available online at https://www.hakirah.org/Vol%203%20Epstein.pdf).

15. For example, James Ussher (1581–1656), one of the earliest scholars who dealt systematically with the issues of chronology in the book of Kings, suggested that Israel's chronology featured two interregnal periods: an eleven-and-a-half-year gap between Jeroboam II and Zachariah, and a nine-year gap between Pekah and Hoshea (Archbishop James Ussher, *The Annals of the World*, revised and updated by Larry and Marion Pierce [Green Forest, AR: Master Books, 2003], 74, 79).

16. Some object to the usage of coregencies in attempting to resolve the chronological issues that exist (arguing that if they existed, there should be an explicit reference). In the case of Uzziah, II Kings 15:5 states that after he was stricken with leprosy, his

2. The two kingdoms utilized two separate counting systems, both
common in the Ancient Near East: (A) an accession-year system
in which the first full year of reign is counted as the king's first
year (used by the Assyrians, Babylonians, and Persians), and
(B) a non-accession-year system, in which the year of the king's
accession is counted as year one (used by the Egyptians, Greeks,
and Romans).[17] The first six decades of the divided kingdom
demonstrate these two systems clearly:

King of Judah	Official Years	King of Israel	Official Years
Rehoboam	17	Jeroboam	22
Abijah	3	Nadab	2
Asa	38	Baasha	24
		Elah	2
		Omri[18]	12
Total	58	Total	62

---

son Jotham managed the palace and governed the people of the land – a straightforward example of a coregency. In Egypt, coregencies were very common (see
William J. Murnane, *Ancient Egyptian Coregencies* [Chicago: The Oriental Institute,
1977]). Dating the pharaohs is a very tricky endeavor, as like the kings in the Tanakh,
the Egyptian records never relate whether it is measured from a coregency. As will
be seen, assumed coregencies was the approach taken already from the time of the
Midrash in *Seder Olam* and followed by Rashi. Nadav Na'aman noted that David set
a pattern by setting his son Solomon on the throne before his death. Na'aman writes:

> Taking into account the permanent nature of the co-regency in Judah from the
> time of Joash, one may dare to conclude that dating the co-regencies accurately is
> indeed the key for solving the problems of biblical chronology in the eighth century
> BCE. (Nadav Na'aman, "Historical and Chronological Notes on the Kingdoms
> of Israel and Judah in the Eighth Century BC," *Vetus Testamentum* 36 [1986]: 91)

17. The second system is the one described in Rosh HaShana 2a:

> The Rabbis taught: A king who ascends the throne on the 29th of Adar must be
> considered to have reigned one year as soon as the first of Nisan comes, but if
> he ascends the throne on the first of Nisan he is not considered to have reigned
> one year until the first of Nisan of the following year.

18. We have omitted the reigns of both Zimri (who ruled for seven days) and Tibni
(who was Omri's rival) from this table, as their rules both began in the same year as
Omri's.

While the totals should be identical, there is a discrepancy of four years, at 58 and 62 years respectively. We can resolve the difference by ascribing accession year dating Judah and non-accession year dating to Israel, so that the year that the king ascends the throne is only counted for the Northern Kingdom. Therefore, the totals agree at 58 years because the actual years for each succeeding king in Israel are a year less (i.e., 22 + 1 + 23 + 1 + 11 = 58).

3. The two kingdoms also began counting the regnal year at different points in the calendar. For example, Thiele argues that the year in Judah was counted beginning in Tishrei (in the autumn), while Israel's regnal year began in Nisan (in the spring), as the reign of Jeroboam over Israel started eight months after the start of the reign of Rehoboam in Judah. However, more recent scholars argue the opposite,[19] in accordance with the Mishnah in Rosh HaShana, which states "There are four new year days: The first of Nisan is the new year for (the ascension of) kings and for (the regular rotation of) festivals," which the Talmud explains as follows:

"R. Hisda says: The rule of the Mishna, that the year of the kings begins with Nisan, refers to the kings of Judah only, but for the kings of other nations it commences from Tishrei."

The last two principles can account for one-year differences between the regnal dates of kings of the north and the south. However, it is the first principle that most use to explain the numerous discrepancies in the text.

DETERMINING THE DATES OF THE KINGS

Part 1: Amaziah and Uzziah in Judah

Dating the early kings of Israel after 841 BCE is relatively simple, as after anointing Jehu as king in 841 BCE, the Northern Kingdom experienced a level of stability it had not enjoyed previously or would since (see above, "A Brief History of Israel and Judah"). Additionally, Jehu received a prophecy guaranteeing that his lineage would sit on the throne for [at

---

19. Galil, *The Chronology*, 9–10, n. 23.

least] "the fourth generation."[20] Though Jehu and his son Jehoahaz faced tremendous political pressures due to the constant encroachment of the Arameans, combined with the relative weakness of Jehu's Assyrian ally during this period, Jehu and his children, bolstered by the divine promise received from Elisha, never faced internal threats to their rule. Thus, we can be relatively confident in determining their dates (Rashi posits a short three-year co-regency between Jehoash and Jeroboam).

In Judah, however, the situation was radically different, as David's dynasty faced the worst threat to its existence. Responding to Jehu's eradication of her family, the house of Ahab, the killer-queen Athaliah murdered every living member of the royal house carrying Davidic blood. Fortunately, the infant Jehoash was spirited away from the palace and hidden in the Temple for seven years before Athaliah was deposed. This was the first break in the Davidic line. Ultimately, both Jehoash and his son Amaziah would be assassinated, the blood of King David was no longer sacrosanct. Despite what should have been inherent stability with David's house ruling Judah, issues of succession arose, thereby lessening the certainty with which we can date the kings of Judah during the eighth century.

We begin with two fateful decisions made by Amaziah and his son Azariah (Uzziah). In both cases, Tanakh's depiction of these events creates tremendous chronological difficulties. Rashi (based on the midrashic tradition) relies heavily on co-regencies to resolve many of the issues. Doing so removes almost forty years from the list of Judean kings.[21] The first time a co-regency occurred was when Amaziah

---

20. That four generations is a minimum, and not a maximum, was explained to me by my teacher Rosh Yeshivat Har Etzion Rav Yaakov Medan, when I asked him whether placing a limitation on the length of Jehu's dynasty violated the principle of free will. He argued – consistent with the approach of the Malbim brought in the book's introduction, which argues that prophecies are best understood as potential outcomes – had the Northern Kingdom and Jehu's descendants been worthy, the dynasty could have lasted longer!

21. The co-regencies Rashi assumes include a fifteen-year overlap between Amaziah and Uzziah and a twenty-five-year overlap between Uzziah and Jotham (and probably Ahaz as well!). Rashi also posits a short three-year overlap between Jehoash and Jeroboam, as noted below, but not the forty years of co-regencies that he suggests for the Southern Kingdom:

succeeded his father, Joash. According to II Kings 14:2, he would reign for 29 years. However, he made a critical error when he chose to attack the Northern Kingdom. He was not only defeated but humiliated, and Israel sacked Jerusalem and the countryside as a result. According to II Kings 14:19, the result was the end of his reign: "And they revolted against him in Jerusalem, and he fled to Lakhish. And they sent after him to Lakhish and assassinated him there."

Rashi suggests that the two events (the fleeing to Lakhish and the assassination) did not coincide, but fifteen years separate them. During this period, Uzziah ruled in Jerusalem while his father was still alive:[22] According to our understanding, we are on solid ground in removing years from Amaziah's reign when coordinating the dates of this era.

"In the thirty-eighth year of Azariah the king of Judah, Zechariah... reigned": From here too it is possible to deduce that Azariah reigned from the time that Joash king of Israel died, fifteen years during the lifetime of Amaziah his father, for if he did not rise until his father died, it follows that he did not rise until the fifteenth year of Jeroboam the son of Joash. Now, since Jeroboam reigned forty-one years, it follows that Jeroboam died in the twenty-seventh year of Uzziah. Now, how does Scripture say, "In the thirty-eighth year"? Rather, we are forced [to admit that] Uzziah and Jeroboam reigned simultaneously, except that Jeroboam reigned three years during the lifetime of his father Jehoash. Therefore, Scripture states (II Kings 13:13), "and Jeroboam had sat on his throne," meaning that he had already sat. Now Uzziah rose when Joash died and Jeroboam reigned as a full-fledged monarch (lit., a full kingship). *I saw in Seder Olam (ch. 19) that Jeroboam reigned one year during his father's lifetime, and I do not know whether it is the copyist's error, for I cannot reconcile [the verse reading,] "In the thirty-eighth year of Azariah... Zechariah... reigned," except in this manner.* (Rashi on II Kings 15:8)

22. Rashi develops this further on in his commentary on II Kings 14:22: "He [Uzziah] built up Elath and restored it to Judah, after king [Amaziah] had slept with his forefathers." "After the king had slept with his forefathers": After the death of his father Amaziah. *From here you deduce that Uzziah reigned during his father's lifetime.* Nevertheless, Elath was not given into his hand until after his father's death, for if he did not reign during his father's lifetime, why was it necessary to state, "after the king had slept with his forefathers?" And when you count the days of the Temple according to the years of the kings, if you do not subtract these fifteen years, which are counted for Amaziah and Uzziah, you will find that it existed four hundred twenty-five years [instead of the traditional four hundred and ten (Yoma 9a)].

His son Uzziah would make a tragic error several years later, as described in II Chronicles 26:16–21:

> And when he became strong, his heart became haughty until he became corrupt, and he trespassed against the Lord his God, and he came into the Temple of the Lord to burn incense on the altar of incense. And Azariah the priest came after him, and with him were priests of the Lord, eighty mighty men. And they stood beside Uzziah the king and said to him, "It is not for you, Uzziah, to burn incense to the Lord, but for the priests, sons of Aaron, who are consecrated to burn [incense]. So leave the Sanctuary, for you have trespassed, and it will not be glory for you from the Lord God." And Uzziah became furious, and in his hand was a censer to burn, and in his fury with the priests, the *tzara'at* [biblical form of leprosy] shone upon his forehead before the priests in the House of the Lord, over the altar of incense. And Azariah, the chief priest, and all the priests turned to him, and behold he was stricken with *tzara'at* on his forehead, so they rushed him out of there, and he too hastened to leave, for the Lord had smitten him. And King Uzziah was stricken with *tzara'at* until the day of his death, and he lived in a house of retirement, for it had been decreed from the House of the Lord, and Jotham his son was over the king's house; he judged the people of the land.

The traditional understanding is that Uzziah lived in seclusion for the second half of his reign, with Jotham (and possibly Ahaz after him) reigning in his stead. Here is Rashi's explanation:

> [Uzziah assumed the throne] "in the twenty-seventh year of Jeroboam": Is it possible to say so? Did not Uzziah and Jeroboam reign simultaneously, as I explained shortly before this (II Kings 14:22)? What, then, is the meaning of the verse, "In the twenty-seventh year of Jeroboam… Azariah… became king"? That from that year, he reigned a plagued kingship. We learn that he was stricken with "tzara'at" in the twenty-seventh year of his reign. (Rashi on II Chr. 15:1)

Additional evidence that Jotham ruled simultaneously with his father is found in 1 Chr. 5:17, which describes a census of the Transjordan tribes: "All these were reckoned by genealogies in the days of Jotham king of Judah, and in the days of Jeroboam king of Israel." This statement indicates that Jotham and Jeroboam II ruled at the same time, which would not be possible unless Jotham was already ruling in the days of his father.

Part 2: After Jehu's dynasty: How many kingdoms of Israel were there?[23]

In its final years, the political instability that plagued the Northern Kingdom mirrors the messy and contradictory chronology of the six kings that ruled during its final three decades. Zechariah ruled for half a year and was murdered by Shallum, whose rule lasted only a month before he was murdered by Menahem. He ruled for ten years, and his son Pekahiah replaced him, ruling two years until Pekah killed him. According to II Kings 15:27–31, Pekahiah ruled for twenty years and was succeeded by Hoshea, who ruled for nine years. Assuming no overlaps, the total amount of years is between forty-one and forty-two years.

However, two dates are clear from within the biblical text itself. First, the fall of Samaria and the end of the Northern Kingdom took place in 722 BCE. Counting backward, Pekah would have had to assume the throne in 751, to rule for twenty years, to be followed by Hoshea. However, during Menahem's ten-year reign (II Kings 15:17), Menahem gave tribute to Tiglath-Pileser of Assyria as is recorded in II Kings 15:19 (Pul there being Tiglath-Pileser's family name),[24] and in Tiglath-Piles-

---

23. Information in this section, in addition to the sources mentioned above, was compiled from H. J. Cook, "Pekah," *Vetus Testamentum* 14 (1964): 121–35, and the following websites: http://www.jewishvirtuallibrary.org/pekah and https://en.wikipedia.org/wiki/Pekah.

24. According to Eugene Faulstich, the Akkadian name-element "Pal" (Pul in Hebrew) was a family name:

> The Hebrew name "Pul" ("pal" is the Akkadian name) was a common dynasty name at this period in Assyrian history. The father of Shalmaneser III was Ashurnasir-pal II. The second son of Shalmaneser was "Shamas-Vul" (Vul = Pul; for the letters v and p are interchangeable in Semitic languages).... Adad-nirari III, the son of Shamas-Vul, was known as Vullush (Pullush).... The name "Pul" is derived from the Assyrian god "Vul," the god of the atmosphere. He would

er's inscriptions.[25] Since Tiglath-Pileser came to the throne in 745 BC, Menahem had to give tribute in 745 or later. If Pekah ascended to the throne in 752, how could Menahem have given tribute and become a vassal of Assyria in 745 BCE (or later)?

Most of the attempts to resolve this issue have focused on the reign of Pekah, in which the biblical evidence is contradictory. Within II Kings, this twenty-year reign is consistent with the statement that Jotham of Judah began to reign in Pekah's second year (II Kings 15:32), and that Jotham's successor Ahaz began to reign in his 17th year (16:1). However, a shorter reign is indicated by II Kings 15:27, which says that Pekah began to reign in the 52nd year of Azariah (Uzziah) of Judah. As noted above, Jotham had already started to reign during the leprosy of his father, making this dating unlikely.

The first scholarly attempt to resolve this difficulty was made in 1887 by Carl Lederer. He proposed two systems in use for reckoning Pekah's reign, one shorter and one longer. The reason for this was a split in the Northern Kingdom, not just the consequence of a personal rivalry between Pekah and Menahem, but over the proper approach that Israel should take to the quickly expanding and threatening Assyrian empire. Menahem, as noted, paid tribute to Tiglath-Pileser. Apparently, upon Tiglath-Pileser III's forces appearing, Menahem took the opportunity to enlist his support by sending a tribute of a thousand talents of silver, with the idea "that he might help him to confirm his hold of the royal power" (II Kings 15:19). While this tribute may have been due to Menahem's sense of insecurity and desire to appease the Assyrian king, it may equally well indicate the presence of a rival. Like a later king, Ahaz of

---

be identical to the Canaanite god, Baal (the letters v and b are the same letter in Semitic languages). (Eugene W. Faulstich, *History, Harmony & The Hebrew Kings* [Spencer, IA: Chronology Books, 1986], 133)

25. Layard 50a, an annalistic text that lists eighteen southeast Anatolian and Syro-Palestinian kings who paid tribute to Tiglath-Pileser, states that *Me-ni-hi-im-me uru Sa-me-ri-na-a+a* (Menahem of Samaria) paid tribute to Tiglath-Pileser. Similarly, the Iran Stela, which came to scholarly attention in the 1960s, the only known stela of Tiglath-Pileser, places Menahem (*Mi-ni-hi-im-me kur Sa-me- ri-i-na-a+a*) third in a list of seventeen kings who paid tribute (Hayim Tadmor, *The Inscriptions of Tiglath-Pileser III, King of Assyria* [Jerusalem: The Israel Academy of Sciences and Humanities, 1994], 68–69; 265–268).

Judah, Menahem of Israel (Ephraim) followed a pro-Assyrian policy, placing himself in opposition to Pekah, who would eventually build a coalition of neighboring states in a futile attempt to oppose the Assyrians; explaining why Menahem felt the need to buy Assyrian support.

In 1954, H. J. Cook added several new factors that support Lederer's thesis. While the Tanakh does not explicitly mention the existence of two rival kingdoms in the north in the latter half of the eighth century BCE, their presence is implied in Hosea. Cook suggests that although "Ephraim" is sometimes used in Tanakh to designate the entire Northern Kingdom, in various passages of Hosea such as Hosea 5:5, "Israel" and "Ephraim" are not synonymous but refer to separate entities.[26] This thesis was supported by Rodger Young, who pointed out that in the Hebrew text of Hosea 5:5, there is a letter *vav* before Israel, followed by another *vav* before Ephraim, which is the Hebrew method of expressing "both... and," implying a distinction in this passage between Israel and Ephraim (the Septuagint translates the verse similarly).[27] Many scholars accept the dual kingdom theory, including Thiele.[28]

Similarly, Stanley Rosenbaum argues that Tiglath-Pileser III's records show the Assyrian king distinguishing between two kingdoms in Israel.[29] Tiglath-Pileser says he united the northern part (restored as Naphtali in the text) with Assyria. In contrast, for the southern region, he wrote, "Israel overthrew their king Pekah and I placed Hoshea as king over them." Though Pekah had served as a leader over parts of Israel for over a decade, either in opposition or as a rebellious subordinate to Menahem, his 12th year (in which he slew Pekahiah) was his first year of sole reign.

Part 3: Jotham and Ahaz

Given that Jotham begins ruling during his father's lifetime, it is impossible to ascertain precisely when Jotham assumed the throne on his, as opposed to serving in his father's stead, and how long he ruled on his

26. H. J. Cook, "Pekah," *Vetus Testamentum* 14 (1964): 121–35.

27. R. C. Young, "When Was Samaria Captured? The Need for Precision in Biblical Chronologies," *Journal of the Evangelical Theological Society* 47 (2004): 581–82, n. 11.

28. Thiele, *Mysterious Numbers*, 120, 129–30.

29. Stanley Rosenbaum, *Amos of Israel: A New Interpretation* (Macon, GA: Mercer University Press, 1990), 26.

own. We suggest that Jotham never ruled independently at all. What should be simple informational verses regarding the length of Jotham's reign appear to contradict each other, as shown here:

> And Hoshea the son of Elah revolted against Pekah the son of Remaliah, and he struck him and slew him, and reigned in his stead, *in the twentieth year of Jotham* the son of Uzziah. (II Kings 15:30)

> In the second year of Pekah son of Remaliah, the king of Israel, Jotham son of Uzziah, the king of Judah, became king. He was twenty-five years old when he became king, *and he reigned sixteen years in Jerusalem*, and his mother's name was Jerusha, the daughter of Zadok. (II Kings 15:32–33)

Another difficulty arises from a simple reading of II Kings – whether the Syro-Ephraimite invasion of Judah, led by Pekah of Israel and Rezin of Aram, took place during Jotham's reign, or during the time of his son Ahaz:

> And the rest of the events of Jotham and all that he did, are written in the book of chronicles of the kings of Judah. In those days, the Lord began to incite Rezin, the king of Aram and Pekah son of Remaliah, against Judah. (II Kings 15:36–37)

> Then Rezin, the king of Aram and Pekah the son of Remaliah, the king of Israel, went up to Jerusalem to wage war, and they besieged Ahaz but could not wage war [with him]. (II Kings 16:5)

Rashi notes these inconsistencies – whether Jotham ruled for sixteen or twenty years and whether the invasion of Judah occurred during Jotham's or Ahaz's reign – to explain an apparent inconsistency in the dating of Israel's final king, Hoshea:

> [And Hoshea … reigned in his stead] … *in the twentieth year of Jotham:* It should have said, "in the fourth year of Ahaz," since Jotham's entire reign lasted sixteen years! However, since Ahaz

> was wicked, Scripture preferred to count them (i. e., the years)
> to Jotham, who was in the grave, rather than to Ahaz, who was
> alive. (*Seder Olam*, ch. 22). (Rashi on II Kings 15:30)

According to Rashi, Jotham's rule only lasted sixteen years. Since the
Tanakh did not wish to acknowledge the evil reign of Ahaz any more
than necessary, it credited Jotham with an additional four years. Two
other possibilities exist to resolve the contradiction, based on a close
reading of the two verses above. First, the absence of the word *lemalkhut*
(of the kingship) from verse 30 is meaningful: "in the twentieth year of
Jotham," and not "in the twentieth year of the kingship of Jotham." Most
times, when discussing kings, the addition of *lemalkhut* is not necessary,
but when dealing with a figure who served as a co-regent, the absence is
probably significant. One possibility to resolve the contradiction is that
Jotham served in his father's place for many years but only assumed the
throne as king near the end of his father's life when it became apparent
that Uzziah would not recover. The second approach, suggested by some
scholars, argues that Jotham was deposed in 736 BCE and replaced by
his son Ahaz, dying twenty years after assuming the throne, but without
the crown four years later in 732 BCE (meaning that his reign was only
16 years). Followers of this theory argue that there was a palace coup
by courtiers who preferred a more conciliatory attitude towards Assyria
than Jotham was willing to countenance. They deposed Jotham, replacing him with the more pliable Ahaz.

Jotham's rule is the last period of quiet Judah would enjoy in the
eighth century BCE. Still, pressures from the steady encroachment of
the Assyrians on the northern border and the resulting pressure from
the countries that surrounded Judah would doom his son Ahaz's reign.
Unfortunately, Ahaz chose to respond to these challenges by embrac-
ing idolatry, as described above in "A Brief History of Israel and Judah."
Modern scholars remain divided as to when Ahaz reigned, whether from
742–727 or 732–716. We reject the later dating for both textual and historical reasons. First, we hold that Ahaz died before the fall of Samaria in 722
BCE, as stated explicitly in II Kings 18:1. Second, we reject the suggestion that Hezekiah took power in 727–726 BCE (per II Kings 18:1) but
allowed Ahaz to remain on the throne for another decade. The usage of

co-regencies to smooth over dating issues cannot be relied upon when the two figures shared such diametrically opposed viewpoints, whether politically (to submit to Assyria or to fight), and more importantly, religiously (to continue Ahaz's policy of supporting Assyrian idol worship as the state religion, or to return to the true worship of God). Hezekiah's program of intensive religious reform, thoroughly described in II Chronicles 29–31 would have been impossible to carry out if he shared a co-regency with his father, the one who introduced idolatry to Judah.

Part 4: When Did Hezekiah Recover from His Illness?

Chapters 18 and 19 of II Kings describe the Assyrian invasion of Judah in 701 BCE. Chapter 20 describes how King Hezekiah suddenly becomes ill and his miraculous recovery, with a divine promise that he would live for another fifteen years. Thus, the question becomes whether this episode occurs after the Assyrian invasion. If this is so, then the date of his death would be 686 BCE, and since II Kings 18:2 tells us that Hezekiah reigned for 29 years, he ascended the throne in 615 BCE. Rashi understands II Kings 20 with Hezekiah's sickness as occurring after Sennacherib, and this is the approach adopted by Thiele and many scholars today.[30] Thus, the midrashic chronology states that there was

---

30. Rashi on II Kings 20:1: "'In those days': Three days before Sennacherib's downfall, Hezekiah became ill, and the third day, when he went up to the house of the Lord, was the day of Sennacherib's downfall, and it was the [first] festive day of Passover."

My teacher, Rabbi Yaakov Medan, suggests that Hezekiah's illness was a direct consequence of the Assyrian invasion. The Tanakh describes how, when facing certain defeat, Hezekiah went to the Temple to pray to God and entreat for Judah's survival – "When King Hezekiah heard, he rent his clothes and covered himself in sackcloth and came to the House of the Lord" (II Kings 19:1). Rabbi Medan speculates that Hezekiah did not simply visit the Temple, but entered the Holy of Holies, as alluded to by the content of his prayer:

Lord, God of Israel, *Enthroned upon the Cherubim*...You alone are God of all the kingdoms of the earth; You made both heaven and earth. Incline Your ear, O Lord, and listen; open Your eyes, O Lord, and see – listen to the words of Sannecherib, those he sent to revile the living God.... But now, Lord our God, save us from his hand, and all the kingdoms of the earth will see that You alone, O Lord, are God. (19:15–19)

Rabbi Medan argues that the usage of the phrase "Enthroned upon the Cherubim" implies that Hezekiah was in the Holy of Holies when he offered this prayer.

less than a decade between the Assyrian invasion, defeat, and the exile of the Northern Kingdom, and Sennacherib's invasion of Judah, which ended in miraculous salvation.

However, doing so creates several problems. First, we accept that Manasseh's rule ended in 641 BCE. Manasseh's reign lasted 55 years, beginning at the latest in 696 BCE. If Hezekiah's rule lasted until 686 BCE, the assumption is that Hezekiah and Manasseh shared the throne in a coregency for the final decade. Upon assuming the throne, however, Manasseh completely reversed every political and religious principle of his father's reign. Therefore, logic demands rejecting the suggestion of a decade-long co-regency.

Second, the Babylonian envoys that Hezekiah meets at the end of II Kings 20 were sent by King Merodach-Baladan of Babylon.[31] Since the Assyrians deposed Merodach-Baladan in 710 BCE, this event almost certainly occurred before Sennacherib's invasion in 701 BCE, not afterward, and therefore at least the second half of chapter 20 occurred before the events in chapters 18 and 19.[32] More likely, all of chapter 20, including

---

31. Isaiah warned Hezekiah against trusted in the Babylon envoys:

> But the prophet Isaiah came to King Hezekiah and said to him, "What did these people say, and from where did they come to you?" "They came from a distant land," said Hezekiah, "from Babylon." "What have they seen in your palace?" he asked. "Why, they have seen everything in my palace," said Hezekiah. "There was nothing in my treasuries that I did not show them." "Hear the word of the Lord," Isaiah said to Hezekiah. "Behold – the days are coming when all that fills your palace and all that your fathers amassed until this day will be borne away to Babylon, and nothing will be left," the Lord has said, "while sons of yours who came forth from you, who were born to you, will be borne far away, castrated slaves in the palace of the king of Babylon." (II Kings 20:15–18)

Tellingly, Hezekiah avoids answering Isaiah's first question, as he knew that Isaiah opposed Judah seeking assistance from or alliances with other nations and not the Lord (cf. Is. 7, in the discussion with Ahaz; also 30:1–5; 31:1–3). As the prophecy given to Hezekiah pertains not to him, but to his descendants ("while sons of yours who came forth from you, who were born to you, will be borne far away" [20:18]), the rationale for placing the events of chapter 20, which occur chronologically before the Assyrian invasion of ch. 18–19, becomes clear.

32. The midrashic interpretation is that the envoys came to visit Hezekiah after the Assyrians' defeat:

> When Hezekiah saw the Babylonian delegates, he became exceedingly conceited [lit., high of heart]. He showed them the royal treasury and the Holy of

both Hezekiah's illness and the visit of the Babylonian envoys, occurred before the events of chapters 18 and 19. Indeed, while Hezekiah's illness is always mentioned after the account of Sennacherib's invasion, it forms an independent unit that is chronologically separated from the preceding text by the non-specific opening statement, "In those days was Hezekiah sick unto death" (2 Kg. 20:1; Is. 38:1; 2).

The final problem is the first that appears in the Bible – the first verse of II Kings 18: "And it was in the third year of Hoshea the son of Elah, the king of Israel, that Hezekiah the son of Ahaz, the king of Judah, became king."[33]

Holies and opened the Ark [of the Covenant] and pointed to the tablets [of stone] and said: "It is with these that we wage war and achieve victory!" (*Pirkei DeRabbi Eliezer*, 51)

More likely, however, is that this international diplomatic mission was sent before the invasion, an attempt by two of Assyria's arch-rivals to create an alliance that would overthrow the Assyrian yoke. In his studies on II Kings, Rabbi Alex Israel writes:

Berodakh Baladan [sic] is a historical figure, and historical records show that he twice attempted to galvanize an anti-Assyrian coalition to terminate Assyria's regional dominance. It seems highly possible that this international diplomatic mission was a consultation in building precisely such a war coalition. Hezekiah's display of his treasury and stores was probably a demonstration of his ability to mount a military campaign, or conversely, to withstand an Assyrian onslaught. (Available online at https://www.etzion.org.il/en/shiur-24-chapter-20-tests-faith, and in *II Kings: In a Whirlwind* [Jerusalem: Maggid Books, 2019].)

33. Reflecting one approach to solve the chronological difficulties, Rashi interprets "the third year of Hoshea" (when Hezekiah ascended the throne) as referring not to the year of his reign, but of his ill-fated rebellion against Assyria. Here is Rashi's approach in full:

A) Commentary on II Kings 17:1:

"In the twelfth year of Ahaz": It is impossible [for us] to say that Hoshea assumed the kingship in Ahaz's twelfth year, for in Ahaz's fourth year, he [Hoshea] assassinated Pekah and took the throne in his stead. See above 15:30, and calculating Pekah's years will demonstrate this. Likewise, it is impossible to say that he [Hoshea] did not reign more than nine years, for he ruled from the fourth year of Ahaz until the sixth year of Hezekiah, when Samaria was captured – which amounts to more than sixteen years. What then does the phrase "nine years" mean? From the beginning of his [Hoshea's] rebellion against the king of Assyria – and this is how it is taught in *Seder Olam* (ch. 23). It is impossible to say that Hoshea started to rebel in the twelfth year of Ahaz for if so, you will count the years of his revolt to include five years during the days of Hezekiah, making eleven years, yet here he states that he reigned nine years...

Hoshea ruled for nine years, from 731 BCE until his defeat by Sargon in 722 BCE, which was the end of the Northern Kingdom. II Kings 18:2 tells us that Hezekiah reigned during Israel's final six years and saw the exile of the ten tribes. As noted, the midrashic account assumed that the time between the two invasions was only fourteen years. However, the Assyrian records are clear that twenty-one years separate the destruction of the Northern Kingdom from Sennacherib's invasion of Judah in 701 BCE. A recent suggestion, which has been finding favor among scholars, splits the Assyrian invasion into two. An earlier invasion occurred in 714–711 BCE. Assyrian sources describe campaigns on Israel's coast, with the Philistines, and in which Hezekiah was appropriately deferential and avoided conflict, as described in II Kings 18:14–16. The second invasion occurred in 701 BCE, in which Hezekiah stood defiantly, beginning with II Kings 18:17. We have chosen to follow the dating that places Hezekiah's reign at 727–696 BCE with this understanding. Accordingly, we place the events in II Kings 20, both Hezekiah's sickness and the visit of the Babylonian emissaries around 711–710 BCE, about a decade before Sennacherib's invasion in 701.

[From here we learn that] the ten tribes were exiled at three different times: (1) in the twentieth year of Pekah, as it is written above, (15:29)…"Tiglath-Pileser the king of Assyria came and took Ijon and Dan…and the entire land of Naphtali (*sic*) and exiled them to Assyria"; which was the fourth year of Ahaz. (2) He [Tiglath-Pileser] then waited eight years and came upon them in the twelfth year of Ahaz and exiled the Reubenites and the Gadites. When Hoshea the son of Elah saw this, he revolted against him and sent messengers to So, the king of Egypt. (3) He [the king of Assyria – Shalmanezzer] waited eight more years [before responding by] coming and laying siege to Samaria. After three years, Samaria was captured, and everyone was exiled. This is the meaning the following verse (in Is. 8:23): "Like the first time, he dealt mildly, the land of Zebulun and the land of Naphtali." [Meaning - just as the king of Assyria dealt mildly with Israel in the first exile by limiting the exile to Zebulun and Naphtali,] so did he deal mildly with the second exile, [again] exiling only two tribes. But "in the last one, he swept (*hikhbid*)" – meaning that he swept everything out [of the northern kingdom] like a person sweeping a house. [Therefore]…the number here refers to] the number of years of his revolt… [for] he did not revolt against him until the fourteenth year of Ahaz: as Ahaz reigned sixteen years, the revolt includes three years of Ahaz and six years in the days of Hezekiah.

B) Commentary on II Kings 18:1: "'In the third year': of Hoshea's rebellion."

Selected Bibliography

Allen, Leslie C. *The Books of Joel, Obadiah, Jonah, and Micah*. Grand Rapids, MI: Eerdmans. The New International Commentary on the Old Testament, 1976.

Alter, Robert, and Frank Kermode. *The Literary Guide to the Bible*. Cambridge, MA: Harvard University, 1987.

Angel, Hayyim. *Revealed Texts, Hidden Meanings: Finding the Religious Significance in Tanakh*. Jersey City, NJ: Ktav Publishing House, 2009.

———. *Vision from the Prophet and Counsel from the Elders: A Survey of Nevi'im and Ketuvim*. Jersey City, NJ: Ktav Publishing House and OU Press, 2013.

———. *Peshat Isn't So Simple: Essays on Developing a Religious Methodology to Bible Study*. Jersey City, NJ: Ktav Publishing House, 2014.

Anglim, Simon. *Fighting Techniques of the Ancient World 3000 BCE–500 CE*. New York: Amber Books, 2013.

Andersen, Francis I., and David Noel Freedman, *Micah: A New Translation with Introduction and Commentary*. New York: Doubleday, 2000.

Assis, Elie. *The Book of Joel: A Prophet Between Calamity and Hope*. The Library of Hebrew Bible/Old Testament Studies (New York: Bloomsbury, 2013), adapted into Hebrew: *Yoel: Bein Mashber LeTikva* (Jerusalem: Maggid, 2015).

Barker, Joel. *Joel: A Discourse Analysis of the Hebrew Bible*. Exegetical Commentary on the Old Testament, 28. Grand Rapids, MI: Zondervan, 2020.

Barker, Kenneth L. "A Literary Analysis of the Book of Micah." *Bibliotheca Sacra* 155 (1998): 437–48.

Barton, John. *Joel and Obadiah: A Commentary.* Louisville, KY: Westminster John Knox, 2001.

Beasley, Yaakov. *Nahum, Habakkuk, and Zephaniah: Lights in the Valley.* Jerusalem: Maggid Books, 2020.

Ben Zvi, Ehud. *The Forms of the Old Testament Literature, Volume 21B: Micah.* Grand Rapids, MI: Eerdmans, 2000.

Boleh, Menachem. *Daat Mikra: Trei Asar, vol.* 2 (Hebrew). Jerusalem: Mossad HaRav Kook, 1990.

Brueggemann, Walter. "Walk Humbly with Your God: Micah 6:8." *Journal for Preachers* 33 (2010): 141–49.

De Roche, Michael. "Yahweh's *Rîb* against Israel: A Reassessment of the So-called 'Prophetic Lawsuit' in the Pre-exilic Prophets." *Journal of Biblical Literature* 102 (1983): 5635–74.

Dorsey, David A. *The Literary Structure of the Old Testament: A Commentary on Genesis to Malachi.* Grand Rapids, MI: Baker Book House, 1999.

Hakham, Amos. *Daat Mikra: Trei Asar,* vol. 1 (Hebrew). Jerusalem: Mossad HaRav Kook, 1990.

Heschel, Abraham J. *The Prophets.* New York: Harper & Row, 1962.

Huffmon, Herbert B. "Covenant Lawsuit in the Prophets." *Journal Of Biblical Literature* 78 (1959): 2852–95.

Hyman, Ronald T. "Questions and response in Micah 6:6–8." *Jewish Bible Quarterly* 33 (2005): 157–65.

Jacobs, Mignon R., *The Conceptual Coherence of the Book of Micah.* Sheffield Academic Press, 2009.

Jensen, Philip Peter. *Obadiah, Jonah, Micah: A Theological Commentary.* New York: Bloomsbury Academic & Professional, 2008.

Laney, J. Carl. "The Role of the Prophets in God's Case against Israel." *Bibliotheca Sacra* 138 (1981): 313–25.

Matthews, Victor H. *The Hebrew Prophets and Their Social World: An Introduction.* Grand Rapids, MI: Baker Academic, 2012.

Redditt, P. L., "The Formation of the Book of the Twelve: A Review of Research." In *Society of Biblical Literature 2001 Seminar Papers,* 58–80. Atlanta, GA: Society of Biblical Literature, 2001.

Sweeney, Marvin A. *The Twelve Prophets.* Volume 1: Hosea, Joel, Amos, Jonah, Obadiah, Micah. Berit Olam: Studies in Hebrew Narrative and Poetry. Edited by David W. Cotter. Collegeville, MN: The Liturgical Press, 2000.

Waltke, Bruce K. *A Commentary on Micah.* Grand Rapids, MI: Eerdmans, 2007.

Wendland, Ernst. https://www.academia.edu/8963455/PROPHETIC_
    RHETORIC_Case_Studies_in_Text_Analysis_and_Translation
https://www.academia.edu/1801675/The_Discourse_Analysis_of_Hebrew_
    Prophetic_Literature_Determining_the_Larger_Textual_Units_of_
    Hosea_and_Joel

Image Credits:

The fonts used in this book are from the Arno family

Maggid Books
The best of contemporary Jewish thought from
Koren Publishers Jerusalem Ltd.